D1195100

In Search of Jewish Community

*Jewish Identities in Germany and Austria,
1918–1933*

Edited by Michael Brenner and Derek J. Penslar

INDIANA UNIVERSITY PRESS

Bloomington and Indianapolis

© 1998 by Indiana University Press
All rights reserved

The paper used in this publication meets the
minimum requirements of American National
Standard for Information Sciences—Permanence
of Paper for Printed Library Materials,
ANSI Z39.48-1984.

Manufactured in the United States of America

Library of Congress Cataloging-in-Publication Data

In search of Jewish community : Jewish identities in Germany and Austria,
1918–1933 / edited by Michael Brenner and Derek J. Penslar.
p.   cm.
Includes bibliographical references and index.
ISBN 0-253-33427-6 (alk. paper). — ISBN 0-253-21224-3 (pbk. : alk. paper)
1. Jews—Germany—Social conditions—Congresses. 2. Judaism—Germany—
History—20th century—Congresses. 3. Jews—Austria—Social conditions—
Congresses. 4. Germany—Social conditions—1918–1933—Congresses.
5. Austria—History—1918–1938—Congresses. 6. Germany—Ethnic
relations—Congresses. 7. Austria—Ethnic relations—Congresses.
I. Brenner, Michael.   II. Penslar, Derek Jonathan.
DS135.G33S35   1998
305.892'4043—dc21   98-8304

1   2   3   4   5   03   02   01   00   99   98

CONTENTS

ACKNOWLEDGMENTS   vii

INTRODUCTION BY MICHAEL BRENNER & DEREK J. PENSLAR   ix

LIST OF ABBREVIATIONS   xvii

1. German Jews between Fulfillment and Disillusion
   The Individual and the Community
   Shulamit Volkov   1

2. *Gemeinschaft* within *Gemeinde*
   Religious Ferment in Weimar Liberal Judaism
   Michael A. Meyer   15

3. *Gemeindeorthodoxie* in Weimar Germany
   The Approaches of Nehemiah Anton Nobel and Isak Unna
   David Ellenson   36

4. Turning Inward
   Jewish Youth in Weimar Germany
   Michael Brenner   56

5. Between *Deutschtum* and *Judentum*
   Ideological Controversies inside the Centralverein
   Avraham Barkai   74

6. *"Verjudung des Judentums"*
   Was There a Zionist Subculture in Weimar Germany?
   Jacob Borut   92

7. Written Out of History
   Bundists in Vienna and the Varieties of Jewish Experience
   in the Austrian First Republic
   Jack Jacobs   115

8. Jewish Ethnicity in a New Nation-State
The Crisis of Identity in the Austrian Republic
Marsha L. Rozenblit   134

9. Gender, Identity, and Community
Jewish University Women in Germany and Austria
Harriet Pass Freidenreich   154

10. The Crisis of the Jewish Family in Weimar Germany
Social Conditions and Cultural Representations
Sharon Gillerman   176

11. "Youth in Need"
Correctional Education and Family Breakdown in
German Jewish Families
Claudia Prestel   200

12. Decline and Survival of Rural Jewish Communities
Steven M. Lowenstein   223

CONTRIBUTORS   243
INDEX   245

ACKNOWLEDGMENTS

This volume is the result of several years of planning and effort by a number of individuals, whom the editors take great pleasure in thanking at this time. In 1992, Robert Jacobs, Executive Director of New York's Leo Baeck Institute, began working with Derek Penslar on the organization of a conference, to be held at Indiana University, on German-speaking Jews during the Weimar period. An organizational committee met in New York in May of 1993; the committee included officers of the LBI (New York President Ismar Schorsch, International President Michael Meyer, and New York Vice-President Fred Grubel), noted scholars (Richard Cohen, Harriet Freidenreich, Marion Kaplan, and Jehuda Reinharz), and representatives from the Friedrich-Ebert-Stiftung (Dr. Dieter Dettke) and the Deutscher Akademischer Austauschdienst (Heidrun Suhr).

There was general agreement that Weimar Jewry and its Austrian counterpart had too long been studied in isolation from each other and that their political, economic, and intellectual elites had received the lion's share of historiographical attention. This conference was seen as an exciting opportunity to open new pathways to the understanding of German-speaking Jews who, although not luminaries, were articulate and left behind moving testimonies of their thoughts, feelings, and deeds. With this agenda in mind, the conference, "Circles of Community: Collective Jewish Identities in Germany and Austria, 1918–1932," was held in March 1996 at Indiana University–Bloomington; it was generously supported by the Friedrich-Ebert-Stiftung, DAAD, and Indiana University's Robert A. and Sandra S. Borns Jewish Studies Program.

The volume before you brings together revised and expanded papers from that conference. In revising those papers, the authors benefited from the responses, offered at the conference, by two Indiana University faculty members, George Alter and Benjamin Nathans, and three invited guests: Marion Kaplan, Ismar Schorsch, and Lee Shai Weissbach. The Friedrich-Ebert-Stiftung offered additional support in the form of a publication subvention, for which the editors are deeply grateful. The editors also thank Carol Kahn Strauss, the current Executive Director of the New York Leo Baeck Institute, for her ongoing interest in this project. And a special expression of gratitude is reserved for Fred Grubel, a *Zeitzeuge* of the events discussed in these papers and a pillar of the Leo Baeck Institute for more than four decades.

At Indiana University, the members of the Borns Jewish Studies Program staff, Patricia Ek, Carolyn Lipson-Walker, and Melissa Deckard, ensured smooth running for the conference and helped ease the trauma of assembling a book manuscript produced by authors on four continents. Last, but certainly not least, the editors want to thank the authors for their prompt and thoughtful responses to the editors' suggested revisions. From the start, the authors expressed a commitment to this volume and its goal: to encourage new ways of perceiving Austro-German Jewish history of the 1920s, a period that, although appearing from our perspective to have been one of impending twilight, seemed to many who lived through it to be the breaking of dawn.

Michael Brenner, Munich
Derek J. Penslar, Toronto

The history of Jews in interwar Germany and Austria is often viewed either as the culmination of tremendous success in the economic and cultural realms, or as the prologue to the road that led to Auschwitz. Some historians point to the significant role individual Jews, such as Max Liebermann, Albert Einstein, Sigmund Freud, and Walther Rathenau, played in culture, science, politics, and the economy; and they emphasize the far-reaching integration of Jews into German society. In the words of Peter Gay, himself both a product and a chronicler of Weimar Germany, "despite the occasional surfacing of antisemitism Jews felt 'at home' in Germany. This was true in the Weimar Republic as well as in the Kaiserreich. There existed an irresistible mixture of a promising historical past and an exciting, and not at all hopeless, present. . . . Jews were, after all, able to realise their ambitions, more or less, without difficulty."[1]

Others stress the dark shadows looming over Weimar Germany. Representing such a view, Daniel Jonah Goldhagen writes in his controversial study of the Holocaust: "Antisemitism was endemic to Weimar Germany, so widespread that nearly every political group in the country shunned the Jews. Jews, though ferociously attacked, found virtually no defenders in German society. The public conversation about Jews was almost wholly negative."[2]

While those approaches focus mainly on the position of Jews within the largely non-Jewish society, the authors of this volume have chosen a different emphasis. They have elected to treat the German and Austrian Jewish communities of the interwar period in their own right, without, however, neglecting the social and political context. In contrast to the plethora of valuable studies on the Jewish communities of Imperial Germany and Austria, not to mention those on the Nazi period, a list of publications on Weimar Germany and the First Austrian Republic is quite brief.[3] Studies in this field have tended to concentrate heavily on the fate of individual Jews and the threat of antisemitism. Only in recent years has the internal development of the German-speaking Jewish community in the two decades after World War One become a focus of scholarly attention. In these works, mostly by younger scholars, the centrality of a reemerging sense of community becomes evident.[4]

The strengthening of communal ties found its expression on two different levels, which are reflected in the German terms *Gemeinde* and *Gemeinschaft*. On one level, there is the expansion and intensification of activities within the framework of the local Jewish communities *(Gemeinden)*. In contrast to the United States and most West European countries, Jewish communities—like Christian churches in Germany and Austria—remained (and remain until today) publicly constituted corporations. They embraced the vast majority of the Jews in any one place of residence and collected from the states tax revenues that Jews were compelled to pay for the maintenance of their religious institutions and services. By the 1920s, large *Gemeinden,* such as Berlin and Vienna, with almost two hundred thousand members each, represented urban administrations with a dense network of social, economic, and cultural institutions, thus reaching far beyond the nineteenth-century limitations of a religious congregation.

On another level, German and Austrian Jews renewed and redefined their identification with the Jewish community at large *(Gemeinschaft)*. In the process of acculturation and religious reform during the nineteenth century, many German Jews had restricted their Jewishness to the private expression of their individual religious faith. German or Austrian citizens of the Jewish faith would differ from their non-Jewish neighbors only in their religious belief and practice. This definition was valid as long as most Jews felt strong ties to their religion. In an increasingly secularized society, however, religion was no longer a unifying factor but a divisive one. Therefore, not only Zionists and the Orthodox, but also Liberal (i.e., Reform and Conservative) Jews looked for new definitions that would include the entire Jewish community. Among the most popular terms employed by Liberal Jews were *Stammesgemeinschaft* (community of common descent) and *Schicksalsgemeinschaft* (community of common fate), both emphasizing ethnic rather than religious community.

As German Jewry was no isolated entity, this search for *Gemeinschaft* must be seen in the broader cultural context, in particular in connection with the enormous impact of Ferdinand Tönnies's sociological study *Gemeinschaft und Gesellschaft* (Community and society, 1887) of the years preceding and following World War One. For Tönnies, *Gemeinschaft* represented "organic" relationships, such as families, neighborly relations, and village communities, whereas *Gesellschaft* expressed itself in "mechanical" relationships, such as business associations or urban administrations. Even a critic of this development like sociologist Helmuth Plessner had to admit that "*Gemeinschaft* is the ideal of our times."[5] For some this ideal meant the search for a revolutionary socialist *Völkergemeinschaft* (community of nations), for others that of a nationalist German *Volksgemeinschaft* (community of the German nation).

Many German Jews shared with their non-Jewish surroundings the need to establish new forms of community. Only a few weeks after the outbreak of World War I, Martin Buber anticipated the strengthening of *Gemeinschaft* among German Jews in a speech later reprinted as the opening essay in his journal *Der Jude:*

> In the tempest of events, the Jew has had the powerful experience of what Gemeinschaft means. . . . The most essential weakness of the Western Jew was not that he was 'assimilated' but that he was atomized; that he was without connection [to the Jewish community]; that his heart no longer beat as one with a living Gemeinschaft. . . . Now, however, in the catastrophic events that he experienced with his neighbors, the Jew discovered with shock and joy the great life of Gemeinschaft. And [this discovery] captivated him.[6]

Together with the discovery of "the great life of *Gemeinschaft,*" the "catastrophic events" of World War I raised new doubts among German and Austrian Jews about their prospects for integration into the larger *Gesellschaft.* Jewish soldiers had entered the war with the hope that finally all barriers to social integration would be overcome. Little remained of this hope after the German census of Jewish soldiers in 1916, the continuing discrimination in the barracks and trenches, and the new wave of postwar antisemitism. To be sure, the new democratic constitutions of Weimar Germany and the Austrian Republic granted Jews total equality, and for the first time they reached high positions both as elected politicians and state officials. Many German-speaking Jews felt more at home within those democratic societies than had their ancestors in the imperial societies. But at the same time, the verbal anti-Jewish threats, which had always existed in those societies, became more violent. This was true especially in Weimar Germany, with the rise of nationalist parties and the turn from antisemitic rhetoric to the expulsion of East European Jews and occasional street riots in front of synagogues.

Political insecurity was not the only threat to German and Austrian Jews during the 1920s. Once solidly rooted in the middle classes, the Jewish community suffered especially severely from the economic crisis. By the end of the 1920s many observers were noting a rapid economic decline of German Jewry and predicted the pauperization and proletarianization of the Jewish masses.[7]

The renewal of Jewish communal life was a response to all those developments: intellectually, it reflected the flight from nineteenth-century individualism and a longing for the restoration of ties with members of one's religious or ethnic group; politically, it was the result

of growing exclusion from a variety of instititutions; and economically, Jewish communities offered shelter and assistance for those
who had lost their secure place in society.

The essays in this volume illuminate the variety of expressions of
Jewish communal life in Weimar Germany and the Austrian Republic.
In the opening essay, Shulamit Volkov sets the stage by reminding us
of the details. She maintains that in focusing on the community, we
should not neglect the fate of the individual. By recalling the background and experiences of her father, who believed himself to be an
assimilated German Jew, she focuses our attention on the group of
people about whom the painter Max Liebermann wrote, in a letter
sent to the Hebrew writer Hayim Nahman Bialik and to Meir Dizen-
goff, the mayor of Tel Aviv, in June 1933: "Like a horrible nightmare
the abrogation of equal rights weighs upon us all, but especially upon
those Jews who, like me, had surrendered themselves to the dream of
assimilation. . . . As difficult as it had been for me, I have awakened
from the dream that I dreamed my whole life long."[8]
   Not every Jew needed the climactic events of 1933 to awaken from
that dream of assimilation. Religious and cultural renewal began well
before the forced return to the ghetto in 1933. With regard to
Germany's Liberal Jews, Michael Meyer elucidates little-known aspects of this renewal and discovers in the Berlin of the 1920s a
precursor to the *havurah* movement, whose informal and intimate
prayer-groups would enrich American Jewish life a half century later.
What emerges from his picture of Liberal Jews in Berlin are islands of
small congregations whose members were dedicated to spiritual creativity in the midst of an ocean of anonymous, often mechanical,
urban community. On the other end of the religious spectrum, David
Ellenson analyzes the development of German Jewish Orthodoxy by
focusing on two of its most prominent representatives, Rabbis Nehemiah Anton Nobel and Isak Unna, and on their attitudes toward the
Einheitsgemeinde, the unified local Jewish community. While both
rejected the path of Samson Raphael Hirsch and refused to establish
secessionist Orthodox communities, Ellenson demonstrates that they
acted for quite different reasons.
   Religion was only one of the ingredients among the far-reaching
activities of the Jewish youth movement. As Michael Brenner shows,
this movement was not only an answer to the exclusion from German
institutional life but a sign of renewed Jewish vitality. By the end of
the Weimar Republic, approximately every third German Jew had
joined a Jewish youth movement, from socialist to Orthodox, from

Liberal to Zionist. Though differing in their ideology, all of those youth groups attempted to implant some form of Jewish identity in their members, who often came from highly assimilated backgrounds.

Religious and cultural pluralism had its counterpart in political and ideological diversity. Using an array of original sources, both Avraham Barkai's analysis of the Centralverein and Jacob Borut's inquiry into the possible existence of a Zionist subculture challenge established notions about the polar division of German Jewry into assimilationists and committed Zionists. As we learn, the dividing line between the two was often blurred, while serious differences remained within the various factions of those two major blocks. In Austria, a third alternative existed outside the Liberal-Zionist political spectrum. Jack Jacobs reconstructs an unknown chapter in Jewish socialism by providing the first scholarly account of the history of Bundists in interwar Vienna. By tracing the ties of Austrian Bundists back to their East European origins he also turns our attention to the constant interchange between East and West in European Jewish history.

The background for Jewish self-definition in the Austrian Republic was quite different from that in Weimar: the former was heir to a multinational empire, the latter to a German national state. Marsha Rozenblit suggests that Austrian Jews hoped to maintain their three-fold self-definition as Austrians by political loyalty, Germans by cultural affinity, and Jews by ethnicity. Those hopes were soon disappointed, and Austrian Jews were faced with an unsolvable paradox of a society that tried to force an ethnic German identification upon them while at the same time excluding them in an atmosphere of rising antisemitism. As a result, Rozenblit shows us, Jews increasingly retreated to the private sphere.

Just as the renewal of Jewish life is one major theme in interwar German Jewish history, the retreat from Jewish life and the deepening sense of crisis and decline are other prominent features. In her study of Jewish women students at German and Austrian universities, Harriet Freidenreich finds that a majority withdrew from any form of corporate Jewish life. Most of these highly educated Jewish women were only marginally involved in matters concerning the Jewish community. The Jewish communal and associational network, which was dominated by men, provided many Jewish men with satisfying means for self-expression as Jews; but these means were denied to their female counterparts.

In their essays, Sharon Gillerman and Claudia Prestel refute the myth of a harmonious German Jewish family life that persisted even under harsh external conditions. Shaken by economic despair and political upheaval, but also by many private tragedies, numerous Jewish families fell apart, and correctional education became a constant feature of Jewish life in the interwar period. The significance of these essays about the Jewish family goes far beyond the Weimar period; it extends to the heart of one of the Jews' most cherished and deep-seated myths and sources of self-identification and self-pride.

Decline and the struggle for survival are at the center of Steven Lowenstein's essay on rural Jewish life in Weimar Germany. Although the vast majority of German Jews lived in big cities during the 1920s and the process of urbanization was still continuing, almost 20 percent of the Jewish population remained in the small towns and villages where their forefathers had lived as cattle dealers and peddlers. While the rural communities struggled with numerical decline, their members were in many cases still able to guarantee their survival as a distinct group within German Jewry.

Taken together, these essays form a mosaic, a complex picture of German Jewry on the eve of its demise. German and Austrian Jews were still split into a variety of communities, but the sense of a single united community became stronger as the external threat increased. Within weeks of the Nazi seizure of power, German Jews created, for the first time in their history, a representative umbrella organization that included all Jewish communities, the *Reichsvertretung der deutschen Juden* (Reich Association of German Jews). On a cultural level, exclusion from German society forced them to found their own *Jüdische Kulturbund* (Jewish Cultural League), where Jewish artists performed for exclusively Jewish audiences. The years between 1933 and 1938 thus constituted a last attempt to build new and more comprehensive circles of community among German Jews. While the groundwork for those new organizations was laid in the days before 1933, they were not merely successors of the earlier circles of community. Their main purpose was to prepare for a new beginning on different ground. For those who stayed behind, the circles of Jewish communal life were broken forever.

Notes

1. English summary of Peter Gay, "In Deutschland zu Hause . . . Die Juden der Weimarer Zeit," in *Die Juden im nationalsozialistischen Deutschland*, ed. Arnold Paucker (Tübingen, 1986), p. 42.

2. Daniel Jonah Goldhagen, *Hitler's Willing Executioners: Ordinary Germans and the Holocaust* (New York, 1996), p. 83.

3. On Imperial Germany, see, for example, Ismar Schorsch, *Jewish Reactions to German Anti-Semitism, 1870–1914* (New York, 1972); Jehuda Reinharz, *Fatherland or Promised Land: The Dilemma of the German Jew, 1893–1914* (Ann Arbor, 1975); Uriel Tal, *Christians and Jews in Germany: Religion, Politics, and Ideology in the Second Reich* (Ithaca, 1975); Steven E. Aschheim, *Brothers and Strangers: The East European Jew in German and German Jewish Consciousness, 1800–1923* (Madison, 1982); Jack Wertheimer, *Unwelcome Strangers: East European Jews in Imperial Germany* (New York, 1987); Marion Kaplan, *The Making of the Jewish Middle Class: Women, Family, and Identity in Imperial Germany* (New York, 1991); Jacob Borut, "'A New Spirit among Our Brethren in Ashkenaz': German Jewry in the Face of Economic, Social, and Political Change in the Reich at the End of the 19th Century," Ph.D. diss. (in Hebrew), Hebrew University of Jerusalem, 1991. On Austria, see Marsha L. Rozenblit, *The Jews of Vienna, 1867–1914: Assimilation and Identity* (Albany, 1983); Robert Wistrich, *The Jews of Vienna in the Age of Franz Joseph* (Oxford, 1989); Steven Beller, *Vienna and the Jews, 1867–1938* (Cambridge, 1989).

4. See, for example, the two volumes produced by the Leo Baeck Institute: Werner E. Mosse and Arnold Paucker, eds., *Entscheidungsjahr 1932. Zur Judenfrage in der Endphase der Weimarer Republik* (Tübingen, 1965), and George L. Mosse, ed., *Deutsches Judentum in Krieg und Revolution, 1916–1923* (Tübingen, 1966); a more recent collection in Hebrew edited by Oded Heilbronner, *Yehudei Weimar: Hevra be-mashber ha-moderni'ut, 1918–1933* [The Jews of Weimar: A society in the crisis of modernity] (Jerusalem, 1994); and Walter Grab and Julius H. Schoeps, *Juden in der Weimarer Republik* (Stuttgart, 1986). A slight departure from the concentration on political and intellectual history in the previous studies was marked in the first and hitherto only attempt to portray Weimar Jewry as a whole: Donald L. Niewyk, *The Jews in Weimar Germany* (Baton Rouge, 1980). More recent studies have shifted their interest to the internal development of different communities within Weimar Jewry. See, for example, Trude Maurer, *Ostjuden in Deutschland* (Hamburg, 1986); Michael Brenner, *The Renaissance of Jewish Culture in Weimar Germany* (New Haven, 1996); Hagit Lavsky, *Before Catastrophe: The Distinctive Path of German Zionism* (Detroit, 1996); and the dissertations by Gabriel Alexander, "Berlin Jewry and Its Community during the Weimar Republic" (in Hebrew), Hebrew University of Jerusalem, 1993), and Sharon Gillerman, "Between Public and Private: Family, Community, and Jewish Identity in Weimar Berlin," Ph.D. diss., University of California, Los Angeles, 1996. On Austria, see Harriet Pass Freidenreich, *Jewish Politics in Vienna, 1918–1938* (Bloomington, 1991). A comprehensive study of Austrian Jewry in the interwar period is still a much needed desideratum.

5. Helmuth Plessner, *Die Grenzen der Gemeinschaft. Eine Kritik des sozialen Radikalismus* (Bonn, 1972), p. 26.

6. Martin Buber, "Die Losung," *Der Jude* 1, no. 1 (1916): 1–2.

7. See, for example, Alfred Marcus, *Die wirtschaftliche Krise des deutschen Juden. Eine soziologische Untersuchung* (Berlin, 1931), and Jakob Lestschinsky, *Das wirtschaftliche Schicksal des deutschen Judentums. Aufstieg, Wandlung, Krise, Ausblick* (Berlin, 1932).

8. Quoted in Michael A. Meyer, *Jewish Identity in the Modern World* (Seattle, 1990), p. 54.

ABBREVIATIONS

ALBI-NY	Archives of the Leo Baeck Institute, New York
BLBI	*Bulletin des Leo Baeck Instituts*
CZA	Central Zionist Archives, Jerusalem
JLZ	*Jüdisch-Liberale Zeitung*
JR	*Jüdische Rundschau*
JZ	*Jüdische Zeitung*
KJW	*Kölner Jüdisches Wochenblatt*
LBIYB	*Leo Baeck Institute Year Book*
ÖW	*Österreichische Wochenschrift*
TJBDG	*Tel Aviver Jahrbuch für deutsche Geschichte*
WMZ	*Wiener Morgenzeitung*

IN SEARCH OF JEWISH COMMUNITY

1

German Jews between Fulfillment & Disillusion

The Individual and the Community

SHULAMIT VOLKOV

Some fifteen years ago my father, a German Jew if ever there was one, suffered a severe brain hemorrhage and a temporary loss of memory. Otto Rudolf Heinsheimer was born in 1908 in the elegant resort town of Baden-Baden in southern Germany, to what was then considered a fully assimilated Jewish family of that proverbial milieu of private bankers, medical doctors, and lawyers—great and small. I was present when the young hospital physician at my father's bedside was trying to assess the damage. The patient was not sure about his whereabouts. He could not give his birth date or any other personal information. Then he was casually asked when he had immigrated to Israel. "1933," came the answer, crystal clear and as quick as lightning. He would never have admitted it—and perhaps it was only a coincidence—but this memory was apparently anchored very, very deeply in his mind.

Despite much scholarly debate, 1933 represented for many German Jews a genuine earthquake. It produced a deep psychic shock, and its reverberations required fundamental reassessment of the most comprehensive type. The presumably secure life-long expectations of these men and women were now totally shattered. No less meaningfully, all accepted views of their near and remote past seemed to have been demolished. A basic reshuffling of all values was now required: a comprehensive reconsideration of all human ties, all professional assumptions, all social and economic prospects. The Jewish collectivity in all its facets—despite its many undertakings, rapid initiatives, and various important supportive functions—could not do much to diminish the pain. In a letter from Berlin, written by the twenty-five-year-old Rudi Heinsheimer on April 25, 1933, we find a description of his visit to the Jewish *Gemeinde*:[1] "There rages an enormous business of mediation and information exchange, organized in emergency but already divided into departments (physicians, lawyers, emigrants, etc.)." He writes, "unimaginably big crowd, a completely full house." But beyond and besides all that "action," things looked worse than ever. The night before, he recounts, he had decided, apparently on the spur of the moment and despite his dark mood, to go to the opera: "In the intermission—foyer: public of the new Germany: completely uniform. Income between 250.– and 1000.– marks per month. Social position: between chief clerk and government counselor, not more than 1 percent Jews. I was so dumbfounded and beaten as I have not been for a long time: about the complete change, about the unheard of uniformity, about the unique contrast to the experience of that previous morning in the Jewish community" (no. 4). Later he has a similar experience at the University of Berlin. Listening to "an extremely weak speech" by the new rector, the "anthropologist and race scientist" Professor Fischer, Heinsheimer notes without further comment that it became clear to him that "in this new university there was no room for us Jews. No. No room. . . ." Then he adds, "Do you remember how I always went to the university and how I used to come back?" (no. 9). How he must have loved the university! How he loved the opera!

In confronting all this, Heinsheimer, naturally enough, found it difficult to write: "No thoughts are being formed," he complains, "nor any words. Only a dark, powerful, strangely effective working is in me, an unrest and quiet simmering." The common words repeated in the letters of these days are "darkness," "uncertain darkness," "wilderness," "wilderness without a way out . . ." (no. 3). "Inside it is completely dark," he writes to his beloved, "and thoughts, sensations, desires, feelings, and everything else rush in ghostlike confusion. Everything is still like a play of shadows upon a half-lit wall, the people who display it cannot be recognized, cannot be grasped." "Not yet," he then adds with a sudden gust of youthful hope, "but soon it will be all right" (no. 4).

The depth of despair of this man can only be appreciated when one reads his letter following Hitler's speech of May 1 at Tempelhofer Feld in Berlin—a letter full of exultation and uncontrolled excitement vis-à-vis the slightest, the farthest, the soon to be proven absurd chance of still, after all, despite everything, being able to join Germany again. The personal context makes his reactions all the more revealing. Heinsheimer's Berlin friends included a number of hard-core Zionists.

His girlfriend, my future mother, was then (as always) unusually clear-sighted. She grew up in a family of Hebrew-speaking Zionists in White Russia and arrived in Germany from the sands of nascent Tel Aviv to study physics and then medicine in Heidelberg and Berlin; by mid-April 1933 she had already left Germany. The letters I am quoting from were written to her—surely not one who would have appreciated Heinsheimer's German nationalist enthusiasm at the time. Here was a man just one step away from a decision to break away from his past forever and for good. He must then have been, as he always was, a self-contained, introverted person, normally strictly rational, and—I can surely vouch for it—very hard to impress. The speech took place only one month after Hitler's announcement of the boycott on April 1, 1933, and followed immediately on the introduction of laws excluding non-Aryans from the civil service, thus practically closing off his own professional future in Germany. But Hitler's speech apparently had an unparalleled effect. It was clearly not only the speech itself—though this was mighty enough. It was the rekindling of hope, irrational to be sure, the reemergence of possibilities already considered lost, that must have made the deepest impression; and then, immediately afterwards, a new wave of confusion, paralyzing indecision, and finally "darkness" once again.

Listening to the speech on the radio, even if it was in "a partially cold and negative milieu," as Heinsheimer reports, must have been an overwhelming experience: "That really was the shattering, crushing, yet still uplifting [aspect] of this speech . . . not the surely important details of the program; not the elegant, organic structure, the rounded flawlessness," runs his explanation, "but the fact that it was an elementary expression of a gigantic natural force, a brilliant testimony of an unshakable faith, the straightforward communication of a visionary, and the thunderous call of a colossal personality" (no. 8). Heinsheimer is then engulfed by new doubts and ever more pressing questions: "What and how much ties you to this place?" he asks himself. "What and how much do you expect here?" And then he raises what is apparently the main point: "Is there really no possibility for a Jew to take part in this thing here? Or if there isn't now, when would it be possible again? Can one wait through this transition time? Should one? . . . What do you give up here? What do you expect outside? Where do you belong? How and where can you set yourself up? What do you look for, after all? What is important for you? Where lie your principles, your capacities, your aims, your ideals? Where, who, how, what? . . . Sometimes it seems to me," he despairingly comments, "as if I could neither live nor die" (no. 8).

There is surely a measure of general, aimless, youthful agony in all this. Nevertheless, this is the voice of one man, of a single Jew reacting to the first signs of what, for him, was a personal, deeply personal catastrophe. He himself was then young and energetic, so that within a couple of months he did finally decide to leave for Palestine. "As much as it seems—theoretically—attractive, to participate in this new and beautiful and great [project] that is apparently being built here . . . ," he writes somewhat later, "so inexorably is it—practically— proven that our cooperation is rejected, prohibited, and despised; so inevitable is the conclusion to turn one's back upon this country" (no. 9). His friends, as so often and in this case, too, mainly Jews, reacted in a variety of ways. Robert was just then marrying a non-Jewish woman and moved to Hamburg before he finally found himself a home on the Pacific coast of California. Fritz was eager to leave for England and had no use for reservations or sentimentality. Edgar was determined to stay. He even finally joined the Verband National- deutscher Juden; but he too finally managed to leave before it was too late. All of them were in their mid to late twenties, relatively well-off, dynamic and resourceful despite that temporary "lethargy" that had seized them all at first, as Heinsheimer reported. But how difficult it must have been! One had to be freed, he explains in yet another letter, from so many "unshakable and unquestionable things," that is, "from the country and your belonging to it, that were till now self-evident; from the language and the culture, that were till now your natural foundations; from the profession of German legal teaching"—and here he refers to his own special case—"in which I grew up till now as if in my inherited air"; also "from that never-doubted urban milieu of Central Europe; from the life habits and lifestyle of an intellectual petit bourgeois; from the climate and seasons of the temperate zone, etc." (no. 12). After all, he writes elsewhere, one should not forget or underestimate "that self-evident certainty with which I was a Ger- man—even if it were a thousand times an error" (no. 15).

The depth of disillusionment cannot be denied. It was a personal tragedy. Moreover, it must be seen in conjunction with that sense of fulfillment and pride in success, likewise personal, that had inspired so many German Jews before. Jacob Toury has recently reminded us of the persistent complacency of most Jewish organizations as well, even as late as 1929.[2] But here I wish to stress neither the story of the leadership nor of the rank and file; I would like to ignore for a moment both organizational and communal activities and concentrate instead on the individual, private Jew. I wish to call to mind the catastrophe of that urban middle-class group of so-called assimilated men and women who felt—"even if it were a thousand times an error"— completely and entirely a part of their non-Jewish environment; men and women who, despite signs of danger, seemed to feel comfortable and secure—that is, as comfortable and secure as anyone could feel in those times of political, social, and economic upheaval in Germany and Austria during the interwar years. The search for Jewish community, it seems to me, cannot be considered apart from or outside this perspective. After all, the process of emancipation had always been directed—primarily and fundamentally—at the individual Jew. And its collapse was therefore most forcefully experienced by the single individual. Assimilation was above all a personal process, one that was crowned, in the most positive cases, with more or less personal success. It is only natural that its abrupt end touched the core of the individual's life—practically, of course, but also in terms of an inner life, sense of self-identity and belonging, and with regard to one's "center of gravity."

In his controversial but highly suggestive book, *Modernity and Ambivalence,* Zygmunt Bauman gives new contours to the eminently individual character of the process of assimilation.[3] The initial principle of emancipation, formulated at the time of the French Revolution, was, after all: "Everything to the Jew as individual; nothing to Jews as a group." And this principle, it has often been argued, was intrinsic to the new social and political order. It was intrinsic to the new type of state, which had been emerging since the late eighteenth century; and it is in fact further intrinsic, according to Bauman, to the *Weltanschauung* of modernity as a whole. Its implications were apparent soon enough. First of all, general, non-Jewish society issued an offer to individual Jews to join in—though this was, to be sure, an offer with a series of conditions attached. Second, that same non-Jewish society, especially its ruling, dominant stratum, insisted on the simultaneous dismemberment of the Jewish community structure, decidedly refusing to integrate it within its own multilayered, far from unified milieu. After all, Bauman's argument notwithstanding, the modern state, while indeed attempting to destroy all corporate arrangements in the area under its jurisdiction, never managed to do that. Instead, it has always allowed a parallel structure of associations to flourish within its boundaries. In Germany, in particular, this network of *Vereine* was very powerful, despite state supervision and occasional police intervention. Still, Jewish communal organizations of whatever type or character were never deemed acceptable within that network. They were neither state supported, nor were they allowed to evolve freely as independent social institutions. The authorities, especially in Prussia, were hostile toward all efforts by Jews to organize beyond the local level of the congregation so that the overall process of Jewish emancipation was often accomplished *out-*

side, if not always explicitly *against,* traditional Jewish community organizations. Furthermore, it was accomplished *against,* and usually *outside,* Jewish community life in general and, most emphatically, *against* Jewish communal identity.

The opposition to emancipation of Jews who saw themselves as spokesmen for organized Jewish life is well known. They openly expressed their fears for the future of that life. It is surely no mere coincidence that early plans for emancipation, both on the part of existing regimes, as in the Austria of Joseph II, and on the part of some private initiators, Jews and non-Jews alike, were given a powerful push at a time when contemporary Jewish communal leadership suffered a severe crisis of legitimation.[4] At this low point of inner-communal cohesion, the campaign against the community, if one agrees to think of it this way, turned out to be particularly effective: not immediately or everywhere, of course, but soon and to an ever-increasing degree throughout the so-called German-speaking world. It is interesting to recall in this context the revealing disagreement between Moses Mendelssohn and Christian Wilhelm von Dohm with regard to the future role of the Jewish community. Dohm, the author of the pathbreaking book *Über die bürgerliche Verbesserung der Juden* (1781), was presumably a spokesman for the strict statist orientation of late Prussian absolutism. He was nevertheless ready, even willing, to leave at least *some* measure of authority in the hands of the Jewish community. Mendelssohn, in contrast, as one modern interpreter has approvingly commented, immediately realized that the safeguarding of communal autonomy, "though it may seem so tolerant and well-meaning, could only strengthen the special status [of Jews]," and that its consequences could finally only be "regressive."[5] The link between full individual equality and the undermining of group authority was inherent in the process and evident, even then and there, to all who truly wished to comprehend its nature.

Bauman gives his formulation a still sharper edge. According to him it was not—or perhaps not *only*—legal, formal emancipation—endowment with equal civil rights—that was bound to destroy the community. The real threat was inherent in what he sees as the "trap of assimilation." Jews, he comments, and Jews in Germany most particularly, fell into this trap "with enthusiasm and abandon." By definition, inaugurating an era of tolerance vis-à-vis the *individual* meant *in*tolerance vis-à-vis the group. "Tolerant treatment of individuals," he summarizes, "was inextricably linked to intolerance aimed at collectivities, their way of life, their values and, above all, their value-legitimating powers." The stigma of being different—and of course inferior as well—was attached to the *collectivity,* he explains, while "the offer of escaping" the stigma was "extended to individuals *qua* individuals." It included an invitation "to the individual members of the stigmatized community," as he puts it, "to desist loyalty to all groups of origin," in fact "to revolt against their power and to renounce communal loyalty."[6]

That this interpretation is only partially true, and that it drastically reduces the complexity of the process, is readily apparent even if we go back only to the familiar and endlessly cited case of Moses Mendelssohn himself. Mendelssohn was indeed willing to pay the *price* of autonomy for the *prize* of being allowed to enter civilized European society and of obtaining equal social and political rights for Jews everywhere within it. At the same time he believed this to be the *only* legitimate price. He certainly was not willing to pay further by denying his Jewish identity, let alone by rejecting the Jewish religion—as he understood it—or even only a Jewish traditional lifestyle. But giving up communal autonomy, often monopolized—as he knew full well—by uninspiring rabbis, was not considered by him to be too high a price. For many at that time it may have seemed an additional bonus. And in this respect, too, Mendelssohn was a forerunner of a major trend in nineteenth-century German Jewry, the trend toward *confessionalism*—toward the turning of Judaism into yet another religious confession in the Germany of that time. Indeed, if anything, this seemed to be the perfect solution for most Jews: it meant pursuing a personal, individual path of integration into German culture and society while maintaining a living (but not too demanding) tie with somewhat reformed (but not too radically reformed) Jewish community life. Finally, attached to this double-edged solution was a third element: an invigorated domestic religiosity, enhancing the role of the much-applauded Jewish family, and therefore easily, almost "naturally," merging with the general norms and ideals of the German *Mittelstand*.[7]

This threefold solution, allowing both private success and communal survival, indeed had an inner logic of its own. Cultural habits adopted by individual Jews in the private sphere of their lives in order to achieve proper and complete integration were, after all, the same basic cultural habits that had to be adopted in communal life, too. The aestheticization of ritual to fit middle-class notions of propriety, for instance, could be seen as merely another face of the aestheticization of private life. Stress on "passing," or adapting and fitting in, was paramount both for the individual and for the new community. In both cases, it required great attention to decorum and a minimum of investment in the inner content of Judaism.

During the early 1820s, efforts by the young, enthusiastic members of the Verein für Cultur und Wissenschaft der Juden to give a new meaning to their Jewishness were rejected by traditionalists as well as by the members of the short-lived Reform synagogue in Berlin. Generally speaking, although reforms of great depth with wide-ranging programs did sometimes enjoy a public response, they were usually of interest to only a small minority. No wonder more radical Reform finally matured in the United States. There, and not in its ideational birthplace, could it become truly meaningful and relevant, since there, and not in Germany, adherence to the community did not, at least did not always, stand in opposition to the demands of equality and integration. In Germany, Reform was not intended primarily to modernize Judaism but to make it acceptable. Better still, Reform was meant to make Judaism as unobtrusive as possible within the context of assimilation. This was deemed appropriate for the purpose at hand and more seemed unnecessary. Through such tactics, the distinction between Jews as private citizens and Jews as members of a religious congregation was made clear, while the process of "passing" could thus continue without interruption. Assimilation that did not include a complete break with the community therefore became possible; it was eventually to be crowned with an astonishing degree of success, despite all hindrances.

By the late nineteenth century and until well after World War I, this combination of "entry" into non-Jewish society and culture along with preservation of constant and convenient ties to a modernized Jewish community and adoption of a fitting style of domestic Juda-ism had become the clearly preferred solution to the dilemma of emancipation. But it had also become apparent that it was not a perfect solution. "Entry" was never quite complete, and communal identity always remained problematic. Antisemitism, though nor-mally not really socially acceptable and ineffective as a social or political force, was nevertheless widespread and never far from the surface. Pockets of discrimination continued to be a cause for disaffec-tion: in the Prussian army, in the upper echelons of the bureaucracy, and in the university professoriate. Still, overall personal and collec-tive achievements seemed truly stunning. Jews could justifiably feel proud of themselves; some even felt slightly embarrassed by it all. What made this imperfect solution finally bearable, often even highly satisfactory, was Jewish success: the rapid economic improvement of so many, the continuous social advancement, and the impressive performance of so many Jews in culture, in the arts and sciences, and even in politics. The dark side of this "arrangement" could easily be forgotten under the circumstances.

A minority, of course, did experience life in a way described by

Bauman, namely, as a testing ground, "a permanent trial period," a nightmare during which one had to prove repeatedly one's belonging and one's no less than perfect "passing." It is easy enough to string together the statements that poured from the pens of disillusioned Jews throughout the "Age of Emancipation." One can thus easily present a continuum that may have characterized a certain group but was never characteristic of German Jewry as a whole. Among intellectual Jews, no doubt, there was never any lack of sensitivity to the predicaments of assimilation. Here we might think of Rahel Varnhagen's bitter words in reaction to the estrangement from her former Berlin "salon" friends following her impoverishment and the emergence of a new type of nationalism in the wake of the Napoleonic wars.[8] Heine's disillusion—first with the efforts of the so-called Culturverein in Berlin to renew Judaism, and then with the consequences, or the lack of consequences, of his own conversion to Christianity—is an even better example.[9] The painful awakening of an aging Berthold Auerbach in view of the open antisemitism in Berlin in 1879,[10] and the traumatic confrontation of Jewish intellectuals with antisemitism in fin-de-siècle Vienna have, if anything, been quoted all too often. But the general mood among Jews at that time was not one of despair or disillusion. It was one of overall satisfaction; indeed, "complacency" would be a better word for it.[11]

Soon, however, new dilemmas became apparent; and some Jews—as always before and after, though now perhaps in increasing numbers—felt forced to draw radical conclusions from them. A minority converted; a somewhat larger group allowed their children to be converted. Others, marrying outside the Jewish fold, simply drifted away; and a considerable group no longer kept any ritual, abandoned all religious habits, allowed all family traditions to become defunct, and sought to become entirely indistinguishable from the bourgeois world of which they had become a part.[12] This was an ongoing process. It is difficult to estimate today how many really felt entirely secure in their new posture. There is evidence to suggest that some, at least, did not. For the early years of the twentieth century and into the time of the Weimar Republic, Walther Rathenau's unease and his continuous inner struggles are well documented and well known.[13] Less well known is the number of those who shared his predicament. More important, however, were the pressures felt by the majority of Jews, who had usually trusted the road they had taken till then and believed they had adequately solved the dilemmas of their German Jewish existence. Most revealing in our context is not their ever-growing realization that a measure of antisemitism and some forms of overt or covert discrimination were apparently there to stay, but their gradually emerging awareness that existing communal links no longer sufficed, no longer supplied them with a meaningful group identity, no longer offered them the kind of modern secular identity they were seeking.

The two last decades of the nineteenth century were a time of great reshuffling and reorganization among German Jews. Various cultural associations were formed, not only for rehearsing the normal, German bourgeois repertoire in the more friendly surroundings of one's own kind, but also in order to establish a new Jewish cultural inventory. This project, previously a matter for a small dedicated nucleus, became increasingly relevant for an ever-growing Jewish public. Politically, too, the establishment of the Centralverein (CV) in 1893 effectively brought to an end—perhaps inadvertently—the previously unchallenged assimilation arrangement. Here was a Jewish organization, pledged to fight antisemitism and organize Jews, and Jews alone, for that purpose and *in public*. This was, indeed, the first major step toward widespread acceptance among German Jews of their existence as a *minority* group—a separate social component with a unique identity that was there to stay. There were earlier beginnings, of course. Men such as Ludwig Philippson, editor of the *Allgemeine Zeitung des Judentums,* had implicitly accepted this fact much earlier. But the inauguration of the CV indicated a major turning point. This was by then no longer an inner-Jewish affair, a kind of meek extension of previous community life. It openly announced the entry of Jews as a collectivity into the general German public sphere. Defense activity was a new departure. It implied a readiness to act collectively for one's own interests, to assert a new kind of consciousness, to publicly endorse a separate Jewish identity. This, to be sure, was not always so interpreted by the protagonists themselves. Most of them surely would have rejected such an interpretation. But what really counted was, after all, not their theory but their practice. Moreover, at the same time, Zionism was also developing its own, explicit version of Jewish communal self-assertion. Continuously engaging in internal controversies with the CV, it was the differences between the two organizations that preoccupied Jewish public opinion at the time and attracted most historians later on.[14] Their *affinity* has thus been too often overlooked. By the end of the nineteenth century, the first phase of Jewish emancipation in Germany had been completed—not only because formal equality was more or less achieved, but also because the first stage of this process, strictly focused upon *individual* achievement, seemed to have advanced as far as possible and to have finally reached a dead end.

The conscious realization of this situation was yet another legacy of the later days of the Kaiserreich to the budding Weimar Republic. Like most of the Republic's other apparent innovations, its true origins went back to the prewar years. The limits of the general, not merely Jewish "project of assimilation," heralded and undertaken by modern bourgeois society and the modern national state in Germany, were made apparent long before the stormy interwar years. Surely more central to its nineteenth-century history than the Jewish chapter was, for instance, the fight against Catholic communal autonomy. No amount of protest on the part of Catholics could ever relieve the stigma of their Ultramontanism, or convince the spokesmen of national uniformity, homogeneity, and perfect inner cohesion of their loyalty. The *Kulturkampf* was no accident; indeed, neither was the Liberal initiative in this matter a coincidence. It was, in fact, the most concerted effort to break up nonnational, nonbourgeois communal identity in modern Germany; and despite its apparent failure, it did have wide-ranging implications for the character of the German state on the one hand, and for Catholic social and political behavior patterns on the other.

Distrust of working-class community life and organization is another case in point. Quite early in nineteenth-century Europe, individual working-class voters were equally acceptable to Liberals and Conservatives alike. Bismarck's introduction of universal male suffrage immediately comes to mind. But the existence of workers' organizations—social or political—had never ceased to be regarded as a real and immediate danger. Trade unions were abhorred, to say nothing of the Social Democratic Party, not only as interest group associations, but also as potential opponents of law and order and outspoken obstructionists of that much sought after and much acclaimed cultural consensus. Assimilation required personal, individual acceptance of norms and values shared by the hegemonic element in state and society. In effect, the poor were expected to get rich, the Catholics to behave like Protestants, and the Jews to convert or at least to minimize their distinctiveness. Insistence on communal links, especially if those meant more than a tactic of "negative integration," was viewed as potentially subversive—indeed, it was subversive under the circumstances. Since pluralism of any kind was inconceivable, all signs of community separatism were dangerous and had to be resisted.[15]

In response, nonhegemonic elements in nineteenth-century "Prussian Germany"—but not only there, of course—had to choose a strategy. Jews, as we have seen, were perhaps particularly eager to take the purely individual road; but they too slowly recognized its limitations. Under the more open antisemitism of the Weimar years, the repeated economic setbacks that characterized it, and its inherent political instability (which often bordered on anarchy), some kind of new communal life seemed more vital than ever. At the same time, war and revolution had practically destroyed the old hegemonic world, and a new one did not seem able to establish itself. The bourgeois world, of which individual Jews were already a part or of which they were striving to become a part, seemed to have lost its footing. In a democratic state, programmatically open to difference, particular communal identity offered at least some anchor. Such an identity had now become not merely legitimate but increasingly indispensable. For many German Jews the stage of ambivalence had long since passed, and a search for a new synthesis was well under way.

The effects of this "return to community" cannot be dealt with here. But I will conclude by recalling those who never managed, even under the pressure of National Socialism, to find their way back, and those for whom such "reentry" into Judaism seemed exceedingly painful. Here, once again, is my father's correspondence from the spring and early summer of 1933. By then it was apparently clear to him that his and his family's previous posture was no longer tenable. "But do you wish that I should also immediately join Judaism," he wrote to my mother on May 19, scarcely three weeks after his Hitler speech euphoria, ". . . I, who know so little of its religion, its history, its language, its culture, etc., and who cannot have, so to speak, a natural [sense of] belonging to it at all?" And since a return to Judaism clearly meant, to him, a turn to Zionism, he adds, "Should I already announce my joining the Zionist Organization? Can I? May I? I think not, since to be a member of such a community is, for me, more than the simple acquisition of a membership card. I do not want to be a Jew, or a Zionist, as long as it is only external circumstances that bring me to it, but only when I am also brought to it, belong to it, from within. I believe with certainty now," he concludes, "that it will come to that" (no. 15). From this new perspective, then, the young Rudolf Heinsheimer looks again at his own previous milieu, describing its fate with both reproach and pity: "I speak of the good bourgeois German Jews," he writes, "—not only the loss of everything, not only the new dispersion. No. A real downfall; a serious, terrible decline. People who have moved upon the partly covered planks of a weak scaffolding and now suddenly see it has all collapsed. Into what do they sink? Into nothingness. Because that is really the most awful thing: they have kept nothing, they have created nothing they could now hold on to . . ." (no. 33).

This is perhaps not entirely fair. It is nevertheless undoubtedly true that despite the existing scaffolding of community life in Weimar

Germany, many individual Jews found themselves completely at a loss when they were forced to face the final test. They must have realized that on that personal, individual level—the most elemental, crucial level, precisely the one on which they had chosen to proceed toward assimilation—their efforts had come to naught. To their total bewilderment, theirs, as my father wrote, turned out to be a cruise on a *Gespensterschiff*—a ghost-ship that was bound to sink.

Notes

1. Here and throughout this paper, I am quoting from a collection of my father's personal letters in my possession, numbered chronologically by him. The passage quoted here is from no. 4.

2. See Jacob Toury, "Gab es ein Krisenbewusstsein unter den Juden während der 'Guten Jahre' der Weimarer Republik 1924–1929?" *TJBDG* 17 (1988): 145–68.

3. See especially Zygmunt Bauman, *Modernity and Ambivalence* (Ithaca, 1991), chapters 4 and 5.

4. See the concise and useful summary in Jacob Katz, *Out of the Ghetto* (New York, 1978), chapter 9.

5. See Horst Möller, "Aufklärung, Judenemanzipation und Staat. Ursprung und Wirkung von Dohms Schrift über die bürgerliche Verbesserung der Juden," *Deutsche Aufklärung und Judenemanzipation*, supplement 3, *TJBDG* (1980): 119–49, esp. 146–47.

6. Bauman, *Modernity and Ambivalence*, p. 106. For this paragraph and the passages cited, see ibid., pp. 106–12.

7. On this affinity, see Julius Carlebach, "The Forgotten Connection. Women and Jews in the Conflict between Enlightenment and Romanticism," *LBIYB* 24 (1979): 67–91.

8. Still the best biography of Rahel, describing her continuous inner struggles, is Hannah Arendt, *Rahel Varnhagen. The Life of a Jewess* (London, 1957).

9. On Heine and Judaism, see especially S. S. Prawer, *Heine's Jewish Comedy: A Study of His Portraits of Jews and Judaism* (Oxford, 1983).

10. See his letter to his brother, November 23, 1880, in *Juden und Judentum in deutschen Briefen aus drei Jahrhunderten*, ed. Franz Kobler (Frankfurt am Main, 1984 [1st ed., Vienna, 1935]), p. 271. And see also Jewish reactions to Treitschke's antisemitic articles at that time, in *Der Berliner Antisemitismusstreit*, ed. Walter Boehlich (Frankfurt am Main, 1965).

11. For a more detailed argumentation, see Shulamit Volkov, "Selbstgefälligkeit und Selbsthass," in *Jüdisches Leben und Antisemitismus im 19. und 20. Jahrhundert* (Munich, 1990), pp. 181–96.

12. Data for conversions are inconclusive. For the Weimar years see Stephan Behr, *Der Bevölkerungsrückgang der deutschen Juden* (Berlin, 1912), and Bruno Blau, "Die Entwicklung der jüdischen Bevölkerung in Deutschland 1800–1945," unpub. ms, ALBI-NY (New York, 1950), pp. 123–24. For information on those leaving the Gemeinde in Berlin, see Peter Honigmann, *Der Austritt aus der jüdischen Gemeinde Berlin 1873–1941* (Frankfurt am Main, 1988).

13. There is a great deal of literature on Rathenau. For a general overview, see Ernst Schulin, *Walther Rathenau. Repräsentant, Kritiker und Opfer seiner Zeit* (Göttingen, 1979). On his problematic position as a Jew and the issue of whether or not it could be considered representative of contemporary Jewry as a whole, see my essay, "'Ich bin ein Deutscher jüdischen Stammes'. Walther Rathenau als Jude," in *Die Extreme berühren sich. Walther Rathenau 1867–1922 (Deutsches Historisches Museum)*, ed. Hans Wilde-Lotter (Berlin, n.d.), pp. 129–38.

14. See, for instance, the presentation in Jehuda Reinharz, *Fatherland or Promised Land: The Dilemma of the German Jew 1893–1914* (Ann Arbor, 1975).

15. Much of the recent literature on all these matters is integrated into the masterly synthesis by H. U. Wehler, *Deutsche Gesellschaftsgeschichte* (Munich, 1995), vol. 3, pt. 6, esp. pp. 848–999. His footnotes provide extensive information on the *Kulturkampf*, the battle with Social Democracy, minorities, and nationalism.

2

Gemeinschaft within Gemeinde

Religious Ferment in Weimar Liberal Judaism

MICHAEL A. MEYER

Form a *Gemeinschaft* that is rooted in the past,
come to terms with the present, and build
for the future. Then will the Jewish
Gemeinde spring back to life and the
house of God become its focus.
—*Levy Rosenblatt*[1]

Gemeinde

The "New Synagogue" on Oranienburger Strasse in Berlin, dedicated in 1866, was an immense and marvelous structure. Its size and opulence paid visual tribute to the rapidly growing and upwardly mobile Jewish community in the Prussian capital. It would long serve Berlin Jewry as a source of private satisfaction and public pride. The Berlin Liberal rabbi Joseph Aub had composed a new three-volume prayer book especially for its worship; the talented synagogue composer Louis Lewandowski wrote new compositions for its cantor and choir. To enter the new synagogue was to experience a sense of awe and aesthetic appreciation. One regular worshipper recalled how "the large, richly atmospheric interior, the illuminated high windows, the mighty organ, the trained choir . . . left an indelible impression."[2] The synagogues built later in the century and up until World War I, both in Berlin and in other German cities, were similarly conceived in that they too were monuments of magnificence to demonstrate Jewish emancipation and affluence. Men entered them wearing a top hat, entirely appropriate attire for a setting that had become distinctly formal and in which decorum was the most perceptible hallmark.[3]

Invariably and increasingly, however, the synagogues became monuments in a stricter sense. The three thousand seats of the New Synagogue (eighteen hundred for men and twelve hundred for women) were filled only for the holidays; for the most part, they remained empty. The parvenu excitement that attended the 1866 dedication could not sustain itself against the gains made by secularization. By the Weimar period even Jews who had remained in the countryside were at best selective in their religious observance and hardly scrupulous about refraining from work on the Sabbath. In larger cities such as Hamburg, Frankfurt, Berlin, and Breslau, the majority of Jews did not attend synagogue at all, even on the High Holy Days; in Hamburg the percentage of women who did not attend reached seventy-four by the late 1920s.[4] In that same commercial city, although there were remarkably few who officially left the community during the Weimar years,[5] barely 40 percent of the members belonged to a religious association *(Kultusverband)*, and from 1925 to 1933, one quarter of all Jews getting married chose a non-Jew for a spouse.[6]

For the most part, Jewish life in the larger communities no longer focused on the synagogues. Political struggles among Liberals, Zionists, and Orthodox absorbed both energies and funds; ideological animosities frustrated cooperative religious endeavors.[7] The relationship between the individual and the community was defined in terms of advocacy of a political program, mostly dichotomized between Zionist and anti-Zionist. Adherence to a religious association was designated by the essentially impersonal and external term "membership" *(Angehörigkeit)*.[8] Inside the synagogue the worshipper became part of an "audience," which either liked or disliked what was offered it, occasionally responding to a particularly fine sermon with applause.[9] Indeed, the rare occasions when synagogues were filled included performances of oratorios and concerts, such as that given in the New Synagogue in 1930, which featured a piece by Bach played on the violin by Albert Einstein.[10]

All of the eleven community synagogues in Berlin in the year 1927 (six of them Orthodox) were centrally administered through a single office in the Oranienburger Strasse. Although there were also local boards for each synagogue, significant decisions affecting religious life

were made by the elected representatives of the organized community, the *Gemeinde,* as a whole. Community rabbis were not consistently associated with a single synagogue but preached in various
locations within either the Liberal or Orthodox sector. Some did try to
exercise a pastoral role by visiting the sick, holding regular counseling
hours, and inviting laypeople to their homes on Friday evenings and
holidays. But as Rabbi Alfred Jospe once said from the pulpit of the
Levetzowstrasse Synagogue in Berlin, where he preached once or
twice a month in the 1930s: "I'm supposed to be a shepherd of souls
[i.e., a pastor], but I hardly know a single soul here."[11] Since rabbis
were responsible to the central leadership of the community for every
word and deed, they were constrained to articulate consensus views
in all matters political and religious.[12]

The mechanical and impersonal character of Jewish religious life
within the Gemeinde of the large city during the Weimar period is well
illustrated by the annual effort in Berlin to accommodate the "three-
day-a-year Jews." Since only a minority of the more than fifty
thousand adult worshippers could fit into the eleven community
synagogues, it was necessary, in the mid-1920s, to rent more than
forty halls for the High Holy Day season. A "Festgottesdienst-Kommission" was given the task of finding and preparing dozens of cantors,
choir directors and members of choirs, organists, and—most difficult
of all—shofar blowers. Since there were not enough rabbis to go
around, rabbinical students from the Breslau seminary and the Berlin
Hochschule were engaged to give the sermons. Robes and birettas
were distributed to the officiants. The liturgy itself was identical in
the auxiliary services with what it was in the Orthodox or Liberal
synagogues and, with few exceptions, it was read and sung in Hebrew.
Although some halls were used repeatedly, new ones had to be rented
as the population shifted westward. A special bureau dealt with the
rental of seats; poorer community members, though they were all
accommodated, could not hope for a place in one of the synagogues
and had to make do with attending services in a *Betsaal.* These prayer
halls included some of the largest public spaces in Berlin, with seats for
as many as two thousand worshippers; among them were such well-
known buildings as the Mozartsaal and even the Philharmonie.[13]
Thus, attendance at High Holy Day services for most Berlin Jews
meant going to a secular hall, probably a very large one; listening to
the sermon of an unfamiliar rabbi or rabbinical student; and hearing
a liturgy with which they were little acquainted, enacted by the
officiants almost entirely in a language they did not understand. Their
fellow worshippers, except by coincidence, were strangers with whom

they had no relationship. As men and women invariably sat separately, families could not participate together. Only the familiar melo-
dies still resonated and provided some continuity from year to year.[14]
Thus, the collective image of Weimar Jewish religious life in the
large cities, especially among Liberal Jews, is one of grand synagogues
built a generation or more earlier and of a bureaucracy serving the
minimal religious needs of an essentially secular and therefore religiously indifferent Jewry. Content with this status quo, however
impersonal, Weimar Jews paid token tribute to their religion by an
annual tax payment and the symbolic act of attending a worship
service once or twice a year. But mostly they just did not want to be
bothered. In its general outlines and for most Weimar urban Jews, this
image is accurate. But it is not the whole story. To a remarkable and as
yet not fully appreciated extent, the status quo in the Gemeinde
aroused contemporary discontent from those active within the seemingly most indifferent sector, that of Jewish religious Liberalism. It was
a discontent that rested upon new ways of thinking and manifested
itself in various ways: in critique, in proposal, and in extraordinary
innovation.

Gemeinschaft

As early as 1887, the sociologist Ferdinand Tönnies had sharply
distinguished between *Gemeinschaft* (community) and *Gesellschaft* (association), finding the latter, with its substitution of institutional ties
for organic ones, to be characteristic of modern times and the former
to be the irrecoverable model of preindustrial ages. By the Weimar
period, Gemeinschaft had ceased to be merely an analytical category
and had become a social ideal, especially for young people and those
on the left of the political spectrum. Among Jews it had become a
favorite concept in the thinking of the young socialist Gustav Landauer, while those who declared themselves to be religious found it
especially in the writings of Martin Buber. Unlike Tönnies, Buber
believed that Gemeinschaft need not be assigned to the past; that it
could be revived, albeit in somewhat different form, even in an age
when the instrumental relationships of Gesellschaft were dominant.
Unlike Landauer, Buber developed a religious conception of Gemeinschaft, in which the presence of God became an essential element.
Buber began to advocate the creation of a "new Gemeinschaft" at
the turn of the century and continued to elaborate the concept as he

moved toward the philosophy of interpersonal relationships represented by his book *I and Thou*. Unlike the old Gemeinschaft, based on
ties of kinship, the new one would be founded upon elective affinities.
Individualism blocked the way back to the natural connectedness of
earlier ages, but it did not obviate the possibility of new forms of
community. "A great yearning for Gemeinschaft courses through all
the souls of soulful people at this life-moment of Western culture,"
wrote Buber in 1919.[15] The state, even a socialist state, could never fill
the role of a community. That was possible only in the intimacy of
small groups and only on the basis of religious relationships. Buber
believed that the longing for Gemeinschaft was a longing for God and
that only where individuals would allow God to exist could they
create a true Gemeinschaft. The quest for community was, religiously
speaking, a quest for redemption.

Yet Buber was consistently critical of the ability of organized
religion to establish community. The religious denomination, he
believed, only wants its own God. "Yet God wants to represent to the
individual the meaning of the world and the eternal ideal; for the
denomination God is but the source of advantage in the world to
come."[16] According to Buber, religious associations, like their secular
counterparts, had taken on the degenerate status of statelike ma-
chines. He foresaw no salvation from the curse of unmitigated Gesellschaft characterizing church and synagogue. What was required, he
argued, was not the reform of existing institutions but a revolution
that would take place outside them.[17] To Buber's way of thinking, the
Jewish Gemeinde, by its very nature as organization, would always
remain Gesellschaft and hence religiously sterile. Nonetheless, Gemeinschaft thinking did penetrate the organized Jewish community,
where it set off a critique of the values represented by the magnificent
monuments and liturgical formalities that were the religious legacy of
the nineteenth century to the Jews of Weimar.

Among the most articulate critics was that most "establishment" of
rabbis, Leo Baeck. In his essay "Community in the Metropolis," Baeck
compared small-town Jewry, where the individual's family was a
piece of the community and his community a large family, with
Jewish life in the city where Jews were "accounted" part of the
Gemeinde but did not "experience" it except upon rare occasions.
"The *baal habbajis* [the householder]," he wrote, "has become the
taxpayer. The personal element has been pushed aside and finally
replaced by the statistical."[18] What had emerged was no longer community but mass, the natural element of politics but not of religion.
Masses want to be impressed, and that was precisely the effect of the

excessively large synagogues that addressed individuals in their mass, not in community. The relations among the individuals, Baeck admitted, had become those of a Gesellschaft, not a Gemeinschaft. Echoing Buber, Baeck noted that young people were looking for religiosity to counter the negative influences of the metropolis; but he offered no suggestions as to what concrete steps the organized Jewish community might take to meet their needs.

There were other critics as well. Jewish Liberals, long-time advocates of individualism, remained wary of collectivism, not only because they were suspicious of socialism but also because it made them think of Zionism. Nonetheless, they had come to realize, at the very least, that something had been lost. For the Liberals, "Gemeinschaft" became an ideal designation for their own understanding of themselves as Jews. It was more embracing than the nineteenth-century self-designation of religious denomination *(Konfession)* yet less than peoplehood. The long-time leader of organized Jewish religious Liberalism in Germany, Heinrich Stern, spoke readily of "communal consciousness" *(Gemeinschaftsbewusstsein)* and "communal work" *(Gemeinschaftsarbeit).*[19] In 1927 the Liberals held a conference, Gemeinschaft und Individuum, where Rabbi Max Dienemann of Offenbach admitted that the individualism of the earlier age had given way to a stronger sense of engagement, especially as a result of the collective experience of the war years. What needed to be done was to reconcile Gemeinschaft with the free will of individuals. Such Gemeinschaft could be spiritual rather than racial or national. In fact, the sense of belonging to a *Geistesgemeinschaft,* a spiritual community, might work to counter the threat of loss through mixed marriage.[20]

It was also increasingly felt that the existing synagogue, rather than furthering a sense of community, tended to be destructive of it. Here, for example, is one layperson's description of the contemporary worship experience:

> As magnificent as our large community synagogues are in many respects, and although much that is beautiful is offered in the services there, they fail to produce any real living effect. It is not the fault of the functionaries but is due to the fact that the Gemeinden in truth are not Gemeinden, not Gemeinschaften. One arrives, one listens to the service more or less passively, one departs. No one knows anyone else; no one plays any active role in the service, either in shaping it or in carrying it out. So, deep down, one remains unmoved.[21]

A leader of the Berlin Liberal movement asks rhetorically: "Hasn't our worship . . . today become theater? We no longer create worship, we the community!"[22]

The critique extended beyond the synagogue to the rabbinate. The rabbis, whom everyone called "Doctor" whether or not they had the title, were tied to pulpit and lectern when, as one writer in Buber's periodical *Der Jude* complained, the need was for religious leaders of the entire people, not obedient pulpiteers. Unfortunately, the rabbi had become the chief religious employee *(erster Kultusbeamte)*—dependent rather than independent, at the edge of the community rather than in its midst.[23]

Among the critics were also women. They too called for Gemeinschaft within the Liberal synagogue, but they had their special agenda as well. In the 1920s, women were beginning to play a larger role in Christian denominations, even as candidates for preaching positions in the Evangelical Church. In Jewish communities, too, a process of enfranchisement was beginning, as in one city after another women were given a vote in community elections and the right to hold office.[24] But their position in the synagogue remained unchanged. In German Liberal synagogues there were no barriers in front of the women's sections and women sang in mixed choirs. In some synagogues women also sat on the same floor as the men; but they invariably sat separate. That was true even for services held in the main building of the religiously radical *Reformgemeinde,* and it was true as well for the oldest Reform institution, the Hamburg Temple.[25] Women could neither participate in the service that preceded their weddings nor in the memorial services held in their homes after the death of a close relative. The confirmation of girls could not take place within a regular religious service but was relegated to a "celebration" *(Feier)* conducted entirely in German without Torah reading or prayer book. Apparently in response to increasing dissatisfaction with the status quo, the *Jüdisch-liberale Zeitung,* in its issue of November 5, 1926, presented a symposium entitled "The Woman in the House of God," which consisted of ten statements regarding the role of women in the synagogue, seven of them by women. Not only did the participants, almost without exception, call for expanded activity by women in community and synagogue governance, but most insisted on enhanced participation inside the sanctuary as well. Of the seven women, four specifically raised the possibility of women rabbis. Their feminine talents, two of them argued, would be especially useful in the area of pastoral work.[26]

The growing desire to include women within the community leadership was paralleled by efforts to embrace young people. The latter, it was realized, as participants in Weimar youth culture, had a particularly lively sense of Gemeinschaft. But attempts to instill a sense of responsibility toward the existing community were of little

avail.[27] Some non-Orthodox Jewish young people were indeed religious, but at the same time alienated from organized Judaism. "One
could almost venture the paradox," wrote the journalist and rabbi's
son Friedrich Thieberger, "that our generation is too deeply religious
to reach the surface of religious life."[28] Recognizing the gap, Jewish
communities tried to provide young people with their own ambience
for Jewish worship. Special services were instituted not only for
children but also for older youth who were encouraged to take over
governance of the *Jugendgemeinde* and officiation at the services.
Recognizing that the cultivation of their own *Gemeinschaftsbewusstsein*
was the condition for the younger generation's participation in religious life, a leader of the Liberal Jewish youth movement urged the
communal celebration of Friday evenings and holidays together in
small homogeneous groups.[29]

Questions also began to arise about the grandiose synagogue as a
model for future construction. Even before the Weimar period the
style of synagogues was beginning to change. The emphasis upon the
street façade lessened; the outward focus gradually gave way to an
internal one. The synagogues built in Essen (1913) and Augsburg
(1917) were still immense, but they differed from their immediate
predecessors in featuring courtyards and vestibules. The apparent
intent was to make the synagogue more of what it had been tradition-
ally—a center of social interchange—rather than, on the Christian
model, solely a sacred space for divine worship.[30]

After the war, the Breslau synagogue architect Alfred Grotte set the
tone for a very different sacral architecture when he wrote in 1922:

> To be sure, the synagogue is a space dedicated to prayer and therefore to
> God. But it lacks that sanctity which, for example, a Catholic church
> possesses on account of its housing a relic and the Host.[31] It is rather a place
> of being together *(Zusammenseins)* for the community praying to God,
> whose preacher is not a consecrated priest and which therefore is a space
> that knows no barrier between clergy and laity. Hence it is justifiable in
> place of the presumptuous designation "house of God" to choose the much
> more appropriate "house of prayer," a concept that came into existence
> long ago and under similar circumstances within Protestantism.[32]

Grotte also believed that in a considerably poorer postwar Germany,
simple, functional structures would be more appropriate than the
grand ones of an imperial age.

Not surprisingly, the language of Gemeinschaft now also enters the
discourse of Jewish synagogue architecture. Another architect, Max
Eisler, sharply reverses the direction of architectural purpose when
he writes in 1926: "The Jewish temple of today wants to gather the

faithful together, surrounding and encasing their silent Gemeinschaft, not directing attention to itself, but helping to focus their devotion inward."[33]

For economic reasons very few new synagogues were actually built during the Weimar period. One of them was the synagogue in Plauen, completed in 1930. In part due to financial constraints, this new building, which was also architecturally the first truly modern synagogue in Germany, became a combination of sanctuary and community center. Here, as one writer noted, *Kult* and *Kultur* were united under one roof so that religion was organically reunited with the rest of Jewish life.[34]

In Berlin the only new structure to be built during the Weimar period was the Liberal synagogue on Prinzregentenstrasse; it was dedicated in 1930. Like its predecessors, it was large (2,300 seats), though almost a third smaller than the New Synagogue. What made it different was that it was the first and only community synagogue in Berlin where men and women sat together. The Liberals had only attained this concession with great difficulty and by a single vote in the assembly of community representatives. Strong opposition had emerged, especially within the Zionist Jüdische Volkspartei, which claimed that the proposal was divisive.[35] The new synagogue was novel in two other respects as well. First, its seating was in the round, rather than in the usual rectangular pattern. Although the stated purpose of the arrangement was to make the pulpit—where liturgy was enacted and sermons given—focal in the structure, it must also have enhanced the sense of community, since worshippers in the spacious balcony could look to each side and see one another's faces. Second, the ark could be separated from the auditorium by lowering an iron curtain, thus allowing the same space to be used for secular Jewish purposes as well.[36]

The last major synagogue structure to be completed before the rise of Hitler was the new Hamburg Temple which, in addition to the main sanctuary, contained school rooms, a Gabriel Riesser Social Hall with adjoining kitchen, and a smaller prayer room. The intentions expressed in the year of its dedication in 1931 clearly indicate how fundamentally the model of the synagogue had changed. Its architect, Felix Ascher, defined the purpose of a contemporary Jewish house of worship as "the real gathering place *(Sammelstätte)* for modern Jews."[37] Its chief cantor, Leon Kornitzer, noted that for too long the congregation's music had neglected the worshippers in favor of the choir; with the new sanctuary, the time had come to introduce more community singing based on traditional Jewish motifs.[38] And the synagogue's rabbi, Bruno Italiener, called particular attention to the role of the

second sanctuary within the structure, the "Kleine Tempel," which
was intended for daily services:

> By creating such a space, the Temple Association, despite the relatively
> large number of its adherents, returns in its work of inner construction to
> the principle of the small community which, as is well known, was for
> centuries the true nucleus for building up Judaism. The outer closer
> connectedness creates the condition for an inner connectedness, the
> external Gemeinschaft bridges the way toward a Gemeinschaft of the soul,
> toward the creation of a new community resting upon common feelings.[39]

But was such a Gemeinschaft really possible in any synagogue that
was part of an organized religious community? Could Gemeinschaft
theory, anchored in a romanticism that rejected religious discipline, be
made the foundation of a faith that stressed the regular performance
of religious duties? In the mid-1920s the intellectual periodical of the
Liberal Weimar Jews, *Der Morgen,* published a number of articles that
addressed this issue. The authors readily admitted that "religiosity," a
concept much stressed by Buber and distinguished by him from
"religion,"[40] could not serve as the basis for religious Gemeinschaft
within the framework of any normative Judaism. It rested on religious
experience *(Erlebnis),* while Judaism rested on religious life *(Leben).*[41]
Experience could not create a "practicing" *(ausübende)* religious community. That was possible only, in the words of Rabbi Emil Schorsch,
on the "unshakable basis of a religious sense of duty that remains
independent of whims and romantic moods."[42] Yet the authors also
recognized that a sense of Gemeinschaft had become a prerequisite if
Liberal Jews were to be attracted to regular prayer, the religious duty
most stressed by Jewish religious Liberalism. Eventually, during the
Nazi years, one German rabbi, Ignaz Maybaum, would translate
Gemeinschaft into the Hebrew word *chevrah* and, following Buber,
understand the concept to mean a sacred community before God. But
he went beyond Buber in insisting that the chevrah needed to be more
than that. It needed regularly to become a *Gebetsgemeinschaft,* a community of prayer in which everyone was a full participant, not merely
a "pious listener" *(andächtiger Zuhörer);* and then, when the Torah was
taken from the ark, it needed to transform itself into a *Lesegemeinschaft,*
a reading community studying the text.[43] Yet all these ideas, articulated by the rabbinical leadership, did not prompt the official organs of
the Jewish community to reform Liberal services in a way that would
bring them nearer the stated goals. It required an initiative emanating
from outside the elected lay establishment and the rabbinate to create
just such a chevrah (what today is often called *chavurah*) within the
skeptical, if not actually hostile Gemeinde of Berlin.

Gemeinschaft within Gemeinde

On Sabbath eve, November 30, 1923, a group of Berlin Jews gathered in the small synagogue of the Baruch Auerbach orphanage located at Schönhauser Allee 162 in the northern section of the city. There they conducted a religious service not authorized by community officials or initiated by any rabbi. The founders and participants were laypeople concerned about the failure of Liberal Judaism to provide the possibility for religious Gemeinschaft. Instead of arguing their case before the recognized organs of the community, they had decided to undertake their own bold experiment.

The moving spirit behind the venture was Hermann Falkenberg (1869–1936), a Jewish educator and Liberal activist who served first as a teacher at the girls and boys middle school of the Berlin community, later as senior instructor at the teachers seminary. Not only was Falkenberg its principal initiator, he was also its chief advocate and supporter.[44] Working closely with Falkenberg was another educator, Professor Josua Falk Friedländer (1871–1942), who taught modern languages, Latin, and Jewish religion in the general schools in Berlin and served on the educational commission of the Berlin Jewish community. Friedländer had studied at Jews' College in London, which was directed by his uncle, Michael Friedländer; and he used his knowledge in arranging the Sabbath liturgy for the new group.[45] The third main figure was Jonas Plaut (1880–1948), like the other two a pedagogue and also director of the orphanage that lent its synagogue to the group.[46]

These Liberal laymen and the others who joined them strongly felt that the service in the "organ synagogues" had become sterile. Having assumed a particular form in the second half of the nineteenth century, it became rigid and development ceased. The liturgy and ambience thereafter remained as fixed as they were in the Orthodox synagogues, unresponsive to shifts in religious thought and feeling. In the words of one member of the group, he too a teacher: "The days may finally be over when people believed that all you needed to do was set up an organ in the synagogue, organize a mixed choir, leave out some prayers, and—presto—you had a Liberal service."[47] On the other hand, they felt that the Reformgemeinde in Berlin, with its radically abbreviated and almost wholly German service, lacked historical roots. They preferred to look to the work of Abraham Geiger, the champion of historical Judaism, who toward the end of his life had served briefly in Berlin. They wanted to restart the process of religious

development that had died with Geiger by incorporating the complementary influences of two more recent thinkers. Hermann Cohen's
rationalism, indispensable for the way of thinking of modern city
people, and Franz Rosenzweig's recognition of the power of faith were
thought to be equally essential.[48] The group hoped to win the three-
day-a-year Jews back to regular participation in prayer.

The services in the orphanage synagogue, which could hold about
two hundred worshippers, differed fundamentally from those in the
official Liberal synagogues. Worship on Friday evenings always began
fifteen minutes to half an hour after businesses closed. People attending services were expected to arrive before they began and remain
until they concluded, and they were expected to attend regularly.
Although the major rubrics of the liturgy were retained, repetitions,
such as of the *kaddish*, were consistently avoided. In contrast to the
practice of the Reformgemeinde, Hebrew was retained for basic
prayers, though there were more prayers recited in German than in
the standard Liberal synagogues. The passages from the Torah were
first read in German and then chanted in Hebrew. Each service was
built around a particular religious theme with songs, sermons, original
prayers, and special readings all reflecting it so that the service in its
totality left the worshipper with a well-defined message. Each Sabbath offered a combination of traditional and novel elements.

But the most radical and remarkable characteristic of these services
was their attempt to create a Gemeinschaft within the Gemeinde by
focusing more on the worshippers than the liturgy. Those who came
to the services were to be full participants, never simply listeners—at
the center, not on the periphery. From the very beginning, women sat
together with men.[49] Although there was a cantorially educated
businessman, a young organist, and a small children's choir to lead the
music, everyone was encouraged and expected to sing the hymns and
responses together. Anything musical in the nature of a performance
was scrupulously excluded. The cantor was to see himself as *sheliach
tsibur,* the representative of the worshippers; the prayer was to be once
more like the old simple *davnen.*[50] Especially in the first years, laypeople conducted the liturgy. Teachers, lawyers, doctors, and students
delivered sermonettes, eight to fifteen minutes in length, until some
dissatisfaction arose with their uneven quality. In order to increase
participation, the full traditional number of seven men was called up
to the reading of the Torah and—in sharp contrast to the Liberal
community synagogues—those called up, especially boys celebrating
their Bar Mitzvah, were trained and encouraged to read from the
scroll themselves. The prophetic selection *(haftarah)* was always read
by a layperson. As many congregants as possible were given other

tasks, such as opening and closing the ark. Family occasions were noted publicly as part of the service.

The orphanage was located in that part of the city some called the "fortress" of Orthodoxy, where the Gemeinde had cared only for the religious needs of traditionalists. It was populated mainly by the poorer elements of Berlin Jewry, "simple, modest people who have to struggle hard for their living."[51] Its members, who had to pay dues (twelve marks per year in 1928) in addition to their community taxes, were principally from the middle and lower middle class. At first, they received no support from the organs of the community and no cooperation from most of the community rabbis. However, financial assistance did come from Liberal organizations and finally from the community as well.

Rabbinical leadership was also soon forthcoming. In 1925, Rabbi Martin Salomonski (1881–1944) moved to the capital, but as a teacher of Judaism, not a community rabbi. He was therefore free to become the regular rabbi of the new synagogue on Sabbaths and holidays. Salomonski, who was also a novelist, poet, synagogue composer, and founder of Jewish old age homes, became associated with the "Liberal Synagogue of the North," as it was soon called, in a more intimate way than community rabbis with the synagogues that they served.[52] In 1928, however, he became a community rabbi, leaving the group to rely once more primarily on lay preachers from its own midst, but also on rabbinical students from the Liberal seminary in Berlin and visiting rabbis from Berlin and other cities.[53]

For a time, the congregation made do by adapting the prayer book used in the New Synagogue, but after four years it printed its own liturgy for the Friday night service.[54] Opening right to left, the little booklet edited by Friedländer began not with a choir selection but with congregational singing *(Gemeindegesang)*. Later, the congregation was expected to join in all of the major responses. Theologically, the highly abbreviated liturgy remained quite conservative, retaining, in Hebrew and German, the faith both in a personal Redeemer and in resurrection. Appended were musical notes for the Hebrew responses and German hymns.

Although the congregation began with Friday evening worship in order to attract those Jews who worked the next day, it soon added services for Saturday morning (less well attended than those on Friday evening, which regularly filled the two hundred or so seats in the synagogue) and for all of the major Jewish holidays. On the High Holy Days the synagogue, not surprisingly, could scarcely hold even half of those who wanted to attend. On the Day of Atonement short introductions explained the special prayers for the day before they were recited. For 1925, we have the impressions of a Professor Leopold Wolff, who came to the Yom Kippur service as a skeptic and left with great enthusiasm. Wolff reported seeing "very many young people and couples" as well as "an imposing circle of older people" among whom he found some wearing both hats and traditional prayer robes (Käppchen und Kittel). As the day progressed, the devotion increased. Wolff concluded: "You must believe me when I say that this Day of Reconciliation reconciled me with Judaism because I again begin to hope."[55]

The congregation made a determined effort to revive active celebration of other holidays and to reinstitute customs neglected by the Liberals. During the week-long holiday of Sukkot, evening and morning services were conducted in the common sukkah; and girls were confirmed during a regular holiday service. For Passover, the congregation conducted a communal seder on the second night and, in time for the holiday in 1929, produced its own Haggadah. The latter, edited by Falkenberg, was specifically directed to those Jews who had given up conducting a seder, those who "have preserved the memory of the seder evening in their hearts but to whom the traditional form no longer speaks or who are no longer able to awaken in their children the seder evening of their own youth."[56] The Haggadah itself differs from its traditional model in two noteworthy respects. First, it distinctly universalizes the message of freedom by extending it to all who are still enslaved and by including the midrash wherein God castigates the children of Israel for rejoicing while the Egyptians are drowning in the Red Sea. And second, it twice incorporates passages from Stefan Zweig's dramatic poem Jeremias, thus lending the volume an aura of contemporaneity.[57]

Recognizing the difficulty of attracting worshippers on weekdays, the congregation focused on observances and celebrations that would not interfere with work times. In 1926, it introduced selichot, the service composed of penitential prayers that takes place on a Saturday night shortly before the High Holy Days. It also developed a similar preparatory service (Einstimmungsgottesdienst) for the Saturday afternoon preceding Passover, concluding it with the havdalah ceremony separating the Sabbath from the rest of the week. These were innovations wholly uncharacteristic of German Liberal Judaism.[58]

Beginning with the High Holy Days in 1927, the group also held youth services, which likewise differed from the rule. Not only were the eves included, but also, to a much greater degree than was customary, the young people, using a specially adapted liturgy, led the service in Hebrew and German and presented the scriptural readings.

A year later the number of those participating had doubled and monthly youth services on Friday evenings were introduced as well.[59] The group wanted to see itself as a *kehillah* (best translated as "congregation," the American term usually inappropriate for Germany, but fitting in this instance), as working to restore the intimacy of the small circle that had once characterized Jewish communities but which the immense Berlin Gemeinde could not itself offer. The group was determined to "build religious life from the bottom up." In the fall of 1925, the congregation published the first issue of a periodical intended to elaborate its point of view, report on its activities, and present subjects of general Jewish religious interest. Not surprisingly, it was called *Die Gemeinschaft*,[60] since from the beginning the group had set itself apart from the synagogues of the Gemeinde as a self-conscious religious community where each "warmed the other with his fire."[61] One writer made the clear distinction: the Gemeinde represents Gesellschaft, the little synagogue in the north of Berlin Gemeinschaft. Some people, wary of too personal involvement, would always prefer the former, the mass, but others would seek out the latter.[62]

The Liberal Synagogue of the North did not confine its activity to conducting worship services. Aside from the Reformgemeinde, it was the only religious organization in Berlin to hold regular "community evenings" *(Gemeindeabende)* at which topics of Jewish interest were discussed and social ties among the members were deepened. There were also Hebrew lessons and concerts associated with Jewish holidays. In 1926, *Die Gemeinschaft* carried an article arguing that religious commitment in Judaism implied social action, a connection rarely made in German Jewry, however characteristic it had become of Reform Judaism in America.[63] Governance was through a board that included women as well as men. Membership grew only gradually, rising from 101 to 138 in the first two years and then to about two hundred by 1928. But the congregation's influence was felt more widely, so that its leaders could claim they were the nucleus of a new movement, an avant-garde within Jewish religious Liberalism. Four years after the establishment of the synagogue community in the north, a similar venture was undertaken in 1927 in the southwest of Berlin, in the Cecilienschule in Wilmersdorf, where three hundred and fifty people attended the first service. Here too, as in the north, regular attendance at services and other functions was made a duty of membership. The Wilmersdorf venture lasted for only three years, however, before being merged into the community's new Prinzregentenstrasse Synagogue, which then absorbed elements from its predecessor. In November 1928 two more synagogue communities of the new type were dedicated, one in the West End (also in a school auditorium) and one in the east.[64] Whereas in the West End the results were disappointing, in the east they surpassed expectations, which had been quite modest given the overwhelmingly conservative character of the lower-middle-class Jewry that lived in that part of Berlin. In the early 1930s, other experimental services on the model of North were undertaken with varying degrees of success in Tempelhof-Oberspree, in the northeast and Reinickendorf/Wedding. The prayer pamphlet for Friday evenings was also used in some synagogues outside Berlin, and *Die Gemeinschaft* reached a readership beyond the congregations.[65]

But the young movement was not to succeed as an independent entity. The Depression led to suspension of *Die Gemeinschaft* in 1930, and only one more double issue appeared in 1933, the year of the tenth anniversary.[66] In that same year Hermann Falkenberg wrote a retrospective of the movement. He concluded with these words, which he underlined for emphasis:

> The year in which the Liberal Synagogue of the North is marking its tenth anniversary has not become a year of jubilation, for it cannot drive away the concern that perhaps the collective work of the Liberal Synagogue in Berlin is endangered, and therewith the blossoming buds of a living religious Judaism.[67]

Nazi Germany would produce its own sense of forced Gemeinschaft among Jews, one hardly anticipated by those who sought, for a time, to create it voluntarily within the Gemeinde.

Notes

1. *Die Gemeinschaft. Hefte für die religiöse Erstarkung des Judentums* 12 (May 20, 1928): 14.

2. Georg Salzberger, "Erinnerungen an Berlin," in *Gegenwart im Rückblick. Festgabe für die Jüdische Gemeinde zu Berlin 25 Jahre nach dem Neubeginn*, ed. Herbert A. Strauss and Kurt R. Grossmann (Heidelberg, 1970), p. 249.

3. See the recollections of Emil Schorsch in *Jüdisches Leben in Deutschland. Selbstzeugnisse zur Sozialgeschichte 1918–1945*, ed. Monika Richarz (Stuttgart, 1982), p. 187, and note this description by James J. Walters-Warschauer of his father, Rabbi Malwin Warschauer, conducting a service at the New Synagogue in Berlin: "For many who attended my father's services, it created an unforgettable impression when he slowly ascended the steps leading to the ark of the Torahs where he stopped below the eternal light and bowed his head before the ark and then proceeded slowly to mount the pulpit. When the last sound of the organ had

died away, an eager congregation waited to listen to him in complete silence" (*LBIYB* 26 [1981]: 199).

4. Jacob Borut, "Religious Life among the Village Jews in the Western Parts of Weimar Germany" (in Hebrew), in *Yehudei Weimar: Hevra be-mashber ha-moderni'ut, 1918–1933,* ed. Oded Heilbronner (Jerusalem, 1994), pp. 90–107. In 1929 it was estimated that in Berlin at least fifty thousand adults did not go to services at all; the majority of the eighty thousand who did go attended only on the High Holy Days. See *JLZ,* February 22, 1929.

5. "It was still the case that society expected everyone to belong to a religion. Where there were churches there also had to be synagogues lest the Jewish community be branded Communist. In many instances this meant doing no more than forwarding the community tax, apart from which the taxpayer simply desired to be left in peace" (recollections of Schorsch in Richarz, *Jüdisches Leben,* p. 184).

6. Ina S. Lorenz, "Die jüdische Gemeinde Hamburg 1860–1943," in *Die Juden in Hamburg 1590 bis 1990,* ed. Arno Herzig (Hamburg, 1991), pp. 86–90; Georg Salzberger, "Die jüdisch-christliche Mischehe," *Der Morgen* 5 (1929): 18–30. The only rabbis who would officiate at a mixed marriage ceremony were those who served the radical *Reformgemeinde* in Berlin.

7. In Danzig a *Gemeindeverein,* established after the war on a neutral basis, was briefly successful in holding well-attended, community-wide Hanukkah and Purim celebrations. But before long politicization (along with other factors) led to its dissolution. See Samuel Echt, *Die Geschichte der Juden in Danzig* (Leer, 1972), p. 103.

8. For example, Ina Lorenz, *Die Juden in Hamburg zur Zeit der Weimarer Republik. Eine Dokumentation* (Hamburg, 1987), vol. 1, pp. 584–85.

9. Alfred Jospe, "A Profession in Transition: The German Rabbinate 1910–1939," *LBIYB* 19 (1974): 52.

10. H. G. Sellenthin, *Geschichte der Juden in Berlin und des Gebäudes Fasanenstrasse 79/80* (Berlin, 1959), p. 67. Most of the items on the program, however, were cantorial music.

11. *Im jüdischen Leben. Erinnerungen des Berliner Rabbiners Malwin Warschauer* (Berlin, 1995), pp. 10–11; Jospe, "A Profession in Transition," p. 52.

12. Alexander Altmann, "The German Rabbi: 1910–1939," *LBIYB* 19 (1974): 33.

13. Salzberger, "Erinnerung an Berlin," p. 249.

14. *JLZ,* September 2 and 9, 1927.

15. Martin Buber, *Worte an die Zeit,* part 2, *Gemeinschaft* (Munich, 1919), p. 17.

16. Paul R. Flohr and Bernard Susser, "Alte und neue Gemeinschaft: An Unpublished Buber Manuscript," *Association for Jewish Studies Review* 1 (1976): 51.

17. For Buber's views on *Gemeinschaft,* see, inter alia, Paul Mendes-Flohr, *From Mysticism to Dialogue: Martin Buber's Transformation of German Social Thought* (Detroit, 1989), and Michael Löwy, *Jewish Libertarian Thought in Central Europe: A Study in Elective Affinity* (Stanford, 1988), pp. 48–55. More broadly on "Gemeinschaft" in relation to "Gemeinde," see Michael Brenner, *The Renaissance of Jewish Culture in Weimar Germany* (New Haven, 1996), pp. 36–65.

18. Leo Baeck, "Gemeinde in der Grossstadt" (1929) in his *Wege im Judentum* (Berlin, 1933), p. 294.

19. "Wie wecken wir das religiöse Interesse?" *JLZ,* February 12, 1926.

20. *JLZ,* October 28, 1927. See also, in the same issue, the lecture by Erich Bayer of Breslau, "Der Kultus, die Gemeinschaft und das Individuum."

21. George Goetz, "'Die Gemeinschaft,'" *JLZ,* October 29, 1926.

22. Ernst Heinrich Seligsohn, "Der 'Laie,'" *Die Gemeinschaft* 3 (March 25, 1926): 10. Seligsohn wanted the rabbi to assume a position within the congregation as *primus inter pares*, not above it, and for worshippers to have the opportunity to address each other since "if everyone knows of everyone else that he has something to say to him here in the house of God, then the community grows together. Indeed, only then does it become a community. . . ."

23. F. L. Bernstein, "Der Rabbiner und die Gemeinde," *Der Jude* 2 (1917/18): 491–93.

24. In Berlin the Liberals secured political equality for women in 1924. In Hamburg women acquired it in the Temple Association the same year, but in the general community the right to hold communal office was delayed until 1930.

25. Even in the new Hamburg Temple building, completed in 1931, women still sat in women's galleries. However, in contrast to traditional synagogues, the specifications called for as many seats for them as for the men. See Harold Hammer-Schenk, *Synagogen in Deutschland. Geschichte einer Baugattung im 19. und 20. Jahrhundert (1780–1933)* (Hamburg, 1981), vol. 1, p. 536.

26. The ten participants were Rabbi Hermann Vogelstein, Else Dormitzer, Hedwig Reiss, Henriette May, Moritz Galliner, Minna Schwarz, Paula Ollendorf, Emil Blumenau, Bianka Hamburger, and Martha Coblenz.

27. Salzberger, "Die jüdisch-christliche Mischehe," p. 30.

28. "Lebensform und religiöse Form," *Der Jude* 8 (1924): 58.

29. Max Vogelstein, "Wir und die andern," in *Zur religiösen Erneuerung des Judentums* (n.p. [Arbeitsgemeinschaft jüdisch-liberaler Jugendvereine Deutschlands], n.d.), p. 23. The *Jugendgottesdienst*, which apparently goes back well before Weimar, was, however, only a partial success in the Orthodox and Liberal synagogues that instituted it. See *Die Gemeinschaft* 13/14 (August 18, 1928): 14. For the High Holy Days the Berlin Community organized thirteen youth services, some in the auditoriums of synagogues, for children from the age of eight to fourteen. These services, of course, had no more sense of community than did their adult counterparts. See *Gemeindeblatt der Jüdischen Gemeinde zu Berlin* 14 (1924): 210.

30. Hammer-Schenk, *Synagogen in Deutschland*, vol. 1, p. 506.

31. This contrasts sharply with the view Jews themselves widely held of the synagogue during the nineteenth century. See Michael A. Meyer, "'How Awesome Is This Place!' The Reconceptualization of the Synagogue in Nineteenth-Century Germany," *LBIYB* 41 (1996): 51–63.

32. "Der Synagogentypus der Nachkriegszeit," *C.V.-Zeitung* 1 (1922): 133; cited in part also in Hammer-Schenk, *Synagogen in Deutschland*, vol. 1, p. 507.

33. "Vom neuen Geist der jüdischen Baukunst," *Menorah* 4 (1926): 521. Eisler also wanted to move the reader's lectern back to the center of the synagogue, its traditional location.

34. Max Eisler, "Neue Synagogen," *Menorah* 8 (1930): 544. Similarly, the Munich architect Fritz Landauer argued the need to bring the organizational life of the Jewish community back into contact with its religious life in a single structure that would serve as a "Gemeindezentrum." See "Jüdische Kultbau von heute," *C.V.-Zeitung* 10 (1931): 342.

35. *JLZ*, February 22, 1929. Rabbinical opinion on this subject, even among Liberal rabbis, was divided. Three rabbis favored mixed seating: Louis Blumenthal, Julius Galliner, and Max Weyl; three were opposed: Juda Bergmann, Julius Lewkowitz, and Malwin Warschauer. Max Wiener and Leo Baeck took intermediate positions. Baeck favored a synagogue that had sections for those who wanted to sit together and for those who wanted to sit separately. The Orthodox

rabbis were unanimously opposed. Still, in 1935 the Liberal rabbi of Frankfurt an der Oder expressed the view that allowing men and women to sit together was distinctly Christian and allowing women to become religious leaders characteristically pagan. See Ignaz Maybaum, *Parteibefreites Judentum. Lehrende Führung und priesterliche Gemeinschaft* (Berlin, 1935), pp. 55–56.

36. Hammer-Schenk, *Synagogen in Deutschland*, vol. 1, pp. 516–17.

37. Lorenz, *Die Juden in Hamburg*, vol. 1, p. 691. Of interest also is Ascher's statement six years later comparing the new structure with its predecessor: "If the old temple in the Poolstrasse was a place exclusively devoted to worship, the new structure in its multifaceted configuration has become a place for the nurture of Jewish community life in its wider sense and constitutes the focus of our Temple community's religious, cultural and intellectual life" ("Der neue Tempel," in *Festschrift zum hundertzwanzigjährigen Bestehen des Israelitischen Tempels in Hamburg 1817–1937*, ed. Bruno Italiener [Hamburg, 1937], p. 45).

38. Lorenz, *Die Juden in Hamburg*, vol. 1, p. 690.

39. Ibid., vol. 1, p. 694. In referring to the social hall, Italiener noted both Christian and the well-known American Jewish precedents.

40. Martin Buber, *Vom Geist der Religion* (Leipzig, 1916), pp. 50–52.

41. Felix Goldmann, "Religiöse Not," *Der Morgen* 2 (1926): 399.

42. "Jüdische Frömmigkeit in der deutschen Landgemeinde," *Der Morgen* 6 (1930): 49.

43. Maybaum, *Parteibefreites Judentum*, pp. 4, 41, 44.

44. *JLZ*, November 20, 1929; Ernst G. Lowenthal, *Juden in Preussen. Ein biographisches Verzeichnis* (Berlin, 1981), p. 60. *Wegweiser durch das jüdische Berlin. Geschichte und Gegenwart* (Berlin, 1987), p. 194, gives the year of his birth as 1869. So closely was the group associated with him that the institution was sometimes called the Hermann-Falkenberg-Synagoge.

45. E. G. Lowenthal, *Bewährung im Untergang. Ein Gedenkbuch*, 2nd ed. (Stuttgart, 1966), pp. 51–53; *Die Gemeinschaft* 21/22 (November 24, 1933): 33. He died in Theresienstadt.

46. Lowenthal, *Juden in Preussen*, p. 181. Like Friedländer and Falkenberg, Plaut was one of the lay preachers. He was able to leave Germany in 1939. Rabbi W. Gunther Plaut, who celebrated his Bar Mitzvah in the synagogue, is his son.

47. *Die Gemeinschaft* 12 (May 20, 1928): 14. The author is Levy Rosenblatt (1888–1944) who, like Friedländer, taught in the Berlin school system. On Rosenblatt, see Lowenthal, *Bewährung im Untergang*, p. 141.

48. Hermann Falkenberg, "Bericht über die 10 jährige Tätigkeit der Liberalen Synagoge Berlin" (mimeographed; n.p., n.d., but almost certainly Berlin, 1933).

49. Of the High Holy Day services it was reported that women declared, "Here for the first time a genuine holiday sentiment *[Jaumtauwstimmung]* had seized them since they had heard the word of God while sitting by the side of husband and child" (*Die Gemeinschaft* 2 [December 11, 1925]: 8).

50. Heinrich Stern, "Einige Gedanken und Anregungen zum Gottesdienst," *Die Gemeinschaft* 21/22 (November 24, 1933): 19.

51. Jonas Plaut, "Ein Jahrfünft Liberale Synagoge Norden," *Die Gemeinschaft* 13/14 (August 18, 1928): 10.

52. Lowenthal, *Bewährung im Untergang*, pp. 142–45. Salomonski died in or on the way to Auschwitz.

53. On August 17, 1928, the synagogue held a festive service on the occasion of the World Union for Progressive Judaism conference in Berlin. The speaker, who addressed the group in English, was Julian Morgenstern, president of the Hebrew Union College in Cincinnati.

54. Entitled *Das Freitagabend-Gebet*, it appeared as issue no. 10 of *Die Gemeinschaft* (December 18, 1927).

55. *JLZ*, November 6, 1925. Wolff may have been an anthropologist.

56. *Die Gemeinschaft* 19/20 (April 11, 1930): 20.

57. *Haggada für die Sederabende*. It appeared as no. 16/17 of *Die Gemeinschaft* (Pesach 1929). Like the earlier Liberal Haggadah by Caesar Seligmann (*Hagada. Liturgie für die häusliche Feier der Sederabende* [Frankfurt am Main, 1913]), on which it was partly based, it omits the call for vengeance *(shefoch chamatcha)* but, in contrast to it, does include the Ten Plagues. The following year Falkenberg gave a course for men and women in the Fasanenstrasse synagogue on how to conduct a seder using his Haggadah (*JLZ*, April 2, 1930).

58. Hermann Falkenberg, "'Erew' oder Die Stunde des Bereitmachens," *Festgabe für Claude G. Montefiore* (Berlin, 1928), pp. 30–34.

59. *Die Gemeinschaft* 12 (May 20, 1928): 13, and *Die Gemeinschaft* 15 (December 7, 1928): 12; Falkenberg, "Bericht," p. 9. There was apparently also an unspecified number of groups of non-Orthodox young people, probably in their twenties, who at this time were privately conducting totally independent, "secret" worship services, probably in private homes. The origins of these groups were almost certainly in the Jewish youth movement, which had taught them that certain acts assume significance only when they are done together. Their conscious intent was to transfer the idea of *Lebensgemeinschaft* to the religious realm—not so much to reform the liturgy as to transform its human context. Deeply under the influence of Buber, they rejected edification as the goal of worship and substituted for it nothing less than "the dialogue of the individual and the Gemeinschaft with God." Such prayer, one of their number held, was always a nonrepeatable, intrinsically valid act. It could not be borne by a collectivity numbering in the thousands but only by "a community that knows itself and has grown together" (eine sich kennende, eine zusammengewachsene Gemeinschaft). The groups had no choir; their prayer leaders and preachers were themselves part of the Gemeinschaft. Those who gave the sermons did not in fact preach but instead articulated feelings the worship experience had aroused in them; or they taught a passage from a classical Jewish text. Some groups used only Hebrew in the service; others included German. They were more radical than the Gemeinde Liberals in that they did not repeat prayers, but they also rediscovered some that the Liberals had thrown out. One such group, it was reported, built its own *sukkah* in the countryside. See Ernst Heinrich Seligsohn, "Gottesdienste der Jugend," *JLZ*, November 25, 1927. Regrettably, I have not been able to find further sources on this interesting phenomenon and therefore cannot judge its extent or duration.

60. The issues generally appeared in advance of Jewish holidays and initially focused on them. Later issues were devoted to community institutions or religious questions. Three issues were dedicated to exemplary figures: Abraham Geiger, Moses Mendelssohn, and Franz Rosenzweig. Altogether twenty-two numbers (some of them double issues) appeared between September 19, 1925, and November 24, 1933. Today it is exceedingly rare. I was able to use a microfilm copy made from the holdings of the Leo Baeck Institute in New York and supplement it with the group's Haggadah in the Hebrew Union College Library in Cincinnati. However, I have not been able to obtain issue no. 18 and part of issue no. 21/22.

61. George Goetz, "Die 'Gemeinschaft,'" *JLZ*, October 29, 1926.

62. [Benno] Gottschalk, "Gemeindeabende," *Die Gemeinschaft* 13/14 (August 18, 1928): 21.

63. The article, "Soziale Pflichten" (*Die Gemeinschaft* 3 [March 25, 1926]: 7–8) dealt with poverty in the Prenzlauer Berg neighborhood in which the synagogue was located and called upon the northern branch of the Liberal Association to instill the conviction "that social work means the fulfillment of religious duty, that social sentiment and social action are the foundations of true Judaism. The obligation of the Liberal associations is not fulfilled by arousing religious feelings through worship. It is just as necessary to sharpen the social conscience, for only out of the union of both does true religious Judaism arise." The author who signed only as B. F. was undoubtedly Bertha Falkenberg, Hermann's activist wife, who was third on the list of Liberal candidates for the Berlin Jewish representative assembly in 1930. See *JLZ*, November 27, 1930. On this subject see also Walter Krojanker, "Judentum und Wirtschaft," *JLZ*, January 14, 1927, where reference is made to the social consciousness of the Jewish Religious Union in England and of circles within international Protestantism.

64. Each of these three synagogues had two women on its governing board of eleven or twelve directors.

65. One source refers to it as "the periodical read by so many" (*JLZ*, November 20, 1929). Still, the very large figure of three thousand copies per issue that is given in the *Jüdisches Jahrbuch für Gross-Berlin* ([1928], p. 149), seems unlikely.

66. It contained contributions not only by the leaders of the group but also by Rabbis Leo Baeck, Benno Gottschalk, and Hermann Sènger; by Professor Ismar Elbogen of the Hochschule für die Wissenschaft des Judentums; and by Heinrich Stern, the leading lay figure among the Liberals.

67. Falkenberg, "Bericht," p. 16. However, Rabbi W. Gunther Plaut, in a letter to me dated September 30, 1995, recalled that services were still being held in the Auerbach Synagogue as late as the summer of 1937. For a recently published recollection of the "Hermann-Falkenberg-Synagogen," see Nathan Peter Levinson, *Ein Ort ist, mit wem du bist. Lebensstationen eines Rabbiners* (Berlin, 1996), p. 37.

3

Gemeindeorthodoxie in Weimar Germany

The Approaches of Nehemiah Anton Nobel and Isak Unna

DAVID ELLENSON

Historians and sociologists of the twentieth century have frequently filtered their discussion and analysis of social and political trends in the modern Occident through the lens provided by the theme of community and its decline. They have asserted that European life at the end of the Middle Ages was marked by an organic sense of community that provided individuals with institutional and cultural patterns, forms, activities, and values that allowed for group solidarity and identification. The premodern community has been depicted as a haven from the existential fears of solitude and individual isolation that are increasingly said to characterize and dominate human life in the modern period.

This view of the transformation in the ideal of community in the West has perhaps best been captured in the writings of the famed sociologist Ferdinand Tönnies. Tönnies saw the history of the West as marked by a move from the intimate face-to-face personal relationships of the premodern *Gemeinschaft* (community) to the rationally ordered and bureaucratically dominated patterns of an impersonal *Gesellschaft* (society). In this transition from a folk to an urban society, traditional frameworks for community—and the patterns of culture, religion, social relations, and politics that supported them—were challenged and often collapsed.

No sociological thinker has contributed more to the creation of a theoretical framework for understanding this change than has Peter Berger. Berger, like many other social theorists, has observed that this transition from Gemeinschaft to Gesellschaft brought in its wake a distinction between public and private spheres. The institutional consequences for religion have included the consignment of religion to the private realm and the subsequent creation of a society in which the structures that formerly supported and sustained religious organizations and beliefs have shifted "from society as a whole to much smaller groups of confirmatory individuals." This "privatization of religion" has permitted pluralism to flourish in the modern setting, for individuals have been able to choose voluntarily those collectivities that promote specific ideologies and that provide highly significant relationships and emotional resources for mediating between the individual and the larger "multi-relational reality 'outside.'"[1]

Berger's writings on this point provide the foundation for illuminating a typology of communal visions that held sway among the German Orthodox during the period of Weimar. Berger reminds us that with the advent of a modern political setting, the traditional *kehillah* (community) and its institutions were altered and in significant ways often dismantled as the Jewish community passed from the corporate political structure provided by the world of medieval European feudalism into the congregational patterns of association that marked religious life in the modern West. The question of how to create a political structure appropriate to the institutional needs of the Jewish community in this passage from medievalism to modernity was a challenge taken up by all segments of the German-Jewish religious world in the modern setting. This essay will be devoted to the way in which two leaders within one camp of the Weimar Orthodox community—Rabbis Nehemiah Anton Nobel and Isak Unna—responded to this challenge in light of diverse religious sensibilities and distinct communal attitudes.

In assessing the stances of these two men, it is essential that we place them in their proper historical context. Some elements within the nineteenth-century German Orthodox camp had put forth an ideal of community in keeping with a modern congregational model of "confirmatory individuals" set apart from the Jewish polity as a whole. For these Jews, the social and religious realities and divisions of the modern Jewish world led to a demand for a *Trennungsorthodoxie,* an Orthodox community that found corporate expression apart from the *kehillah.* From the moment Rabbi Samson Raphael Hirsch successfully engineered the passage by the Prussian Diet of the 1876 *Austrittsgesetz,* which allowed Orthodox Jews to establish independent *Austrittsgemeinden* (separatist communities), it was clear that a significant body of Orthodox Jews no longer affirmed the traditional notion that a sufficient ground for the creation and maintenance of a unified Jewish community was provided by the fact that Jews constituted what was widely regarded as an *Abstammungsgemein-schaft*, a common community of descent. Nor, more importantly, did these Jews assert that all Jews were part of a *Schicksalsgemeinschaft*, a community of shared destiny. Instead, these Orthodox Jews—like many of their Reform peers in the nineteenth century—viewed Judaism in terms that were almost exclusively based in religious dogma. They held that only a sense of common religious purpose and vision could foster community. As Rabbi Hirsch phrased it, "All the institutions and establishments in the care of a community are religious in nature." Only the separatism demanded by *Trennungsortho-doxie* could facilitate the construction of an Orthodox Jewish community marked by a genuine fidelity to the tenets and teachings of Judaism.[2]

Other Orthodox German Jews dissented from this position and clung to the notion that the modern Jewish community demanded institutional expression in the traditional structure of an *Einheitsge-meinde*, a united community. Yet, even here the reasons put forth to justify such a position were radically different from the attitudes held by communal leaders in the past. This essay will explore two such positions by examining selected writings of two prominent exponents of Gemeindeorthodoxie during the Weimar period—Nehemiah Anton Nobel of Frankfurt am Main (1871–1922) and Isak Unna of Mannheim (1872–1948).

Nobel, though born in Nagymend, Hungary, was raised in Halberstadt, where his father served as *Klausrabbiner* (rabbi of an endowed study house). He attended the rabbinical seminary of Esriel Hildesheimer in Berlin during the 1890s and was ultimately selected as *orthodoxer Gemeinderabbiner* in Frankfurt. In accepting this post, Nobel positioned himself as heir to a legacy of Gemeindeorthodoxie bequeathed to him by his predecessor, Rabbi Marcus Horowitz. Rabbi Unna was born in Würzburg; he was the grandson of Seligman Bär Bamberger, the *Würzburger rav* and great German Talmudist who refused to support Hirsch's notion that Orthodox Jews were duty-bound in all instances to secede from Einheitsgemeinden. As a young man, Unna journeyed to Frankfurt, where he studied with Marcus Horowitz. Like Nobel, Unna was ordained at the Berlin rabbinical seminary, and he too argued for a united Jewish communal structure that would include both Orthodox and non-Orthodox Jews. Indeed, Unna constructed rather elaborate statements on the structure and framework of the *jüdische Gemeinde* during the modern era. Yet, his arguments on behalf of Jewish communal unity were distinct from those of Nobel and represent an alternative vision of community among the Orthodox of this time and place. Seen against the backdrop of a larger Occidental context, the presentation and analysis of their approaches to the issue of community will provide insight into the two dominant visions of Gemeindeorthodoxie that reigned during the Weimar period.

Nobel: Vision and Ideals

Gemeindeorthodoxie in early Weimar found its most charismatic spokesman in the person of Nehemiah Anton Nobel, the Orthodox rabbi of Frankfurt am Main. Ordained at the rabbinical seminary in 1895, Nobel possessed a stellar reputation as a Talmudist. Indeed, Mordechai Breuer has identified Nobel as a "star pupil of [Esriel] Hildesheimer."[3] However, Nobel's academic talents were not limited to the realm of rabbinic literature. He also journeyed to Marburg in 1900 and there studied philosophy under Hermann Cohen. So accomplished did he become in the field of philosophy that Alexander Altmann was able to describe Nobel years later "as the only true philosopher amongst German-Jewish Orthodoxy."[4] Others have shared this assessment.[5]

For our purposes, what is more significant is that Nobel maintained "a long-lasting and close friendship" with Cohen until his teacher's death in 1918, despite the considerable religious differences in their views of Judaism. Nor were his relationships and encounters with Liberal and secular Jews limited to Cohen. As we shall see, Nobel had many such associations.[6] Moreover, his ability to sustain such encounters with non-Orthodox Jews reflects more than the openness and warmth of his personality. It indicates that he saw non-Orthodox Jews as persons of integrity and knowledge, and it provides evidence of his judgment that such persons—whatever his condemnation of and dissent from their religious positions—were his brethren and as such part of his community. This conviction was characteristic of Nobel throughout his life. It informed his myriad activities within the Jewish community, and it guided his writings on the nature of that community both before and after Weimar.

None of this should obscure the fundamental Orthodox postures Nobel affirmed. Indeed, his religious orthodoxy led him to offer a sharp critique of Reform and its theological postulates. He was particularly agitated by *Die Richtlinien,* guidelines of a program for Liberal Judaism issued by sixty-one German rabbis for adoption as a statement of principles and beliefs by a conference of the Union for Liberal Judaism held in Posen in 1912. His response to this statement is paradigmatic of attacks he made on Liberal Judaism throughout his career. Nobel was disturbed by the claim put forth in the guidelines that Jewish law was subject to historical processes and, as such, could be amended or abrogated in light of academic research or the needs of the time. The Liberals claimed that "every generation adopted the faith of the fathers through its own particular religious concepts and expressed it in its own particular forms." *Die Richtlinien* continued:

> Liberal Judaism therefore recognizes the validity of evolution, which gave Judaism in every age the right and duty to abandon certain historically conditioned beliefs and forms, or to develop them, or to create new ones, while safeguarding its own essential content. This duty speaks with special urgency to our time. Through the entrance of Jews into the . . . community of this age, . . . many traditional concepts, institutions, and customs have evaporated and disappeared and thereby lost both content and significance.

Some ordinances, the Liberal rabbis contended, remained obligatory for modern Jews, while others could simply be abandoned. For example, in addressing the issue of the Sabbath, these rabbis held that whatever "disturbs [the] solemnity [of the Sabbath] must be avoided and, conversely, whatever does not disturb it cannot be considered as prohibited." Liberal Judaism, the rabbis concluded, "recognizes as worthwhile only that which for the individual has the power to elicit pious sentiment, to advance moral action, and to recall religious truths and experiences vividly."[7]

It was this emphasis on the law as historically conditioned and subject to the will of the individual that so disturbed Nobel's Orthodox sensibilities. He acknowledged the purity and sincerity of the Liberal rabbis' intentions. Nevertheless, Nobel condemned the sentiments contained in *Die Richtlinien* as springing from the soil of a "Protestant communal consciousness." They constituted a "war against the Halakhah," against the system of "statutes and judgments" that lay at the heart of authentic Judaism.[8] For Judaism, as Nobel had asserted in an article in *Die jüdische Presse* years before, "could never have become a universal religion had it confined itself to a system of abstract thought."[9] The Halakhah permitted the moral values of Judaism to become manifest in life.

Unlike the Liberals and individuals in the Jewish past, for example, Paul of Tarsus, the prophets themselves—whom the Liberals loved to cite in support of their antinomian posture—never, Nobel claimed, opposed the Law. They only opposed its rote performance by those who observed it in a "superficial and external manner." Like the German Liberals, Nobel asserted that there could be no authentic "religion without morality." However, the Liberals in *Die Richtlinien* failed to realize that the Law was eternal and that genuine Jewish observance of the Law did not result from heteronomous coercion but from an internal state of freedom that permitted the Jew to accept God's commandments autonomously. Law and ethics were not opposed in Judaism. On the contrary, they were complementary. The Law, as Nobel put it, did not impose an onerous "yoke" upon the freedom of the Jew. Instead, the faithful Jew observed the Law with joy and celebration.[10] Observance of the Law was not a mark of bondage, it was the essence of Judaism. Law was not transitory but eternal, and the Liberals, in striking at the Law as they did in *Die Richtlinien,* threatened "the existence of Judaism itself."[11]

In view of the sharp rebuke Nobel aimed at the Liberals in response to *Die Richtlinien,* it is significant that he refused to join in the attacks his Orthodox colleagues immediately mounted at Liberals upon publication of *Die Richtlinien.* The Vereinigung der traditionell-gesetzestreuen Rabbiner Deutschlands (Union of Traditional and Torah-Faithful Rabbis of Germany), of which Nobel was a member, "laid emphasis on the problems that would occur in the future in the joint work of *Einheitsgemeinde.*" Religious instruction offered by Liberal "rabbis and based on the 'Guidelines' would constitute 'a danger for Jewish youth.'"[12] When 111 of his Orthodox colleagues in the Vereinigung signed a circular condemning the Liberals for *Die Richtlinien,* Nobel, in the words of Mordechai Breuer, "went so far in his tolerance that he did not sign the protest of the traditionalist rabbis of Germany against the liberal *Richtlinien,*"[13] despite, as we have seen, his disdain for its content. By his refusal to participate in this protest against *Die Richtlinien,* Nobel signaled his determination to maintain a united Jewish community in spite of religious differences that might divide its members. For Nobel, the community could not be reduced to a congregation of "confirmatory individuals." His allegiance to communal Orthodoxy and to the traditional structure of an Einheitsgemeinde could not be shaken even in the face of Liberal impieties.

Nobel supplied a rationale for his posture early in his career. On April 30, 1897, in a letter to the Synagogengemeinde Köln, he offered his view of rabbinical office. Nobel wrote:

I hold that a rabbi can fulfill his task successfully only if he stands above all parties within and outside his community. He himself must have a firm and unflinching standpoint—one not given to appeals—on all the religious issues of his time. For myself, this standpoint is that offered by Judaism in its historical tradition. This alone seems to me to guarantee the proper development toward a sound future. But, I consider it my duty to examine every religious trend within Judaism, to meet it with objective arguments only, and to treat the representatives of opposition movements and viewpoints with the kind of respect we owe to ardent opponents. I want to lay greater stress in my public activities on that which unites different trends than on those causes which separate them. . . . This is my ideal of the rabbi as I see it, and to strive for its realization is my life's task.[14]

Nobel remained faithful to this vision of the rabbinical office and the institutional expression of a united community it entailed throughout his career. His communal activities and attitudes gave practical expression to these commitments. Preeminent among these activities was Nobel's active participation in the Allgemeiner deutscher Rabbinerverband. Indeed, Nobel was elected president of the organization in 1921, the first Orthodox rabbi to serve in that capacity. Organized by Orthodox and Liberal rabbis, this rabbinical union affirmed a unique sense of solidarity among all Jews despite doctrinal differences that might separate them in the religious realm. Nobel was also constantly involved in serious outreach to non-Orthodox students and intellectuals, and he engaged actively with them even if they did not affirm his own stance of religious Orthodoxy. His power and charm as a preacher and lecturer were legendary, and he attracted hundreds of listeners—Orthodox and non-Orthodox alike—to the lectures he delivered each year at the Frankfurt Lehrhaus that Rosenzweig had established during the early years of Weimar.[15] At the same time, he established a circle of young Jewish intellectuals—including not only Rosenzweig but Ernst Simon, Erich Fromm, and Nahum N. Glatzer, among others—"whose impact rejudaicised broad circles outside Orthodoxy."[16]

Nobel was also an active Zionist, and despite his attachment to Mizrachi, accorded nonreligious Zionists such as Chaim Weizmann the same respect and concern he displayed toward non-Orthodox Jews in the communities of Germany. At the Twelfth Zionist Congress held in Karlsbad in 1921, Nobel sought, as he did elsewhere, to emphasize the commonalities shared by secular and religious Zionists.[17] In taking this stance toward the Zionist movement and nonreligious Zionists, Nobel displayed fidelity to the principles he had articulated and the actions he had taken in connection with the whole of the Jewish community throughout his life. Nevertheless, the uniqueness of his stance in the Orthodox world is summed up well by Mordechai Breuer when he writes, "N.A. Nobel stood virtually alone in the [German] Orthodox rabbinate as an advocate of association with the Zionist movement and as a co-founder of Misrachi."[18]

Nobel was a charismatic and scholarly individual whose insistence on Gemeindeorthodoxie was fueled, in Leo Baeck's words, by his "lively feeling for Jewish community wholeness *(Gesamtheit).*"[19]

Rachel Heuberger sums up Nobel's position well when she observes, "His belief, that there existed a Jewish entity and a Jewish solidarity resulting from it, was fundamental. The feeling of obligation to *Klal Yisrael* . . . made him a strict adversary of separatist community politics."[20] In this way, Nobel stood in absolute opposition to views in support of Orthodox separatism expressed by both Samson Raphael Hirsch and his teacher Esriel Hildesheimer when the Law of Secession was passed in the 1870s. Hirsch, the chief architect of the policy of secessionist Orthodoxy, had written, "The divergence between the religious beliefs of Reform and Orthodoxy is so profound that when an individual publicly secedes he is only giving formal expression to convictions which had long since matured and become perfectly clear to himself." Separatist Orthodox congregations were mandated, Hirsch maintained, for "all the institutions and establishments in the care of a community are religious in nature, and they are . . . intimately bound up with the religious law." Hildesheimer, though he did not insist as Hirsch did on a policy of Orthodox institutional separation from Liberal Judaism in every community, did support Hirsch's position on the passage of the *Austrittsgesetz*. In a letter to the Prussian Diet, Hildesheimer wrote, "The gulf between the adherents of traditional Judaism and its religious opponents is at least as deep and wide as in any other religious faith and, in fact, is larger than in most."[21] Nobel, in contrast, wrote, "Both trends [Liberal and Orthodox] have enough in common, so that the consciousness of belonging together and forming one entity can develop its social, political, and religious creative strength. The majority of German Jews take the Solomonic view that the maternal love of conviction proves itself in its love to the whole."[22]

Nobel's policy of Gemeindeorthodoxie emanated from an open and broad personality that fostered an attitude of tolerance and respect, even for those with whom he disagreed on religious grounds. However, that personality emerged from and was informed by a principled commitment to the classical rabbinic teaching that God is exalted when all Israel is united in a single fellowship and that Jews should not needlessly divide themselves into factions. Drawing upon Leviticus 19:1, "Speak unto to *all* the congregation of Israel,"[23] Nobel was able to assert that the proper task of the Jewish leader was to serve all the people—observant and nonobservant alike—for all were part of the Jewish community. "Party slogans," as Eugen E. Mayer has pointed out, were alien to Nobel. As "a protagonist of 'Klal Yisrael,'" Nobel believed, "in Solomon Schechter's felicitous phrase, [in] catholic Judaism."[24] This conviction caused him to conclude that the religious imperatives of Judaism frowned upon an institutionalized

Orthodoxy apart from the Einheitsgemeinde. In advocating such a policy, Nobel resisted significant trends in the modern world that combined to splinter and transform the Jewish community from its status as a unified medieval legal corporation to a quasi-voluntary association or group of associations of individuals in twentieth-century Germany. Nobel, unlike the advocates of Trennungsorthodoxie, refused to see Judaism solely as a religious confession. He did not regard membership in the Einheitsgemeinden of modern Germany as a matter of voluntary consent. The traditional Jewish communal ethos he had internalized led him to view all Jews—regardless of the religious orientations they advocated—as members of one body. The concept of Klal Yisrael demanded institutional expression in Einheitsgemeinden.

Unna: Principles and Pragmatism

Nobel was not alone among the Orthodox in adopting this position. As Donald Niewyk has observed about the Jewish world of Weimar, "In most urban centers unified Jewish communities governed all the local Jewish congregations, from the most conservative to the most liberal."[25] For some of the proponents of Gemeindeorthodoxie, the attacks on communal Orthodoxy that emanated from the separatist Orthodox circles of Samson Raphael Hirsch and his ideological descendants demanded a Jewish legal response. An examination of the halakhic arguments advanced by Rabbi Isak Unna on behalf of communal Orthodoxy will display the nature of this response and present a more complete spectrum of the views advanced by the Orthodox advocates of this policy during Weimar.

Unna's legal writings on behalf of Gemeindeorthodoxie must be seen against the backdrop of internal events and divisions within the ranks of German Orthodoxy in particular and European Orthodoxy in general. In 1885 Samson Raphael Hirsch established the Freie Vereinigung für die Interessen des orthodoxen Judentums (Free Union for the Interests of Orthodox Judaism) as an institutional vehicle for the promotion of Orthodoxy. Many of its members were supporters of Trennungsorthodoxie. Solomon Breuer, the son-in-law of Hirsch as well as his successor in 1888 as rabbi of the Israelitische Religionsgesellschaft, along with his son Isaac Breuer, a Frankfurt attorney, and Jakob Rosenheim, another prominent member of the Frankfurt Austrittsgemeinde, were all active members of this union and they were the chief proponents of the notion that Orthodox Jews in Germany were obligated to be members—where possible—of separatist Orthodox congregations.

When, on March 28, 1912, an international assembly of Orthodox Jews took place in Kattowitz for the express purpose of uniting Orthodox Jews from East and West institutionally under the banner of Agudas Yisroel, Solomon Breuer attempted to extend the Hirschian principle of separatism to this international body. He supported the proposition that Orthodox Jews who were not connected to the Austrittsgemeinde that existed in their place of dwelling not be allowed to hold office in the international group. Breuer's position met with severe opposition and was not adopted at the Kattowitz conference. However, in Vienna in 1923 a Great Assembly *(Kenesiyah ha-Gedolah)* of the Agudah was convened. There the Agudah—at the initiative of Breuer and his group as well as some Hungarian colleagues—did adopt an article that imposed an ideological test for determining membership. While the article did not deal specifically with the matter of separatism, Breuer's opponents on this issue seized the opportunity to establish an alternative Orthodox organization that would not be identified with Trennungsorthodoxie. Hence, on December 26, 1923, Achduth-Vereinigung gesetzestreuer Juden Deutschlands (Union of Torah-Faithful Jews in Germany) was formed. Rabbi Unna, who was a member of Agudas Yisroel and who had participated in the 1923 Assembly in Vienna, was among its founders and was its first leader.[26]

Rabbi Unna's speech at the founding assembly of Achduth, "Der Gedanke der Arewuth in seiner praktischen Bedeutung" (The practical meaning of the idea of "mutual responsibility"), was directed toward an Orthodox audience. It both surveyed the struggle between separatist and communal Orthodoxy in Germany during the previous half century and offered a Jewish legal defense of Gemeindeorthodoxie.[27] Unna began by pointing out that from the moment Reform became a force in German Jewish life during the first half of the nineteenth century, an Orthodox minority came to be subject to scorn and derision by a dominant Reform majority in virtually every community in Germany.[28] The Reformers consistently and deliberately refused to respond to Orthodox requests for communal support of Orthodox institutions, and this fostered a desire among the Orthodox to be freed from the shackles and intolerance of Reform-dominated communities. The mechanism for achieving this aim was secession, and when the Austrittsgesetz was passed on July 28, 1876, the Orthodox minority had the means it needed to compel the Reform-dominated Gemeinden to accede to their requests lest the unity of the community be destroyed. As a result, the Liberals, in virtually every

Jewish community in Germany, surrendered to Orthodox demands. Despite this, Hirsch ruled that secession was a religious obligation thrust upon every Orthodox Jew regardless of the newfound willingness of the Einheitsgemeinde to finance Orthodox Jewish religious institutions and needs. Bamberger disagreed with Hirsch and asserted that if the administration of a unified community was both willing to support Orthodox institutions and prepared to have these institutions be supervised by Orthodox Jews, then there was no obligation for Orthodox Jews to secede.[29]

In a polemical thrust clearly directed at Breuer and Breuer's desire to apply Hirsch's 1876 demand to Orthodox Jews in 1923, Unna pointed out that secession was never a practical possibility—even in Hirsch's day—for most Orthodox Jews in Germany. Their numbers in most communities were simply too small to maintain separatist Orthodox institutions. What was true in Hirsch's time was all the more true later. Nevertheless, Hirsch, and later Breuer, as well as many in their camp, persisted in claiming that authentic Judaism demanded Orthodox secession from the Einheitsgemeinde in every instance. This caused division among the Orthodox, with the supporters of Austritt going so far as to seek separation from the proponents of Gemeindeorthodoxie. Unna thundered against the application of this position and condemned the Hirschian ideology that warranted it as "sectarian dogmatism" *(Parteidogma)*.[30]

Unna then went on to the heart of his argument. He maintained that the halakhic principle of *'areivut* had been unjustifiably ignored by the Separatists in their rulings and actions on this matter, and he contended that this notion had to be assigned decisive weight in guiding Orthodox policy on the question of secession from the Einheitsgemeinde. This principle, based on Sanhedrin 27b, held that "all Israel is responsible for one another." In assessing its significance, Unna stated, "I emphasize at the start that what we have before us [in this principle] is no mere sermonic flourish [keine homiletische Floskel] concerning the solidarity of all Jews. Rather, it is a halakhic principle of decisive practical importance."[31]

Unna continued by offering an exegesis of Deuteronomy 29 from the weekly Torah portion *Nitzavim* to support his assertion that the principle of 'areivut should be applied by the Orthodox to the challenges posed by the existence of Reform throughout Germany. The biblical chapter begins with an admonition concerning the sins of individuals and goes on to warn of the punishments that will befall the entire people should such individuals sin. Why should the community suffer because of the transgressions of isolated individuals? The explanation is to be found in the principle of 'areivut. For the concluding verse of the Torah portion (Deuteronomy 29:29), which states that "The secret things belong unto the Lord our God, but those things which are revealed belong unto us and our children forever," indicates that when the community is capable of preventing the public sins of an individual and does not, then it is culpable for the sins of that single person. "The reciprocal responsibility that *Klal Yisrael* possesses for one another is here established."[32]

Unna further cited Rabbi Isaac Elchanan Spektor of Kovno, Eastern Europe's greatest halakhic authority, to buttress his case concerning the import and dimensions of this principle. Unna wrote of Rabbi Spektor:

> He has demonstrated from a survey of the sources themselves that the sin of the individual is the sin of *Klal Yisrael* and therefore attached to every single person among the people Israel in accord with the notion of reciprocal responsibility. And this principle . . . obligates us to become involved in every instance where we are capable of preventing transgression. . . . In so doing we not only attempt to act for the benefit of the sinner himself, we also grant merit to ourselves and *Klal Yisrael*. This *'areivut*, this solidarity, includes the people of Israel in all its branches, even those who have abandoned their faith. . . . The law of *'areivut* excludes only those who have actually apostasized to another religion.[33]

Unna maintained that Spektor's position was conclusive for Orthodox Jews on this matter. The law of *'areivut* extended to Liberal Jews. Consequently, the Orthodox were halakhically bound to maintain relations with them in Einheitsgemeinden so long as these Liberal Jews—regardless of their motives—allowed for Orthodox institutions under Orthodox control in their communities. These people—albeit "sinners" whose disbelief and nonobservance could only be abhorred by those faithful to the Law—remained part of Klal Yisrael. By participating in the Einheitsgemeinde, the Orthodox Jew increased the opportunities for engagement with these people. In so doing, the Orthodox Jew could both promote Orthodox concepts and organizations to a larger public and engage more directly in a war against Reform. Furthermore, through Orthodox supervision of communal institutions, the proponents of Gemeindeorthodoxie were better positioned than their colleagues in the camp of Trennungsorthodoxie to prevent non-Orthodox Jews from sinning through their insistence that communal institutions comport to the dictates of Halakhah. In this way, the supporters of Gemeindeorthodoxie displayed a greater fidelity to the requirements of *'areivut* and Jewish law than did the advocates of separation.

Unna also dismissed two other criticisms that the advocates of

Trennungsorthodoxie commonly hurled at the proponents of Gemeindeorthodoxie. The first criticism maintained that the participation of Orthodox Jews in an Einheitsgemeinde granted recognition
and religious legitimacy to Liberal Judaism. Unna cited the example of
Shimon ben Shetach as a warrant for this dismissal. In seeming
violation of the Law, Shimon ben Shetach had once entered the
Sanhedrin, in which Sadducees participated. However, he did so in
order to combat the Sadducees and to purify the Sanhedrin. Unna saw
the position of the communal Orthodox as identical to that of Shimon
ben Shetach. The Talmudic sage's actions admitted of only one conclusion. Unna wrote, "We will be able to work for the authority of Torah
and combat those erroneous tendencies connected to Judaism only if
we are found in the midst of the community." Unna also asserted that
Orthodox participation in the Einheitsgemeinde did not violate the
rabbinic prohibition against abetting sinners (she'lo l-sa'yei'a ov'rei
'aveirah). Such a prohibition only applied in instances where the
sinner could perform the sin only with the direct aid of the abettor.
This condition did not obtain in the communities of Germany where
the Orthodox by and large constituted a small minority. Indeed, it
could only apply in a community where the Orthodox had complete
control. Interestingly, Unna added parenthetically that if such were to
be the case, then the Orthodox, in full conscience, "could not permit
Reform institutions" (Reformeinrichtungen).³⁴

Unna's essay indicates that his policy of Gemeindeorthodoxie was
not without textures and ambivalence. It was informed in large
measure by a sense of commitment and obligation to the religious
well-being of the entire community of Israel. After all, as Unna
observed at the conclusion of his article, "Israel cannot be redeemed
until it is united in a single fellowship."³⁵ Nevertheless, the main
thrust of Unna's essay indicates that his advocacy of Gemeindeorthodoxie sprang primarily from pragmatic considerations. The exi-
gencies of the day, not a principled commitment to the unity of the
Jewish people, demanded tolerance of Liberal Judaism and participation in the Einheitsgemeinde. It was a tactic that best advanced the
interests of Orthodox Judaism in the contemporary situation.

Unna's approach to Gemeindeorthodoxie clearly distinguished him
from Nobel. He was informed with a different sensibility than Nobel,
and he did not accord even a modicum of integrity to the religious
positions advanced by Liberal Jews. A fuller picture of the distinctive
posture Unna adopted is apparent when we turn to another essay,
"Das Trennungsprinzip und die Zusammenarbeit der Gesetzestreuen"
(The principle of secession and the cooperation of the Orthodox),
which Unna wrote in 1924.³⁶ Here, as in his speech before the

founding assembly of Achduth, Unna addressed himself principally to his Orthodox coreligionists—supporters and critics alike. At the outset Unna distinguished between *'edah* and *kahal,* two terms for community in Jewish tradition. The former term signified unity of religious purpose, while the latter referred to the entirety of the people in a civil sense. In the period of the Second Temple, no distinction was made between these two dimensions of community, and "the civil and religious community was one" (die bürgerliche und die religiöse Gemeinde [war] eins). All residents of the city *(b'nei ha-ir)* were by definition members of the community and every member of the community was responsible, according to the Mishnah (*Nedarim* 5:5), for providing for public needs. In Babylonia, the notion reigned that the civil and religious community were congruent and that all members of the community *(Gemeindemitglieder)* were also partners *(Gesellschafter [shutafin])* in the institutions and property of the community. This situation persisted through the Middle Ages, and the Jews of this period constituted "a state within a state."[37]

With the advent of the modern era, the unity of the civil and religious dimensions of the Jewish community was shattered. The Jewish community was reduced to a religious Gemeinschaft in civil law. The community no longer constituted a "state within a state." It ceded its civil authority to the state and was now legally assigned the status of a *Privatkirchengesellschaft.* As such, its members were no longer Gesellschafter, shutafin, from a Jewish legal point of view.[38]

This point was crucial to Unna. The Einheitsgemeinde of the contemporary era was legally distinct from the Jewish community of premodern Jewish history. Its members were no longer shutafin, legal partners. Consequently, the supporters of Gemeindeorthodoxie were not halakhically responsible—as all premodern Jews would have been in the period when the Jewish community constituted a "state within a state"—for every appropriation the Einheitsgemeinde made.

While this was a necessary argument for the defense of Gemeindeorthodoxie, Unna does not seem to have regarded it as sufficient to respond to the attacks of the Trennungsorthodoxen. He admitted that Gemeindeorthodoxie was disturbed by the Einheitsgemeinde's establishment of non-Orthodox religious and educational institutions despite the lack of Jewish legal responsibility the Orthodox members of the Gemeinde had for such institutions. Gemeindeorthodoxie had been made possible, in Unna's opinion, only because each Einheitsgemeinde in Germany had agreed that tax money paid to the community by Orthodox Jews would be used solely for social, not religious or cultural, purposes. Hirsch believed that such a distinction was specious.[39] He contended that Orthodox Jews who maintained member-

ship in the community were—protestations to the contrary notwithstanding—in actuality supporting Liberal religious and educational
programs. Unna disagreed and stated that this conclusion was un-
founded. He pointed out that if one could not pay taxes to the
Einheitsgemeinde on the grounds that money was being designated
for institutions and programs that were suspect or forbidden in the
eyes of Jewish law, then each Jew would have to stop paying taxes to
the government of Germany itself. After all, the German state appropriated tax dollars for the support of non-Jewish religions which, in
the eyes of Jewish law, may well have promoted *avodah zarah*,
idolatry. In addition, it was unquestionably true that the government
financed educational institutions that taught biblical criticism, a topic
whose content was surely forbidden by the Halakhah. Yet, no Orthodox Jew would refuse to pay taxes for those reasons. Even the
suggestion of such a thing was ridiculous! Therefore, the Gemeindeorthodoxen were justified in designating tax funds for one purpose in
the united community while refusing to apply them for another.[40]

Unna also supplemented the argument he had made in his earlier
address concerning the issue of "siyua' y'dei 'ovrei 'aveirah" (abetting
sinners). He repeated his previous claim that the Orthodox were in the
minority in every community in Germany. Consequently, Reform
Jews did not need the aid of Orthodox Jews. Rather, the Orthodox
needed the aid of the Reformers to maintain Orthodox institutions.[41]
In an astonishingly candid vein, Unna even pointed out that the
Gemeindeorthodoxen were in fact diminishing the support for Reform institutions by participating in Einheitsgemeinden. After all,
money spent by the Reform majority that would have been used for
the support of Reform institutions was now being appropriated for
the support of Orthodox ones. Orthodox participation in an Einheitsgemeinde certainly did not constitute a violation of the rabbinic
dictum of "hahzakat y'dei 'ovrei 'aveirah" (strengthening the hands of
sinners). Indeed, wrote Unna, "It is well known that we do not affirm
their deeds. We emphasize repeatedly our opposition to them. We do
not enter their synagogues, nor do we join in their prayers or religious
ceremonies. We remain with them in one community only because
they maintain those institutions that we need in accord with traditional forms."[42] Gemeindeorthodoxie aided Orthodoxy while weak-
ening Reform.[43]

Unna conceded, as he had in his speech to Achduth, that secession
from the unified community had been necessary for the nineteenth-
century Orthodox. The stringent stance on this matter taken at that
time by the great scholars of Hungary constituted "an emergency
measure" *(l'migdar milta)* designed to check the lawlessness of early

Reform. Nevertheless, this policy was not in the best interests of contemporary Orthodoxy. An Orthodox Jew would certainly have preferred to be in a community with like-minded Orthodox individuals. However, given the minority status of Orthodox Jews in Germany, such an option was impossible to attain—for economic reasons. To insist upon Austritt was to "impose a decree upon the community that the majority could not abide" (gezei'rah she-'ein rov ha-tzibur y'kholin la-'amod bah).[44]

Unna concluded his essay on a note of Orthodox triumphalism. Fifty years earlier many had seen secession as the only way to preserve Orthodoxy. However, in the atmosphere of Weimar, such a policy was no longer necessary. Liberal Jews were no longer as strident in their antinomianism as they had been, and many Reform rabbis even embraced, in a reversal of the position advocated by their nineteenth-century predecessors, the cause of Jewish nationalism from a religious perspective. Still other non-Orthodox Jews acknowledged, despite their nonobservance, the failure of Reform. Third and fourth generation descendants of Reform Jews no longer felt as their ancestors did, and Unna heralded the fact that many in the younger generation sought to return to traditional Judaism. The goals and interests of Orthodoxy could best be served by participation in Einheitsgemeinden and by a rejection of the policy position put forth by Trennungsorthodoxie.[45]

Unna, like Nobel, supported Gemeindeorthodoxie. However, the tenor of his arguments could hardly have been more distinct. Unna displayed neither the tolerance nor the respect for the concept of the Einheitsgemeinde that Nobel did. Indeed, his Jewish sensibilities seem rather distinct from those of Nobel. His Gemeindeorthodoxie did not embrace a "lively feeling of Jewish community wholeness." It was instead informed by a sense of pragmatism and opportunism. His vision of community was directed at his opponents in the Orthodox camp, and it was they whom he addressed in offering his defense of Gemeindeorthodoxie.

Conclusion

The manifold changes that marked the modern West as it moved from Gemeinschaft to Gesellschaft were accompanied and informed by the process that sociologists have labeled secularization. As sociologists employ the term, secularization does not signify the disappearance of religion. Rather, it points toward the constriction of religion and the compartmentalization of life. A distinction between the public and private spheres arises and religion becomes increasingly consigned to a private realm. Religion no longer plays the role it previously did in informing the beliefs and guiding the activities of either persons or entire communities. In the wake of such a process, traditional religious beliefs sometimes collapse. At other times, such beliefs are altered to accommodate and adapt to a novel reality. In either case, they are surely challenged. Nobel and Unna, like other Jewish religious leaders of their time and place, were compelled to construct an institutionalized framework for the jüdische Gemeinde in a world where the political realities of the modern era had transformed Jews into citizens of the German state. The intimacies as well as the communal structures that had characterized the traditional jüdische Gemeinschaft had become severely attenuated, if not, in many instances, completely obliterated.

As Orthodox Jews, Nobel and Unna had sworn fidelity to Jewish religious tradition. Nevertheless, theirs was a world where political, cultural, social, and religious changes had long since dismantled the structure and nature of the premodern Jewish community. Nobel and Unna were both fully cognizant of this, and both attempted to provide a vision of community for the Jews of Weimar that would maintain proper faith with the past while adapting Judaism to the communal realities of the present. For both men, this meant that their conceptions of community had to be rooted in Jewish tradition. Yet, as we have seen, each man understood the dictates and applications of that tradition in distinct ways.

While both Nobel and Unna supported a policy of Gemeindeorthodoxie, Nobel supported a vision of and framework for community informed by the primacy of kinship. The Jewish people constituted a single entity, and the group solidarity that characterized the Jewish people was absolute. As the teachings of Judaism demanded an institutional pattern of community in keeping with this holistic vision, Nobel held that the only form of community that would appropriately embody these teachings was the Einheitsgemeinde. The changes that the modern world introduced into the Jewish situation could not alter Nobel's belief that the concept of Klal Yisrael demanded institutional expression in a united community.

A different vision informed the stance of Isak Unna. Like the proponents of Austrittsorthodoxie, Unna embraced a vision of Gemeinde attuned to the dictates of a modern setting that differentiated between religious and communal spheres. He, like his opponents in the separatist camp, viewed Judaism essentially, though not exclusively, as a religious confession.[46] His approach to community arose from a recognition that the religious and ethnic components of Jewish identity and status had been torn asunder by the realities of the modern world. His Gemeindeorthodoxie ultimately distinguished between religious dogma and ethnic solidarity and accorded the former primacy over the latter. Considerations of prudence—the practical benefits that would accrue to the Orthodox through their participation in the political structure of the Einheitsgemeinde—were the factors that led Unna to embrace Gemeindeorthodoxie. His commitment to this policy was instrumental.

The writings of Nobel and Unna on the issue of community indicate that both men were wedded to the imperatives of Jewish law and teachings as well as to the application of those imperatives and teachings in a contemporary communal setting. At the same time, their writings testify to the power of adaptation and the manner in which even religious traditionalists advance visions of community in response to the dictates of an age. Their views illuminate the pluralism that characterized the Orthodox camp in Germany during Weimar. Study of their views illuminates some of the dynamics that have informed the development and evolution of Judaism in the modern age.

Notes

I would like to express my thanks to both Professors Modechai Breuer and Yaakov Zur for their careful reading of an earlier draft of this essay.

1. Peter Berger, Brigette Berger, and Hansfried Kellner, *The Homeless Mind: Modernization and Consciousness* (New York, 1973), pp. 80, 186.

2. For the passage from Hirsch and an extended treatment of his views as well as those of his colleagues on this subject, see David Ellenson, "Traditional Reactions to Modern Jewish Reform: The Paradigm of Jewish Orthodoxy," in *The Routledge History of Jewish Philosophy,* ed. Oliver Leaman and Daniel Frank (London, 1996), pp. 751ff.

3. Mordechai Breuer, *Modernity within Tradition: The Social History of Orthodox Jewry in Imperial Germany* (New York, 1992), p. 246.

4. Alexander Altmann, "Theology in Twentieth Century Germany," *LBIYB* 1 (1956): 211.

5. Rachel Heuberger, "Orthodoxy versus Reform: The Case of Rabbi Nehemiah Anton Nobel of Frankfurt a. Main," *LBIYB* 27 (1992): 47.

6. Ibid.

7. As translated in W. Gunther Plaut, *The Growth of Reform Judaism* (New York, 1965), pp. 69–71.

8. Nehemia Anton Nobel, *Hagut v'Halakhah* (Meditations and Halakhah) (Jerusalem, 1969), pp. 66–70, 89.

9. Quoted in Eugen Eliahu Mayer, "Nehemia Anton Nobel," in *Guardians of Our Heritage*, ed. Leo Jung (New York, 1958), p. 567.

10. Nobel, *Hagut v'Halakhah*, p. 90.

11. Ibid. For my treatment of these writings in a different context, see David Ellenson, *Between Tradition and Culture: The Dialectics of Modern Jewish Religion and Identity* (Atlanta, 1994), pp. 19–21. For Heuberger's presentation of these sources, see her article, "Orthodoxy versus Reform," pp. 52–55.

12. Heuberger, "Orthodoxy versus Reform," p. 53.

13. Breuer, *Modernity within Tradition*, p. 246.

14. Nobel, *Hagut v'Halakhah*, p. 138. This text, so crucial for elucidating Nobel's attitudes toward the Jewish community and the role of Orthodoxy in it, is also cited and translated in Mayer, "Nehemia Anton Nobel," p. 576; and Heuberger, "Orthodoxy versus Reform," p. 51.

15. See Michael Brenner, *The Renaissance of Jewish Culture in Weimar Germany* (New Haven, 1996), p. 84; Breuer, *Modernity within Tradition*, pp. 152–53; and Ernst Simon, "N.A. Nobel as Preacher," in Hebrew translation in Nobel, *Hagut v'Halakhah*, pp. 11–14.

16. Heuberger, "Orthodoxy versus Reform," pp. 48–49.

17. For Nobel's attitudes and activities as a Zionist, see the brief description of this dimension of his life by Yeshayahu Aviad, "Rabbi N.A. Nobel," in Nobel, *Hagut v'Halakhah*, pp. 29–38.

18. Breuer, *Modernity within Tradition*, p. 370.

19. Cited in Heuberger, "Orthodoxy versus Reform," p. 57.

20. Ibid.

21. These citations from the work of Hirsch and Hildesheimer are taken from David Ellenson, *Rabbi Esriel Hildesheimer and the Creation of a Modern Jewish Orthodoxy* (Tuscaloosa, 1990), p. 87.

22. Cited in Heuberger, "Orthodoxy versus Reform," p. 57.

23. See Mayer, "Nehemia Anton Nobel," p. 578, for a discussion of the content and style of Nobel's sermons as well as the citation of this particular biblical passage.

24. Ibid., p. 570.

25. Donald L. Niewyk, *The Jews in Weimar Germany* (Baton Rouge, 1980), p. 122.

26. This information on the background of Unna's statements in defense of Gemeindeorthodoxie is taken from Moshe Unna, "Isak Unna: The Man in His Generation," in Isak Unna, *For the Sake of Unity and Uniqueness* (in Hebrew) (Jerusalem, 1975), pp. 64ff. On the debate between Hirsch and Bamberger over the question of Austritt, see Leo Trepp, "Segregation or Unity in Diversity," in *Bits of Honey: Essays for Samson H. Levey*, ed. Stanley Chyet and David Ellenson (Atlanta, 1993), pp. 289–310.

27. Isak Unna, "Der Gedanke der Arewuth in seiner praktischen Bedeutung," *Jüdisches Wochenblatt* 1 (March 13, 1924), pp. 4–5.

28. In making this claim, Unna was repeating a story concerning the plight of German Orthodoxy during this period that was commonly told in German Orthodox circles. As Robert Liberles has written in his insightful study *Religious Conflict in Social Context: The Resurgence of Orthodox Judaism in Frankfurt am Main, 1838–1877* (Westport, 1985), pp. 19–20, "This picture . . . [was] put forth by the German Orthodox themselves. . . ." He argues that "this view derived from a hagiography greatly influenced by the writings and teachings of Samson Raphael Hirsch [himself]." Thus, whatever its historical accuracy, this perspective on the

past and the ill-treatment accorded Orthodoxy by a dominant Reform majority from the period beginning in the 1820s until the passage of the Law of Secession in 1876 was one commonly held in German Orthodox circles even during the 1900s. Unna, in this particular statement, was simply echoing this view.

29. Unna, "Der Gedanke der Arewuth in seiner praktischen Bedeutung," p. 4.

30. Ibid.

31. Ibid.

32. Ibid.

33. Ibid., p. 5.

34. Ibid.

35. Ibid.

36. Isak Unna, "Das Trennungsprinzip und die Zusammenarbeit der Gesetzes-treuen," *Jeschurun* 13, no. 7/8 (1924): 403–18.

37. Ibid., pp. 404–406.

38. Ibid., pp. 406–409.

39. Ibid., p. 409. For Hirsch's position in his own words, see Samson Raphael Hirsch, *The Collected Writings*, vol. 6 (New York, 1990), pp. 193–97.

40. Ibid., pp. 412–13, 410.

41. Ibid., p. 410.

42. Ibid., p. 413.

43. In taking this stance, Unna foreshadowed an argument that was to be made decades later in the United States by Rabbi Moshe Feinstein. In one responsum, Rabbi Feinstein was asked whether it was permissible for Orthodox Jews to contribute funds to Jewish Federations inasmuch as such funds were generally administered by non-Orthodox Jews and portions of the funds were appropriated to the religious institutions of the *kofrim* (heretics), Reform and Conservative Jews. Rabbi Feinstein was disposed not to allow Orthodox Jews to contribute to these charities. However, he indicated that it was permissible for Orthodox Jews to do so if the moneys designated by the charity for Orthodox institutions exceeded the contributions made by Orthodox Jews. In this way, Orthodoxy and its institutions would be strengthened and Reform and Conservative Judaism and their institutions would be diminished. See Feinstein's *Iggerot Moshe, Yoreh Deah*, no. 149. The last paragraph on pp. 298–99 speaks directly to this point.

44. Ibid., pp. 413–15.

45. Ibid., pp. 416–17.

46. Unna's support of Zionism, as well as the approbation he offered those Liberal rabbis who embraced the cause of Zionism, indicates that Unna did not reduce Judaism to a religious confession alone. However, it is important to bear in mind that his own advocacy of the Zionist cause arose from what he deemed a religious imperative. The Zionism of Unna was completely removed from the secular nationalism of Herzl and his followers.

4

Turning Inward

Jewish Youth in Weimar Germany

MICHAEL BRENNER

Generations in Conflict

"After the war," writes Peter Gay in his eloquent essay on Weimar Culture, "German youth, restless, bewildered, often incurably estranged from the Republic, sought salvation in the poets, but it also found other, more prosaic if not less strenuous guides. The youth movement, which had its modest beginnings at the turn of the century and flourished mightily through the twenties, collected among its ranks and preserved among its graduates many would-be thinkers hunting for an organic philosophy of life."[1] One of the central motives behind the rise of the German youth movement was filial rebellion against a bourgeois world characterized by a lack of vitality and ideals.

Young Jews in Weimar Germany were no exception when it came to a revolt against the established notions of their parental world. Against what appeared to them to be the shallowness of their parents' bourgeois values, they emphasized genuine emotions, authenticity, and political and social engagement. For some, the departure from an intact middle-class world led to socialism or communism, for others to spiritual utopias. Overall, there can be little doubt, however, that the Jewish youth revolt was a rather conservative one—a revolt that emphasized a return to Judaism and Jewishness.

What started out during the war and immediate postwar years as a revolt of Jewish youth against an established older generation soon became an integral and constructive part of the Jewish community at large. An emphasis on spiritual renewal and community, a hunger for genuine forms of Jewish life, and attempts to reform Jewish learning were significant elements in the struggle of youth against the Jewish establishment in the early 1920s. By 1930 all those elements, including the youth groups themselves, were receiving the full support of the established Jewish community. What seemed like a provocative challenge to a Jewish community in times of relative comfort was recognized as a source of relief in times of crisis.

As is the case with its Gentile counterpart, the roots of the Jewish youth revolt can be traced back to at least a decade before the crumbling of the old regime. When Martin Buber delivered his celebrated "Three Addresses on Judaism" to the Jewish student society Bar Kochba in Prague between 1909 and 1913, he had already established himself as a kind of cult figure for those Jews who rejected what for their parents still looked like the natural trend in modern German Jewry: a path leading away from Judaism (without official renunciation of it) and straight into German society. On the eve of World War I, this path no longer represented a desirable or realistic option to many young Jews, who were confronted with growing antisemitism and "volkish" ideology in schools, universities, and youth organizations.

Some, at least theoretically, chose the radical remedy offered by Zionism, though in most cases without accepting the bitter pill of emigration that Zionism prescribed. Others engaged in revolt on their own home ground. They happily embraced the very notions of Jewishness that their ancestors had thrown overboard. Franz Kafka's enthusiasm for Yiddish theater, Franz Rosenzweig's excitement when he stumbled into a "disorderly" Orthodox prayer service, and Walter Benjamin's troubled encounters with the strange Hebrew language may be taken as the most famous examples, the mere tip of an iceberg. The reaction of Arthur Scholem to young Gerhard's endeavors in Jewish Studies took the form of a radical, but not exceptional, response: "The wasted time is a pity." And he reprimanded his son: "An even greater pity is the working capacity and intellectual energy wasted in this unproductive manner."[2] The domestic peace in the Scholem household had already been destroyed when Scholem père, furious about his son's Zionism and pacifism in the middle of the war, sent his son a note stating, "I have decided not to provide for you anymore, and inform you of the following: You have to leave my apartment by March 1, and you won't enter it again without my permission."[3]

Considered a "martyr of Zionism" by like-minded German Jews, Scholem fils also became a fierce critic of the Zionist youth movement. Just after he had to leave his parents' home in February of 1917, he published the following lines in Martin Buber's new journal, *Der Jude:*

In recent years and up to this very hour, we have not had among us a Jewish youth movement: no movement which would be felt and sustained by young people as Jews. We have this and that organization, and we often and at length hear talk of them and their programs as the embodiments and standards of the Jewish youth movement; but what one looks for in them in vain is often not only Judaism and youth, but rather, again and again, movement. Without exception these organizations, the great and small ones, lack the characteristics of a movement: wholeness, spirit, and greatness.[4]

Scholem was, of course, not unbiased; nor was he a typical representative of German Jewry. However, his voice is important as a counterweight to the numerous contemporary and later accounts that tend to glorify the German-Jewish youth movement. In fact, most literature written on the German-Jewish youth movement stems from the pen of former members, including Scholem, and exhibits all the advantages and shortcomings of insider reports.

The generational conflict was perhaps the most delicate issue for the Orthodox youth movement. On the one hand, there were Orthodox Jewish values such as study and reverence for one's parents, and on the other hand the central elements of both the German and German-Jewish youth movements that usually included the rejection of home and school. But it is important to note that, as in many other youth groups, rejection of home and school did not necessarily imply criticism of family and study. What the Orthodox youth movement rejected was the shallowness of their own education and the bourgeois spirit identified with Samson Raphael Hirsch's ideology of *torah im derekh erets* (Jewish learning and observance combined with general social and political engagement). When they criticized a whole generation of Orthodox parents, they did so because, in their opinion, their parents were not fulfilling their parental obligations as Orthodox Jews. Likewise, they reprimanded Jewish schools because they were not Jewish enough. It was not a revolt against too much authority but against too little; where they expected guidance, they often received only empty words.

Ideas and Ideals

The *German* youth movement, which emerged from hiking associations such as the Wandervogel, came into existence around the turn of the twentieth century and clung to a blend of romanticism, teetotalism, volkish thought, and strong belief in the principle of leadership.

When antisemitism became a palpable element in the German youth movement shortly before World War I, Jews founded their own youth movements. The first one was Blau-Weiss (established in 1907 in Breslau, in 1912 nationwide), a Zionist organization that transformed elements of German nationalism into Jewish nationalism. The influence of the German Wandervogel youth movement on Blau-Weiss was obvious. Hiking tours and songs expressed a romantic love of nature and collective experience. During the Weimar period, a whole range of other Zionist youth movements were founded, often with a more rigorous program. They ranged from the socialist-oriented Jung-Jüdischer Wanderbund to the religious-Zionist Zeirei Misrachi.

Orthodox Jewish youth movements were soon to follow. The first to organize were the religious Zionists, who formed the Misrachi Youth in 1910. Not coincidentally, Hamburg was the center of their early activities. Rabbi Nehemiah Anton Nobel, then serving in Hamburg, was the group's spiritual mentor, and one of his disciples, Oskar Wolfsberg, became its first leader.[5] After World War I, other groups followed; the most important was Esra (founded in 1918), which issued two periodicals: the *Führerschaftsblätter* for the organization's leaders and a journal for the younger members. In 1927, Esra had local associations in twenty-six German cities and towns.[6] Some of them, like Esra itself, were more hesitant about Zionism; others, like the Torah ve-avodah, were active in propagating Zionism and founded a *kibbutz* in Rodges (Hesse) for the purpose of agricultural preparation for immigration to Palestine *(hakhsharah)*.

Young Liberal Jews, just like their Zionist and Orthodox peers, were looking for new organizational structures in a society they considered particularist and "atomistic"; like other groups of Jewish youth, the Liberals had their own youth movements, modeled after the German Bünde. Their first organization, the Kameraden, was established during the war, in 1916. During the Weimar years it was joined by other groups, such as the Jewish Scouts' Association. Altogether, more than thirty thousand young German Jews joined the various Jewish youth movements during the Weimar years.[7] Thus, by 1933 at least every third young Jew in Weimar Germany had at some point been a member in a Jewish youth organization.

What were the main causes for the establishment of a separate German-Jewish youth movement? Without question, the antisemitism of many (though not all) German youth organizations and the resulting exclusion of Jewish members played a crucial role in the formation of specifically Jewish organizations. Eva Marcuse, a member of the Jewish Liberal Youth group (Jüdische Liberale Jugend, JLJ) "Oliva" in Berlin summed up the background and motives of many of her colleagues when she wrote, "Most of us come from homes which were entirely indifferent toward Judaism, partly from circles which consciously tried to keep out any Jewish influence. They have no or little knowledge of Judaism and come to the JLJ for different reasons: some because they are beaten up, others because they are lonely; then there are those who want to hike; and finally those who come to get to know things Jewish. Our task should be first and foremost: to implant Jewish knowledge into those people."[8]

It would indeed be misleading to reduce the existence of a Jewish youth movement to the purely negative factor of exclusion. We cannot close our eyes to the fact that the Jewish youth movement was not merely a reaction to volkish ideology; instead, it grew out of related roots. Like their Gentile counterparts, members of the Jewish youth movement posed a radical challenge to the rational and individualistic ideologies associated with their parents' world, and they evoked a new sense of community *(Gemeinschaft)*. In a discussion of the Jewish youth movement, Glenn Richard Sharfman correctly observed that all youth movements in Weimar Germany "rejected liberalism, rationalism, materialism, and solutions that revolved around the individual. Youth movements were grounded in romanticism and collectivism."[9] This held true for Jewish as well as for non-Jewish youth.

Another feature common to both the general and Jewish youth movements was the immense admiration of spiritual leaders. What Gustav Wyneken or Hans Blüher had been for the Wandervogel movement and the Bünde, Martin Buber was to Jewish youth, both Zionist and non-Zionist.[10] His revival of Jewish mysticism was exactly what the Jewish youth movement believed it needed. Without taking Buber's philosophy too seriously, the youth movement picked out his romanticism, his call for originality, and saw in the East European Hasidim an equivalent to the German peasant ideal. Buber's appeal to Jewish youth has been widely documented, and I shall mention here only one example of specific interest in our context.

Hermann Gerson was a young student enrolled at the Berlin Liberal Rabbinical Seminary (Hochschule für die Wissenschaft des Judentums) when he addressed Buber in November of 1926. After stating that he was a member of the Kameraden and an admirer of Gustav Wyneken, he continued: "Last Monday I was privileged to see and hear you in Berlin for the first time. I felt much more personally and fatefully touched and responded quite differently from the way one does to a merely 'good' lecture. And thus I plucked up the courage to turn to you and ask you a question. I believe it sometimes happens that a guide *[Führer]* gives direction to another one, or is torah to him [in Buber's sense of *Weisung*, 'guidance']." Gerson concludes his letter by asking Buber to meet him and decide if he would pass on his guidance to him.[11] Gerson was received in Buber's Heppenheim home shortly thereafter. A few years later, Gerson had become one of the most active leaders of the non-Zionist German youth movement. For the Orthodox, the personality of Rabbi Nehemiah Anton Nobel had a similar aura until his untimely death in 1922. As the historian Joseph Walk, himself a former member of the Orthodox youth movement, writes: "The teaching of their master united them all in a common cause."[12]

Not only the ideal of the leader but also the terminology of the Jewish youth movement was an imitation of the German youth movement. There were Jewish *Knubbel* and *Pimpfe, Führer* and *Schwarze Haufen*. Military language played an important role in communication. That was true for both the right-wing groups, such as Das Schwarze Fähnlein, and for Zionist organizations such as Blau-Weiss. During the national meeting in Prunn in 1922, Blau-Weiss leaders constructed the ideal of an imaginary army. As their periodical, the *Führerzeitung,* reported, "Our powerful task needs leaders *(Führer)* and armies. Leaders to give orders, armies to serve, altogether a tight, Germany-wide organization. The era of the initial, undisciplined *Sichausleben* is over, the plea to Blau-Weiss means now the beginning of an eternal obligation."[13] In letters of 1925 among members of the Kameraden, the greeting *Heil* was still commonly used. It was partially replaced by the Hebrew *Shalom* in later years.[14]

Among the Jewish student fraternities, even the Orthodox Vereinigung jüdischer Akademiker created a bizarre combination of *Kommersen* (drinking bouts) and *shiurim* (Talmud study). The novelist Selig Schachnowitz enthusiastically described this atmosphere, which he himself had experienced as a student, in one of his books:

> Salvaging from a lost youth a little joy and happiness, he sang the *Gaudeamus* heartily and participated in the drinking bouts. But then he felt a particular magic, when out of the same throats, from which he first had heard joyous student songs, he now heard the learning, the old learning, out of the old books. . . . Here those [Samson Raphael Hirsch's] firm principles became reality. Knowledge and religion, Judaism and *Kultur* celebrate their union.[15]

Isaac Breuer, the most adamant spokesman for interwar Orthodox German Jewry, scoffed at Jewish and non-Jewish fellow students who wore colorful uniforms and were ready to fight in duels against each other. For him this seemed like a "permanent Purim."[16] But while rejecting the outward forms, he accepted many of the ideological values characteristic of student organizations, which were based on the principle of strong Gemeinschaft. As a cofounder of the Strasbourg Bund jüdischer Akademiker chapter and its first leader, Breuer later adopted the title of a *Fuchsmajor* and used the common student fraternity language.

Perhaps the most striking parallel between the German and the German-Jewish youth movements was the centrality of hiking. Even the Zionist Blau-Weiss stressed that its emphasis on hiking was something particularly German, something that distinguished the German (and German-Jewish) youth movement from counterparts in other countries, for example, the British Boy Scouts. One might even say that for young Jews, hiking tours had a higher value than for their non-Jewish counterparts. To be sure, both rejected urban life as decadent and idealized the countryside as the place where they could return to more original forms of life. But for young Jews, hiking tours meant much more. No other group had undergone as rapid an urbanization as German Jews in the nineteenth century. Though they lived almost exclusively in villages and small towns at the beginning of the nineteenth century, a hundred years later German Jews were concentrated in big cities.

In practical terms, hiking tours into the countryside meant sleeping in cold, wet stables or under the sky (tents were rejected as too comfortable), using one's own cooking utensils over open fires, and an occasional encounter with the remnants of rural Jewish life in Germany. Like the *Ostjuden* (East European Jews), German *Landjuden* (rural Jews), who had preserved their customs, were celebrated as the embodiment of Jewish authenticity. For the Zionist Blau-Weiss, one of the most important aspects of hiking tours was the projected physical rejuvenation of the Jewish people. Thus, Blau-Weiss leader Moses Calvary claimed in a speech of his organization's 1916 national meeting that "Zionism as an educational task means striving for nobility, masculinity, and naturalness. Hiking has to become a necessary component of the [Zionist] movement. For Zionism means: To put Judaism back on a natural basis. To be sure, the other [Jews] are also hiking today. But for them, the Orthodox and the Liberals, hiking is a pleasure or an attraction, but not the center of their Jewish education."[17]

Masculinity, as mentioned by Calvary, was not an undisputed ideal in the Jewish youth movement. As in the German youth movement, most Jewish organizations of this kind adored men and muscles. The circle around Stefan George, one of their idols, was among the most prominent *Männerbünde* of its time, and some Jewish youth groups adopted a purely male concept of Gemeinschaft. Even the young

Scholem, whom we encountered as a critic of many of the youth movement's characteristics, did not object to their predominantly male character. Quite the contrary—he protested against the involvement of women in intellectual discussions among the Jewish youth groups he joined. In his recently published diary, there are quite a few remarks that show the biases of young Scholem, culminating in his conviction that women are not interested in deep intellectual discussion: they attend lectures only "when the lecturer lays it on thick." When Scholem went to a lecture by the historian Zalman Rubaschoff (known as Zalman Shazar after he later became Israel's president), he deliberately arrived late, "since—*has ve-shalom*—this time girls were invited, which I could not prevent, although I decisively opposed this until the last minute. . . ." Noting the women's comments on Rubaschoff's accent, Scholem continues, "it naturally gave some of the females *[Weiber]* cause for inattentiveness and mischief, and since I sat just behind three such nymphs, I became quite upset."[18]

The youth rebellion was, however, not only a revolt of the son, as Peter Gay puts it, but also a revolt of the daughter. As becomes clear from Scholem's own remarks, women did participate in at least certain segments of the Jewish youth movement. In many cases they had their own separate girls' divisions. Some voiced angry protest when attempts were made to exclude them. Thus, in response to a Hanukkah article in Blau-Weiss's paper, which stated, "We look into the flames and we swear to become men," one Elsa Rosenblüth replied: "And we, we girls? Do you think we will [stand] aside and notice that the flame is yellow and blue or that it would burn better if the wood were drier? Or what? Herr Redakteur did not know what we shall swear? Well, then I will tell you what we will become: we will become women, Jewish women. If you all want to become Maccabeans, where will we [find] the Maccabean women? . . . Weren't there any heroines in the time of the Hasmoneans? Don't you know Hannah, who sacrificed her seven children for the sake of her country and who died for liberty and faith?"[19]

By the late years of the Republic, the Jewish youth movement was separated by not only gender but also ideology. The Kameraden were split into those who emphasized their Jewish "blood" and those who stressed their ties to the German homeland. But both expressed their affiliations in similar terms; while the "German Jews" gathered around their campfires and recited Martin Buber's *Hasidic Tales*, the "Jewish Germans" met at medieval castles and read Stefan George. Liberal Jewish youth organizations rejected the Zionist idea of a Jewish nation but adopted much of the Zionist agenda of a revival of Jewish group solidarity. If they read Buber or George (and most read both), they did it as Jews who were in search for a new sense of Gemein-schaft, one that no longer was phrased in the intellectual language of rationalism.

In the waning days of the Republic, the emphasis on Jewish consciousness became an ever more visible ingredient even among the non-Zionist organizations (with the exception of some radically German nationalist splinter groups), and the gap between Zionist and non-Zionist ideology seemed to narrow. Thus, Hermann Gerson, representing the part of the Kameraden that emphasized their Jewish heritage, had to clarify his position in a letter to the membership in October 1932: "Dear Friends! Again and again I hear your question: 'Why aren't we Zionists?' That means, Why aren't we going to Palestine? I will try here to answer this legitimate question. We assimilated ones have gradually grown more Jewish. And now the question arises: Why shouldn't we be entirely Jewish, why shouldn't Jewish life be complete for us? And here [in the Diaspora] it can't be [complete]. It is no coincidence that we, too, speak of 'galuth' [exile] today, not only—as we once did—of 'Germany.' For we don't forget that we live in the galuth, with all it strains and sorrows." Palestine, however, as Gerson concluded, could offer no solution to the Jewish problem at this time.[20]

Not all of Gerson's colleagues in the Liberal Jewish youth move-ment shared his views. When the Kameraden split on the eve of the Nazi takeover, some became increasingly socialist-Zionist, others ad-hered to German nationalist ideology. However, to those for whom emigration was no option and the current situation in exile was unsatisfactory, the most obvious response to ease the pains of exile was to intensify the bonds of Jewish community and to deepen Jewish knowledge. While the foundation of youth movements outside the established communities and against the established notions of a middle-class society represented such a response in the early days of the Republic, by the late 1920s new forms of youth community had emerged. They were characterized by pragmatism, attempts at unity, and increasing integration into the institutions of the Jewish commu-nity at large.

Toward a Jewish Youth Community

An excellent example of this new approach were the Schulen der jüdischen Jugend (Schools of Jewish Youth), established in the late 1920s in Berlin, Frankfurt am Main, and Cologne. While they drew heavily on the model of Franz Rosenzweig's Lehrhaus (House of Study [for Jewish adult education]), they were established and administered by youth organizations themselves. They also brought together representatives of a broad variety of youth organizations. In Berlin, representatives of most major Jewish youth organizations, ranging from the Liberal JLJ to the Zionist Kadimah, were represented on the commission governing its affairs. Religious and ideological differences were not to be downplayed but presented side by side by the various teachers. As in the Lehrhaus, pure transmission of knowledge was the least important aspect of the teaching at the Schulen der jüdischen Jugend. "Everything that shall be taught and studied should be deeply influenced by the personality of the 'teacher' and the Jewish-human attitude of the 'student.' . . . This task requires a peculiar type of teacher. He has to have a lively relationship to youth and must be able to understand them. His field of knowledge . . . has to represent a life task for him."[21] Emphasis in class was to be directed toward "lively discussion" rather than lecturing. During the fall of 1930, four hundred students attended the twenty-four courses of the Berlin Schule der jüdischen Jugend. The Spring 1931 trimester listed twelve courses, among them an introduction to general Jewish knowledge, a survey of Jewish folk tales, a course entitled "Hasidic Traditions and Their Importance for Young Western Jews," a Jewish music hour, handicrafts lessons for producing modern Jewish ritual objects, and study groups on sociology and socialism. In addition, the program offered eleven Hebrew language and literature courses and a general introductory lecture course on "The Jewish Cultural Heritage."[22]

Some Zionists criticized the Schule der jüdischen Jugend, not because it was not good enough but "because there exists a danger that it might become too good," as one of them claimed. Liberal German Jews, this anonymous Zionist continued, "succeeded and still succeed at providing our people with a Jewish fulfillment and at creating a clearly defined Liberal Jewish cultural ideal, which in my opinion will succeed in achieving a Jewish galuth ideal. . . . I see the greatest danger in the fact that it will really become possible, on an individual level, to live a Jewish life in the galuth. . . . Under no circumstances should we cooperate in such attempts at this time."[23] This opinion expressed an old Zionist dilemma, which had existed since the days of Theodor Herzl: Should Zionists become active in *Gegenwartsarbeit* (present-day work) and thus help to strengthen the Zionist camp in the Diaspora, or should they reject any attempt to create a comfortable positive basis for Jewish life in the Diaspora? In Weimar Germany, most young Zionists chose the first option and supported such institutions as the Schule der jüdischen Jugend.

This endeavor must be seen in the larger context of integrating diverse Jewish youth movements and their activities under one roof and within the framework of the Jewish community during the last years of the Weimar Republic. The foundation of youth communities in several cities was the most visible expression of those attempts. In Mannheim the young rabbi Max Grünewald had established a *Jugendgemeinde* (youth community) as early as 1925: "We want to raise a *Gemeindejudentum* rather than a *Richtungsjudentum*," he wrote in a programmatic statement.[24] All Jewish youth groups in Mannheim were housed in the Jewish community building, and they received almost all of their financial support from the Jewish community budget.[25] Similarly, in Leipzig the various Jewish youth organizations formed a Jüdische Jugendring in 1929; it included Orthodox, Zionist, and Liberal groups with a total membership of about twelve hundred and fifty. A year later, the Jewish community established a youth committee, which financially supported the youth organizations.[26] The Jewish community of Breslau established a *Jugendheim* (youth center) which became the focus of a rich cultural program with a library and a number of special events in music, literature, and sports;[27] and in Hamburg the Jewish *Jugendamt* (youth office) of 1921 was followed by a *Landjugendheim* (youth camp) ten years later.[28] By 1933, the demand of the Brunswick rabbi Paul Rieger that Jewish communities should grant generous financial subsidies for youth activities and establish permanent centers for Jewish youth was realized in most major communities.[29]

Among the activities of a Jugendgemeinde were the study of Hebrew, the organization of youth services, excursions, and hiking. The staging of plays that represented both Jewish tradition and German literature was especially popular among Jewish youth groups. In Leipzig, the Jung-Jüdischer Club not only organized a trip to the Dessau Bauhaus and a lecture by Martin Buber, it also initiated a "Literary Trial . . . against Judas Iscariot for moral treason against Jesus of Nazareth."[30] The Mannheim Jugendgemeinde arranged a short version of Stefan Zweig's *Jeremiah* for Hanukkah 1925, just after Rabbi Grünewald's arrival. When amateur actors of a Liberal Jewish youth group in Düsseldorf staged the same play in 1930 at their annual conference in Munich, the author himself honored them with his presence.[31]

In some cases, youth rabbis and youth communities initiated educational programs and reforms among the Jewish communities at large. Thus, a few years after the staging of *Jeremiah*, Grünewald organized a huge Hanukkah event, which drew its inspiration from Bertolt Brecht's innovative musical form, the *Lehrkantate* (educational cantata), with hundreds of adult Mannheim Jews performing in the most distinguished local music hall. Grünewald was also instrumental in establishing a Lehrhaus for the adult Jewish population of Mannheim, as was Max Elk, who was employed as a youth rabbi in Munich.

The impact of the youth movement on German-Jewish life cannot be measured merely by looking at membership numbers or the movement's activities. By the end of the 1920s, when the youth movement had become a substantial element of the cultural life of German Jews, its programs were increasingly integrated into the institutional framework of the Jewish community at large. The Jewish youth movement, which had arisen on the eve of World War I in opposition to the established Jewish organizations and institutions, had by the end of the Weimar period significantly contributed to the transformation of the Jewish establishment itself. They had turned inward not only in the sense of Jewish renewal but also with regard to the organized Jewish community.

The most significant development with regard to Jewish youth, reaching beyond the scope of the Schule der jüdischen Jugend and the youth community, was the expansion of regular Jewish schools in most major cities and their integration into the framework of the local Jewish community. No other question since the introduction of organs into synagogues during the nineteenth century had divided the Jewish public as much as the discussion about Jewish schools. The official Liberal position advocated attendance at nondenominational schools by Jewish pupils as the best way to secure their integration into German society. Zionists and Orthodox, on the other hand, were in favor of Jewish schools, which would provide the much-needed Jewish education in a specific Jewish context and an atmosphere free of antisemitism. Looking only at statistics, the Liberals could claim that they had won the battle. The Liberals could point to the number of Jewish schools in Germany, which was reduced dramatically from 492 in 1898 to 141 in 1932. It was not only the ideological battle against Jewish schools that led to this decline but, perhaps more importantly, rapid urbanization. Thus, most schools that closed during the Weimar period were located in small towns and had only a handful of pupils left. Orthodox and Zionist advocates of Jewish schools, however, were eager to correct the statistics. While the total number of Jewish schools was further reduced in Weimar Germany, this tendency was reversed in the big cities. In Berlin, the opening of five Jewish elementary schools between 1919 and 1927 marked a clear revival of separate Jewish education. In other cities, such as Munich, Nuremberg, and Duisburg, where for decades no Jewish schools had existed, such institutions were reestablished during the

1920s, either by the Jewish community or by Orthodox associations. In some Jewish communities with old, established Jewish school systems—for example, Hamburg, Frankfurt, and Cologne—about every second Jewish child attended a Jewish school in 1932.[32]

Most of the new Jewish schools were established by the Orthodox separatist communities, which refused to contribute their members' tax money to the Reform-minded communities, or were the result of private Zionist initiative. By the end of the Weimar period, because of the general economic crisis, only a few of them could exist exclusively on private resources and they therefore turned to the Gemeinden for financial support. In general, the response was positive. Thus, the Cologne Jewish community concluded a contract with the Orthodox Jawne high school in 1928 that guaranteed annual subsidies for a period of five years in exchange for community control over the school.[33] In Hamburg, the girls' high school of the Jewish community grew from 350 to 600 pupils during the Weimar years because it absorbed the students of a private Jewish girls' school that had to be closed.[34] In Berlin, one private school was integrated into the community framework during the Zionist domination of the late 1920s, and two new schools were established under the auspices of the community. The Liberals cut the subsidies after they regained power in 1930, but they did not change the schools' status as community-run schools. By then, antisemitism had driven quite a few pupils from Liberal homes out of nondenominational schools and into Jewish schools. As Joseph Walk, a graduate of the Breslau Jewish school, wrote in 1931: "How happy is the Jewish child who spends his time free of the hatred of Gentile companions."[35]

In Search of "Muskeljuden"

A similar process of expanding the framework of the Jewish community was also visible in sports, another important area of organized youth activities. With the flourishing of Jewish youth organizations during the Weimar period, more young Jews joined Jewish sports clubs. To be sure, most would still participate in non-Jewish clubs, but there were now for the first time non-Zionists who founded separate Jewish clubs. This indeed marked a sharp deviation from the prewar period, when Jewish community leaders encouraged youth to join general sports clubs as a means of social integration within German society. Thus, at the turn of the century, the request of Bar Kochba— the first Jewish sports association in Berlin—to use the gymnasium of the Jewish school was rejected by the Jewish community leadership of Berlin, and the Jewish athletes had to practice instead in a gymnasium provided by the city. In the same spirit, leaders of the Hanover Jewish community advised the members of the newly founded local Jewish sports club in 1904 to dismantle their association and to join a German one.[36] In spite of this opposition, the Zionist-oriented Jüdische Turnerschaft grew from the initial ten clubs in 1903 to more than thirty in the 1920s.

More significantly, Jewish sports clubs were now accepted even among some Liberal German Jews, and by the mid-1920s the Reichsbund Jüdischer Frontsoldaten, the association of German-Jewish war veterans, had established its own network of sports clubs. This step constituted a radically new phenomenon among Liberal German Jews. "All this has grown out of absolutely nothing," the Reichsbund journal, *Der Schild*, reported in 1926 on the fifth anniversary of their first Jewish sports organizations and in response to the rapid spread of Schild clubs.[37] While only two decades earlier Liberal Jewish leaders had reprimanded Zionists for forming their own sports associations, a spokesman of the Reichsbund, which consisted of Liberal German Jews, now claimed: "It is of incomparably higher importance if a Jewish soccer club wins against a non-Jewish one than if thirty good Jewish soccer players would spread over all kinds of different clubs and Jews would not appear prominently."[38] It was not in soccer, however, where Jewish athletes excelled most. It is highly symbolic that the only discipline in which athletes from a Jewish sports club actually held any German championships was the defensive sport jujitsu.[39]

Entering the Establishment

The discussion of Jewish youth in Weimar Germany cannot be restricted to their own organizational framework but has to note the role young Jews and former youth leaders played within major Jewish organizations. Even the Centralverein deutscher Staatsbürger jüdischen Glaubens, the major association representing Liberal German Jews and perhaps the most "established" Jewish organization in Weimar Germany (usually associated with bald-headed lawyers smoking thick cigars), was by 1930 "infiltrated" by young German Jews, some of whom had grown out of the youth movement and tried to integrate parts of its ideology. To be sure, by the eve of World War I, the Centralverein had undergone a redefinition from an *Abwehr-*

verein (defense organization) mainly interested in combatting anti-semitism, to a *Gesinnungsverein* (association of sensibility), in which the spread of Jewish knowledge and the strengthening of Jewish identity assumed at least equal importance. This tendency was emphasized even more strongly in the Weimar days. What tends to be overlooked is the central role young leaders played in this process, especially outside Berlin.

In Munich, for example, twenty-eight-year-old Werner Cahnmann was appointed *Syndikus* (legal representative) of the Bavarian Centralverein branch in 1930, despite his known pro-Zionist stance. This appointment marked a decisive change, because at the same time the long-time president and the vice-president of the Munich Centralverein—in Cahnmann's words, "both German nationalists and assimilationists"—resigned. They were followed by Dr. Alfred Werner, who was not only a Social Democrat but also viewed the pro-Zionist Jewish Agency with much sympathy. But even on the national level, Cahnmann recalled that "a small-scale internal revolution took place" in the Centralverein during the late 1920s.[40]

The main representatives of this revolution on the national level were two young Centralverein leaders, Ludwig Tietz and Friedrich Brodnitz (whose father Julius was the president of the Centralverein).[41] Tietz, who had been elected to the board of the Centralverein in 1921 at the age of twenty-four and who became its vice-president in 1932, was one of the most active and charismatic adult leaders of Liberal Jewish youth. He founded the Deutsch-Jüdische Jugendgemeinschaft in 1921 in order to activate the still unorganized Jewish youth, and he was the major force behind the Reichsausschuss der jüdischen Jugend, which was established six years later with the aim of uniting the already existing Jewish youth organizations in Germany under one roof (it was later led by Brodnitz). As Centralverein leaders, Tietz and Brodnitz were among the authors of a programmatic statement called "Der Central-Verein der Zukunft" (The Centralverein of the future) (1928), a passionate appeal for the renewal of Jewish spirituality and Gemeinschaft among Liberal German Jews. The influence of youth movement ideology lurks behind such statements as, "Only what really is alive deserves to be called life. Not some misty 'Jewishness' *(Jüdischkeit)* but lucid and life-spending 'Judaism' *(Judentum)*."[42] The paper then goes on to welcome the construction of a Jewish homeland in Palestine and basically reflects the views of the newly established Jewish Agency. It was a logical consequence that Tietz, along with some older members of the Centralverein board such as Leo Baeck and Otto Hirsch (but over the protests of many others), became a member of the Initiative Council of the Enlarged Jewish Agency in 1929.

In retrospect, a leading German Zionist, Robert Weltsch, called the appearance of a figure such as Tietz in the camp of the Centralverein a "revolutionary phenomenon. . . . He regarded the strengthening of *Jewish* self-consciousness and will of life, rather than the perpetual emphasis on *German* patriotism, as the most effective reaction [against growing antisemitism]. Therefore he became the initiator of genuinely Jewish education and knowledge, especially among the Jewish youth organizations; he understood immediately that the ephemeral differences among the Jewish positions had become meaningless in the face of a crystallizing Jewish *Schicksalsgemeinschaft*."[43]

When, in March of 1933, Weltsch wrote his famous appeal to Jews to wear the yellow badge with pride, he knew all too well that he would not be heard among Zionists alone. Thanks to the initiatives of a younger generation of German Jews and the youth movement in particular, the renewed sense of community, the spread of Jewish knowledge, and the support of the construction of a Jewish homeland had found open ears among a growing segment of non-Zionist Jews as well. The groundwork for bringing the divided parts of German Jewry closer together had been laid in the later Weimar years.

Notes

1. Peter Gay, *Weimar Culture: The Outsider as Insider* (New York, 1968), p. 77.

2. Betty Scholem and Gershom Scholem, *Mutter und Sohn im Briefwechsel, 1917–1946*, ed. Itta Shedletzky (Munich, 1989), pp. 79–80.

3. Ibid., p. 13.

4. Gershom Scholem, "Jewish Youth Movement," in idem, *On Jews and Judaism in Crisis: Selected Essays* (New York, 1976), p. 49.

5. Joseph Walk, "The Torah ve-Avodah Movement in Germany," *LBIYB* 6 (1961): 243–44. On Rabbi Nobel, see the essay by David Ellenson in this volume.

6. *Führerschaftsblätter des Esra*, no. 1/2 (n.p., Teweth 5687 [= 1927]).

7. Georg Lubinski, "Die jüdische Jugendbewegung in Deutschland," *Jüdisches Jahrbuch für Gross-Berlin* (Berlin, 1928), p. 64.

8. Bundesarchiv Potsdam, 75 C Arl/1 (JLJ Gruppe Oliva).

9. Glenn Richard Sharfman, "The Jewish Youth Movement in Germany, 1900–1936: A Study in Ideology and Organization," Ph.D. diss., University of North Carolina, 1989, p. 436.

10. See Chaim Schatzker, "Martin Buber's Influence on the Jewish Youth Movement in Germany," *LBIYB* 23 (1978): 151–71.

11. *The Letters of Martin Buber: A Life of Dialogue*, ed. Nahum N. Glatzer and Paul Mendes-Flohr (New York, 1991), p. 346.

12. Walk, "The *Torah ve-Avodah* Movement in Germany," p. 249.

13. *Blau-Weiss Blätter,* Führernummer, vol. 3 (1922), p. 26.

14. Bundesarchiv Potsdam, 75 C Wa 1 (Wanderbund Kameraden), folder 16.

15. Selig Schachnowitz, *Luftmenschen. Roman aus der Gegenwart* (Frankfurt am Main, 1912), p. 179.

16. Isaac Breuer, *Mein Weg* (Zürich, 1986), p. 94.

17. *Blau-Weiss Blätter,* Führernummer, vol. 1 (June 1917), p. 1. Quoted in Irmgard Klönne, *Deutsch, Jüdisch, Bündisch. Erinnerung an die aus Deutschland vertriebene jüdische Jugendbewegung (puls. Dokumentationsschrift der Jugendbewegung 21,* 1993), p. 10.

18. Gershom Scholem, *Tagebücher nebst Aufsätzen und Entwürfen bis 1923,* vol. 1: 1913–1917, ed. Karlfried Gründer and Friedrich Niewöhner (Frankfurt am Main, 1995), pp. 138, 283–84.

19. Quoted in Klönne, *Deutsch, Jüdisch, Bündisch,* p. 12. See also Claudia Prestel, "Frauen und die zionistische Bewegung (1897–1933). Tradition oder Revolution?" in *Historische Zeitschrift* 258 (1994): 70–71.

20. Ibid., p. 40.

21. *Der junge Jude* 1, no. 6 (November 1928): 190–91.

22. "Schule der jüdischen Jugend: Arbeitsplan Januar bis März 1931," *Private Archives Benjamin Ravid,* Simon Rawidowicz Papers, Newton, Massachusetts. The Cologne Schule der jüdischen Jugend was founded in 1932. See *Gemeinde-Blatt der Synagogengemeinde zu Köln,* October 14, 1932, p. 252. See also Chanoch Rinott, "Major Trends in Jewish Youth Movements in Germany," *LBIYB* 19 (1974): 86–87.

23. *Der junge Jude* 1, no. 6 (November 1928): 195.

24. Max Grünewald, "Zur Einrichtung der Jugendgemeinde," *Die Jugendgemeinde: Beilage zum Israelitischen Gemeindeblatt Mannheim,* no. 4, February 25, 1926, p. 1.

25. Max Grünewald, "Jüdische Jugend und jüdische Gemeinde," *Jüdische Wohlfahrtspflege und Sozialpolitik* 2 (1931): 69.

26. Hans Oesterreicher and Fritz Grübel, "Der Jüdische Jugendring Leipzig," *Jüdisches Jahrbuch für Sachsen* (Leipzig, 1931/32), pp. 97–101.

27. *Jüdisches Gemeindeblatt Breslau* 8, no. 2, February 1931, appendix.

28. Ina Lorenz, *Die Juden in Hamburg zur Zeit der Weimarer Republik: Eine Dokumentation* (Hamburg, 1987), pp. 869–93.

29. YIVO-Archives, RG 6, Simon Bernfeld Collection, folder 41: "Die jüdischen Jugendvereine und die Gemeinden. Leitsätze von Landesrabbiner Dr. Rieger" (n.d.).

30. ALBI-NY 7126, Jung-Jüdischer Club Leipzig.

31. *Die Jugendgemeinde: Beilage zum Israelitischen Gemeindeblatt Mannheim,* no. 2, December 11, 1925, pp. 1–2. *Bayerische Israelitische Gemeindezeitung,* July 1, 1930, pp. 209–10.

32. For more details, see Michael Brenner, *The Renaissance of Jewish Culture in Weimar Germany* (New Haven, 1996), pp. 59–65.

33. Adolf Fürst, "Die höheren jüdischen Schulen Deutschlands," *Monatsschrift für Geschichte und Wissenschaft des Judentums* 75 (1931): 57–58.

34. Lorenz, *Juden in Hamburg,* vol. 2, pp. 413–14.

35. Joseph Walk, "Dank an die jüdische Schule," *Jüdische Zeitung für Ostdeutschland,* vol. 8, no. 12, March 27, 1931 [n.p.]. See also Chaim Schatzker, *Jüdische Jugend im zweiten Kaiserreich: Sozialisations- und Erziehungsprozese der jüdischen Jugend in Deutschland, 1870–1918* (Frankfurt am Main, 1988), pp. 83–89.

36. George Eisen, "Zionism, Nationalism, and the Emergence of the Jüdische Turnerschaft," *LBIYB* 28 (1983): 255.

37. *Der Schild,* vol. 5, no. 44/45, November 1, 1926.

38. Quoted in Ulrich Dunker, *Der Reichsbund jüdischer Frontsoldaten: Geschichte eines jüdischen Abwehrvereins* (Düsseldorf, 1977), p. 99.

39. Paul Yogi Mayer, "Equality-Egality: Jews and Sport in Germany," *LBIYB* 25 (1980): 224. On sports activities, see also the essay by Jacob Borut in this volume.

40. Werner Cahnmann, "The Jews of Munich: 1918–43," in idem, *German Jewry: Its History and Sociology* (New Brunswick, 1989), p. 114. See also idem, "The Nazi-Threat and the Central-Verein: A Recollection," p. 6 (unpublished manuscript, Werner Cahnmann Collection, ALBI-NY, AR 556). See also idem, "Judentum und Volksgemeinschaft," *Der Morgen* 2 (1926): 291–98.

41. On Tietz's and Brodnitz's involvement in the CV activities in a different context, see the essay by Avraham Barkai (chapter 5) in this volume.

42. Quoted in Friedrich Brodnitz, "Kampf um die Jewish Agency," in *Jüdische Jugend im Übergang: Ludwig Tietz, 1897–1933. Sein Leben und seine Zeit,* ed. Gustav Horn (Tel Aviv, 1980), p. 288.

43. Robert Weltsch, "Die kritische Epoche der deutschen Judenheit: Von der Parteispaltung zur Kooperation," in *Jüdische Jugend im Übergang,* ed. Horn, pp. 29–30. Emphasis in original.

5

Between
Deutschtum & Judentum

Ideological Controversies
within the Centralverein

AVRAHAM BARKAI

In purely legal terms, the period of the Weimar Republic is considered the heyday of Jewish emancipation in Germany; but the political and social reality was quite different. During the first, turbulent years of the Republic, antisemitism reached a new peak in political and public life. It was disseminated in an unprecedented flood of popular pamphlets, novels, and pseudoscientific racist publications, and it erupted in violent outbreaks on the streets. Then, after a few, more peaceful years between 1924 and 1929, economic and political upheaval caused the rise of the Nazi party and its neoconservative right-wing satellites, and the so-called Jewish Question became a major political topic.

Historians have long been aware that despite increasing pressure from the outside, which should have enhanced unity and the closing of ranks, internal Jewish conflicts did not diminish. The editor of the *Jüdische Rundschau,* Robert Weltsch (1891–1982), has argued that "at this time, despite—or probably because of the danger from outside—the party differences among the Jews were not laid aside and were indeed not irrelevant. Each of the two leading groups believed its policy was right and that of the others injurious."[1] Nowadays one may doubt if this is a sufficient explanation.

Probably the most violent polemical clashes occurred during the election campaigns of 1926 and 1930 for the leadership of the Jewish community of Berlin, where one-third of all German Jews lived at that time, and for that of the Prussian Association of Jewish Communities (Preussischer Landesverband jüdischer Gemeinden, PLV). The temporary loss of the "Liberal" majority to a coalition of Zionists, Orthodox Jews, and organizations of East European Jews in 1926 was a severe shock to the members and followers of the Centralverein deutscher Staatsbürger jüdischen Glaubens.[2] Despite these conflicts, the leadership of the principal nationwide Jewish political organizations, the Zionistische Vereinigung für Deutschland (ZVfD), and the Centralverein, succeeded in creating a united election committee for the Reichstag elections of September 1930 in order to support the democratic parties and to counter antisemitic propaganda. On the other hand, although the Liberals regained their position in the Berlin community in the elections of November 1930, the alliance between the two organizations was not renewed before the far more crucial general elections of 1932.[3] Although the power struggles in Berlin and other communities did play some role in aggravating internal Jewish conflict, the real reasons for the radicalization of the two sides' ideological and political positions are the internal disputes within the two main political camps, the Zionists and the Centralverein.

Neither the CV nor the ZVfD campaigned in community elections. The main, though not the only, Zionist list was the Jüdische Volkspartei (JVP), while most followers of the CV voted for the Vereinigung für das Liberale Judentum (VLJ). In the case of the Zionists, recent research has disclosed that this was not just a functional "division of labor" produced by tactical considerations. The leadership of the JVP and that of the ZVfD was not identical. Their prominent spokesmen differed in their sociological, occupational and, in part, in their educational backgrounds, as well as in their political orientations.[4] So far, no adequate study exists of the VLJ leadership and its relations with the CV. I would suggest, however, that although all the activists and most of the voters of the VLJ were members or supporters of the CV, substantial differences in political outlook and ideological tenets are discernible between these two organizations.[5]

The founding of the Centralverein deutscher Staatsbürger jüdischen Glaubens (CV) on March 28, 1893, was a reaction to a renewed wave of antisemitism in Imperial Germany.[6] Two years earlier, the hoary blood libel had reappeared at Xanten. In 1892, overtly antisemitic tenets were incorporated into the Tivoli program of the Conservative Party. In the parliamentary elections of 1893, the antisemitic parties won sixteen seats in the Reichstag. That same year, Raphael Löwenfeld (1854–1910), a well-known writer and the founder and director of the popular Schiller Theater in Berlin, published a pamphlet called *Schutzjuden oder Staatsbürger?* that was to become the most important "founding paper" of the CV. Löwenfeld's brochure argued

against the intentions of the executive board of the Jewish community in Berlin to appeal to the Kaiser for protection against rising
antisemitic propaganda.

The CV's intention to fight antisemitism via an open and public
confrontation ("im Lichte der Öffentlichkeit") had to overcome the
opposition of community leadership, both Liberal and Orthodox,
mainly in Berlin and other large cities.[7] Taking up Löwenfeld's rhetoric, the new organization declared its aim of refraining from the
traditional political practices of pre-emancipation Schutzjuden: no
more behind-the-scenes petitioning and buying of the protection of
sympathetic or self-interested Gentiles. Instead, the Jews themselves
should fight openly, as German citizens, for their full and equal rights
and against antisemitic slander and discrimination. The CV claimed
these rights not only on the basis of the constitutional emancipation of
1869 but also on the basis of the centuries-old history of the German
Jews and their allegiance to the sacred and time-honored values and
predominant nationalist ideals of *Deutschtum;* this allegiance had been
proclaimed and proven under the fire of war by their forefathers and
by themselves.

Very soon, however, the ideological tenets of the movement went
beyond those of a mere defensive organization. The CV's most prominent ideologue, Eugen Fuchs (1856–1923), led the way in the definition of the CV as not only an association of defense *(Abwehrverein)* but
also as one of conviction *(Gesinnungsverein)*. Outlining this theory of a
unifying conviction in 1917, in a famous polemic against Kurt Blumenfeld, Fuchs stressed his German identity: "I speak German and feel
German. I am more fulfilled by German culture and German spirit
than by Hebrew poetry and Jewish culture. When abroad, I yearn for
Germany, for German nature, and German *Volksgenossen. . . .*"[8] But in
the same article he also declared: "If it were so that the Centralverein
enhances apostasy and the disintegration of Judaism, and that Zionism furthers antisemitism, I would not hesitate for one moment to
move with flying banners into the Zionist camp . . . because, compared with apostasy, I regard antisemitism to be the lesser evil."[9]

There is no doubt that Eugen Fuchs's Jewish consciousness, so aptly
expressed in these declarations, voiced the sentiments of a significant
number of his contemporaries in the CV's leadership.[10] But I doubt
that this consciousness deeply penetrated the ranks of the CV's
members and followers. Around 1900, the Deutschtum element in
the ideological formula was indeed played down in the guidelines in
favor of more Judentum, but this was less prominent in the widely
circulated publications of the CV.[11] During and after the war, under the
dual pressure of antisemitism and Zionism, the CV's public rhetoric

increasingly featured extremely nationalistic pronouncements of German patriotism.

During the interwar years, the task of an ideological redefinition of the synthesis between Deutschtum and Judentum was taken over by Ludwig Holländer (1877–1936), who from 1908 on was the *Syndikus* (legal counsel) and later the director of the CV and its most outstanding spokesman. Holländer presented his interpretation of the synthesis in a set of nine theses and a lengthy lecture at the convention of the CV in February 1928. An extended version was published the following year by the organization's publishing house (Philo-Verlag), founded by Holländer in 1919.[12] Aware of the politically charged connotations of Deutschtum under the prevailing conditions, Holländer went out of his way to justify the CV's continuous adherence, since 1893, to the main ideological commitment in the first paragraph of the statutes of the CV, the "cultivation of German sentiment" (die Pflege deutscher Gesinnung):

> I remember . . . that in this question there were always differences of opinion. . . . But as friends who are seeking the truth I have to tell you that the term "cultivation of German sentiment" is justly an extraordinarily multifaceted one to this very day. The development of our present public circumstances has created so many possible interpretations in this direction that clarity cannot easily be found, . . . because these emotionally inflated, irrational definitions are open to thousands of possible mental modifications.[13]

Holländer found himself in perhaps even deeper waters when he tried to redefine the contents of Judentum. If the CV wanted to be an association of conviction and "not only call itself so, it has to face the questions of *our connection with Jewry and Judaism.*" Holländer's first and leading principle with regard to this connection was a negative one: denial of the unity of these two entities. "We regard the absolute unity of Jewry in the whole world to be not even a beautiful aim, not to mention an existing reality. . . . Even the Middle Ages could not unify the Jews in the diverse ghettos of the world."[14] The ideal of Jewish unity was to be sought only in the spiritual sphere of Judaism, that is, in "the unity of religious conceptions and moral perception that lead us to conceive the unifying idea of God and unifying morals as essential to Judaism and thereby for us."[15]

Holländer had to admit that even this broad definition of Judaism was subject to different interpretations. He could not ignore the fact that a sizeable portion of the German Jews of that time, whom the CV claimed to represent, had little interest in religion. A good number even regarded themselves as atheists who nonetheless belonged to the German-Jewish entity and wanted to remain part of it. "Today we can no longer cling to the principle that their religion alone distinguishes the Jews of a country from their fellow citizens. . . . We recognize that the viewpoint of a community of fate and common descent also creates important cohesion . . . we know today that the question, 'Why are we and why do we remain German Jews? has to be asked and explored again and again. . . ."[16]

The concept of a "community of fate" *(Schicksalsgemeinschaft)* was Holländer's contribution to an ongoing process of ideological clarification in the search for a new definition of modern Jewish identity. The "community of common descent" *(Stammesgemeinschaft)* had already been introduced before the war by Eugen Fuchs in an important speech at the CV's convention in March 1913: "Judaism is for me a community of religion and of common descent, not a nation. . . . It would be insincere to deny that as a Jew I possess a special peculiarity, that my Jewish origin and Jewish home bestowed on me not only a religious but also a special spiritual, maybe also physical, stamp . . . but in the national sense this kind of tribal stamp does not separate me any more from the German Christian . . . than the tribal stamp separates the Frisian peasant from the Rhenish industrial worker or from the proletarian of Berlin."[17]

Fuchs's conception of the Jews as a *Stamm* (literally, "tribe") was aimed at integrating the German Jews, at placing them beside and making them equal to the other German tribes in the entity of not only the German state but the German folk as well. In a lecture of December 1932, Ludwig Holländer went further when he spoke of a common Jewish Stamm, united across national borders by millennia of a "heritage of memory" *(Erinnerungserbe).* Jews had been a folk in the past, but being today a part of the German folk they, "like every other German Stamm, have to be proud of our tribal history."[18] Hans Bach (1902–1977), one of the editors of *Der Morgen,* went even further, reconnecting the German-Jewish Stamm to its ancient historical origins: "Since the Babylonian exile they have not been a *Volk.* They are less and more: A *Stamm.* Only as a *Stamm* can . . . the *unity* of blood and spirit, of character and religion, of physical and metaphysical cohesion that is peculiar to Judaism be created and preserved."[19]

Eugen Fuchs's definition, and almost all the following, soul-searching efforts to reduce the tension between Deutschtum and Judentum, appeared in the context of anti-Zionist polemics. Considering the relatively small membership of the ZVfD in 1913, and even in the early 1930s, one wonders why it was that Zionism occupied the minds and aroused the wrath of CV spokesmen. After all, they could rightly claim to represent the vast majority of German Jews. Even most CV followers who were members or supporters of the ZVfD did not regard this as a contradiction of their German patriotism. The undeniably defensive note of the arguments in some articles by Eugen Fuchs and Ludwig Holländer suggests that the dispute with the Zionists reflected differences of opinion within their own ranks. The more the CV conceived of itself as a Gesinnungsverein, rather than as a mere Abwehrverein, the more important internal ideological conflicts became.

In the lecture by Fuchs quoted above, he reacted to the radicalization of the ZVfD, led by Kurt Blumenfeld, at its convention in Posen in June 1912. The CV convention then countered the Zionist challenge with a decision to "separate ourselves . . . from those Zionists who deny a German national sentiment, regard themselves as guests of a [foreign host people], and feel themselves to be only Jewish nationals."[20] The resolution reiterated the CV's commitment to the maintenance of *deutsche Gesinnung,* but the selective differentiation among Zionists allowed for quite a flexible interpretation of that concept. In fact, although the ZVfD reacted with a declaration that from then on, simultaneous membership in the ZVfD and in the CV was no longer tenable,[21] many Zionists ignored this directive, and there is no evidence of massive ejections from the CV on its own initiative.

The growing antagonism between the CV and the Zionists in the interwar years reflected increasing differences of opinion within the CV's own ranks. The Balfour Declaration and the League of Nations mandate for the British administration of Palestine bestowed a new aura of feasibility on the Zionist "utopia." At the same time, the rise of antisemitism dashed hopes for a full integration into German society in the near future. Although the Zionist movement still had not attained a large mass membership, its influence and self-assurance were increasing, especially among the younger generation. In this situation it was unavoidable that the tension between Deutschtum und Judentum, and the attitude toward the construction of the developing Jewish national home in Palestine, became major sources of internal dispute within the CV.

Immediately after the war the differences of opinion between the CV and the ZVfD appeared to have diminished. Reactions on both sides to an American Jewish initiative for the establishment of a Jewish congress, and even to the idea of seeking internationally granted and supervised minority rights for the Jews of certain countries, were quite similar. Some CV leaders, led by Eugen Fuchs, did not entirely exclude the possibility of a German Jewish congress to support the minority rights of Jews in Eastern Europe, and even as a common platform for the representation of German Jewry. On the other hand, most Zionists showed little sympathy for the idea of assuring the status of national minority for the Jews in Germany. For a while, a rapprochement between the positions of the two main opposing parties within German Jewry seemed possible.[22]

But very soon the antagonism gained new and stronger momentum. In my view, the greater share of responsibility for this must be attributed to the Palestinocentric orientation of the ZVfD leaders at Berlin's Meinekestrasse. Some of them believed that the rattled ideological self-confidence of the CV opened the way to recruiting support for Zionism among the CV's membership, especially among the younger followers of the organization, by means of intensified polemical attacks.[23] To some extent these tactics could claim success, though it may well be that a more objective and conciliatory tone might have resulted in even greater influence than was actually exerted.

But what concerns us here is the discussion of principles inside the CV that, in my opinion, would have occurred in any case. As a result of the changing situation, the "radicalization of Jewish aims and perceptions" inside the CV that had already begun between 1907 and 1913[24] now continued even more vigorously among the younger members of the CV, as it did among the Zionists. And as before, this process did not bridge ideological and political differences. On the contrary: it increased the tensions between the two camps and inside each of them.

Reassessment of the priority of Deutschtum or Judentum was a major subject of dispute not only within the youth movements that still identified with the CV, such as the Deutsch-Jüdische Jugendgemeinschaft (DJJG) and the Kameraden. Some of the younger members of the CV also challenged what they regarded as the exaggerated "German-oriented" or "assimilationist" tendencies of an older generation that still comprised the vast majority of members. In early 1927, Ludwig Foerder (1885–1954) replied to an anti-Zionist pamphlet by the chairman of the CV in Chemnitz, Georg Mecklenburg (1869–1932); it had been distributed by the CV main office. Foerder claimed that it endangered "the unity and concord of German Jewry, which are an important condition for our fight."[25] Quoting the first article of the CV bylaws, Foerder stressed the unchanged and unequivocal agreement on the first part, the "safeguarding of German Jews' civic equality"; but he criticized current interpretations of the second part on the "cultivation of German sentiment."

Foerder objected in particular to the demand that all present or new members declare their allegiance to Deutschtum because the CV was first of all an "association for the cultivation of German senti-ment." Instead, he argued, the positive attitude of each member to his German nationality should be taken for granted, but in a purely legal sense, while his German sentiment should remain no more a matter for concern than his Jewish beliefs. "The special demand for *deutsche Gesinnung* would violate the parity of *Deutschtum* and *Judentum* that has rightly always been underlined. We do not demand any Jewish *Gesinnung* . . . but are satisfied with the formal Jewish confession. . . . Do we have any right to act differently with regard to *Deutschtum?*"[26]

One year later, much more outspoken voices emanated from a circle of active members of the younger generation. In a programmatic brochure for the forthcoming convention, Friedrich Brodnitz (1899–1997), Kurt Cohn (1899–1987), and Ludwig Tietz (1897–1933) set out to sketch the guidelines for the "Centralverein of the future":

> We, together with the generation of young men, have first of all the true desire not to be compelled any longer to speak of our *Deutschtum*. . . . [In situations or environments] where we are among ourselves we have no need to speak of it. This seems to be obvious, but closer observation shows that there are many among us who can never sufficiently overemphasize their conscious *Deutschtum*. . . . We believe that one can assume *deutsche Gesinnung* as an unconscious function of life, especially among the young generation. . . . For us this is the basis of our work in the CV, but not the principle of work. . . . On this basis we now demand the unperturbed cultivation of our *Judentum*. . . . A *Judentum* that Jewish youth deeply yearns to see become a really insoluble part of its life.[27]

What did the protagonists of more Judentum really have in mind? Was it a mere demand for sentimental *yiddishkeit* in the movement's educational programs, or for a return to religious beliefs and practices in the spirit of Liberal Judaism? A close examination will show that, essentially, it was neither of the two but rather a search for identity and a sense of belonging. As we have seen, the spiritual leaders of the CV had grappled with this problem from its very beginnings. Starting with definitions of German Jewry as a mere confessional *Religions-* or *Glaubensgemeinschaft*, they had advanced to concepts of a historical and ongoing *Schicksals-* or *Stammesgemeinschaft* without marking the boundaries of this community of fate or common descent. This is probably the reason their propositions now appeared to be unsatisfac-tory in the eyes of some, mostly younger members.

We should keep in mind, however, that this group constituted a very small minority within the CV. Just how small it was became apparent in the Berlin community elections of 1930, in which Tietz and Brodnitz appeared as a separate "Postiv-liberale Liste" and gained

723 votes, less than one percent of the total.[28] Nevertheless they were not lacking influence. Tietz was elected deputy chairman of the CV and, together with Brodnitz, held leading posts in nationwide Jewish youth and welfare organizations. After 1933 Brodnitz became the official spokesman of the Reichsvertretung der deutschen Juden (National Representation of German Jews).

The real target of the young opposition was not the CV's top leadership, which actually tried to find a conciliatory middle way. Rather, the target was the host of second-rank functionaries in the CV's regional *Landesverbände* and its local chapters in the provinces, among whom the most ardent defenders of an explicitly nationalist and conservative concept of Deutschtum were to be found. The practical political issues, discussed at the national conventions of 1926 and 1928, were the motions to join the German section of the Keren Hayesod and later the non-Zionist German representation in the enlarged Jewish Agency. Both motions were, time and again, defeated by the majority of delegates from the provinces. They did not have enough power to explicitly prohibit the personal membership of outstanding personalities such as Leo Baeck (1873–1956), who served on the executive boards of both the CV and the Keren Hayesod. Baeck, Tietz, Otto Hirsch (1885–1941), and other prominent members of the CV's board of directors also became members of the Jewish Agency after its establishment in 1929. But the bulk of the provincial delegates manifested their misgivings and suspicions by passing riders that expressed "expectations" that these "individual delegates" would always represent the CV's true "patriotic sentiments" *(vaterländische Gesinnung)* in all places and on all occasions.

The most ardent anti-Zionists found it hard to live with this compromise. The local chapter of the CV in Chemnitz circulated a brochure in which the anonymous author criticized a decision of the CV executive, according to which "it trusts all its members to defy any Jewish-national propaganda . . . in the Jewish Agency."[29] He explained, not without reason, that this contradicted the legal basis of that organization, namely, the Palestine Mandate based on the Balfour Declaration. The Jewish Agency, he argued, was nothing other than the political executive of the Zionist movement, and the Keren Hayesod was its financial tool. Therefore, the Chemnitz chapter demanded the immediate resignation of all CV members from the Jewish Agency.

This did not happen, of course, but the argumentation in this brochure reveals an interesting reaction, shared by many members of the CV, to the rising tide of antisemitism:

The duty of the CV is to fight antisemitism. Zionism nurtures antisemitism. . . . The CV demands equal rights for the Jews because they belong to the *German people* . . . and [it] fights the libelous allegation that the Jews are a foreign people in Germany. The Zionists declare themselves to be a part of this foreign people. . . . Our defense is constantly weakened by compromises, based on some cloudy sentiments, between these two absolutely contradictory ideologies.[30]

This was an almost verbatim repetition of the Mecklenburg Resolution, which passed by a small margin against the opposition of most of the CV's prominent leaders, at the CV's general convention of 1928.[31] Georg Mecklenburg may well have been the author of the unsigned paper. It was certainly no coincidence that this appeal emanated from a community in which native German Jews were the minority and to the very end led a vigorous and successful fight against granting equal voting rights to the majority of Ostjuden.[32] It was also no coincidence that the paper referred approvingly to a strongly worded decision of the Vereinigung für das liberale Judentum (VLJ), dated February 1929, against participation in the Jewish Agency.

The history of the VLJ is still to be written, and one can only surmise that this organization contained the staunchest, most inveterate defenders of an extremely nationalistic Deutschtum among the German Jews, outdistanced only by the vociferous but quantitatively insignificant Verband nationaldeutscher Juden led by Max Naumann (1875–1939), or the even less significant Deutscher Vortrupp of Hans-Joachim Schoeps (1909–1980), whose affiliation with or membership in the VLJ is not clear.

The VLJ was founded in 1908, following an appeal signed by Liberal rabbis and laymen. On the face of it, the proclaimed aims were purely religious: the adjustment of the Jewish faith and its practice to modern life, as a barrier against religious indifference and apostasy. These were without doubt the objectives of the Liberal rabbis, organized since 1898 in their own Vereinigung der liberalen Rabbiner.[33] Very soon, however, they detected that their lay cofounders, who from the beginning secured the majority in all forums, were less seriously concerned with religious problems and used the Vereinigung as a political instrument to assure their hold on the administration of the Jewish communities. These differences had already appeared in 1912 at the convention of the VLJ in Posen, where rabbis Caesar Seligmann and Leo Baeck presented a set of guidelines for Liberal ritual and observance after it had been ratified by a convention of Liberal rabbis. The lay majority rejected the institution of "a liberal *Shulkhan Arukh*" (the ritual code of Orthodox Jews) and arranged for what Seligmann later described as "a first-class burial" of the guidelines.[34]

In 1912, the militant anti-Zionist attitude of the VLJ came to the fore when its chairman, Bernhard Breslauer, initiated the establishment of a Reichsverband zur Bekämpfung des Zionismus, afterwards renamed Antizionistisches Komitee, at the VLJ's offices in Berlin. The two most prominent leaders of the CV, Eugen Fuchs and Maximilian Horwitz, who were discreetly approached, declined to be connected with this initiative, but Ludwig Holländer seems to have supported it.[35] At the CV convention of May 1913, Holländer demanded a clear break and the expulsion of Zionists, but he had to give way to his more moderate elders, who advocated the already mentioned "selective" anti-Zionist decision.

After the war, the movement's monthly, *Liberales Judentum*, edited in Frankfurt am Main by Seligmann, was transferred to Berlin and became the weekly *Jüdisch-Liberale Zeitung*, edited by Bruno Woyda, a member of the Berlin Reformgemeinde and an ardent German nationalist. The new weekly was transformed into a mouthpiece of the Liberal factions in the communities. Caesar Seligmann had fought this transfer and, like many Liberal rabbis, distanced himself from the activities of the VLJ and its weekly, as both "descended to become mere instruments of community politics in a purely anti-Zionist vein." In March 1927, a conciliatory resolution of the Association of Liberal Rabbis, leaving the attitude toward Zionism to the personal decision of each Liberal rabbi or layman, provoked the wrath of the lay leadership of the VLJ. The weekly's editors declared that the rabbis had ceased to be the leaders of Liberal Judaism, and from then on, most rabbis refrained from participating in the VLJ's activities and publications.[36]

The VLJ was, from early on, an essentially political organization, not a religious one. Its "lay leadership was composed mainly of community politicians whose interest was often limited to gaining and holding onto positions of power in their communities. . . ."[37] Although most of its leaders and followers were at that time members of the CV, the political orientation of the two organizations differed in some important respects. Actually, this was more evident in the prewar period. As we have seen, the CV established its policy and tactics of Abwehr against antisemitism in opposition to the liberal "notables" who governed the communities. During the Weimar years, both organizations underwent substantial changes. The CV shed the character of a mere, absolutely neutral Abwehrverein, while the VLJ withdrew almost entirely from religious matters and became primarily an instrument for political power struggles in the Jewish communities. It remains to be determined why, in this process, many leaders of the VLJ appear from the very beginning to have been the most radical German nationalists and extreme anti-Zionists in the ranks of the CV. In any case, perusing the pages of the *Jüdisch-Liberale Zeitung*, one understands whom Leo Baeck had in mind when he deplored, in a letter to Seligmann thought to have been written in 1926, "the spiritual dreariness of some CV members who try to create from their Deutschtum a kind of substitute religion."[38]

The confrontation with the JVP in the election campaigns of the 1920s are at best only a partial explanation. There may also be sociological reasons: as in the case of the *Gemeindezionisten*—but even more distinctly—the "Gemeinde Liberals" who belonged to the CV were the second tier of the movement's leadership. The first-tier leaders of the CV and the ZVfD were professionals with a broader intellectual and ideological outlook, while among those of the JVP and certainly of the VLJ there were many middle- or upper-class businessmen. But despite these perhaps superficial and schematic similarities, some differences in attitude are perplexing: among the Zionists, the most radical opponents to closer cooperation with the CV were Kurt Blumenfeld and Siegfried Moses of the ZVfD, while men such as Alfred Klee or Max Kollenscher of the JVP took a more conciliatory stand. As we have seen, the opposite is true in the case of the CV, where the Gemeinde Liberals outvoted the leaders at the top on issues such as the Keren Hayesod, the Jewish Agency, and financial assistance to Hechaluz.

Also of interest are the different attitudes of the young generation in the two camps. In the CV, as we have seen, Ludwig Tietz, Friedrich Brodnitz, and their followers had consistently fought for internal Jewish rapprochement and, though a minority, achieved growing influence on the board. In contrast, inside the VLJ, the young spokesmen of the Jüdisch-Liberale Jugendvereine (JLJ) outdid their elders in German nationalism and radical anti-Zionism.[39] During the election campaign of October 1930, their column in the *JLZ* accused the JVP of hiding its Zionist commitment behind false pretenses; the JVP was compared to the Nazis: "Through fanaticism, phrases, and unrealistic yet idealistic-sounding programs, the National Socialists have brought people over to them who, according to their mentality, belong somewhere quite different. The same phenomenon manifests itself with the Jewish-Nationals. Here, too, fanaticism and idealistic programs, which must affect every 'feeling.'" Moreover, the populist ring of the name of the Jüdische Volkspartei was akin to that of the NSDAP, which called itself a *workers'* party.[40] These Liberal youth groups seem to have attracted only a small membership in some larger communities and had almost no influence on the young Jewish generation of the Weimar period. Still, these differences in attitude deserve further study in future research.

The community elections of 1926 and 1930 in Berlin coincided in time with the rising political crisis and the upsurge of antisemitic propaganda. It is difficult to determine the role of these developments in the aggravation of inter-Jewish conflicts, including the tensions between the VLJ and the CV. In any case, toward January 1933, and even more so during the first month of the Nazi regime, the *Jüdisch-Liberale Zeitung* and the official declarations of the Liberals adopted an ever more pronounced right-wing nationalist and anti-Zionist vocabulary. This was without doubt influenced by the vociferous public campaign launched in the press and on the street kiosks by the Verband nationaldeutscher Juden.[41] Naumann and his followers believed their time had come, and Liberals such as Bruno Woyda or his successor as editor of the *Jüdisch-Liberale Zeitung*, George Goetz (1892–1968), were dangerously close to them. In April 1933, Naumann convinced even the leaders of the veterans organization, the Reichsbund jüdischer Frontsoldaten (RjF), to join his Verband along with the right-wing Jewish youth movement Schwarzes Fähnlein and other marginal groups in an effort to unite all German-Jewish nationalists in an Aktions-Ausschuss der jüdischen Deutschen, but the coalition fell apart after only a few weeks.[42]

This was not the end of Liberal initiatives to accommodate the new regime, nor of their attacks on the CV's leaders, who at that time took part in the establishment of the Reichsvertretung der deutschen Juden. George Goetz openly accused them of "letting the German Jews down" and of handing over the provisional chairmanship of the CV to a man (evidently Ludwig Tietz) "whose position on the question *Deutschtum* and *Judentum* has never been . . . in the tradition of the CV and who, to our taste, has always been too much interested in Palestine."[43]

This was the overture to a concerted campaign against allegedly increasing Zionist influence among the leading ranks of the CV. In October Bruno Woyda published, in the *Berliner jüdisches Gemeindeblatt,* what he defined as "programmatic guidelines" for the future of the Jews in Germany. His main thesis was that the German Jews expect "to have their rights granted only by . . . the German *Volk* and its leaders . . . therefore the German Jews must not hesitate to integrate themselves into a state organism that is compelled to restrict their rights, because it regards a certain community of blood the condition for the community of the *Volk*. . . ." Woyda stressed that he was speaking only of those "who have only one fatherland, one homeland: Germany," not of those who want to emigrate, or of Jewish foreigners, who can only expect to be treated like other foreigners.[44] The publication of Woyda's article led to the resignation of the chairman of the ZVfD, Siegfried Moses (1887–1974), from the executive board of the Jewish community of Berlin. The community's Liberal chairman, Heinrich Stahl (1868–1942), declared in response that Woyda's conceptions "were by no means obsolete . . . and are agreed on by the majority of the Jews of Berlin and of Germany."[45]

In November 1933 Bruno Woyda and a few like-minded friends founded a Revival Movement of Jewish Germans *(Erneuerungsbewegung der jüdischen Deutschen)*. In its first, and to my knowledge only, public appeal the movement acknowledged the fundamental change in the situation of the German Jews, who evidently "had lost their equal standing and equal rights, but not their consciousness of being and remaining Germans who are connected, for better or worse, with the fate of our German fatherland." In the name of those Jewish Germans the initiators of the appeal demanded complete separation from the "Zionists of all shades, who should be left to attend to their own affairs" while the "Jewish Germans unite and subordinate under the discipline and order of a determined German-Jewish leadership."[46]

This appeal was an open call for war against the newly established Reichsvertretung and a short-lived attempt to cotton to the new rulers who, as in the case of Naumann's approaches, showed little interest.[47] In this case the executive of the Berlin Jüdische Gemeinde, replying to repeated accusations by Siegfried Moses, distanced itself from Woyda's Revival Movement and declared its loyalty to the Reichsvertretung.[48]

In the current of historical events, the Jewish Germans and their most radical leaders inside the JLV fought a losing battle. The *Jüdisch-Liberale Zeitung* had to restrict publication to twice a month, and even after it adjusted to the new reality and, under a new editor, changed its name to *Jüdisch-Allgemeine Zeitung*, its readership constantly declined. The CV also had to fight the desertion of growing numbers of its members to the Zionist camp.[49] But for the last years of the Weimar period it is still difficult to discern which group, the intransigent "Jewish Germans" in the provinces or the more moderate leaders in Berlin, could more rightfully claim to represent the majority of the CV's membership. Nor do we have a clear sense of those German Jews, those who had already severed substantive connections with any Jewish establishment or organization, even if formally they still belonged, and paid their taxes, to the Jewish communities. Now, following the discovery of the CV's files in Moscow and the addition of other sources, until recently inaccessible, from other archives, we may hope that a younger and more distanced, or less biased, flock of historians will be able to answer these, and similar, still open questions.

Notes

1. Robert Weltsch, 'Schlussbetrachtung,' in *Entscheidungsjahr 1932. Zur Judenfrage in der Endphase der Weimarer Republik*, ed. Werner Mosse and Arnold Paucker, 2nd ed. (Tübingen, 1966), p. 555.
2. See Gabriel E. Alexander, "Berlin Jewry and Its Community during the Weimar Republic (1919–1933)," Ph.D. diss., Hebrew University of Jerusalem, 1995 (in Hebrew), esp. pp. 214ff.; Michael Brenner, "The Jüdische Volkspartei: National Jewish Communal Policies during the Weimar Republic," *LBIYB* 35 (1990): 219–43. I am grateful to Gabriel Alexander for letting me use his unpublished thesis.
3. See Arnold Paucker, *Der jüdische Abwehrkampf gegen Antisemitismus und Nationalsozialismus in den letzten Jahren der Weimarer Republik*, 2nd ed. (Hamburg, 1969); idem, "Der jüdische Abwehrkampf," in *Entscheidungsjahr 1932*, ed. Mosse and Paucker, pp. 423–24.
4. I wish to thank Michael Brenner for letting me use his unpublished M.A. thesis, *Die jüdische Volkspartei–Nationaljüdische Gemeindepolitik in der Weimarer Republik*, Hochschule für Jüdische Studien, Heidelberg, 1988. His article "Jüdische Volkspartei" (see note 2 above) summarizes his findings.
5. Alexander's chapter on the VJL in "Berlin Jewry," pp. 97–119, is a commendable, pioneering study on the history of this organization.
6. A comprehensive history of the CV is still outstanding. For the pre–World War I period, see Paul Rieger, *Ein Vierteljahrhundert im Kampf um das Recht und die Zukunft der deutschen Juden* (Berlin, 1918). Informative for the same period is Ismar Schorsch, *Jewish Reactions to German Anti-Semitism, 1870–1914* (New York, 1972). See also Jehuda Reinharz, *Fatherland or Promised Land: The Dilemma of the German Jew, 1893–1914* (Ann Arbor, 1975), which deals mainly with the ideological controversies between the CV and the Zionists. Arnold Paucker, "Zur Problematik einer jüdischen Abwehrstrategie in der deutschen Gesellschaft," in *Juden im Wilhelminischen Deutschland*, ed. Werner Mosse and Arnold Paucker (Tübingen, 1976), pp. 479–548, contains an account of the political activities of the CV during these years.

Two outstanding leaders of the CV who survived the war, Eva and Hans Reichmann, produced some important but fragmentary contributions on the internal discussions and developments within the CV; see Eva Reichmann, "Der Bewusstseinswandel der deutschen Juden," in *Deutsches Judentum in Krieg und Revolution, 1916–1923* ed. Werner Mosse and Arnold Paucker (Tübingen, 1971), pp. 511–612; Hans Reichmann, "Der Centralverein deutscher Staatsbürger jüdischen Glaubens," in *Festschrift zum 80. Geburtstag von Rabbiner Dr. Leo Baeck* (London, 1957), pp. 63–75. Elsewhere, Hans Reichmann has lamented the lack of archival sources that makes the writing of an objective, scientifically adequate history of the CV extremely difficult. He explained that in March 1933 none other than Hermann Göring advised the leaders of the CV to destroy the material that they had collected in their campaigns against the Nazi party. This had partly already been done before, at the CVs own initiative. On the other hand, the files of Jewish organizations were confiscated by the Gestapo and other National Socialist agencies because the Nazis wanted to efface the traces of their terrorist regime. (See Reichmann's essay "Der drohende Sturm" in the volume *In zwei Welten. Siegfried Moses zum 75. Geburtstag*, ed. Hans Tramer (Tel Aviv, 1962), pp. 557–58.) Reichmann was wrong: some years ago, a stock of more than 4,300 files, containing what is believed to be the main body of the archives of the CV main office in Berlin, was discovered in the Moscow Sonderarchiv and may now enable the writing of the history of the largest and most important political organization of German Jewry.

7. Paucker, "Zur Problematik einer jüdischen Abwehrstrategie," pp. 486ff., quotes the *Leitsätze* of the new organization as "closely relying upon Löwenfeld's theses, yet divested of any religious polemic." The proviso refers to the attacks against Orthodoxy and the Talmud in Löwenfeld's brochure; according to Paucker, this proves that "he was not exactly a spiritual giant" (p. 488); Jacob Borut, "'A new Spirit among Our Brethren in Ashkenaz,' German Jewry in the Face of Economic, Social, and Political Change in the Reich at the End of the 19th Century," Ph.D. diss. (in Hebrew), Hebrew University of Jerusalem, 1991, esp. chapter 6, pp. 198–236, and, within that discussion, pp. 216ff. See also idem, "The Rise of Jewish Defense Agitation in Germany, 1890–1895: A Pre-History of the C.V.?" *LBIYB* 36 (1991): 59–96.

8. Eugen Fuchs, *Um Deutschtum und Judentum. Gesammelte Reden und Aufsätze (1894–1919)* (Frankfurt am Main, 1919), p. 251.

9. Ibid., p. 258.

10. Schorsch, *Jewish Reactions*, pp. 112ff.

11. Ibid., p. 137.

12. Ludwig Holländer, *Deutsch-Jüdische Probleme der Gegenwart* (Berlin, 1929).

13. Ibid., pp. 10–11.

14. Ibid., p. 21.

15. Ibid., p. 23.

16. Ibid., p. 9.

17. Fuchs, *Um Deutschtum und Judentum*, pp. 252–53.

18. *JR*, December 16, 1932.

19. *Der Morgen* 8/1 (April 1932): 14. For the passages referred to here and in note 18 and for an insightful analysis of them, see Kurt Loewenstein, "Die innerjüdische Reaktion auf die Krise der deutschen Demokratie," in *Entscheidungsjahr 1932*, ed. Mosse and Paucker, pp. 354–55.

20. Fuchs, *Deutschtum und Judentum*, p. 249.

21. See *Dokumente zur Geschichte des deutschen Zionismus 1882–1933*, ed. Jehuda Reinharz (Tübingen, 1981), pp. 111–12.

22. See Jacob Toury, "Organizational Problems of German Jewry: Steps towards the Establishment of a Central Jewish Organization (1893–1920)," *LBIYB* 13 (1968): 57–90, esp. 84ff.; *Dokumente*, ed. Reinharz, pp. 235ff. The positive approach of Eugen Fuchs appeared in his article "Was nun?" in the *Neue jüdische Monatshefte* (1919): 137ff., reprinted in Fuchs, *Deutschtum und Judentum*, esp. pp.

269–70. The negative reaction of the majority of the CV to the Jewish Congress initiative appeared in an anonymous brochure under the title *Zeitfragen, Die Kongresspolitik der Zionisten* (Berlin, 1919).

23. See *Dokumente*, ed. Reinharz, pp. 390–91: Anlage I – Streng vertraulich! – . . . 30. Oktober 1927: *Unsere Stellung zu den jüdischen Organisationen in Deutschland*.

24. Evyatar Friesel, "A Response," *LBIYB* 33 (1988): 110. This article concludes a discussion of the same author's theses presented in "The Political and Ideological Development of the Centralverein before 1914," *LBIYB* 31 (1986): 121–46.

25. Ludwig Foerder, *Die Stellung des Centralvereins zu den innerjüdischen Fragen in den Jahren 1919–1926* (Breslau, 1927), p. 1.

26. Ibid., p. 8.

27. Friedrich Brodnitz, Kurt Cohn, Ludwig Tietz, *Der Central-Verein der Zukunft, Eine Denkschrift zur Hauptversammlung 1928* (n.p., n.d.), p. 12.

28. Alexander, "Berlin Jewry," p. 220.

29. *Aufklärungsschrift der Ortsgruppe Chemnitz des Centralvereins deutscher Staatsbürger jüdischen Glaubens* (n.p., n.d.), pp. 2–3. The decision of the board of directors at its session of February 16, 1930, read: "Der Hauptvorstand . . . hat das Vertrauen, dass alle seine Mitglieder jede national-jüdische Propaganda auch im Rahmen der Jewish Agency abweisen."

30. Ibid., pp. 15–16.

31. CV calendar, 1929, p. 62.

32. See Trude Maurer, *Ostjuden in Deutschland 1918–1933* (Hamburg, 1986), pp. 621ff.

33. The organization of the Liberal rabbis continued to exist after 1908 and had ninety-four members in 1933. See Walter Breslauer, "Die 'Vereinigung für das liberale Judentum in Deutschland' und die 'Richtlinien zu einem Programm für das liberale Judentum.' Erinnerungen aus den Jahren 1908–1914," *BLBI* 9 (1966): 302ff. The following discussion is based on this article and on Michael A. Meyer, "Caesar Seligmann and the Development of Liberal Judaism in Germany at the Beginning of the Twentieth Century," *Hebrew Union College Annual* 40/41 (1969–1970): 529–54; on Caesar Seligmann, *Erinnerungen*, ed. Erwin Seligmann (Frankfurt am Main, 1975); and on Alexander, "Berlin Jewry," esp. pp. 97–119.

34. Quoted in Meyer, "Caesar Seligmann," p. 545n.; see also Seligmann, *Erinnerungen*, pp. 146ff.

35. Schorsch, *Jewish Reactions*, pp. 198–99; Marjorie Lamberti, "From Coexistence to Conflict—Zionism and the Jewish Community in Germany 1897–1914," *LBIYB* 27 (1982): 78ff.

36. Seligmann, *Erinnerungen*, pp. 159–60; Meyer, "Caesar Seligmann," pp. 552–53.

37. Meyer, "Caesar Seligmann," p. 547.

38. See the facsimile copy of the letter in *LBIYB* 2 (1957): 44ff.

39. Breslauer, "Die 'Vereinigung,'" pp. 312–13.

40. "Aus der ILI-Bewegung," *JLZ*, October 8, 1930.

41. See Carl J. Rheins, "The Verband nationaldeutscher Juden," in *LBIYB* 25 (1980): 243–68, esp. 265ff.

42. See Klaus J. Herrmann, *Das Dritte Reich und die deutsch-jüdischen Organisationen 1933–1934* (Cologne, 1969), pp. 12–13.

43. George Goetz, "Gefahren, Versäumnisse, Aufgaben. Eine notwendige Kritik," *JLZ*, May 1, 1933, supplement.

44. Bruno Woyda, "Um die künftige Stellung der deutschen Juden. Programmatische Richtlinien," *JLZ*, October 31, 1933, supplement.

45. Stahl to Moses, October 18, 1933, in *JLZ,* October 24, 1933, supplement.

46. "Erneuerungsbewegung der jüdischen Deutschen," *JLZ,* November 14, 1933.

47. See Herrmann, *Das Dritte Reich,* pp. 70ff.

48. "Berliner Gemeinde für Einigkeit," *JLZ,* November 21, 1933.

49. See Avraham Barkai, "Der CV im Jahre 1933: Neu aufgefundene Dokumente im Moskauer 'Sonderarchiv,'" *TJBDG* 28 (1994): 233–46.

6

"Verjudung des Judentums"

Was There a Zionist Subculture in Weimar Germany?

JACOB BORUT

"We are currently suffering from a 'Jewification' of Jewry" (Verjudung des Judentums), complained an avowed Liberal Jew from Cologne, Siegfried Braun, in early 1928.[1] "We are rapidly approaching a situation that we overcame more than a century ago and that is adequately characterized by the term 'spiritual ghetto.'"

During the Weimar period, the range of Jewish organizations and associations in Germany reached proportions that have been described in recent scholarship as "astounding"[2] and that aroused the concern of some Jewish contemporaries who were afraid that Jews were willingly returning to a self-erected spiritual ghetto. "With accelerating frequency come requests to attend Jewish lectures, courses, and gatherings of all kinds," explained Braun. "Jewish writings, in the form of newspapers, journals, pamphlets, and books, are steadily growing, and reading only a small part of them takes up a considerable portion of our time. Jewish public life, which is constantly branching out, creates dozens of organizations that compete for public participation in meetings and conferences. In brief, there reigns everywhere among the Jews an industriousness that can hardly be surpassed and that captivates many of us to such an extent that there declines both the possibility and the inclination to devote oneself to the cultivation of non-Jewish culture."[3]

During the Weimar period the Jewish organizational system did indeed attain its largest size and range since the decline of the traditional Jewish subculture of premodern times. This essay will examine that organizational system and will compare one of its parts, the Zionist movement, with the others. The Zionists openly advocated the creation of a separate Jewish sphere—a nightmare for Liberals such as Braun—whereas the organizations of the majority of German Jews, such as the Centralverein deutscher Staatsbürger jüdischen Glaubens (CV), or the Reichsbund jüdischer Frontsoldaten, though they took an active part in the formation and expansion of the Jewish organizational system, were opposed to the creation of a "spiritual ghetto." Profound differences in target groups and aims were expressed by the leaders of the Zionist and Liberal organizations,[4] and conventional historiographical wisdom holds that such differences permeated the rank-and-file. In this essay we will investigate whether the associational life of both the Zionist and Liberal currents did in fact correspond with the aims attributed to them by their leaders.

The broad array of Jewish organizations has been described by several scholars as a "subculture." This term requires closer analysis. Subcultures in Weimar Germany took the form of a wide matrix of societies, organizations, and other sociopolitical institutions (such as newspapers) that spanned most walks of life "from cradle to grave." These organizational systems encouraged contacts between members of specific groups, reinforcing their members' loyalty for common purposes. The subculture segregated and protected its members from the surrounding society, which was in many cases hostile, and integrated them into a world of their own.[5] In this context, special attention should be given to newspapers (a neglected subject in most studies), because they created the framework of an "imagined community" for their readers, a nationwide community of people who were thought to be part of a single camp. This community consisted of people whom the readers had never met but about whose existence they learned through the paper, and the newspapers thus created a large group with whom readers could—and did—identify.[6]

The major German subcultures assumed popular, mass-based form in the 1890s, grew rapidly until World War I, and reached their widest proportions, as measured by the numbers of organizations and membership figures, during the Weimar period. This was achieved in spite of the many ruptures and power struggles within them, especially within the former socialist camp. Indeed, these ruptures had probably contributed to the subcultures' growth, as opposing groups such as Social Democrats and Communists created rival organizational networks and made efforts to strengthen them.

Did the array of Jewish organizations constitute a "subculture"? Until the modern period, Jewish society did resemble a subculture, quite distinct from the society surrounding it. From the time of the Enlightenment, some parts of Jewish society had undergone processes of assimilation and acculturation that led Jews "out of the ghetto" and toward the majority society into which they sought to be integrated. These tendencies spread gradually and finally encompassed the great majority in Jewish society. They led to the disintegration of the Jewish subculture, whose only remnants, apart from the communities, were for the most part charitable organizations—one area in which Jewish autonomy was encouraged by the German authorities, since they preferred that the Jewish poor be helped by Jewish, rather than public, funds.[7]

A reversal of this tendency occurred in the 1890s (with signs of that change already visible in the 1880s), as a new network of Jewish societies and organizations began to emerge. The most notable phenomenon of that period was the establishment and almost immediate rise to power of the CV, but this was one facet of a much wider process that included the rise of a flourishing network of Vereine für jüdische Geschichte und Literatur (Societies for Jewish History and Literature) and, in general, a strong development of Jewish societies. (Peter Pulzer has described this phenomenon as a Jewish "organizational renaissance.")[8] The CV and the Societies for Jewish History and Literature became, in the early twentieth century, giant organizations with tens of thousands of members. While only adult males could become members, it can be assumed that other family members also adhered to their principles and that they therefore represented the majority of the Jewish population. In addition to these associations, Jews founded networks of specifically Jewish student fraternities, youth movements, women's organizations, and athletic societies. This network of organizations expanded in size and scope with time.

This system cannot, however, be described as a "subculture." Without getting entangled in the web of scholarly definitions, let us say that a "subculture" denotes something that encourages the social separation of its members from majority society and other subcultures.[9] A main constituent of the subculture is—especially according to historical research about subcultures in Germany and Austria—the existence of a Lager,[10] an organizational system whose aim is to shield its members from outside influences. A subculture attempts to bring all or most areas of life into its scope. David Sorkin, the major proponent of the use of the term "subculture" to describe modern German Jewish society,[11] bases his opinion on the assertion that German Jews created an associational network parallel to that of their Gentile counterparts, thereby rendering Jews similar to the German bourgeoisie while remaining separate from it. Sorkin, however, fails to prove this point, because the types of Jewish societies that he argues covered all needs "from cradle to grave"[12] were by and large charitable societies, catering to the lower echelons—that is, to a minority of Jews. Even though these societies were run and supported by bourgeois Jews, the time and effort they required were hardly substantial. Hirsch Heimann, an important notable in Berlin and leading member of several welfare societies, wrote that "the members of the directorial boards were not extraordinarily occupied with routine administration. They had at most six meetings annually. . . ."[13] Although it might be claimed that these societies were helpful in the construction of a bourgeois German Jewish identity, they most certainly did not fulfill any significant role in bourgeois German Jews' daily life or social habits and do not, by themselves, constitute a subculture.[14]

What was clearly lacking were Jewish parallels to the German social as well as professional societies. There were no Jewish parallels to the many choral, gymnastic, and local history societies, or to the professional associations of merchants and attorneys. This was because the Jews did not want their own subculture; they strove to be a part of the existing bourgeois subculture. The CV, the major organization of German Jewry, was heavily involved in the founding of various Jewish organizations, yet it explicitly stated that it supported the creation of Jewish societies only in fields in which Jews were discriminated against and not where equality prevailed.[15] This sentiment led to concrete action when, in the early twentieth century, Zionists and other Jewish activists started forming Jewish athletic and team gymnastics societies, which encountered strong opposition from Liberals.[16]

Leaders of most Jewish organizations, and the Jewish public in general, had no intention of forming an all-embracing system constituting a Lager or a subculture. What they wanted, and actually created, was a less encompassing organizational system that can be defined as a *Teilkultur* (partial culture).[17] This term describes either a system of organizations encompassing only a limited number of realms (one that thus prevents its members from being isolated from the surrounding society), or a system in which the commitment of the members to their own kind is not total (they thus do not desire self-imposed isolation from the majority society). These two cases can affect each other, as a sector with a low amount of commitment would find it hard to develop a wide array of organizations. There is often, but not always, a high degree of overlap between them; a system with highly committed members could become a Teilkultur, and not a subculture, if it developed only a limited number of organizations because of hostile government pressure or a small number of potential supporters (as was the case, e.g., with the organizational system of the Social Democratic Party in small and medium-sized towns).

A good example of the meaning of the Teilkultur is the realm of Jewish education. The system of Jewish schools, separate from Christian schools, was in decline throughout the second half of the nineteenth century; the majority of Jews preferred to send their children to schools in which they could mix with German children and receive a general education. The Jewish population did not desire a return to the former system of Jewish schools, as would have been the case in a subculture, since a separate educational system was viewed as Jewish self-seclusion and as an abandonment of the desire to integrate into German society. On the other hand, toward the end of the nineteenth century, many Jews wished their children to receive a Jewish education that would provide them with some knowledge of Judaism and that would reinforce the Jewish facet of their identity. The solution was found in the demand to strengthen Jewish religious education within the general educational system, and especially to ensure that it would be provided in every school that had Jewish pupils. Such demands had become a major issue in Jewish public opinion in the 1890s and had, in fact, led to the defeat of the ruling Liberal party in the Jewish community elections in Berlin in 1895. German Jews felt that their children should receive Jewish education—not in separate Jewish schools, whose numbers were dwindling, but in Christian schools.

The new tendency within Judaism was based on a perception that sought a synthesis between *Deutschtum* and *Judentum,* without giving away, or belittling, the Jewish facet of German-Jewish identity.[18] It saw Deutschtum and Judentum not as opposite poles, which would have meant that approaching one necessarily entailed withdrawing from the other, but as mutually supplementary and reinforcing. The Jew who is not ashamed and neglectful of his Jewish identity, so the idea went, would also be a better German.

The CV exemplifies how the will of some Jews to advance Jewish integration within the surrounding society led them to strengthen and emphasize their self-perception as Jews, as a specific group protecting its needs and values. From the 1890s onward, Jewish activists had noted the success in German politics and society of group action led by specific population sectors, such as the agrarians, who advanced their demands through the creation of interest groups and united action against the authorities. Activists felt that if Jews wanted to remove the obstacles blocking the way to successful integration (e.g., acceptance into governmental and official posts), they had to act as a united group and fight together for their needs. Thus, if they acted like "better

Jews," not ashamed of demonstrating group unity, they could also be "better Germans" and better serve their fatherland.

The Zionist world view was very different from that of the majority of German Jews.[19] Like the Orthodox, the Zionists clearly wanted to create a full-fledged Jewish subculture that would encompass all walks of Jewish life. The new generations of leaders that came to dominate German Zionism before World War I felt that Deutschtum and Judentum were opposite poles that made necessary a choice between them.

During the Weimar period Jewish activities reached an unprecedented level. There was an immense growth in the number and size of Jewish organizations. For example, of the twenty youth organizations that existed in Frankfurt am Main in 1932, sixteen were founded during the Weimar period.[20] Jewish organizational life was stimulated by the presence of significant numbers of Jews from Eastern Europe *(Ostjuden)* in the Jewish communities. In general, this period was characterized by a huge increase in the organizational activities of minorities and various sectors in Germany, thanks to the unprecedented tolerance shown by German authorities toward minorities, a tolerance that included official assistance for their public activities. This combination of factors enabled the Zionist activists in the communities, sometimes with the help of the authorities and with the Ostjuden as a base of support, to increase substantially the dimensions of Zionist activities and to develop new Jewish institutions, for example, Jewish schools financed by local German administrations.[21]

We can now turn to an examination of the spectrum of Zionists activities at the local level in comparison with the activities of majority, pro-Liberal Jewish society. Such study must be based on local sources, and we will therefore concentrate on one part of Germany—the western part, consisting of the Prussian provinces of Rhineland and Westphalia, the Saargebiet, and the Bavarian Palatinate.

To begin with, the Jewish associational life of Zionists as well as of Liberals concentrated only on leisure-time activities. Unlike the leaders of the Socialist/Communist, Catholic, and Liberal subcultures, Jews developed no trade unions and few professional Jewish organizations. It was not for lack of numbers—there were enough Jewish merchants, lawyers, and doctors in any big town to form a professional association—but because the Jews preferred to be members of the local German associations, mainly the Liberal ones, in which some of them reached very respected positions. There were, however, some Jewish professional organizations. This was a relatively new phenomenon that emerged around the turn of the century. The strongest such organizations were those of the artisans.[22] The Verein selbstständiger

Handwerker jüdischen Glaubens (Association of Independent Craftsmen of the Jewish Faith), founded in 1895, and especially the Zen-
tralverband jüdischer Handwerker (Central Union of Jewish Craftsmen), founded in 1905, had local chapters in the major communities
and sometimes fielded candidates for the community's representative
council, on which they managed to win some seats. Their membership
seems to have consisted mainly of Ostjuden. Another professional
organization was the Verein jüdischer Hotelbesitzer und Restaura-
teure. It was much weaker than the artisans' associations, and its
members often complained about their financial situation, even in the
relatively better economic atmosphere before 1929.[23] These professional groups remained outside the sphere of the competing ideological currents, as they cared mainly for the economic and material
interests of their members and shared little common ground with
organizations based on ideology. In fact, the involvement of the
artisans' organizations in community politics made them competitors
of both the Zionists and the Liberals. There were a few attempts to
organize Zionist associations among younger employees in com-
merce. These efforts "from below" did not achieve significant success.
Zionist academics were organized mainly as *Alte Herren,* that is, as
groups of former members of student fraternities. This, however, was
a spare-time, not a professional, activity. The field of professional life
remained outside the scope of Zionist associational life.

The major difference between Zionists and Liberals lay in their
stand on a separate Jewish educational system which, in general,
Zionists supported and Liberals opposed. There were, however, some
exceptions. The Liberal community leadership of Frankfurt had kept
alive the Jewish Liberal school, the Philantropin, using large sums
from the community budget, in spite of Orthodox and Zionist demands to close it down.[24] Still, the majority of German Jews—even in
Frankfurt—preferred to send their children to non-Jewish schools.[25]
Due to a combination of ideological and financial factors, the dwindling of the Jewish educational system that began in the nineteenth
century continued into the Weimar period.

In some towns, however, we find a reversal of this tendency. The
increased presence of Ostjuden created a demand for new Jewish
schools and strengthened existing ones.[26] This demand was supported
by the Zionists and the Orthodox within the communities and sometimes by other groups such as the B'nai B'rith.[27] In some places in
western Germany, such as Essen, Duisburg, and Recklinghausen, new
Jewish schools were opened.[28] These efforts were supported by the
tolerant attitude of local government toward the Jews: municipalities
agreed to recognize Jewish schools as municipal schools, to provide

buildings, and to pay teachers' salaries, which represented a major financial benefit for the community.

Against this background, the resolute stand of the Liberals against Jewish schools is all the more noteworthy. One example is their fight in Duisburg, where they represented a minority on the community's representative council, which decided, in 1928, to open a Jewish school. The local Liberals called protest meetings, distributed brochures, and protested against the decision at various governmental levels, but to no avail.[29] Michael Brenner notes that in some places the Liberals "gradually accepted" Jewish schools "as necessary institutions in times of virulent antisemitism";[30] but such developments occurred only in the early 1930s and encompassed only a part of the Liberal Jewish population.

Only a minority among the Zionists themselves used separate Jewish educational systems where they existed. A Zionist leader in Berlin declared proudly that in 1930, after years of Zionist control over the community and heavy investment in its educational system,[31] one-seventh of the Jewish pupils in Berlin studied in Jewish schools. This share, much smaller than the share of the Jüdische Volkspartei in the community elections, was a cause for pride.[32] Among fifteen Jewish schools listed in an official document in Rhineland and Westphalia, none had more than forty pupils, even in communities that had thousands of members. We should note, however, that the great majority of Socialists also avoided sending their children to the "free" (that is, without religious instruction) schools that were created in the Weimar period by the socialist movement, preferring to send them instead to confessional or *Simultanschulen* (non-confessional schools).[33]

Some associations included all the currents of Jewish life in Germany: youth movements,[34] student fraternities, and women's associations. Even before 1914 each ideological current had its own student, youth, and women's groups, either because new ones had been created or organizations that grew up from below had been "adopted." The student movements and the first youth movements were based on preexisting Liberal and Zionist student and youth groups for which *Dachverbände* (umbrella organizations) were created; and these, in turn, worked hard to establish new groups. Each current invested plenty of resources and effort in maintaining and developing such societies.

For the women's organizations, the picture was somewhat complicated. The major Jewish women's organization, the Jüdischer Frauenbund, was part of the Liberal Jewish majority Teilkultur. On the one hand, it rejected the Zionist notion that the Jews were a *Volk* and claimed that its members were part of the German nation. Still, it had a Zionist membership and "was sensitive to the feelings of its Zionist members."[35] Therefore, the Zionists did not create a separate women's movement and could cooperate with the leading organization. Nevertheless, some Zionist women had created and organized their own women's groups, such as Lina Tauber-Wagner's National-jüdische Frauenvereinigung in Berlin, or the groups for supporting settlements in Palestine, such as the Verband jüdischer Frauen für Kulturarbeit in Palästina.[36]

A leading motive behind the development of the youth and student groups was competition with other Jewish ideological currents.[37] Such competition helped the founders of the non-Zionist and non-Orthodox youth movements that were connected with the Liberal Teilkultur to overcome the initial opposition within that current to the founding of a Jewish youth movement, which many members felt was not fully compatible with the principles for which they stood. Thus, internal Jewish competition led to a gap between theory and practice within the Jewish Liberal Teilkultur.

Organizational development within those realms was not a unique Jewish phenomenon but was common to the German subcultures from the 1890s onward. In fact, the organization of youth and women, formerly neglected by the social and political organizational network, was a major characteristic of the change within German society and politics that began in the 1890s.[38]

One realm that was especially developed by the Zionists at the local level was sports. In every community that had a large enough Zionist group, an athletic society, Bar Kochba or Maccabi, was formed.[39] The most popular types were *Turnen* (team gymnastics), which had a long German tradition, soccer, track and field, and in some places also boxing. At first, local Zionist societies competed against German sports associations in their locality or region, mainly societies associated with the workers movement. As the number of Zionist organizations grew in the late 1920s, they could also compete against each other without traveling too far. In western Germany, a West German District was formed, and from 1930 onward it sponsored a soccer mini-league.

In this regard the Zionists were an exception among the ideological currents within German Jewry. For them, athletic activities had a significance beyond recreation or physical fitness. They were a vehicle for creating a new youth, far different from the traditional Diaspora Jew. Zionist athletic societies had an educational and ideological mission, and a large share of their activity was pedagogic in nature. Moreover, in the late 1920s those societies proved to be an excellent means for drawing young members to the Zionist movement. Indeed, the 1929 Zionist Delegiertentag (Delegates' Assembly) in Jena accepted a resolution calling on local groups to give "powerful support" to athletic societies and for their communal representatives to ensure financial assistance for the societies, since this was required by their "erzieherische und propagandistische Bedeutung [educational and propagandistic importance]."[40]

The Zionists were not alone in the field of Jewish sports. In large Jewish communities and many of the medium-sized ones, there were many other Jewish athletic societies. Most of these were neutral, not connected with any ideological current, and some were affiliated with the Liberal Teilkultur. Unlike the Zionists, however, the Liberals did not support sporting activities in separate Jewish athletic organizations. Most of the athletic organizational network of the Reichsbund jüdischer Frontsoldaten—Der Schild—was created during the Nazi period.[41]

The ambivalence displayed by the leadership of Liberal organizations toward Jewish sports left the field open to local initiatives that made possible a rare cooperation between Jewish sportsmen of different ideological views. On April 26, 1925, representatives of eleven Jewish athletic associations in western Germany gathered in Essen and agreed to create a large regional organization called Vintus, which was declared to be a neutral organization. The meeting was initiated by a Zionist group, Hakoah Essen, and among the eleven associations, three were Zionist, while three were affiliated with the RjF.[42] Thus, we have a field in which Jews from various groups—Zionist, Liberal, and neutral—cooperated under one umbrella organization.

But there was even more cooperation. In Dortmund, for example, the founder, and an honorary member, of the local Zionist boxing club was none other than the teacher Siegmund Nussbaum, an active Liberal leader, cofounder and vice chairman of the local group of the Vereinigung für das liberale Judentum. He founded the Zionist group in his function as Athletics Director of the RjF.[43] It is also noteworthy that the *Jüdisch-Liberale Zeitung* published reports about cooperation with the Zionists without any comment, even though such cooperation clearly contradicted the newspaper's standpoint and in spite of the warning it published itself about Zionist attempts to win the allegiance of Jewish youth through athletic activities.[44]

To understand the circumstances that made possible such cooperation, we need to explore the ambivalent relations between the Liberal leadership and such athletic groups. The leadership found it hard to encourage them, because it was the field of sports that led to controversy between Zionists and Liberals when the first Jewish athletic clubs were founded in the early twentieth century. On the other hand, it found it hard to discourage them, because it could not ignore the needs of youth for athletic activities in an increasingly antisemitic society. Thus, in this field there is evidence of cooperation between local activists of various ideological shades, without outside hostile interference or even criticism, which led to the creation in western Germany of a neutral umbrella organization encompassing Zionists and Liberals alike. I believe that the existence of non-Zionist frameworks such as Vintus and the many neutral athletic societies made it possible for the Liberals to remain—in the realm of sports—loyal to their theory and to refrain from creating an organizational system of their own. Otherwise, they might well have chosen to enter that field so that the Zionist challenge would not go unheeded.

One field that saw hardly any Jewish activity prior to 1933 was that of high culture, especially music and the theater. Under Nazi rule, when the Jews were driven out of German cultural life, wide-ranging cultural activities were organized, mainly under the auspices of the Kulturbund. There were Jewish orchestras, theatrical performances, and artistic exhibitions. There were many Jewish artists in Germany, in all areas of culture, and the Jewish presence in German cultural life as spectators, financial contributors, and benefactors, and also as active participants, exceeded by far their share of the population. But until the Nazi era there were hardly any institutionalized German-Jewish groups working in the realm of high culture and the arts.

There was one exception. The field of literature saw strong Jewish activity from among all ideological currents. There was a wide variety of books on Jewish subjects for all ages and levels, including a relatively large supply of fiction.[45] Liberals as well as Zionists had publishing houses, for example, the Philo-Verlag and the Jüdischer Verlag. Competition drove these publishers to formulate various commercial strategies, such as book clubs, to increase the circulation of their books.[46] There was also, in the Weimar era, a great expansion of Jewish libraries formed by communities, B'nai B'rith lodges, and other organizations.[47]

Descending from "high culture" to more popular forms of culture, a realm in which there was very wide activity in German associational life was that of singing. German *Gesangvereine* existed practically everywhere, even in the smallest villages, and they were very popular among the German bourgeoisie as well as among various subcultures in Germany, from Catholics to Communists. Many Jews all over Germany were active members of local bourgeois Gesangvereine. The Jews had something like an equivalent in the synagogue choirs (although those hardly belong to the field of "popular culture"),[48] but those groups were quite small and did not attract much of a following among the Jewish public. Such choirs sometimes performed in public, mainly for charity, but that happened only once or twice a year, and attendance was not always satisfactory.[49] Their popularity cannot be compared with that of the Gesangvereine among the Jews. In fact, the choirs' numbers greatly dwindled during the Weimar years.[50] The Zionists were the only ideological current within German Judaism to form some Gesangvereine, but their activity within that realm was limited. The same is even more true of most other forms of popular culture. Jews had a strong presence in German cabarets, as artists and as spectators, and a glance at the local Jewish paper of Cologne shows that local cabarets, as well as cinemas, made a real effort to advertise in its pages. Still, apart from a Jewish cabaret in Berlin—the Caftan, which was run by and for Ostjuden—there were no Jewish cabarets or cinemas in Germany. It seems that this domain, like that of high culture, was also, for most Jews, a "neutral society."[51]

Concerts and theater are public events, and in this public domain, all Jews, including Zionists and Orthodox, preferred to participate as Germans rather than as Jews. This also explains the relatively high demand for recordings of Jewish liturgical music as opposed to synagogal concerts.[52] It seems as if the emancipated German citizens of the Jewish faith unconsciously adopted Jehuda Leib Gordon's celebrated dictum of the Haskalah period and were—culturally speaking —(partly) Jewish in their homes and Germans when they went out.

The desire of pro-Zionist ideologues and artists to create a culture befitting the "Jewish Renaissance"[53] found no echo among the Zionist rank and file in western Germany. Some members of the younger generation did not like it. The young Yeshayahu Leibowitz, a member of the Zeirei Misrachi, described the theater as a symbol of degeneration and assimilation for Jewry, but he offered no practical alternative to it, except for Hebrew theater, which was inaccessible to almost all German Jews.[54]

Toward the end of the Weimar period, there was a slow change in another cultural field, that of the visual arts, especially painting. Although there were no Jewish galleries, the number of exhibitions of work by Jewish painters increased throughout Germany. Such exhibitions took place in the early years of Weimar as well, but they were quite rare.[55] In the final years of the Republic, their numbers began to grow. In this particular domain, it seems that Jewish Liberals, rather than Zionists, took the lead—not as Liberals but in their capacity as community leaders, since the communities were the main sponsors of such exhibitions. In fact, the 1930 opening of the large traveling exhibition of work by Jewish artists in Dortmund was seized on as an occasion for a meeting of the Westphalian section of the Vereinigung für das Liberale Judentum since most Liberal community leaders were present.[56] The same applies to the Jewish museums that were founded in some of the bigger communities.[57]

Jewish cultural life existed among the Ostjuden in Germany mainly, though not exclusively, in Yiddish.[58] Stage plays were performed before sympathetic audiences, and Cologne and Essen were homes to successful theatrical companies that appeared in various places throughout the Rhineland and Westphalia.[59] Ostjuden organized concerts and shows and produced records. Artists and groups from Eastern Europe also came to Germany, sometimes achieving tremendous successes, as did the then-Russian Ha-Bimah theater.[60] Zionists supported this cultural activity in principle, and encouraged it on the local level, but it had no formal connection with Zionist activities. Nor was there any Zionist content in the plays themselves.

Apparently, the world of arts, especially concerts, the opera, and theater, was for German Jews a "neutral society" where one not only could, but also should, integrate with European culture and the German people (in fact, with the German bourgeoisie), and not be segregated. The Zionists (apart from Ostjuden) were no exception in this respect.

Some of the more modern and popular arts, such as film and jazz music, did penetrate the Zionist movement before 1933. In Berlin, a small Zionist group produced short films. In Cologne, a jazz group was formed within the Bar Kochba sports group, in what was called the "music division." It is worth noting that Zionist leadership, on the national as well as on the local level, used these activities purely for propaganda purposes and showed little interest in their cultural aspects. The same is true for Liberal Jewish society: some films were produced for propaganda, such as one entitled *Friday Evening*, which promoted contributions to welfare organizations. None of these films was presented to non-Jewish audiences.

The Zionists cooperated, unofficially, with the Liberals in the expanding field of Jewish adult education. The Vereine für jüdische Geschichte und Literatur, which spread throughout Germany after the 1890s, continued their operations but had passed their peak,[61] because lectures on such subjects became a regular part of the activity of practically every Jewish organization (apart from the welfare societies). An unprecedented phenomenon was the growth of adult education institutes for Judaism, the most famous of which was Frankfurt's Lehrhaus, which set an example copied by many communities.[62] In such schools highly qualified experts delivered courses in various fields of Judaism. In comparison with the Vereine für jüdische Geschichte und Literatur, these schools required a far greater commitment in time, effort, and money for the acquisition of "a deeper knowledge of the cultural treasures of our *Gemeinschaft.*"[63] (The participants paid for the courses, which were sometimes quite expensive.)[64] We should note, however, that only a minority of the Jews participated in these schools: the largest number of participants in Frankfurt was eleven hundred in 1922/23, which represented 4 percent of the local Jewish population. In Breslau, there were five hundred participants in 1924.[65]

In these institutions, Zionists participated along with others. Although some Zionists had qualms about the spirit of such organizations and the tendency of most lectures to strengthen Jewish-German identity and reassure the Jews of their place within German culture, they did not attempt to form a competing system.[66]

The picture of Zionist activities that emerges shows them as run by and for the younger generation. The fields that were actually covered, sports and the newer art forms, as well as youth and student organizations, were fields that attracted the young, especially youth who were less "established" than the average bourgeois German Jew. The fine arts, which attracted the traditional bourgeois public and more prominent and wealthier groups, did not attract the Zionists as a group (although some Zionists were attracted to them on an individual basis).

The differences between Zionists and Liberals were quite small and were apparent primarily in sports and in the field of education. The differences became even smaller after 1929, following the deep economic crisis, when Jewish communities and organizations increased their activities among Jewish youth[67] because of a real threat that many young Jews affected by the crisis might drift away from Judaism. The controversy between Zionists and Liberals concerning the role of the Jewish community—with the Zionists claiming that the community should be a *Volksgemeinde*—was mainly theoretical; in reality there was not much difference between the two currents.[68] The real divide within German Jewry in that respect was between Ostjuden and Westjuden, and the issue was origin rather than ideology. One can hardly describe the system of Zionist organizations as a separate subculture. If there was something like a Zionist subculture, it was developed mainly by and for Ostjuden and was based on their subculture.[69]

An excellent example of the connection between Zionism on the local level and the system of *ostjüdische* organizations was the Essen Zionist *Ortsgruppe* (local chapter), which was constantly plagued by inner discord. The local Jüdische Volkspartei found it very hard to achieve any influence in communal representative bodies because of the constant conflicts among its members.[70] In June 1931, after great pressure from below, the elections committee of that party was dissolved and replaced by the *ständiger Ausschuss* (standing committee) of the Jüdische Volkspartei. The Ausschuss consisted of representatives from eight local associations and took control of the work of the Volkspartei and its elected members in community organizations. Zionist local organizations, including the Zionist Ortsgruppe itself, constituted only half of the associations that formed the committee. The other half was made up of various groups of Ostjuden; these groups had no formal political affiliation. There was the Ostjudenverband, the Verband ostjüdischer Frauen, and the Yiddish theatrical group Hazamir, which was the driving force behind the creation of the Ausschuss. Interestingly enough, the fourth group was the Verein Bikur Cholim; this is the only case I know of where a welfare society, among more than a thousand such Jewish societies that existed in Germany,[71] took a political stand and identified openly with one of the warring factions within German Jewry.[72]

An independent Zionist subculture crystallized among the younger generation of Zionists, especially among the hard core of youth movement activists. For them, the feelings of Gemeinschaft and comradeship prevalent in the German youth movement had a decisive influence. Gabriel Loewenstein from Duisburg called for the creation of a strong Zionist social life, claiming that there should be social differentiation between Zionist activists and their environment.[73] Alfred Landsberg called for an "intensity of Zionist experience" that would lead to a concept of "a great Zionist confrontation" with Jewish Liberals.[74] The new activist generation, for example, took the study of Hebrew much more seriously than did the older generations of Zionists; and particularly in the youth movements, it was beginning to create a cultural life in Hebrew through singing groups and discussion evenings. This was clearly leading toward the establishment of an almost full-fledged Zionist subculture, isolated from surrounding society; but we should mention that the numbers of those involved in such efforts were rather small.

An interesting question, when dealing with subcultures and Teilkulturen, is the extent to which members and participants in the various groups and associations identified with the ideological principles of their group. Researchers working on the socialist subculture have, since the 1980s, turned their attention to the relations between the working class and the socialist movement;[75] they claim that the influence of the socialist subculture was "limited to a strong minority among the workers, mainly in the big towns, and apparently among the more established."[76]

One study of the socialist organizations in the Weimar period classifies workers in three groups and uses, as its main indicator, attitudes toward Weimar's mass culture (especially its cabarets and Hollywood-style sentimental films), which was rejected out of hand by socialist ideologues; the study compares these attitudes with those toward socialist cultural values set by the Socialist Party and its spokesmen.[77] The categories of workers found by the study are: a) hard core activists, deeply involved in subculture activity and regular participants in it; b) supporters on the periphery who participated in the activities of the organizations of the subculture but not on as regular a basis as the first group; and c) supporters of the subculture among the group addressed by its activities, even if the degree of participation was low. While members of the first category were immune to outside influences, remaining faithful to the ideals dictated by subcultural values, the members of the other categories were influenced, to varying degrees, by the values of the surrounding society.[78]

Another study, based on the results of an oral history project about workers' lives in the Ruhr basin, revealed that workers moved freely between Catholic, Socialist, Communist, and Nazi organizations without heed to their ideology, and that they were sometimes simultaneously members of organizations with contradictory ideologies, such as those of the Nazis and the Communists. The reasons for joining an organization, or moving from one to another, were trivial: personal relations with other members, proximity to the home or favorite pub, etc. It is interesting that such people were not only members but could also be functionaries: one could be treasurer of a Nazi bowling club while belonging to a socialist Gesangverein, and vice versa.[79]

Could such circumstances exist among the Jewish organizations? I have found such examples. The secretary of the Maccabi boxing club of Cologne actually held Liberal views and supported the ideology of the Reichsbund jüdischer Frontsoldaten. He joined the Maccabi because some friends in the Zionist movement offered him the post because of his great skills as an organizer. His son, himself a non-Zionist, joined the soccer group of Maccabi Cologne because his father's friends insisted that the son of a secretary in Maccabi should be a member of that club, not a rival organization. A girl who grew up in Cologne and also joined the Zionist youth movement without being a Zionist, claimed that the main reason for choosing a youth group among the local youth was the appeal of the recruiters.[80]

Such cases of non-Zionists joining Zionist organizations for social reasons show that Zionism in Cologne was socially acceptable. Unlike the picture painted by several studies about German Jewry, or by memoirs of leading Zionists, we see that Zionists were not socially isolated. Most studies and memoirs refer to the high-ranking functionaries and leaders among the Zionists and the Liberals, and it seems that among them, tensions and mutual opposition were strong, sometimes unbearable. Those were the ideologically committed, the equivalent of the first category described by Loeshe and Walter. But at the lower levels, ideology clearly played a lesser role and was sometimes overshadowed by social considerations in the choice of an organization. The picture of the Zionists as a closely knit and isolated group, described by studies that concentrate on the higher echelons, becomes more complicated. (We must remember, however, that Cologne Jews prided themselves on the good relations between Jews of opposing world views, so this community might not be typical.)

The theoretical gap between the Zionists, who wanted to form a closely knit subculture, and the Liberals, who wanted to integrate into the surrounding German society, existed more on paper than in real life in Rhineland and Westphalia in the Weimar period. Here, theory did not match reality. There were several reasons for this. The Zionists did not have a sufficiently large and committed following to constitute a full-fledged subculture. Only members of the younger generation constituted the elements of a Zionist subculture, while most Zionists, including those who were older and wealthier, had no intention of forsaking their German cultural habits. Indeed, formation of a "German-Jewish cultural sphere" was not even discussed in that area, although the Zionists were fully aware of attempts by Socialists and Catholics to create independent cultural spheres for their members and were of course familiar with the Jewish cultural spheres created in Eastern Europe. The Zionists among the Ostjuden participated in their own cultural sphere, with hardly any attempts to give it Zionist undertones.

The Liberal Teilkultur, on the other hand, created an organizational system far wider than it originally intended. Competition with the Zionists played a major part. Jewish isolation within German society grew greater over time, and Jews were driven out of German societies, contrary to the hopes of Liberal leaders. Moreover, the socialist and communist subcultures opened their gates fully to Jewish youth. Thus, growing numbers of Jews were looking for alternatives to German Vereine, and the Liberals, faced by the dual competition from Zionists and socialists, had to offer their own alternatives. Hence, both Liberals and Zionists had their organizational networks. In the middle, in some special cases, a neutral field took its place, a field in which both sides cooperated. Such was the case in the field of sports, the Frauenbund, and the charitable network (with few exceptions, mainly organizations of Ostjuden), which developed enormously during the Weimar period and especially toward its end. The process of "Verjudung des Judentums" advanced greatly during the Weimar period, but there was no danger of a "geistiges Ghetto," as some avowed Liberals had feared. Yet the organizational networks that were created proved to be a solid base on which to construct a full-fledged subculture when the Nazis forced German Jews into a ghetto that was much worse than a spiritual one.

Notes

I would like to thank Till van Rahden for reading the manuscript of this essay and for his useful comments.

1. Siegfried Braun, "Wege und Abwege," *JLZ,* January 6, 1928, supplement, p. 4. Braun was the editor of the Cologne affiliate of the *JLZ,* the *Kölner Jüdisch-Liberale Zeitung.*

2. Monika Richarz, ed., *Jüdisches Leben in Deutschland. Selbstzeugnisse zur Sozial-geschichte 1918–1945* (Stuttgart, 1982), p. 32.

3. Braun, "Wege und Abwege," p. 4.

4. Such expressions are far too numerous to be cited here. To cite just one example, in September 1932, Kurt Blumenfeld summed up the difference between the Zionists who fought for a "new orientation of the Jews in Jewish matters," and the majority Jewish society in which "the Jewish component is deposited in the private sphere and the German component in the public sphere." See Jehuda Reinharz, ed., *Dokumente zur Geschichte des deutschen Zionismus 1882–1933* (Tübingen, 1981), pp. 539–40. For a Liberal Jew describing the Jewish medieval autonomous community as identical with the Zionist ideal of a *Volks-gemeinde,* see *JLZ,* May 18, 1928, 2nd supplement, p. 1.

5. See, for example, Ursula Mittmann, *Fraktion und Partei: Ein Vergleich von Centrum und Sozialdemokratie im Kaiserreich* (Düsseldorf, 1976), pp. 10–11, 80–81.

6. The important term "imagined communities" was used in a study about modern nationalism but can also be applied in our context. See Benedict Anderson, *Imagined Communities: Reflections on the Origins and Spread of Nationalism* (London, 1983), pp. 15–16, 32–40.

7. See Helga Krohn, *Die Juden in Hamburg: Die Politische, Soziale und Kulturelle Entwicklungen einer Jüdischen Grossstadtgemeinde nach der Emanzipation 1848–1918* (Hamburg, 1974), p. 50; Derek J. Penslar, "Philanthropy, the 'Social Question' and Jewish Identity in Imperial Germany," *LBIYB* 38 (1993): 59.

8. Peter Pulzer, *Jews and the German State* (Oxford, 1991), pp. 13–14.

9. For a brief discussion of this point, see James F. Short, "Subculture," in

The Social Science Encyclopedia, ed. Adam Kuper and Jessica Kuper (London, 1985), p. 839.

10. A. von Plato, "'Ich bin mit allen gut ausgekommen', oder: war die Ruhrarbeiterschaft vor 1933 in politische Lager zerspalten?" in *"Die Jahre weiss man nicht, wo man die heute hinsetzen soll." Faschismuserfahrungen im Ruhrgebiet*, ed. L. Niethammer (Berlin, 1983), pp. 31–33; D. Schott, *Die Konstanzer Gesellschaft 1918–1924* (Konstanz, 1990), pp. 18–21; Dirk Berg-Schlosser and Ralf Rytlewski, "Political Culture in Germany: A Paradigmatic Case," in idem, eds., *Political Culture in Germany* (London, 1993), pp. 7–8.

11. David Sorkin, *The Transformation of German Jewry, 1780–1840* (New York, 1987), esp. chapter 5. See also Trude Maurer, *Die Entwicklung der jüdischen Minderheit in Deutschland (1780–1933): Neuere Forschungen und offene Fragen* (Tübingen, 1992), chapter 10 ("Teilintegration und Ausbildung einer deutschjüdischen Subkultur"). On Sorkin, see ibid., pp. 157–60.

12. Sorkin, *Transformation of German Jewry*, p. 122.

13. Aron Hirsch Heymann, *Lebenserinnerungen*, ed. Heinrich Loewe (Berlin, 1909), p. 310.

14. Penslar, "Philanthropy," pp. 58–60, 75.

15. See, for example, *Im deutschen Reich* (henceforth *IDR*) 9, no. 10 (October 1903): 606.

16. The founders of the first Zionist Turnverein stated that they wanted to be in a Jewish Verein in order to strengthen sinking Jewish self-awareness and feelings of *Zusammengehörigkeit* (belonging). See Reinharz, ed., *Dokumente*, p. 55. The founding of Jewish athletics societies and Liberal opposition in the years 1902–1903 needs to be researched. See, in the meantime, the *Jüdisches Volksblatt* (Breslau), August 8, 1902, p. 302; September 19, 1902, p. 363; and November 21, 1902, p. 446.

17. For a more detailed discussion of this subject, see Jacob Borut, "'A New Spirit among Our Brethren in Ashkenaz.' German Jewry in the Face of Economic, Social and Political Change in the Reich at the End of the 19th Century," Ph.D. diss. (in Hebrew), Hebrew University of Jerusalem, 1991, pp. 16, 131–35, 269–74. My concept of this term is very similar to that of Till van Rahden, who uses the term "situative ethnicity," but I put more emphasis on the associational framework. See Till van Rahden, "Weder Milieu noch Konfession. Die situative Ethnizität der deutschen Juden im Kaiserreich in vergleichender Perspektive," in *Religion im deutschen Kaiserreich*, ed. Olaf Blaschke and Frank Michael Kuhlmann (Gütersloh, 1995), pp. 415–40.

18. On the Liberal Jews' perception, see Donald L. Niewyk, *The Jews in Weimar Germany* (Baton Rouge, 1980), chapter 5.

19. On the Zionist perception, see Niewyk, *Jews in Weimar Germany*, chapter 6, and Michael Brenner, *The Renaissance of Jewish Culture in Weimar Germany* (New Haven, 1996), pp. 51–52. Brenner's important book covers many of the aspects discussed in this essay (though not from the perspective of Liberal vs. Zionist activities), and I have referred to it often in the notes. See also the sources mentioned in his book.

20. List published in *KJW*, August 19, 1932, p. 3.

21. On that subject, see Trude Maurer, *Ostjuden in Deutschland 1918–1933* (Hamburg, 1986), pp. 589–604, 679–80.

22. See Uta Lohmann, "'Auf der Organisation ruht die Zukunft des Handwerks': The History and Activities of Jewish Artisans in Berlin," *LBIYB* 41 (1996): 126–33.

23. See, for example, *KJW,* October 5, 1928, p. 1.

24. On community support for Jewish schools in Hamburg, Cologne, and Frankfurt, see Brenner, *Renaissance,* pp. 61–62. His picture of the Philantropin is, however, too rosy. Reports in the Jewish press show that the school had a disappointingly small number of pupils through most of the Weimar period, and only in the last years before the Nazi takeover did the numbers rise sharply, apparently as a result of growing antisemitism. At that time, however, it was threatened with a sharp cut in community financial support; the cut was eventually reduced as a result of protests by parents. On this episode, see Henry Wassermann, ed., *Pinkas Hakehillot Germania,* vol. 3 (Jerusalem, 1992), pp. 646–47.

25. For the numbers of Jewish pupils in Frankfurt, see Paul Arnsberg, *Geschichte der Frankfurter Juden seit der französischen Revolution* (Darmstadt, 1983), vol. 2, pp. 503–504.

26. In the old Talmud Thora of Cologne, 105 of the 150 pupils were from East European families, in addition to a separate East European Talmud Thora that existed in Cologne. See *KJW,* vol. 8, no. 43, October 24, 1930, p. 4.

27. See Brenner, *Renaissance,* pp. 59–61. On Zionist support for Jewish schools, see Michael Brenner, "Die jüdische Volkspartei–nationaljüdische Gemeindepolitik in der Weimarer Republik," M.A. thesis, Hochschule für Jüdische Studien, Heidelberg, 1988, pp. 58–62.

28. See materials about this subject in the Central Zionist Archives in Jerusalem (CZA), A101/89. A governmental document counted fifteen Jewish schools in Rhineland and Westphalia (Yad Vashem Archives, JM/2963). The list is not complete.

29. See CZA, A101/79.

30. Brenner, *Volkspartei,* p. 61.

31. Ibid., p. 152.

32. Aron Sandler's memoir in *Jüdisches Leben in Deutschland,* ed. Richarz, p. 192. Brenner, *Volkspartei,* p. 152, writes that the number of pupils in Jewish schools grew fourfold between 1926 and 1930.

33. F. Walter Loesche, "Zwischen Expansion und Krise. Das sozialdemokratische Arbeitermilieu," in *Politische Teilkulturen zwischen Integration und Polarisierung: Zur politischen Kultur in der Weimarer Republik,* ed. D. Lehnert and K. Megerle (Opladen, 1990), p. 185.

34. Jewish youth movements in Germany have received wide attention from modern researchers. The most recent publications in the field are Hannah Weiner, *Youth in Ferment within a Complacent Community: Zionist Youth Movements and Hechalutz in Germany,* vol. 1 (Jerusalem, 1996) (in Hebrew); and Yehoyakim Doron, *The Jewish Youth Movements in Germany 1909–1933* (Jerusalem, 1996) (in Hebrew). See also Michael Brenner's essay (chapter 4) in this volume.

35. Marion Kaplan, *The Jewish Feminist Movement in Germany. The Campaigns of the Jüdischer Frauenbund, 1904–1938* (Westport, 1979), pp. 20–23. On the consideration for Zionist stands and feelings, see ibid., pp. 200, 206n. 8 (which is the source of the quotation).

36. Although originally founded at The Hague, this was mainly a German organization. On its founding and first activities, see *1. Bericht des Verbandes jüdischer Frauen für Kulturarbeit in Palästina* (Berlin, 1909).

37. See Marjori Lamberti, "From Coexistence to Conflict—Zionism and the Jewish Community in Germany 1897–1914," *LBIYB* 27 (1982): 62–64 (student organizations), 65–69, 71 (youth groups).

38. For the appeal to youth from the 1890s onward, see Jürgen Reulecke, "The Battle for the Young: Mobilizing Young People in Wilhelmine Germany," in *Generation Formation and Conflict in Wilhelmine Germany,* ed. Mark Roseman (Oxford, 1995), pp. 97, 100. For an overview of the whole process, see Borut, "'A New Spirit,'" chapter 3, esp. pp. 126–30.

39. See Robert Atlasz, *Barkochba: Makkabi – Deutschland 1898–1938* (Tel Aviv, 1977), esp. pp. 86–109; on local groups in Germany, see Paul Yogi Mayer, "Equality—Egality: Jews and Sport in Germany," *LBIYB* 25 (1980): 227–30.

40. *JR,* January 10, 1930, p. 21.

41. Ulrich Dunker, *Der Reichsbund jüdischer Frontsoldaten 1919–1938. Geschichte eines jüdischen Abwehrvereins* (Düsseldorf, 1977), pp. 96, 102–104, 164; Mayer, "Equality—Egality," pp. 230–31. For a local study proving this point, see the detailed description in Günter Erckens, *Juden in Mönchengladbach* (Mönchengladbach, 1988), vol. 1, pp. 559–68. On the Jewish sports movement, see also Michael Brenner's essay (chapter 4) in this volume.

42. *JLZ,* May 15, 1925, 1st supplement, p. 3; August 21, 1925, 1st supplement, p. 3.

43. *JLZ,* December 24, 1926, supplement, p. 1.

44. *JLZ,* July 16, 1926, p. 2.

45. See Brenner, *Renaissance,* chapter 5.

46. On the *Zionistischer Bücherbund,* see *KJW,* July 8, 1929, p. 6.

47. See Brenner, *Renaissance,* pp. 56–59, which refers only to community libraries. For an example of the wide range of Jewish libraries, the large majority of which were founded during the Weimar period, see Ulrike Schmidt, "Jüdische Bibliotheken in Frankfurt am Main. Vom Anfang des 19. Jahrhunderts bis 1938," *Archiv für Geschichte des Büchereiwesens* 29 (1987): 235–67.

48. See Brenner, *Renaissance,* pp. 156–59.

49. See, for example, *KJW,* April 19, 1929, p. 7.

50. Niewyk, *Jews in Weimar Germany,* p. 103. Brenner also admitted that concerts of Jewish music attracted small audiences: see *Renaissance,* pp. 219–20.

51. See Ruth Klinger, *Die Frau im Kaftan: Lebensbericht einer Schauspielerin,* ed. Ludger Heid (Gerlingen, 1992); see also *KJW,* March 14, 1930, p. 6.

52. Catalogues of record companies had no fewer than 1,325 titles of "Jewish" musical recordings in 1928, the majority of which were of liturgical music. See Brenner, *Renaissance,* p. 160. Such a large number, in relation to the number of Jews in Germany, indicates quite a substantial interest for that topic in the record market.

53. See Inka Bertz, *"Eine neue Kunst für ein altes Volk." Die jüdische Renaissance in Berlin 1900–1924* (Berlin, 1991); idem, "Politischer Zionismus und jüdische Renaissance in Berlin vor 1914," in *Jüdische Geschichte in Berlin, Essays und Studien,* ed. Reinhard Rürup (Berlin, 1995), pp. 149–80.

54. *JR,* February 14, 1930, p. 90.

55. See, for example, *JLZ* (Breslau), January 14, 1921, p. 3 (report from Görlitz).

56. See *JLZ,* March 19, 1930, p. 4 (the meeting) and p. 5 (the exhibition).

57. See Brenner, *Renaissance,* pp. 177–81.

58. See Maurer, *Ostjuden,* pp. 679–80, 717–41.

59. On the founding and activities of the Klub jüdischer Theaterfreunde in Cologne (in spite of its name, it was a regular theatrical group), see *KJW,* April 29, 1926, p. 3. On its situation during the economic crisis, see *KJW,* May 2, 1931, p. 4. On Ha-Zamir of Essen, see *JR,* August 12, 1924, p. 464. Those groups were far

more successful than the theater groups in Berlin described in Brenner, *Renaissance*, pp. 192–95.

60. On the success of its 1926 tour of Germany, not only among Ostjuden, see Brenner, *Renaissance*, pp. 190–91.

61. A Jewish paper wrote that the "once flourishing literary societies now lead only a shadowy existence" *(Kölner Jüdisch-Liberale Zeitung*, July 6, 1928, p. 2).

62. The adult education institutes in the communities, and especially that of Frankfurt am Main, are described in Brenner, *Renaissance*, chapter 3.

63. *Breslauer jüdisches Gemeindeblatt*, September 23, 1924, p. 23.

64. Franz Rosenzweig in Frankfurt had intentionally set high prices for courses in the Lehrhaus, mainly because he wanted it to be financially independent but also because he believed that "well-to-do bourgeois would rather attend expensive courses than cheap ones" (Brenner, *Renaissance*, p. 85).

65. For Frankfurt, see R. Heuberger and H. Krohn, eds., *Hinaus aus dem Ghetto* (Frankfurt am Main, 1988), p. 165; for Breslau, see the *Breslauer jüdisches Gemeindeblatt* as cited in note 63 above.

66. See Jacob Borut, "Vereine für Jüdische Geschichte und Literatur at the End of the 19th Century," *LBIYB* 41 (1996): 109–11, 113–14; for a cynical Zionist view of these societies, see Sammi Gronemann's song, published in Jehuda Reinharz, *Fatherland or Promised Land: The Dilemma of the German Jew, 1893–1914* (Ann Arbor, 1975), pp. 235–37.

67. See Brenner, *Renaissance*, p. 49; for other examples, see *JR*, February 7, 1930, p. 75, and *KJW*, February 7, 1930, p. 2.

68. During the election campaign to the Preussischer Landesverband jüdischer Gemeinden, an internal Zionist circular noted that the Liberals were using the term *Volksgemeinde* as a code word to scare voters away from the Zionists. The circular claimed that what the Zionists defined as a Volksgemeinde had become a reality in the Jewish communities, which no longer limited themselves to the older definitions of community duties: "There is no Jewish community in Germany that does not fulfill duties outside the religious sphere" (Wahlbureau der vereinigten Jüdischen Volkspartei und Konservativen Partei für Rheinland und Westfalen, Rundschreiben [circular] no. 17 [Duisburg, January 19, 1925], CZA, A101/126).

69. On the various organizations of the Ostjuden, see Maurer, *Ostjuden*, pp. 678–741.

70. See, in great detail, the documents in CZA, A101/3.

71. On the Jewish welfare societies, see Penslar, "Philanthropy."

72. On the formation of the Ständiger Ausschuss, see the *Jüdische Gemeindeblatt Essen*, June 15, 1931. Copy in CZA, A101/3.

73. *JR*, October 29, 1926, p. 610.

74. *JR*, November 12, 1926, p. 640.

75. This was part of the move toward the writing of *Alltagsgeschichte*, as the emphasis in study of the German working classes shifted from Socialist ideology and party history to the life of German workers. For a review of the outstanding works in that field, see Michael Schneider, "Gibt es noch ein Proletariat? Aktuelle Beobachtungen zu einer alten Kategorie," *Archiv für Sozialgeschichte* 28 (1988): 517–24; and see Geoff Eley, "Joining Two Histories: The SPD and the German Working Class, 1860–1914," in idem, *From Unification to Nazism* (Boston, 1986), pp. 171–99; idem, "Labor History, Social History, Alltagsgeschichte: Experience, Culture and the Politics of the Everyday—a New Direction for German Social History?" *Journal of Modern History* 61, no. 2 (June 1989): 297–343.

76. See Josef Mooser, *Arbeiterleben in Deutschland 1900–1970* (Frankfurt am Main, 1984), pp. 187–90; the quoted passage is from p. 188.

77. Peter Loesche and Franz Walter, "Zur Organisationskultur der sozialdemokratischen Arbeiterbewegung in der Weimarer Republik. Niedergang der Klassenkultur oder solidargemeinschaftlicher Höhepunkt?" *Geschichte und Gesellschaft* 15 (1989): 4, 511–36, esp. 520–21, 533–36.

78. Ibid., p. 536. On the *Solidargemeinschaft,* see also p. 534.

79. Von Plato, "'Ich bin mit allen gut ausgekommen,'" pp. 31–65.

80. Barbara Becker-Jackly, ed., *Ich habe Köln doch so geliebt . . .* (Cologne, 1993), pp. 130–31, 235–36.

7

Written Out of History

Bundists in Vienna and the Varieties of Jewish Experience in the Austrian First Republic

JACK JACOBS

In her solid and dependable book on Jewish politics in Vienna between 1918 and 1938, Harriet Freidenreich mentions in passing that there was a very small Bundist organization in Vienna between the two world wars, that this Bundist grouping never achieved political significance, and that it never played a role in the organized Jewish community, the *Israelitische Kultusgemeinde*.[1] All of these things are true. Nevertheless, it is worth devoting attention to Bundists in Vienna, because by doing so we can gain some insight into the multifaceted Jewish experience in Vienna during the period of the First Republic. I hope to demonstrate, first of all, that there was a moment in time—immediately after the end of World War I—when the Bundists of Vienna had a critical mass of followers and were on the verge of having a political impact. I also hope to demonstrate that the Bundists never played a role in the Kultusgemeinde because, first and foremost, the Kultusgemeinde was of no interest to them.[2] They were keen on playing a role not in the organized Jewish community of Vienna but in the socialist movement, and they may actually have played a marginally greater role in the latter than the existing secondary literature would lead us to believe. One of the lessons of this exercise, therefore, may well be that studies with a focus primarily on the activities of the Kultusgemeinde, while helping us to understand a key part of the Jewish experience in interwar Vienna, need to be complemented by additional works that include Jews who lived and worked outside the parameters of the organized Jewish community.

The tale of the Bundists in Vienna does not begin with the creation of the First Republic but at the turn of the century. The Bund—the General Jewish Workers' Union in Russia and Poland—was founded in Vilna in 1897 and was the largest Jewish socialist party in Europe in the first four decades of the twentieth century. The Bund was characterized, in the first few years of the twentieth century, by its commitment to Marxism, its advocacy of Jewish cultural autonomy, its secularism, and its anti-Zionism. Its intent was to organize Jewish workers and to work arm in arm with non-Jewish socialist parties in their efforts to overthrow the czar.

Because the Bund feared government oppression in Russia in the years leading up to World War I, it occasionally used Vienna as a base from which to engage in activities that would have been far riskier in the Bund's home territories. When, for example, the Bund decided in 1911 to begin to issue a legal weekly newspaper, it also decided to locate the editorial staff of the paper outside of the Russian Empire in order to escape the prying eyes of the Okhrana, the Russian secret police.[3]

One might have expected that Switzerland would be chosen as the home base for such an undertaking, for there were already a number of Bundists in Switzerland at that time. Switzerland, however, was too far from Russia to make it a feasible base of operations. The Austro-Hungarian Empire, on the other hand, bordered on Russia. It was relatively easy, moreover, to smuggle illegal political literature or confidential correspondence across the border separating the Austrian and Russian empires. Until 1910, the conservative and monarchist government of Austria had been highly suspicious of Russian revolutionaries. In the years 1910–1911, on the other hand, as tensions mounted between Austria and Russia, the Austrian police ceased harassing Russian revolutionaries in the imperial capital. It was ultimately decided, therefore, that the editors of the proposed Bundist newspaper would live in Vienna, and the editorial staff—which included many of the most prominent Bundist writers—gathered in that city by the spring of 1912. Bronislav Groser, a.k.a. Slavek, was already living in Vienna. He was joined there by Abramovich (Rafail Abramovich Rein), who arrived from Zürich; Vladimir Medem, who had been living in Geneva; and A. Litvak (Chaim Yankev Helfand), who arrived directly from the Russian Empire. All three of these men moved into Slavek's crowded and poorly furnished room on the outskirts of the city. This room thereupon became the editorial office of a new Bundist organ, *Lebensfragn*, as well as the living quarters of the editorial board; and it was in this room, crowded with books and manuscripts, that the material for the inaugural issue of *Lebensfragn* was discussed and prepared.[4] Only one issue of the periodical appeared, however, and it was promptly confiscated by the czarist regime.[5]

With so many of its leading figures already gathered in Austria, Vienna became the logical location in which to convene the Bund's ninth conference. This conference, which took place in June 1912, was attended by a total of seventeen voting delegates, including not only Abramovich, Medem, Litvak, and Slavek, but also Mark Liber (Mikhael Isaakovich Goldman), Noyakh (the party name of Yekutiel Portnoy), and Ester Frumkin, among others.[6] The Vienna gathering, in other words, while not large in size, was attended by the leading activists of the largest Jewish socialist movement of that era.

In the wake of this conference, Slavek was called back to Russia by the Bund's Central Committee. The Bundist writers remaining in Vienna, however, simply regrouped, and they tried once again to produce a legal weekly. Slavek was replaced by yet another very prominent Bundist, M. Olgin, who moved to Vienna early in 1913. The Bundists living there then reconstituted themselves as the editors of a periodical called *Di tsayt*, which was written primarily in Vienna but was officially published in St. Petersburg (where the censors were apparently much more easygoing than were those in Warsaw).

A number of the Bundists in Vienna eventually wrote highly revealing memoirs about this period of their lives. Vladimir Medem, for example, wrote that he had found Vienna to be "truly a remarkable city." Vienna, Medem continues, in a passage well worth quoting at length,

> was attractive, pulsating, hospitable. After spending no more than a few weeks there, one felt like a native. . . . In other large cities one must first develop a feeling of being at home; and the loss of that sense of strangeness frequently takes years. But I arrived a total stranger . . . and after only a short time began to feel like a denizen, to feel just as if I were at home. . . . In comparison with the condition of the Jews in Russia, life in Austria was idyllic. The depression and fear that weighed like a heavy burden upon the Jews in Russia were experienced neither in Vienna nor in Galicia. Feeling much freer, and more stalwart in their demeanor, the Jews of Austria bore themselves with a certain pride and independence. I loved Vienna deeply.[7]

Abramovich's memoirs of this Vienna period in his life are equally revealing. He points out that in addition to the members of the editorial collective there were other Bundists in Vienna during this era, and he writes that there was not only a Bundist club functioning in the city at that time but a Russian Social Democratic club, with which Trotsky, Bukharin, and Riazanov were affiliated. Moreover,

Ber Borochov, the leading theoretician of the Jewish Social Democratic Workers' Party Poalei-Zion also lived in Vienna, and Abramovich reports that he met Borochov very frequently.[8]

Every Saturday night, Abramovich indicates, the leading Austrian
Social Democrats would gather in the Cafe Central, on the Herren-
gasse, and the socialist emigrés—including the Bundists—would
gather with them. Wilhelm Ellenbogen, Rudolf Hilferding, and Otto
Bauer were regulars, Abramovich suggests. "Through this contact
with Austrian Social Democrats . . . ," Abramovich concludes, "our
colony too was pulled deeper into international politics and raised to
a higher level of political consciousness and culture."[9]

Abramovich only mentions the Bundist club of Vienna in passing.
It can be safely assumed, however, that he was referring to the
Jüdische Arbeiter-Bildungsverein "Ferdinand Lassalle," and that the
rank-and-file membership of this club was made up not of Russian
Bundists, who tended to stay in Vienna only for relatively brief periods
of time,[10] but of individuals who were members of the so-called
Galician Bund, the Jewish Social Democratic Party of Galicia, often
known as the ZPSD (the party's initials in Polish).

The ZPSD was created on May Day, 1905. While it insisted that only
an independent Jewish socialist organization would be capable of
organizing and representing the Jewish proletariat of Galicia, it clearly
wanted to affiliate itself with the All-Austrian Social Democratic
Workers Party. The executive body of the Austrian socialist party,
however, unanimously resolved that the ZPSD contradicted the Brünn
Program and the organization of the Gesamtpartei itself.[11] This rebuff
notwithstanding, the ZPSD continued its organizing activities, continued to think of itself as a social democratic group, and did in fact
succeed in attracting a significant and growing membership in Galicia.
By the time the ZPSD held its second party congress, which took place
in Lemberg in 1906, the delegates represented 2,800 organized Jewish
workers. The party claimed to represent 3,500 members in 1908, and
4,206 members in 1910. The membership grew again when, in 1911,
the grouping known as the Jewish Social Democracy in Galicia (an
affiliate of the Polish Social Democratic Party of Galicia) merged with
the ZPSD;[12] membership reached its peak when the Bundist group of
Bukovina merged with the ZPSD to found the Jewish Social Democratic Party in Galicia and Bukovina.[13]

The ZPSD—not surprisingly—was defined by its positions for Jewish national cultural autonomy, for socialism, and against Zionism. In
1910, the party coordinated a popular mass campaign to allow Yiddish
to be listed as a mother tongue in the Austrian census. Though there

were, to be sure, certain differences between the Bund in Russia and the ZPSD—including the fact that the Russian Bund was illegal for most of the period under discussion while the ZPSD was a legal organization—the positions of the ZPSD clearly paralleled those of its sister party.

The most prominent individuals sympathetic to the ZPSD in Vienna before World War I, it should be noted here, were not workers but East European Jewish students (some of whom attended the University of Vienna), such as Henryk Grossmann and Feliks Gutman.[14] Grossmann, born in Cracow in 1881 into an acculturated family, had attended a gymnasium in Cracow and subsequently furthered his education by studying law, political economy, and economic history at the universities of Cracow and Vienna. Grossmann, a leading figure in the ZPSD, was one of the eight signatories of the official letter inviting the executive committee of the Austrian Social Democratic Workers Party to the ZPSD's founding convention. He wrote for the Yiddish language organ of the ZPSD, *Der sotsialdemokrat,* published a justification of the policies of the ZPSD entitled "What Do We Want?" in 1905, and, two years later, published a short work on Bundism in Galicia.[15] However, Grossmann eventually left Galicia for an extended stay in Vienna, where, it would appear, he initially continued to maintain contact with like-minded individuals.[16]

A ZPSD member, Dr. Maurerer, initiated the formation of a ZPSD grouping in Vienna to supplement the work of the Lassalle club.[17] However, there were not enough Bundist sympathizers in Vienna before the end of World War I to create a viable political organization. Thus, it was primarily via the Ferdinand Lassalle club, which was a Jewish socialist grouping but was educationally and culturally oriented, not via the ZPSD per se, that Bundists who found themselves in the Austrian capital during the first years of the twentieth century were able to exchange and develop their views. For these socialists, the Lassalle club provided a little taste of home. On Saturday evenings or Sunday afternoons the Lassalle club would regularly sponsor lectures in Yiddish on literary, cultural, political, and economic themes.[18] The activities of the Lassalle club, however, were modest in scope. The club did not have the resources, before the beginning of World War I, to recruit East European Jews who had not already had affiliations with the socialist movement before arriving in Vienna; nor was the club capable of conducting political activities on its own.[19]

The number of Bundists in Vienna, however, jumped markedly during and immediately after the war. By the time World War I began, Vienna already had a larger Jewish population than any other city in Western or Central Europe. More than 175,000 Jews lived in the capital of the Austro-Hungarian Empire in the years immediately preceding the war, approximately 20 percent of whom had migrated to Vienna from the eastern provinces of Bukovina and Galicia.[20] The war led to a sharp increase in the number and percentage of East European Jews living in the capital, for, in the wake of the Russian invasion of Galicia, military authorities ordered civilians to evacuate from the battle zone. A large wave of refugees, made up dispropor-tionately of Jews, fled west in search of a safe haven. Seventy-seven thousand of these Jewish refugees went to Vienna—thereby (tempo-rarily) increasing the size of the Jewish population of that city by almost 50 percent.[21]

A second stream of East European Jews, which arrived several years later as the war was winding down, was made up of soldiers who had served in the Austrian army (particularly on the Italian front).[22] For many of these ex-soldiers, the road home went through Vienna. Home itself, however, proved to be temporarily inaccessible. Thus, many Galician and Bukovinian Jewish soldiers who had served in the Austro-Hungarian army and who made it to Vienna in 1918 were forced to remain in the capital while awaiting a more propitious time for continuing their journeys—thus resulting in yet another increase in the number of so-called *Ostjuden* in the capital city. A good number of the Jewish war refugees did in fact go back to their homes in the East as soon as their native provinces were evacuated by the Russians. Some 35,000 of the newly arrived East European Jews, however, were still in Vienna when the war ended in 1918.[23]

East European Jewish refugees, many of whom were Yiddish-speaking and some of whom dressed in Hasidic garb, were relatively easy to identify and encountered vicious antisemitism. As Joseph Roth later put it, "there is no harder fate than that of alien Eastern [European] Jews in Vienna. For the Christian Socials they're Jews; for the German nationalists they are Semites. For the Social Democrats they are unproductive elements."[24]

The Ostjuden found themselves ostracized not only by much of the non-Jewish population but also by many native-born Jews. The attitudes of Viennese-born Jews who had internalized the prejudices of their neighbors toward the most recent Jewish arrivals in their city were often characterized by disgust, scorn, and resentment.

During and immediately after the war, conditions in Vienna were harsh, of course, not merely for East European Jewish refugees and demobilized soldiers but for virtually everyone. Food, fuel, and hous-ing were all in short supply. As Paul Hofmann has pointed out, the Viennese were eating . . . ersatz meat made in part with the pulverized bark of birch trees, beet jam, and vile-tasting make-believe 'chocolate'. . . . Bread was mostly of cornmeal and more questionable ingredients. . . . The trouble was that the stores quickly ran out of supplies and often were unable to honor ration cards. Hungry and shivering people, mostly women, were lining up all night for the scant rations."[25]

When the war ended, unemployment grew rapidly. There were 24,000 people unemployed in Vienna in December of 1918, nearly 114,000 unemployed in February, 1919, and 131,500 in May of that year.[26]

These conditions helped fuel the radicalization of the Austrian working class. A series of strikes and mass actions took place in Vienna in 1917 and 1918, creating a potentially revolutionary situation.[27] There were 42,000 industrial workers on strike in Vienna in May of 1917. Additional strikes took place that summer in other Austrian cities. In January of 1918 the most powerful strike action in the history of the Austrian working class soon transformed itself into a mass political movement demanding immediate peace on all fronts. Nearly 1,000,000 workers throughout the Austro-Hungarian Empire participated in actions in support of this demand between January 14 and January 22.[28] *Soviets*, that is, workers councils, were founded during this period, mostly by left-wing socialists; by November of 1918, such councils existed throughout the country.[29] A revolutionary atmosphere developed in Vienna, fanned by the creation of a soviet republic in Hungary on March 21, 1919, and by the establishment of a soviet regime in Bavaria in April. The Communist Party of Austria, which was founded on November 3, 1918, repeatedly attempted to emulate the Hungarian and Bavarian examples in the months follow-ing its creation—notably on April 17 and June 15—but was soundly defeated in each of its attempts.[30]

Conditions in Vienna during and immediately after the end of World War I, the radicalization of the Austrian workers movement, events elsewhere, and the treatment of Ostjuden by both the non-Jewish and native-born Jewish populations all contributed to the alienation and radicalization of Ostjuden in Vienna. While it is all but certain that most of the East European Jews in Vienna were not sympathetic to revolutionary ideologies, a minority of the East Euro-pean Jewish refugees who had been members of the ZPSD in their Galician homes had arrived in Vienna as committed socialists. More-over, the conditions discussed above led some East European Jews who had not been socialists before the war to embrace the Bundist perspective. At this point, the Viennese Bundists created a new organization, the *Veker* [The awakener] group, which engaged in political activities and which published a periodical of the same name. "From the small, prewar, educational association of Galician and Bukovinian Bundists 'Ferdinand Lassalle'" a Bundist source later wrote, "there suddenly grew [at war's end] a powerful Bundist organization [in Vienna] with a party organ of its own, *Veker*, with large meetings, with a caucus in the Workers Council of Vienna, with a presence in all the large workers demonstrations."[31]

Lippe Rosenmann, who was born in Podhaytse [Podhajce], in eastern Galicia, around 1892, and who studied first at the University of Lemburg and later at the University of Vienna, became a leader of the Viennese Bundists during this era—the heyday of the Bund in the Austrian capital.[32] Deeply concerned with the plight of East European Jewish refugees and demobilized soldiers, Rosenmann threw himself into work on their behalf. In the years immediately following the end of World War I, whenever it was anticipated that Bundist meetings in Vienna might be disrupted by political opponents, Rosenmann, who was a good public speaker, was chosen as chair. His tact and energy, it was later reported, prevented these meetings from being broken up. When efforts were undertaken to evict war refugees from Vienna— efforts, I would stress here, that were endorsed by the representatives of the Austrian Social Democratic Workers Party to the Viennese city council—Rosenmann, an attorney by profession, was regularly a member of the delegations to various governmental entities hoping to stay these evictions.

In November of 1918, a Jewish National Council for German Austria was created.[33] The Bundist organization in Vienna initially joined this council and had five representatives on it. However, when Zionist representatives to the council endorsed a resolution demanding a "Jewish home," and when all those in the council except the Bundists voted for this resolution, the Bundists decided to leave this new Jewish nationalistic organization. "We were not able to stomach sitting at the same table as the bourgeois [representatives]," these Bundists later reported. "The Zionists exhibited such hatred toward socialism that it was simply impossible to work with them."[34] Lippe Rosenmann was given the task of reading a strongly worded condemnation of the policies of the Jewish National Council at a council session. Repeatedly interrupted by catcalls and jeers, Rosenmann denounced the members of the council as "servants of British imperialism," thereby provoking even angrier reactions from those assembled. It was only because a group of workers protected the Bundist delegates that these delegates succeeded in leaving the meeting unharmed. Significantly, the Bundists then delivered their declaration before a large meeting of Jewish workers, who warmly endorsed the stance taken by Rosenmann and his comrades.

During this same period of time, workers' councils were active in the working-class districts of Vienna, and a citywide workers' council, chaired by Friedrich Adler, met regularly. Bundists did well in initial elections to these councils. In both the 2nd and the 20th districts, there were so many Bundists elected that the Bundists were able to form their own caucuses, made up of ten or more representatives. Lippe Rosenmann was chair of the Bundist caucus in the workers council of the 20th district (which is immediately adjacent to Leopoldstadt).

The Bund had representation not only on the district-level workers councils but also on the workers council of Vienna as a whole. Its representative to the citywide council—and the most prominent Bundist in Vienna during this stormy period—was Josef Kisman. Kisman, born in Paltinose [Paltionoase], Bukovina, in 1889, was the son of pious businesspeople.[35] He studied traditional Jewish subjects until the age of fifteen, attended gymnasium in Surat, and later studied jurisprudence at the University of Vienna. From 1910 to 1912 he was co-editor of the ZPSD's organ, *Der sotsial-demokrat*. In 1913 Kisman finished his studies, and he and his wife, Leah, settled in Bukovina. They moved to Vienna after World War I.

Josef and Leah arrived in the capital at a point in Viennese history when it felt as if revolution was in the air. A biographer of Leah described this period as follows: "Day and night there marched through the streets columns of workers in military uniforms and in civilian clothing, with revolutionary chants, with revolutionary songs. The cobblestones sang of freedom and brotherhood."[36]

Josef held a number of posts. He did not merely represent the Bund on the city's workers council but also edited Vienna's first and only Bundist periodical, *Der veker*, which had an office on Novaragasse in the 2nd district. The first issue of *Der veker* appeared on June 20, 1919, only days after the Communist Party had called on the People's Militia to demonstrate, weapons in hand, in favor of an Austrian soviet republic and the Social Democratic government had responded by arresting 115 members of the Communist Party. Though it did not mention these actions in its inaugural issue, *Der veker* was harshly critical of the Austrian Social Democratic Workers Party (the SDAP), and strongly supportive of the Bolshevik regime in Moscow. "From Moscow," the introductory editorial in the first issue of this periodical begins, "there is resounding over the whole world the call of the Third International for the liberation of all humanity. Help us, working men and women, to carry this fighting call into the ranks of the Jewish proletariat in Vienna."[37] Another article in this inaugural issue accuses the SDAP of acting as if its most important task was the salvation of capitalism.[38]

There had quite clearly been a marked turn to the left by the Bundists of Vienna. When, in February of 1919, elections had been held to the Constituent National Assembly, the Bundists had worked on behalf of Social Democratic candidates by calling meetings, distributing flyers, etc. By June of that year, the Bundists were disillusioned with their erstwhile comrades who, having emerged from the elections as the single strongest party, promptly formed a coalition government with the middle-class Christian Social party.[39] *Der veker* was critical of the SDAP first of all because it believed that the leaders of the Austrian party were putting de facto brakes on the revolution rather than taking part in it. From the point of view of the Bundist organ, the SDAP had placed itself in the camp of the right-wing Social Democrats of Germany, who had allied themselves with Field Marshal von Hindenburg, suppressed the Spartacist uprising, and created an atmosphere that encouraged the murderers of Rosa Luxemburg, Karl Liebknecht, and Leo Jogiches.

The Bundist organ of Vienna was harshly critical of the SDAP not only because of the nonrevolutionary stance taken by that party but also because of the Austrian Social Democrats' opportunistic use of anti-Semitic sentiment. "They know," *Der veker* pointed out, "that in Vienna one can still drum up business with antisemitism."[40] This sense that SDAP leaders were willing to pander to antisemitism was reinforced by the fact that many Social Democrats in the Viennese City Council favored a decree expelling Galician war refugees from the capital.[41] Indeed, from the Bundist point of view, Austrian Social Democratic support for the expulsion of purportedly foreign proletarians from Vienna was one of the saddest aspects of this sordid story.[42]

In addition to participating in the Jewish National Council and in the general Workers Council of Vienna, the Bundists of Vienna at the end of World War I also participated in the Polish Workers Council, which protected the interests of both non-Jewish Polish workers and Polish Jewish workers living in Vienna. This council, which contained representatives of two Polish socialist organizations and of the Bund, stressed the solidarity of all workers, worked to prevent the expulsion of its members from Vienna, and also obtained food for it constituents during a period when many Viennese were near starvation. The council vigorously protested the expulsion of Polish and Polish Jewish refugees from Austria by sending delegations to a variety of officials and by sponsoring mass meetings and demonstrations, one of which was attended by three thousand people.[43] The Bund was represented in the Polish Workers Council by a large number of members. More-over, Leah Kisman acted as co-chair of the council itself.[44]

Leah, born in 1889, was from Kitef [Kuty], eastern Galicia, and was involved in socialist and union activities beginning with her teenage years. She was deeply affected by the revolutionary spirit she found in Vienna when she arrived in that city. "Leah acted as if intoxicated by the revolutionary tide," one source notes. "Bitter need, hunger and cold ruled Vienna. Leah felt none of this. She was ruled only by the feeling that freedom had come. Socialism was on the way. The most beautiful dreams of her youth were in the midst of being realized. It was these exalted feelings that bore her work in the Viennese organi-zation of the Bund."[45] Nearly forty years later, Leah confirmed the enormous impression this period made on her by recounting specific details of Vienna's May Day parade of 1919, in which the Jewish workers of Vienna participated as a distinct bloc, and during which short talks were held in Yiddish, Polish, and German.[46]

The Bundists of Vienna—like their counterparts in Poland, Russia, and other lands—had a strong sense of Jewish identity and were deeply concerned with the fate of the Jewish masses of Europe. The Bund, however, located the linchpin of contemporary Jewish iden-tity not in continued adherence to Jewish religious belief or practice, nor in the movement to obtain a Jewish homeland, but in secular Yiddish culture. Their Jewishness was rooted in a sense of belong-ing to a distinctive Jewish people, in empathy for Jewish workers, in the language spoken by the overwhelming bulk of East European Jews, and in the secular literature, music, and theater created in that language.

The years 1919 and 1920, which were very clearly the highpoint for revolutionary socialists of all kinds in Central Europe, were also the highpoint for the subset of this group with which we are con-cerned, Bundists in the Austrian capital. These were the years during which there crystallized a network of political, cultural, and trade union institutions, all of which were located in Vienna and all of which were supported primarily by left-wing Yiddish speakers. Along-side the Lassalle club and the Bundist periodical, there emerged a tailors' union local *all* of whose members were affiliated with the Bund,[47] and a Jewish workers' kitchen (Yidisher arbeter-kikh)[48] based in the 2nd district. A Yiddish theater group—the Freye yidishe folks-bine—not only put on performances (in the workers' kitchen and in other locations)—but also gave acting classes to members of an amateur's club.[49] A group for students (the Bund farayn fun yidish-sotsialistishe studenten un akademiker), a workers' chorus, and an educational section sponsoring courses (including one on reading and writing Yiddish and a second on "the communist program") also operated in Vienna in 1919.[50] The Yiddish writer Melekh Ravitch [Zekharye Bergner], who was close to the Jewish workers movement and who had first moved to Vienna in 1913, helped, six years later, to found a publishing firm known as Der kval (The Well) in that city.[51] This firm, initiated by Moyshe Zilburg (who had been arrested in Russia in 1912 on the false charge that he was a member of the Bund) not only issued a series of books but also published a literary monthly, Kritik.[52]

A significant number of Yiddish writers and journalists lived in Vienna in 1920–1921. All of these men, who were, to be sure, not Bundists and not united on political matters, affiliated themselves with Zilburg's new periodical.[53] It should also be noted here that the Left Poalei-Zion published a Yiddish-language periodical in Vienna, Avangard, in 1920 and 1921, and that the Right Poalei-Zion also had a Yiddish-language organ in Vienna, Unzer vort, during these same years. Harriet Freidenreich has claimed that "the capital of German-Austria, unlike Warsaw, Paris, or New York, possessed a constellation of factors that rendered the Bundist program largely irrelevant. In this German cultural mecca, Yiddish was ignored as a separate language."[54] In fact, Vienna did have a fragile Yiddish-speaking subculture—made up in part of individuals sympathetic to the Bund—throughout the era of the First Republic.[55] This subculture was, however, larger at the beginning of this era than it was at its end.

In 1920, the revolutionary fervor that had existed in Vienna as World War I ended dampened considerably. Both the Hungarian and the Bavarian soviet regimes had fallen. Moreover, a large proportion of the East European war refugees who had fled to Vienna had left by mid-1920, many under pressure to do so from the Austrian authorities. The Bundist organization shrank in size once again. In the summer of 1920, at the request of the Bundists in Czernowitz, Romania, Josef and Leah Kisman moved to that city.[56] Der veker ceased publication, and the activities of the Bundist group in Vienna diminished in intensity.[57]

Just as in Germany, Bundist activity in Austria went through a process of rise and decline during this period; however, a small number of Bundists remained in the Austrian capital.[58] Among them, the role of a spokesman was apparently taken by Lippe Rosenmann. But despite Rosenmann's efforts, the ranks of the remaining Bundists were thinned in the years of the First Republic, not only by the outflow of East European Jews from Vienna and by the ebbing of revolutionary fervor, but by a political split within the Bund itself.

The twelfth conference of the Russian Bund, held in Gomel in April of 1920, had resulted in a parting of the ways between the left- and right-wing factions within that organization. The left, which had a majority of votes at the Gomel conference, called for the Bund to enter the Russian Communist Party and renamed their organization the Kombund. The right, which walked out of the twelfth conference, established the Social Democratic Bund as an alternative organization.[59]

Similar splits in the ranks of Bundist organizations occurred elsewhere. In Vienna, for example, one faction within the Bundist organization proposed that the word "Bundist" be removed from the masthead of the party's Austrian organ (as a step, it may be presumed, toward fusing the Bundist organization in Vienna with the Communist Party). Rosenmann was initially the only member of the Bundist intelligentsia in Vienna who did not endorse this perspective.[60] At a stormy and crowded meeting chaired by Rosenmann, however, 75 percent of those voting ultimately resolved to keep the word "Bundist" in the masthead. Some of those on the losing side eventually left the mainstream Bundist movement and formed a group of their own, the members of which later tended to join the Austrian Communist Party.[61]

But Rosenmann's victory over these "Kombundists" was pyrrhic, for the Bundist group itself kept shrinking in size as ever more of its members left Vienna. Rosenmann therefore ultimately led the remaining Viennese Bundists into the Austrian Social Democratic Workers Party, in which he became an activist and lecturer.[62] He worked throughout this period as an attorney for the Austrian metal workers union and wrote for the Bundist press in Poland.[63] He died of a heart attack in 1932.

Rosenmann's death left Yitzhok Blind as the most visible Bundist in Vienna. Blind, who was born in Lemberg around 1866 into a working-class, religious home and who received a traditional education, had remained in Vienna after the bulk of the war refugees had returned to the East; he had become known as the unofficial Bundist Counsel in the Austrian capital.[64] When Polish Bundists visited Vienna in the years of the First Republic, they were received and aided by Blind.[65] Moreover, when a large delegation of Bundist youth attended an international gathering of socialist youth in Vienna in the summer of 1929, Karl Seitz, the Social Democratic mayor of Vienna, designated Blind the official host of this delegation, and Blind marched at the front of the Bundist delegation in the parade of participants in this large-scale event. Blind—who had participated in Polish socialist affairs when in Galicia and in the Hungarian socialist movement when in Budapest—was active not only in Bundist affairs while living in

Vienna but also in the Austrian Social Democratic Workers Party. Though already in his late sixties at the time of the Austrian civil war of February 1934, Blind, who had participated in the Schutzbund, was on the barricades of Vienna during the fighting. Blind was arrested after the Social Democratic fighters were defeated, spent seven months in prison, and was released with the understanding that he would leave Austria.[66] Rank-and-file Bundist workers who did not attract the attention of the authorities remained in Austria through the period of the Anschluss, if not longer.[67]

What then, are we to make of this tale? There was a Bundist presence in Vienna more or less continuously from the first few years of the present century to 1938. For much of this period, the number of Bundists was small. The individuals I have discussed, moreover, were not born in Vienna and rarely died there. Nevertheless, Vienna was more than a mere way station in their lives. Vienna was a place of refuge, sometimes for only a few months, in other cases for years or even decades. For Vienna was, until 1934, also the home of a powerful socialist and workers movement; as such, it was a source of hope and inspiration. Moreover, when the First Republic was created, there appear to have been hundreds of Bundist sympathizers in Vienna, maybe as many as a few thousand (as evidenced by the numbers of Jews reported to have taken part in certain Bundist-sponsored demonstrations). The Bundist movement took an active part in a variety of forums and had a genuine presence among the East European Jewish workers resident in that city. Like a comet in the summer sky, there was a fleeting moment during which the Bundist movement of Vienna was red-hot, visible, and moving rapidly forward. Like a comet, its tail lingered long after the movement had reached its Viennese apogee. And, like a comet, it soon went over the horizon.

Studies of Viennese Jewry that concentrate first and foremost on the Kultusgemeinde—the major constellation of organized Jews in Vienna—necessarily neglect the Bundists, for the Bundists were present in another part of the sky. The Bundists of Vienna during the years of the First Republic allied themselves not with the non-working-class Jews who dominated Jewish organizational life in interwar Austria, but rather with the socialist movement. Fritz Adler, Otto Bauer, Max Adler, and other nationally prominent Austrian Social Democrats were certainly aware of the presence of Bundists in the Austrian capital and no doubt discussed and debated political affairs with their Bundist acquaintances. The leadership of the Kultusgemeinde, on the other hand, had no contact with and no interest in the Bundists living in Vienna, nor did those Bundists have any particular interest in bourgeois German-speaking Jews. The Yiddish-speaking socialists of Vienna, I conclude, formed a separate subculture. It is only by acknowledging and studying such subcultures that we will be able to fully describe the range of Jewish experiences in German-speaking Europe between the two world wars.

Notes

1. Harriet Pass Freidenreich, *Jewish Politics in Vienna, 1918–1938* (Bloomington, 1991), p. 86. My thanks to John Bunzl, Dan Diner, Rick Kuhn, Edith Rosenstrauch, and Yfaat Weiss for their valuable comments on earlier drafts of this paper.

2. In making this claim I do not mean to suggest that Bundists elsewhere were never interested in participating in the organized Jewish community. The Bund in interwar Romania and interwar Poland did in fact run lists of candidates in specific Jewish communal elections.

3. Vladimir Medem, *The Life and Soul of a Legendary Jewish Socialist,* ed. and trans. Samuel A. Portnoy (New York, 1979), p. 481.

4. Sophie Dubnow-Erlich [Sofie Dubnov-erlikh], "Bronislav groser," in *Doyres bundistn,* ed. Jacob S. Hertz [I. Sh. Herts], vol. 1 (New York, 1956), pp. 332–33.

5. Medem reports that a second issue was prepared. When it became clear that censors in Warsaw would not permit the distribution of *Lebensfragn,* a decision was made to publish the material that had been gathered for this second issue in the form of an anthology. See Medem, *Life and Soul,* p. 484.

6. S[ophie] Dubnow-Erlich [S(ofie) Dubnov-erlikh], "In di yorn fun reaktsie," in *Di geshikhte fun bund,* vol. 2, ed. G. Aronson, S. Dubnow-Erlich [S. Dubnov-erlikh], J. S. Hertz [I. Sh. Herts], E. Nowogrudski [Novogrudski], Kh. Sh. Kazhdan, and E. Scherer [Sherer] (New York, 1962), p. 585.

7. Medem, *Life and Soul,* pp. 482–83.

8. Raphael Abramovitch [Rafail Abramovich Rein], *In tsvey revolutsies. di geshikhte fun a dor,* vol. 1 (New York, 1944), p. 350.

9. Ibid., p. 351. Cf. Helmut Gruber, *Red Vienna: Experiment in Working-Class Culture, 1919–1934* (New York, 1991), p. 33.

10. Medem, for example, left Vienna for Kaunas (Kovno) at the end of June 1913.

11. Jack Jacobs, *On Socialists and "The Jewish Question" after Marx* (New York, 1992), p. 92.

12. Y[ankef] Bros, "Tsu der geshikhte fun der i.s.d.p. in galitsie," *Royter pinkes. tsu der geshikhte fun der yidisher arbeter-bavegung un sotsialistisher shtremungen bay yidn,* vol. 2 (Warsaw, 1924), pp. 46ff.; V[iktor] Shulman, "25 yor. tsum yobiley fun der yidisher s. d. partay in galitsie ("galitsianer bund") 1–ter may 1905–30," *Naye folkstsaytung,* April 30, 1930, p. 5.

13. Yoysef Kisman, "Di yidishe sotsial-demokratishe bavegung in galitsie un bukovine," in *Di geshikhte fun bund,* vol. 3 (New York, 1966), p. 460.

14. On Gutman, who served as vice-chairman of the Union of Socialist Students, see Feliks Gutman, "An arraynfir-vort in shaykhes mit der antshteyung un antviklung fun z.p.s.d. bizn yor 1911," p. 16, typescript, Bund Archives of the

Jewish Labor Movement [henceforth Bund Archives], YIVO Institute for Jewish Research, New York. Gutman eventually emigrated to Mexico (Kisman, "Di yidishe sotsial-demokratishe bavegung," p. 372). Though Grossmann appears to have studied at the University of Vienna with Carl Grünberg, the university has no extant records corroborating that Grossmann was ever formally enrolled as a student (Rick Kuhn to Jack Jacobs, February 21 and 26, 1996).

15. See Willem van Reijin and Gunzelin Schmid Noerr, eds., *Grand Hotel Abgrund. Eine Photobiographie der Frankfurter Schule* (Hamburg, 1990), p. 48; Zalmen Reyzen, *Leksikon fun der yidisher literatur, prese un filologie,* vol. 1 (Vilna, 1926), p. 616.

16. In 1910, for example, Grossmann was scheduled to deliver a lecture on the economic history of Jews in Galicia to the Ferdinand Lassalle club (Bund Archives, MG 2 #130).

17. Gutman, "An araynfir-vort," p. 15.

18. Moyshe Olgin—who became famous years later as the editor of New York's Yiddish-language, pro-Communist daily the *Morgn frayhayt*—was invited to deliver such a lecture in 1910, as were less well-known speakers such as J. Klammer, M. Krüger, M. Korkes, K. Haskler, H. Frenkel, T. Weinstein, and L. Weinstein (Bund Archives, MG 2 #130).

19. "Fun unzer organizatsie," *Der veker,* July 4, 1919, p. 7. For a discussion of factors that may help to explain the relative weakness of the Jewish socialist movements of Vienna before World War I, see Klaus Hödl, *Als Bettler in die Leopoldstadt. Galizische Juden auf dem Weg nach Wien* (Vienna, 1994), pp. 172–77. Unfortunately, Hödl's discussion is marred by errors, such as his claim that Engelbert Pernerstorfer was a Jew (ibid., p. 175).

20. Marsha L. Rozenblit, *The Jews of Vienna, 1867–1914: Assimilation and Identity* (Albany, 1983), pp. 5, 17, 19.

21. Bruce F. Pauley, "Political Antisemitism in Interwar Vienna," in *Jews, Antisemitism and Culture in Vienna,* ed. Ivar Oxaal, Michael Pollak, and Gerhard Botz (London, 1987), p. 153. Cf. Beatrix Hoffmann-Holter, *"Abreisendmachung." Jüdische Kriegsflüchtlinge in Wien 1914 bis 1923* (Vienna, 1995).

22. Y[oysef] K[isman], article on Leah Kisman, in *Doyres bundistn,* ed. Jacob S. Hertz [I. Sh. Herts], vol. 3 (New York, 1968), p. 310.

23. Since the overwhelming bulk of the Galician and Bukovinian Jews who arrived in Vienna during the war were impoverished, and since Vienna had experienced a severe housing shortage even before the crisis caused by the war, the Jewish refugees were generally forced to squeeze into substandard housing with relatives and friends. In the Viennese district known as Leopoldstadt—the so-called Matzoh Island—into which many of these Ostjuden moved, the average density reached six individuals per room (George E. Berkley, *Vienna and Its Jews: The Tragedy of Success, 1880s–1980s* [Cambridge, 1988], p. 138).

24. As quoted in Robert S. Wistrich, "Social Democracy, Antisemitism and the Jews of Vienna," in *Jews, Antisemitism and Culture in Vienna,* ed. Oxaal et al., p. 111.

25. Paul Hofmann, *The Viennese: Splendor, Twilight, and Exile* (New York, 1988), p. 161.

26. Charles A. Gulick, *Austria from Habsburg to Hitler,* vol. 1 (Berkeley, 1980), p. 70.

27. Members of the Poalei-Zion played leading roles in the strike of January 1918 (John Bunzl, *Klassenkampf in der Diaspora. Zur Geschichte der jüdischen Arbeiterbewegung,* Schriftenreihe des Ludwig-Boltzmann-Instituts für Geschichte

der Arbeiterbewegung, vol. 5 [Vienna, 1975], pp. 126ff.; Hans Hautmann, *Die verlorene Räterepublik. Am Beispiel der Kommunistischen Partei Deutschösterreichs* [Vienna, 1971], passim). It should be pointed out, however, that the office of the Poalei-Zion was apparently also used by many activists who did not actually belong to that movement (John Bunzl, "Arbeiterbewegung, 'Judenfrage' und Antisemitismus. Am Beispiel des Wiener Bezirks Leopoldstadt," *Bewegung und Klasse*, ed. G. Botz, H. Hautmann, and H. Konrad [Vienna, 1978], p. 752). Hautmann's discussion of the history of the Poalei-Zion (in *Die verlorene Räterepublik*, p. 167)—in which he asserts, for example, that the ZPSD was "the Galician section of the Austrian party" and that a leftist group made up primarily of members of the ZPSD crystallized within the Poalei-Zion around 1917—contains a series of historical misunderstandings.

28. Hans Hautmann and Rudolf Kropf, *Die österreichische Arbeiterbewegung vom Vormärz bis 1945. Sozialökonomische Ursprünge ihrer Ideologie und Politik*, Schriftenreihe des Ludwig-Boltzmann-Instituts für Geschichte der Arbeiterbewegung, vol. 4 (Vienna, 1974), pp. 122–23.

29. Gulick, *Austria*, p. 71; Helmut Gruber, *International Communism in the Era of Lenin: A Documentary History* (Garden City, 1972), pp. 177ff.

30. Anson Rabinbach, *The Crisis of Austrian Socialism: From Red Vienna to Civil War* (Chicago, 1983), pp. 23–24; Hofmann, *The Viennese*, p. 165.

31. Yoysef Kisman, "Gefaln a kemfer. tsum toyt fun kh' dr. l. rozenman," *Naye folkstsaytung*, May 29, 1932, p. 3.

32. Ibid.

33. Freidenreich, *Jewish Politics in Vienna*, p. 38.

34. "Fun unzer organizatsie," *Der veker*, July 4, 1919, p. 8.

35. J[acob] S[holem] Hertz [I. Sh. Herts], article on Yoysef Kisman, in *Doyres bundistn*, vol. 3, pp. 306–308.

36. "Leah kisman," unpublished typescript, p. 10, Bund Archives, ME 40–92.

37. "Tsu unzere lezer un fraynd!" *Der veker*, June 20, 1919, p. 2.

38. M.R., "Revolutsionere shturmen," *Der veker*, June 20, 1919, p. 3.

39. "Fun unzer organizatsie," *Der veker*, July 4, 1919, p. 8.

40. "Politishe shtrikhen," *Der veker*, July 4, 1919, p. 3.

41. See Hoffmann-Holter, "*Abreisendmachung*," pp. 190ff., for a full discussion of Austrian Social Democratic policies toward the Jewish war refugees.

42. "Di oysvayzungen," *Der veker*, September 24, 1919, p. 3.

43. "A masenferzamlung akegen di oysvayzungen," *Der veker*, August 15, 1919, p. 6; "Unzer masenferzamlung vegen di oysvayzungen," *Der veker*, September 24, 1919, p. 4.

44. Y[oysef] K[isman], article on Leah Kisman, in *Doyres bundistn*, vol. 3, pp. 310–11.

45. "Leah kisman," unpublished typescript, op. cit., p. 10.

46. Leah Kisman, "Ershter may in kamf far fridn (a bintl zikhroynes)," *Der veker* (New York), May 1, 1958, p. 15.

47. "Fun unzer organizatsie," *Der veker*, July 4, 1919, p. 8.

48. *Der veker*, November 21, 1919, p. 8.

49. *Der veker*, October 24, 1919, p. 8; Mendl Naygreshl, "Di moderne yidishe literatur in galitsie," *Fun noentn over*, vol. 1 (New York, 1955), pp. 395–97; Sh. I. Harendorf, "Yidisher teater in estraykh tsvishn di yorn 1918–1938," *Yidisher teater in eyrope tsvishn beyde velt-milkhomes*, vol. 2 (New York, 1971), pp. 242–44.

50. *Der veker*, December 5, 1919, p. 8.

51. On Ravitch, see Reyzen, *Leksikon*, vol. 4 (1929), p. 85.

52. On Zilburg, see Reyzen, *Leksikon*, vol. 1, p. 1070.

53. *Kritik*, February 25, 1921, p. 2; Naygreshl, "Di moderne yidishe literatur," pp. 383–87; Melekh Ravitsh, *Dos mayse-bukh fun mayn lebn. fun di yorn: 1908 biz 1921* (Buenos Aires, 1964), pp. 486–99. For additional information on the Yiddish writers of Vienna, see Sol Liptzin, *A History of Yiddish Literature* (Middle Village, 1972), pp. 238ff.

54. Freidenreich, *Jewish Politics in Vienna*, p. 86.

55. The best recent study of the Yiddish-speaking writers and cultural institutions of Vienna, Gabriele Kohlbauer-Fritz's *In a Schtodt woss schtarbt. In einer Stadt, die stirbt. Jiddische Lyrik aus Wien* (Vienna, 1995)—from which I have benefited greatly—notes that "despite the difficult political and legal situation of the 'Ostjuden' in Vienna, in the early 1920s there developed in the coffee houses and cellar theaters of the 2nd and 20th districts a flourishing Yiddish cultural scene. Yiddish periodicals were published and presses established; the Yiddish theater, which had already begun in Vienna some decades previously, experienced a florescence; and even Yiddish films were produced in Vienna" (p. 12). A Yiddish weekly, *Di naye tsayt*, began publishing in Vienna in 1924. A monthly, *Yidish*, began to appear in the Austrian capital in 1928. Yiddish books were published in Vienna as late as 1938. Among the Yiddish writers who remained in Vienna in the 1930s were Moyshe Gros, Ber Horovits, Melekh Khmelnistki, and Mendl Naygreshl. The silent films starring Yiddish actors and actresses that were produced in Vienna were released primarily between 1918 and 1923 (J. Hoberman, *Bridge of Light: Yiddish Film between Two Worlds* [New York, 1991], pp. 59–71).

56. The Kismans later emigrated to New York, where Kisman worked for the Jewish Labor Committee. Leah died in 1964, and Yoysef died in 1967.

57. Of course, not only those in the Bund but also a susbstantial portion of the Yiddish-speaking community in which they had operated tended to leave—or were forced out of—Austria around this time or shortly thereafter. Melekh Ravitch left Vienna in 1921 and settled in Warsaw. Zilburg moved to Vilna in 1923.

58. Khayim Zakhariash, "Di bundishe grupn in daytshland beys der velt-milkhome," *Naye folkstsaytung*, November 19, 1937, p. 23. My thanks to Gertrud Pickhan for alerting me to the existence of this source. East European Jews living in Berlin during World War I founded a Perets *farayn*—named after the Yiddish writer Yitzkhok Leybush Perets—as a literary organization devoted to education; it attracted from seven hundred to eighteen hundred members. Bundists dominated this group in its period of greatest strength. The question as to why the Bundists seem to have been proportionately stronger in Berlin than in Vienna in 1920 is relatively easy to answer. The East European Jews in Vienna were primarily from Galicia—which was not an area dominated by the Bund. The East European Jewish workers in Berlin, on the other hand, were primarily from the Russian Empire, which was, of course, the Bund's home base.

Just as they did in Austria, the Bundists in Germany launched a periodical after the end of World War I. The first issue of *Der morgnshtern. tsaytshrift far politik un sotsiale fragn* was dated December 12, 1920. One Anna Stern—otherwise unknown—was listed as "Verantwortlicher Redakteur." The first issue reports on the second conference of Bundist groups in Rheinland-Westphalia, which took place on November 28, 1920, in Essen; it was attended by representatives of Bundist groups in Essen, Duisburg, Hamburg, Elberfeld, and Gladbeck, among other cities. Representatives of groups from such areas as Düsseldorf, Dortmund, and Herne were unable to attend. "The conference showed," the report in *Der morgnshtern* concluded, "that there exists among the Jewish workers who have emigrated an attachment to the Bund, which will lead them, in closed ranks, to communism, to the Third International."

Neither the Bundist periodical nor the local Bundist organizations represented at the 1920 Essen conference survived long into the Weimar years.

59. Zvi Y. Gitelman, *Jewish Nationality and Soviet Politics: The Jewish Sections of the CPSU, 1917–1930* (Princeton, 1972), p. 195.

60. "Kh' dr leyb roz[e]nman," *Naye folkstsaytung,* May 20, 1932, p. 9.

61. Naygreshl, "Di moderne yidishe literatur," p. 388.

62. Jacob S. Hertz [I. Sh. Herts], "Dr. lipe rozenman," in *Doyres bundistn,* vol. 3, pp. 248–49.

63. See, for example, L. Rosenmann, "Marsz na Wieden," *Nasza Walka* 1, nos. 2–3 (1928): 54–56.

64. "Kh' yitskhok blind 70 yor alt," *Naye folkstsaytung,* October 16, 1936, p. 10; B. Bigelmeyer, "52 yor in der sotsialistisher bavegung. tsum 70-yorikn yobiley fun kh' y. blind," *Argentiner lebn,* October 20, 1936, p. 4; Maks Speyzer, "Yitkhok blind—der revolutsiener un sotsialistisher veteran," *Argentiner lebn,* October 20, 1936, p. 5; Jacob S. Hertz [I. Sh. Herts], "Yitskhok blind," in *Doyres bundistn,* vol. 3, pp. 246–48.

65. Three hundred members of the Bundist youth group of Poland, the Tsukunft, and of the Polish Bundist sports organization, Morgnshtern, visited Vienna in 1931 in order to take part in the second international workers sports olympics (I. Sh. Herts, "Der bund in umophengikn poyln, 1926–1932," in *Di geshikhte fun bund,* vol. 5, p. 136). In the same year, a delegation of Bundists took part in a congress of the Labor and Socialist International, which was held in Vienna (ibid., p. 84).

66. Blind went from Vienna to Poland and later moved to Argentina, where he died in 1947.

67. For example, Avrom Yitskhok Khaykin, chair of the Bundist caucus in the workers council of Vienna's 2nd district, the district that had the highest concentration of East European Jews ("Avrom yitskhok khaykin," *Unzer tsayt,* January 1970, p. 37). Khaykin arrived in Vienna in 1914 and did not leave the city until after the Nazis had come to power. He emigrated to New York in September 1939. He was connected with the Bundist organization in New York and was also a member of the Workmen's Circle. Khaykin died in 1969. After the suppression of the SDAP, Bundists allegedly did work within Jewish organizations and even participated in the last prewar elections to the Kultusgemeinde (Edith Rosenstrauch to Jack Jacobs, February 22, 1996).

8

Jewish Ethnicity in a
New Nation-State

*The Crisis of Identity in the
Austrian Republic*

MARSHA L. ROZENBLIT

When he arrived in Vienna in late 1918 to register at a university already filled with fellow demobilized soldiers, the Galician Jew Joachim Schoenfeld noticed that "everyone was in a hurry to finish his education, get a job, marry, and forget the events of the war. And so was I."[1] Such notions—the desire to return home, resume work, and create or recreate family life after the horrors of World War I— were widespread, at least among those who wrote memoirs of their experiences.[2] Minna Lachs, whose family had fled to Vienna from Galicia in 1914 when the Russians invaded, recalled her mother's response when her father returned from the army in November 1918. Laughing and crying at the same time, she sobbed, "I could no longer bear it alone. . . . Now that you are here, it will all be better." Lachs's father, however, realistically replied, "It will first become worse."[3]

The father's prescience was not just about the impact on his family of the food shortages, overcrowded housing conditions, and terrible economic difficulties of the immediate postwar years. The devastation of war, followed by the deprivations and dislocations of the next few years, would create a prolonged crisis all over Central Europe. Minna Lachs's father probably also worried about the disastrous conse-quences for the Jews of the collapse of the Habsburg monarchy. As a Galician Jew who had just served in Austria-Hungary's multinational army, he may have sensed not only that the postwar turmoil would lead to an upsurge in antisemitism but also, and more importantly, that the Jews of the former monarchy now faced a grave crisis of identity. No longer members of a relatively tolerant multinational society, the Jews now confronted theoretically homogeneous nation-states that demanded a very new kind of loyalty from them.

Jews in the new republic of Deutsch-Österreich (German-Austria, as it was known at first) faced a serious dilemma. The new state, founded at the end of October 1918, saw itself as German and expected that its citizens consider themselves members of the German nation, the German *Volk*. Indeed, the majority of people in the new state, largely consisting of the German-speaking Habsburg hereditary lands, sought *Anschluss*, union with Germany, a merger that the victorious powers at Versailles would not permit.[4] Jews in the new Austria, essentially the Jews of Vienna and later the Burgenland, had adopted the German language and culture as they modernized in the nineteenth century. But they did not necessarily regard themselves as members of the German Volk. Instead, they had developed an identity as "Austrians," as members of the German *Kulturnation*, as Viennese, and as Jews.[5] They now had to reconstruct a new identity in a state that demanded the unity of national, cultural, ethnic, and political loyalty. Austria-Hungary had allowed the Jews the luxury of separating these loyalties, but the new nation-state would not prove so tolerant. Indeed, Jews had to reconstruct a new identity against the backdrop of rising antisemitism and radical nationalist insistence that the Jews could never form part of the German or German-Austrian nation even if they wanted to.[6]

Austrian Jews responded to the crisis by emphasizing their Jewish ethnic identity. Despite intense identification with German culture, Austrian Jews could not define themselves as Germans in the national or ethnic sense, as members of the German Volk. Most Jews hoped that they could continue to define themselves as they had in the days of the Habsburg monarchy: as Austrians by political loyalty, as Germans by cultural affinity, and as Jews in an ethnic sense. Since the new Austria did not develop a national identity of its own, many Jews hoped that the old Habsburg formula might work. Unfortunately it could not. Without a viable new overarching Austrian political identity to replace the old Habsburg Austrian one, Jews, who did not see themselves as ethnic Germans, increasingly identified primarily as Jews, as members of the Jewish people. The reality of antisemitic exclusionism only intensified their commitment to a Jewish ethnic identity. Jews regularly asserted their loyalty to the new Austrian Republic and their full participation in German culture, but they also insisted on a Jewish ethnic identity, not a German national one. As antisemitism grew and the Austro-German polity increasingly shunned Jewish participation, Jews responded by asserting their Jewish ethnic identity even more vigorously. In this context Jewish nationalism flourished.

At the same time, the interwar years also witnessed a retreat into private life. After the devastations of war, the turmoil of the postwar years, and the uncertainties of national-political identity for all Austrians, it was only natural that people sought comfort and identity within the family. In the case of the Jews, the combination of political crisis and public hostility made the family an especially alluring retreat.

In order to understand the crisis that confronted Austrian Jews in 1918–1919, it is best to begin with a short description of Jewish identity in the Habsburg monarchy. In the decades after their emancipation in 1867, the Jews of Austria-Hungary, and in particular the Jews of the Austrian half of the monarchy, had developed a comfortable tripartite identity that had allowed room for a large measure of Jewish ethnic assertiveness. Jews all over Austria insisted that they were Austrian by political loyalty, German or Czech or Polish by cultural identity, and Jewish by ethnic attachment. Such a tripartite identity had been made possible by the very nature of Austria itself, which was not a nation-state like Germany or France where national and political loyalties were co-terminous.

Austria-Hungary was a dynastic state that contained eleven recognized nationalities or *Volksstämme*—Germans, Hungarians, Czechs, Poles, Ruthenes, Italians, Romanians, Slovaks, Slovenes, Croats, and Serbs.[7] Hungarian nationalism had been assuaged by the compromise agreement of 1867, which granted Hungary the quasi-sovereignty that allowed it to function as a nation-state. Thus, Hungarian Jews affirmed their membership in the Magyar nation as they embraced Magyar culture and Hungarian patriotism. In "Austria"—which included such diverse regions as the German-speaking Habsburg hereditary lands; the Czech- and German-speaking provinces of Bohemia and Moravia; Polish and Ruthene Galicia; German, Ruthene, and Romanian Bukovina; Italian Trieste; and Croatian and Slovene Dalmatia—Jews eagerly asserted their Austrian state patriotism, even developing a veritable cult of the emperor, Franz Joseph.[8] They remained devoted to the Austrian *Gesamtstaat* to the very end, recognizing that only it protected them from the fierce antisemitism that raged among the radicals in all the national camps. Yet this Austrian loyalty, a loyalty shared perhaps only by the emperor, his army, and the bureaucracy, did not require them to adopt an Austrian national identity, which did not exist.[9]

Moreover, although modernizing Jews in Habsburg Austria warmly adopted German or Czech or even Polish culture, they did not thereby become Germans or Czechs or Poles in the national sense. Jews in

Vienna or Prague, for example, spoke German, loved the German classics, regarded German culture as superior to all others, but did not really consider themselves Germans, members of the German Volk.[10] Jews in Austria identified as members of the Jewish people. Although the authorities did not recognize the Jews as one of the *Völker* of Austria,[11] and most modern Jews rejected the Zionist claim that the Jews formed a nation, Jews in pre–World War I Austria, traditional and modern alike, articulated a large measure of Jewish ethnicity. Jewish leaders insisted that the Jews were members of the Jewish *Volk* or *Stamm* (lit., "tribe," best rendered as "community of common descent"), even if their defense of Jewish peoplehood varied in accordance with their ideologies. Modern rabbis surely emphasized the religious dimensions of Jewish solidarity, while other spokesmen understood Jewish cohesiveness in terms of history and fate. Zionists insisted that the Jews were a nation with political aspirations, while the religious traditionalists simply asserted that the Jews were a nation in exile awaiting divine redemption. But virtually all Jews agreed that the Jews formed a coherent albeit unusual group in Austria.

The nature of World War I itself strengthened this tripartite identity of the Jews. Indeed, in Austria, as in most belligerent countries, the early years of the war witnessed an outpouring of patriotic fervor, not least among the Jews. Austrian Jews eagerly participated in the war effort, convinced that the struggle against Russia was waged both on behalf of the Austrian state and the Jewish people. After all, Russia had invaded Austria in August 1914, occupying the provinces of Galicia and Bukovina, from which hundreds of thousands of Jews had to flee because of real or feared persecution at the hands of the Russian army. The struggle against Russia was therefore a "just cause" against the enemy of Austria and the Jewish people. World War I became a war of revenge against the Russia that persecuted the Jews and a war of liberation for the Jews of Galicia and Eastern Europe. Jews fought for Austria and participated actively on the home front, confident of the identity of Austrian and Jewish war aims. They regarded the charitable assistance they extended to the Galician Jews who had fled to Bohemia, Moravia, and Vienna as a simultaneous act of Jewish charity and Austrian patriotism. While sharing the ultimately naive hope of German Jews that the war would end antisemitic animosity, they also hoped that the brotherhood of arms would end the nationality conflict in Austria.[12]

Unfortunately, the resumption of normal parliamentary activity in Austria in May 1917 led to an intensification of the nationality conflict. At the same time, the relaxation of the *Burgfrieden,* the internal political truce, at a time of increasing food shortages and widespread war weariness led to a proliferation of antisemitic invective. Fearful of both the rise of antisemitism and nationalist agitation, the Jews fervently hoped for the continuity of the multinational Austrian state as their only protection from nationalist antisemitism. They regularly reiterated their loyalty to the Austrian Gesamtstaat and its Habsburg rulers. In February 1918, for example, the Viennese Liberal Jewish newspaper, the *Österreichische Wochenschrift,* noted that the war had irrefutably proven the "unbroken loyalty and unshakable devotion" of the Jews, who were the "state-upholding element *[staatserhaltendes Element]* of proven reliability."[13] By July 1918 the paper conceded that the Jews were "the only Austrians in the monarchy loyal to the state."[14] In October, when the dismantling of the old Austrian state appeared imminent, the editor reminded his readers that the Jews had always been "the strongest, most trustworthy, most unconditional supporters of the state and the dynasty," and he expressed his anxiety over the consequences for the Jews of the possible dissolution of the monarchy. In particular the editor feared for the safety of the Jews of Galicia now that they were at the mercy of the Poles.[15] Orthodox Jews likewise fervently hoped for the continuity of Austria down to the very end because they understood that only it "corresponded to the interests and desires of the Jews of the monarchy, whose salvation is also their salvation."[16] Only the central government, the Orthodox newspapers insisted, could protect the Jews from the scourge of antisemitism, and only it allowed the Jews the proper room to develop their own culture.[17]

Zionists as well desired the continuity of the multinational monarchy till the very end. Like the Liberals, they feared that antisemitism would proliferate, especially in Galicia, without the monarchy's protection. In addition, they wanted to keep the monarchy united because the multinational state suited their political agenda far better than a German-Austrian nation-state ever could. Zionists shared President Wilson's love affair with the concept of national self-determination, and they sought to win recognition for Jewish nationality in Austria. Needless to say, such recognition was only plausible in old Austria, which might conceivably be reorganized along national lines. New nation-states, however, would leave no room for Jewish nationalist aspirations. Thus, in June 1918, the *Jüdische Zeitschrift,* the organ of the Austrian Zionist organization, insisted that "the idea of the Austrian state is an indubitable necessity."[18] In line with their 1906 Cracow program, the Zionists continued to urge that Austria be reorganized as a federation of nationalities that would recognize the Jews as an autonomous nationality.[19] The leading spokesman for such a reorganization was Hermann Kadisch. In September 1918 he issued a plea for the continuity of the Austrian multinational state because only it could serve "the common interests of all citizens for cultural and social progress" and guarantee their rights. Arguing that territorial autonomy was a bad idea, he supported the Social Democratic goal of an Austrian federation of nationalities based on personal affiliation.[20]

When the monarchy finally collapsed at the end of October 1918, *Österreichische Wochenschrift* columnist Heinrich Schreiber wondered if the day on which Deutsch-Österreich was created would be a new ninth of Av, a day of Jewish mourning. While the nations of Austria-Hungary cheered for their newly won rights of national self-determination, Schreiber expressed his grief over the dissolution of the monarchy:

> We acknowledge openly and honestly the deep pain in our hearts about the gloomy and painful transformation and upheaval. It is with the deepest sadness and depressed feelings that we bid farewell to the united Fatherland, standing shocked before the grave of old, familiar, honorable memories and feelings, holier and more cherished traditions that a day of calamity has dashed into ruins. We can only take comfort from the fact that we Jews are guiltless for this event.[21]

Galician-born Viennese Jew Erna Segal recalled later in her memoirs how sad she felt the day the Republic was declared: "We were raised with deep respect for the dynasty, we loved Austria and its rulers and now with one blow everything had come to an end. What now? I asked myself."[22] She and her family worried greatly about the fate of the Jews in the new, uncertain political situation.[23]

Despite changed conditions in November 1918 the Zionists continued to seek Jewish national self-determination in the Austrian successor states. Zionists hastily created Jewish National Councils to demand that the new states recognize the Jews as a nation and accord them autonomy and minority rights, including the right of representation in all elected bodies.[24] So eager were Zionists in their new task that they forgot to mourn the Austrian state for whose continuity they had so recently prayed. In Czechoslovakia, itself a multinational state of Czechs, Slovaks, Germans, Hungarians, and Jews, the Jewish National Council at least had some hope for official recognition of Jewish national rights. But the Jewish National Council in Deutsch-Österreich persisted in demanding official recognition of the Jewish nation even though such recognition was never even remotely possible. From its inception on November 4, the Council demanded that the new state recognize the Jews as a nation and guarantee them national rights in addition to individual rights as citizens.[25] Many Zionists recognized immediately that such national rights were impossible in the new nation-state, but others, especially Robert Stricker, the leader of Viennese Zionists in the interwar period, remained utterly committed to a program of Jewish national rights in Austria.[26]

Such demands reflected the fact that the Zionists continued to adhere to the notion that they could be Austrian by political loyalty, German by cultural affiliation, and Jewish by nationality even when the political basis for such a tripartite identity had disintegrated. The Jewish National Council of Deutsch-Österreich, under the leadership of Robert Stricker, insisted that Jewish nationalists valued German culture and the German people "in whose language we think and feel" and certainly would always be loyal citizens of the new state.[27] Despite this cultural Germanness, the Jewish nationalists did not regard themselves as members of the German Volk. Indeed, the Hebrew title for the Jewish National Council of Deutsch-Österreich—Moetzet Leumit LiYhudei Austria Ha'Ashkenazit[28]—which avoided the modern Hebrew term for German (Germanit) and preferred instead the medieval Hebrew Ashkenazit—reveals the fact that the Zionists did not want to view Austria as a German nation-state and much preferred to see it as German only in the cultural sense.

The council did, however, define the Jews as a nation, seek Jewish national rights in the new state, and run candidates to represent the Jewish nation in the Austrian national assembly and Viennese city council in 1919. When Stricker won a mandate from a largely Jewish area in Vienna, the Zionists exulted in the victory of the Jewish national idea.[29] During the election campaign, Stricker and the Zionists had made their position clear. In an article in early February 1919 in his daily newspaper, the *Wiener Morgenzeitung*, Stricker argued that Jews belonged to two communities: the state in which they lived and the Jewish people, and he insisted that these two loyalties posed no conflict at all. Jews in Deutsch-Österreich, he argued, lived in two spheres "as members of the Jewish people, whose center is in Palestine" and "as members of the German-Austrian state, in whose blossoming [the Jew] takes an active interest." Jews can be the best citizens of the state specifically because they have no territorial interests elsewhere in Europe and because they do not have their own language. At the same time he consoled the Germans of Austria that they surely formed part of the German Volk even if they did not share a state with all other Germans.[30] Later that year, Stricker urged the government to count Jewish nationality in the census.[31]

Throughout the turbulent history of the First Republic, the issue of

Jewish national rights remained central to Austrian Zionism. By the mid-1920s many Austrian Zionists recognized the futility of seeking Jewish national autonomy and understood that such an agenda merely squandered Zionist resources, which would best be used to develop the Jewish national home in Palestine. Moreover, the proliferation of intense antisemitism in interwar Austria required the Jews, they realized, not to waste their votes on Zionist candidates who had no chance of winning but to use their votes to prevent the antisemitic parties from coming to power. Nevertheless, Robert Stricker and his stalwarts, who dominated the Austrian Zionist Federation, succeeded in maintaining its devotion to a political agenda developed during the monarchy but no longer viable in the new nation-state. They remained wedded to the Jewish nationalist ideology of their youth and paid no attention to the fact that there was no possibility whatsoever that such an ideology could be implemented in nationally homogeneous German-Austria. The Jewish nationalists achieved virtually no electoral successes. They won only one parliamentary seat, and that only in 1919, and three city council seats in 1919 and one in 1923. But they continued to run candidates, convinced of the moral virtue of such tactics. When in 1930 the majority of Austrian Zionists decided on pragmatic grounds no longer to run Jewish national candidates, Stricker put forward his own candidate list and denounced the Austrian Zionist Federation for renouncing its heritage.[32]

Of course not all Jews in Austria wanted the government to grant them national minority rights. Nor were they united in thinking that the Jews formed a distinct nation deserving self-determination. Yet even Liberal Jews—those who had abandoned much of traditional Judaism, had adopted a German-cultural orientation, sought integration in Austrian society, and distanced themselves from Jewish nationalism—had an extremely difficult time constructing a new identity when Austria-Hungary collapsed and German-Austria came into existence. Although they affirmed their loyalty to the new state and absolutely identified with German culture, they too did not really think themselves to be members of the German Volk, and so they too had a hard time adjusting to the realities of German-Austria. Jews who had long regarded themselves as German-Austrians had a particularly difficult time coping with the fact that the term "German-Austrian" now had a new meaning. Whereas before 1918, at least for the Jews, it had meant an individual of German culture who was loyal to Austria, it now required something more, an affirmation of belonging to the German nation or Volk. Such affirmation was difficult for Jews. No matter how utterly devoted they were to the German

Kulturnation, they also had a strong sense of belonging to the Jewish people, a commitment that became even stronger in the confusing and difficult period after World War I.

At the very end of October 1918, Heinrich Schreiber articulated the dilemma of most Austrian Jews in his article "The Jews and the German-Austrian State" in the *Österreichische Wochenschrift*. Schreiber bemoaned the death of the old Austria while affirming Jewish loyalty to the new state. He sadly insisted:

> We are citizens, indeed loyal and state-supporting citizens of the community in which our ancestors lived and worked, in which they died, in whose culture, economic, and political improvement they participated, to whose blossoming they contributed, for whose best they gave themselves, for which we ourselves live and die, often winning only ingratitude, hatred, and persecution, but from which we also have reaped and continue to reap thanks, good fortune, honor, and proper consideration.

Schreiber hoped, of course, that the new state would be based on principles of equality. While utterly rejecting the Zionist demand that the state recognize the Jews as a nation and fearing that such recognition would only encourage antisemitic plans to stigmatize and persecute the Jews, he insisted that the Jews feel and think Jewish and want to be known as Jews. Nowhere did he assert the German national identity of Jews. He concluded: "We are Jews, we are Austrians, and when that is too little, we are German Austrians, by birth and customs, education and culture, disposition and feeling."[33]

In the first few months of the new republic, Liberal Jews endlessly debated the nature of their identity as Jews, Germans, and Austrians. They certainly all agreed on the need to be loyal citizens of the new state, but the professions of loyalty had a formal quality, like the statements of medieval vassals declaring their fealty to a new lord. Austrian Jews simply transferred their old Habsburg loyalty to the new republic, and understood their Austrian identity not in grand political terms but in very basic, human terms. By ignoring the German nationalist dimension of the new Austrian identity, Jews could find a place for themselves in the new republic. One anonymous Jewish woman, who claimed to write on behalf of other women who shared her views, insisted:

> Yes, we have a Fatherland, a *Heimat*! For this [homeland] we have uncomplainingly given our husbands, sons, and grandsons; for this Fatherland they fought bravely, sacrificed their blood and their lives; and for this, our beloved, poor, and now trampled down Fatherland, for German Austria, we live and die. This land, whose language we speak and understand, this

land, where our families, our existence, and our dear graves are located, this is and remains our *Heimat*.[34]

Other spokesmen took for granted that the Jews would be good citizens of the new state, but they were nervous about the extent to which the antisemites would dominate politics there.[35] In particular, they feared the proposal that citizenship in the new state be restricted to those who professed membership in the German nation.[36]

Liberal Jews had trouble coming to grips with the meaning of Germanness in the new state. They continued to cling to a cultural definition of German identity and could not adopt a more *völkisch* one. A group of Liberal Jewish notables, including leaders of the Austrian-Israelite Union (a defense organization against antisemitism), B'nai B'rith, and Jewish religious communities, issued a formal declaration of their views on December 2, 1918. Rejecting the Zionist claim that the Jews formed a separate nation, they insisted instead that "We feel German through *Heimat*, language, and education." Naturally they also reiterated their desire to be fully equal citizens of the German Austrian Republic.[37] A week later, a delegation of such Jews formally announced their Germanness to the government.[38] These Liberal Jews understood their assimilation in utterly cultural terms. In the words of one writer, they had assimilated not in a *deutschvölkisch* sense, but in a purely cultural way.[39]

The transformation of Austria, coupled with Zionist assertiveness, goaded Liberal Jews into rethinking the meaning of Jewishness in modern society. Rejecting the Zionist contention that the Jews constituted a political nation,[40] they reiterated the classic Liberal notion that the Jews merely formed a religious community.[41] Yet virtually all Liberal spokesmen recognized that Jewish identity transcended religious faith and included membership in the Jewish people. Such views had already found articulate expression in the late nineteenth century, but post–World War I Liberals seemed far more insistent on Jewish ethnic attachments than Liberal spokesmen of an earlier era. The ethnic dimension of Jewish identity was well expressed by Rabbi David Feuchtwang, who insisted that all Jews in the world agreed with Zionist founder Theodor Herzl's declaration that the Jews were "a people—one people." True, Jews were not a nation like other nations. Jewish national identity was not political but moral, religious, and cultural. Jews were a Volk because of their religious idea. Yet at the same time, Feuchtwang stated that it was "false, unhistorical, and erroneous" to say that Jewish identity was merely religious. Jews formed a *Religionsvolk*, a nation that embodied the ideals of the prophets.[42]

Throughout the early months of the republic, Liberal Jewish spokesmen articulated this religio-ethnic definition of Jewish identity. Although they were often confused about which terms best served their purposes, they nevertheless agreed about the meaning of terms. In an open letter to Vienna's chief rabbi in late December, S. Ortony argued that Jews were united by far more than religion. While rejecting nationalism, even going so far as to declare that he felt no national bonds with Eastern European Jews because they did not share the same territory, language, or culture, he nevertheless regarded himself in primarily Jewish terms, not as a national Jew, and not as a Jew by religion, but simply as a German-Austrian Jew, united with other Jews by ties of sentiment, family, shared persecution, and honor.[43] Another writer in early 1919 went even further, insisting that all Jews consciously or unconsciously harbored a national-religious sense of Jewish identity.[44] A spokesman for the Austrian Israelite Union denied that Jews formed a full-fledged Volk, yet he argued that Jews formed "one ethnic group (Stamm) and one blood group with our brothers in the East." Jews were united therefore by religion and ethnicity.[45] Even the B'nai B'rith, which insisted in early 1919 that its members were "Jews of German nationality" and that Jewish identity was purely religious, also acknowledged that their religion formed the Jews into a Volk. The Jews were "a nation of believers in the eternal ideas of Judaism. . . . united by common descent, common history, commonly suffered persecution, and especially profession of Judaism."[46]

The strongest voice to assert Jewish ethnicity in the new nation-state was, as usual, Josef Samuel Bloch, the feisty editor of the *Österreichische Wochenschrift*. Bloch, the Galician-born rabbi in the Viennese suburb of Floridsdorf, had a reputation as an aggressive opponent of antisemitism both in the courts and in parliament. He had long articulated his commitment to a multinational Austria and to a staunchly ethnic definition of Jewish identity.[47] In the new republic Bloch continued to insist on Jewish ethnicity. In a series of articles in his paper in the summer of 1919, Bloch provided the most clearly articulated version of this identity, declaring that Jews were a race, a nation, an ethnic group, and a religious community all at once. Jews, he noted, possessed the "ethnological isolation, individuality, and exclusivity of a race." Yet they were best labeled an ethnic community, a *Stammesgemeinschaft*, a community of people tied to each other because of their shared descent from the biblical Jacob. At the same time he acknowledged that they formed "a metaphysical-ethical God-community," which would bring blessings to all mankind. In short, for Jews religion and nationality were "intimately connected" because "the Jewish religion is national and the Jewish nation is a people of God."[48]

Orthodox Jews likewise joined this debate on Jewish identity in the new Austria. They too rejected the Zionist contention that Jews formed a nation in the political sense, and they did not want the Zionists to speak in the name of all Jews;[49] but they certainly assumed that Jewish identity contained a national dimension alongside the primary religious content of Judaism.[50] At a meeting on December 5, 1918, a group of Orthodox Jews in Vienna, led by the Adas Yisroel Schiffschul, publicly resolved that they were both loyal citizens of the new state and "through our descent, through our many thousands of years of history and especially through our holy religion . . . a closed national community *[Volksgemeinschaft]*."[51]

Obviously the political crisis precipitated by the end of World War I and the collapse of the multinational Habsburg monarchy led Jews to assert their ethnic identity more forcefully. Jews at the time perceived that the war and the immediate postwar situation, including the rise of vicious antisemitism, had heightened their Jewish identities. Anitta Müller, a Viennese Jewish social worker and Zionist activist who worked tirelessly on behalf of Galician Jewish refugee women and children, felt that the new situation had strengthened Jewish folk solidarity *(Volkszugehörigkeit)*, especially among returning soldiers and women.[52] Minna Lachs remembered that as a young girl in postwar Vienna she came to recognize her firm attachments to the community of fate *(Schicksalsgemeinschaft)* she shared with other Jews.[53]

Jews in Germany also experienced a heightened sense of Jewish ethnicity during and immediately after World War I, largely in response to antisemitism and the encounter with East European Jews.[54] For Austrian Jews, however, such rising ethnicity was not only a response to antisemitism but also, more importantly, the result of the struggle to construct a new identity in a period of crisis. Building on already established Habsburg Jewish traditions, which had always emphasized Jewish ethnicity, Austrian Jews asserted the ethnic dimension of Jewish identity even more forcefully than in the past. It should come as no surprise that Jews preferred to assert a separate Jewish identity in a new nation-state that was unsure of its own national identity and that contained many radical German nationalists who were unwilling to allow Jews membership in the German national community.

The interwar period, with its terrible economic and political crises—inflation, depression, political turmoil, civil war, political assassination, the rise of Nazism, the creation of the right-wing corporate state in 1934, and the Anschluss with Nazi Germany in 1938—only strengthened the consciousness of Jewish ethnicity among most Austrian Jews. The popularity of antisemitism and official support lent to it by the ruling Christian Social Party created an environment in which the most comfortable solution for the Jews was to cling to a Jewish ethnic identity, especially since they had always understood their identity in such terms. After 1934, the new "German-Christian" state, dominated by the Fatherland Front, viewed the Jews as neither Germans nor Christians. Thus, Jewish status in the state became problematic, even if the official church felt uncomfortable with racial antisemitism. Obviously, then, Jews were simply Jews, and most seemed proud of that fact, even if they remained divided over how best to deal with the challenge of antisemitism.[55] Harriet Freidenreich has amply demonstrated that in the First Republic all Jewish groups —the Liberals, the Zionists, the Socialists, and the Orthodox—upset with the futile political situation in Austria, turned their attention away from the public sphere and toward the Jewish community itself.[56]

Interestingly, by identifying themselves primarily as Jews rather than as integral members of the surrounding nation, and by turning their attention to the Jewish community because the possibility of full integration did not exist, the Jews of interwar Austria more closely resembled the Jews of other successor states in East Central Europe than they did the Jews of Germany or France. The analogy must not be overdrawn. After all, Austrian Jews had embraced German culture and had played leading roles in the Viennese cultural scene. Jews in Poland, no matter how avidly they spoke Polish or lauded Polish culture, were unable to achieve anywhere near the same level of cultural integration that the Jews of Austria took for granted. Nevertheless, the resemblance is striking: in Austria as in other countries in East Central and Eastern Europe in which antisemitism flourished and authoritarian regimes enforced or tolerated antisemitic measures during the interwar period, Jews identified themselves primarily as Jews.[57] But it was not only the antisemitic environments that fostered Jewish insistence that their primary identity was as Jews. The legacy of Habsburg Jewish identity, which had always allowed the Jews a much larger measure of ethnic assertiveness than was possible in the nation-states of Western Europe, also played a role in defining Jewish life in all of the Habsburg successor states, including the rump German-Austria.

Besides defining themselves in ethnic terms, Jews in interwar Austria coped with the political crises they faced by focusing on the private sphere, on the family and personal life. The family served many purposes. In addition to fulfilling its normal role, the family could also insulate Jews from the threat of antisemitism and anti-semitic exclusionism and, at the same time, foster Jewish identity.[58] Zionists such as Anitta Müller recognized the potential power of the family. She urged Jewish mothers to take the lead in inculcating Jewish national consciousness within the family.[59] But for all Jews, the family provided an important source of refuge from the dilemmas of life in the new German-Austria. In such circumstances, most Jews sought comfort and support within the family and Jewish community.

The centrality of the family, both as protector and as incubator of Jewish identity, was most clearly recognized by memoirist Nina Lieberman. A psychologist by profession, Lieberman sensitively described how her family provided her with the security to deal with antisemitism in interwar Austria. Born in Jaroslaw, Poland in 1921, she spent the first eight years of her life in Tachov, in the Sudetenland region of Czechoslovakia, where, she insists, tolerance for diversity, and for the Jews, prevailed. Only in Salzburg, where her family moved in 1929, did she encounter fierce antisemitism, which grew more vicious in the late 1930s. In this intense antisemitic atmosphere, she notes in her memoirs, the nuclear family, important to everyone, became much more important to her: "We moved as a family unit to three different countries. In times of persecution and stress, the family was a fortress in whose walls I found protection."[60] At the same time, Lieberman, whose father was a rabbi, felt that Jewish tradition also provided her with security. She noted: "In my wanderings from country to country, the concrete symbols of Judaism as well as my consciousness of being Jewish had a stabilizing effect and made it easier for me to settle down in the different cultures."[61]

Measuring the role and impact of the family is a difficult task. The best sources for family life are memoirs, but memoirs from all periods, especially those of nonfamous people, always focus on family and personal matters. Moreover, most Jewish memoirs written after the Holocaust tend to romanticize the time before as happy and personally satisfying, especially in comparison to the Nazi period. Those written by people who were children during the interwar period deal of necessity only with the family in that period, emphasizing loving parents and idyllic childhood experience, often presented in stark contrast to the horrors of life after the Nazis came to power. Despite the problems with the sources, a close reading of a large number of Austrian Jewish memoirs leaves the reader with the distinct impression that the family did indeed take center stage in the period between World War I and the Anschluss. This was a period of at least imagined tranquility, when life could flourish and families grow. The same memoirs that deal at length with political issues before and during World War I, and certainly in the Nazi period, ignore politics to focus on personal life—career and family—in the interwar period.

The memoirs of Jewish life in interwar Austria offer significant testimony to the centrality of family in those years and the ways that family life served to provide escape from the problems that Jews faced in the First Republic. Memoirs written by adults emphasize the satisfactions of family life. Wood merchant Otto Friedman, for example, who moved for business reasons from Vienna to Salzburg in 1926, insists that he and his family lived "very happily in our house" until March 1938.[62] His family life was so happy that he did not even notice Salzburg's anti-Jewish hostility. Memorists discuss the satisfaction they found in career, children, family outings and vacations, culture, and social life. Hella Roubicek Mautner, who moved to Vienna in 1923 from Prague, noted that in "the years between the two world wars, we had a very interesting and scintillating life."[63] Those who were children in the interwar period similarly emphasize their happy, carefree, satisfying childhoods and their summer vacations.[64] Meir Neeman remembered his childhood in Vienna in the 1920s and early 1930s in terms of music lessons, soccer, summer vacations in the mountains, family meals, the Sabbath, Passover, his Bar Mitzvah, and his sister's wedding. School was the only place where he encountered antisemitism.[65] Freda Ulman Teitelbaum, who was born in 1924 and grew up in an observant home in Vienna's Leopoldstadt, contrasted her "near-perfect childhood within a tightly knit family circle" with the horrors of post-Anschluss Austria. Her extended family made her feel as if she were "enveloped in a cocoon of love, warmth, and acceptance."[66]

Even those who present a less rosy picture of life in the turbulent years of the First Republic still indicate the happiness of their family life in that period. Erna Segal, who felt a sense of great foreboding at the end of the war and who described the postwar years as "terrible and difficult times," or as "the beginning of a catastrophic, creeping danger," nevertheless describes the happy childhood of her son, born in 1921, who spent his summers in Styria and his winters in Vienna.[67] Even for those for whom family life was not positive—Esti Freud, for example, who felt increasingly alienated from her husband, Freud's son Martin[68]—the family, private life, career, and not grand political events, formed the basis of experience.

Certainly after the Anschluss families bonded together even further to cope with the uncertainties of Nazi persecution and emigration abroad. Freda Ulman Teitelbaum expresses this reality best. In 1938, she noted in her memoirs, the already "warm kinship" she shared with her family "became even stronger . . . when the family drew tightly together in the face of a common danger."[69] Family and Jewish identity was all that was left to the Jews lucky enough to leave Austria altogether for new homes in America, England, and Palestine. But long before the Nazis utterly deprived Jews of their right to an Austrian or German identity, the Jews of Austria had crafted an identity based on Jewish ethnicity. Remaining loyal to the Austrian state and to German culture, they nevertheless fully understood that their primary identity was as Jews and not as Germans or even Austro-Germans. The antisemitic environment of interwar Austria surely strengthened the commitment to Jewish ethnicity, but it did not create it. Rather, the Jews of Austria built on an identity already established in the time of the monarchy. The existence of the new nation-state, German-Austria, undercut the scaffolding of that identity, which had set Jewish ethnicity within the context of an Austrian political loyalty and a German, or some other, cultural one. Now asked to identify with the German nation and at the same time denied the right to do so, Jews responded by emphasizing their Jewish ethnic identity even more than they had previously. This identity served them in good stead later, when they had to leave.

Notes

1. Joachim Schoenfeld, *Jewish Life in Galicia under the Austro-Hungarian Empire and in the Reborn Poland 1898–1939* (Hoboken, 1985), p. 179.

2. See, for example, many of the unpublished memoirs located at the Leo Baeck Institute (LBI), New York, especially those of Otto F. Ehrentheil, "Part of the Honors"; Philipp Flesch, "Mein Leben in Deutschland vor und nach dem 30. Januar 1933"; Joseph Floch (no title); Otto Friedman, "Lebenserinnerungen"; Arnold Hindls, "Erinnerungen aus meinem Leben"; Fritz Lieben, "Aus meinem Leben"; and Adolf Mechner, "My Family Biography." See also Manès Sperber, *God's Water Carriers: A Trilogy,* trans. Joachim Neugroschel (New York, 1987), pp. 151–52.

3. Minna Lachs, *Warum schaust du zurück. Erinnerungen 1907–1941* (Vienna, 1986), p. 90.

4. On the creation of the Austrian republic see Barbara Jelavich, *Modern Austria: Empire and Republic, 1800–1986* (Cambridge, 1987); Charles A. Gulick, *Austria: From Habsburg to Hitler,* 2 vols. (Berkeley, 1948); K. R. Stadler, *The Birth of the Austrian Republic, 1918–1921* (Leiden, 1966).

5. On Jewish identity in prewar Vienna, see Marsha L. Rozenblit, *The Jews of Vienna, 1867–1914: Assimilation and Identity* (Albany, 1983); Robert S. Wistrich, *The Jews of Vienna in the Age of Franz Joseph* (Oxford, 1989); William O. McCagg, Jr., *A History of Habsburg Jews, 1670–1918* (Bloomington, 1989), esp. pp. 47–64, 140–58, 195–200.

6. On Austrian antisemitism in the interwar period, see Bruce F. Pauley, *From Prejudice to Persecution: A History of Austrian Anti-Semitism* (Chapel Hill, 1992).

7. On the nationalities and the nationality conflict in Austria, see Adam Wandruszka and Peter Urbanitsch, eds., *Die Habsburgermonarchie 1848–1918*, vol. 3, *Die Völker des Reiches* (Vienna, 1980); Robert A. Kann, *The Multinational Empire: Nationalism and National Reform in the Habsburg Monarchy, 1848–1918*, 2 vols. (New York, 1950); Oskar Jászi, *The Dissolution of the Habsburg Monarchy* (Chicago, 1929, reprint 1961).

8. On the "cult" of the Emperor Franz Joseph, see Wistrich, *Jews of Vienna*, pp. 175–81. See also such memoirs as Sperber, *God's Water Carriers*, trans. Neugroschel, p. 74; Lachs, *Warum schaust du zurück*, pp. 20, 22, 51.

9. The Austrian loyalty of the Jews is well known and documented. McCagg, *History of Habsburg Jews*, pp. 57–64, 100, argues that the absence of an Austrian national identity facilitated the "national 'self'-denial" of the Jews, but I would argue the opposite: that the absence of an Austrian national identity allowed the Jews room to assert their own ethnicity even as they modernized. On the supranational nature of Austrian patriotism in general, see István Deák, *Beyond Nationalism: A Social and Political History of the Habsburg Officer Corps, 1848–1918* (New York, 1990).

10. Martin Broszat, "Von der Kulturnation zur Volksgruppe. Die nationale Stellung der Juden in der Bukowina im 19. und 20. Jahrhundert," *Historische Zeitschrift* 200 (1965): 572–605, esp. 579–84; Wistrich, *Jews of Vienna*, pp. 30–31, 132–35; idem, "Liberalism, *Deutschtum*, and Assimilation," *Jerusalem Quarterly* 42 (Spring 1987): 100–102.

11. Wolfdieter Bihl, "Die Juden," in *Die Habsburgermonarchie 1848–1918*, ed. Wandruszka and Urbanitsch, vol. 3, *Die Völker des Reiches*, part 2, pp. 880–948; Gerald Stourzh, "Galten die Juden als Nationalität Altösterreichs?" in *Prag-Czernowitz-Jerusalem: Der österreichische Staat und die Juden vom Zeitalter des Absolutismus bis zum Ende der Monarchie*, ed. Anna M. Drabek, Mordechai Eliav, and Gerald Stourzh (Eisenstadt, 1984) = *Studia Judaica Austriaca* 10 (1984): 73–116.

12. I am currently working on a book about the impact of World War I on the Jews of Austria-Hungary. On German Jews in World War I, see Werner Mosse, ed., *Deutsches Judentum in Krieg und Revolution 1916–1923* (Tübingen, 1971).

13. *ÖW*, February 15, 1918, p. 97.

14. *ÖW*, July 19, 1918, p. 442. For other references to the loyalty of the Jews to the dynasty and the Fatherland in 1918, see *ÖW*, August 2, 1918, p. 474, and September 6, 1918, p. 557.

15. *ÖW*, October 4, 1918, p. 25.

16. *Jüdische Korrespondenz*, October 3, 1918, p. 1.

17. *Jüdische Korrespondenz*, November 1, 1918, pp. 1–2.

18. *JZ*, June 14, 1918, p. 1. The World Zionist Organization (WZO), then headquartered in Berlin, also thought that Jewish interests were best served by continued Austrian unity. See the letter of the Berlin Zionist Office to Robert Weltsch, then a representative of the WZO in Vienna, October 8, 1918, in CZA, Z3/850.

19. See, for example, *JZ*, July 12, 1918, p. 1; July 26, 1918, p. 1; August 30, 1918, p. 4; October 4, 1918, pp. 1–2; October 11, 1918, pp. 1–2; October 18, 1918, p. 1; October 25, 1918, pp. 1–2. For the history of these demands, see Rozenblit, *Jews of Vienna, 1867–1914*, pp. 170–74; Adolf Gaisbauer, *Davidstern und Doppeladler: Zionismus und jüdischer Nationalismus in Österreich, 1882–1918* (Vienna, 1988);

Adolf Böhm, *Die zionistische Bewegung*, 2 vols., 2nd rev. ed. (Tel Aviv, 1935–1937), vol. 1.

20. *JZ*, September 6, 1918, pp. 1–2; Hermann Kadisch, *Die Juden und die österreichische Verfassungsrevision* (Vienna, 1918). Kadisch was merely repeating what he had been arguing in books, pamphlets, and newspaper articles for decades.

21. *ÖW*, October 25, 1918, p. 673. McCagg, *History of Habsburg Jews*, pp. 201–22, insists that the Jews did not mourn the demise of the monarchy, but that is most certainly not the case.

22. Erna Segal, "You Shall Never Forget" (in German), unpublished memoir, ALBI-NY, p. 26.

23. Ibid., p. 27.

24. Letter of the Jüdische Nationalrat für Deutsch-Österreich to the government, November 4, 1918, in CZA, L6/366; Report, December 10, 1918, in CZA, L6/93; Memorandum, November 4, 1918, in CZA, Z3/214; *JZ*, October 25, 1918, p. 1, and November 1, 1918, pp. 1, 2, 5.

25. *JZ*, November 8, 1918, pp. 1–3, and November 15, 1918, pp. 1–2; *WMZ*, January 19, 1919, p. 3, and April 9, 1919, pp. 1–2.

26. As early as late October 1918, Robert Weltsch, a Prague Zionist sent to Vienna by the World Zionist Organization, recognized that the old programs would no longer work; but he was not able to stop Stricker. See correspondence between Weltsch and Leo Herrmann, October 28, 1918, in CZA, L6/366 and CZA, Z3/850.

27. *JZ*, December 6, 1918, p. 5.

28. Hebrew title on stationery of the Jewish National Council. See, for example, the letter of November 25, 1918, in CZA, L6/358 or CZA, Z3/180.

29. See *JZ*, February 21, 1919, p. 1. See also *WMZ*, February 7, 1919, p. 3; February 10, 1919, p. 1; February 17, 1919, p. 1; February 18, 1919, p. 1. Stricker's tenure in the National Assembly was short-lived. He was not elected to the Austrian parliament in 1920. In addition, three Jewish nationalists won seats on the Vienna city council in the spring of 1919 (see *JZ*, May 9, 1919, p. 1; *WMZ*, May 5, 1919, p. 1).

30. *WMZ*, February 11, 1919, p. 1.

31. *JZ*, May 16, 1919, p. 1, and October 24, 1919, p. 3.

32. Harriet Pass Freidenreich, *Jewish Politics in Vienna, 1918–1938* (Bloomington, 1991), pp. 48–72.

33. *ÖW*, October 25, 1918, pp. 673–75.

34. Letter from "L.W.," *ÖW*, November 1, 1918, p. 696.

35. See, for example, *ÖW*, November 8, 1918, p. 705; November 15, 1918, p. 721; December 6, 1918, pp. 779–80; January 3, 1919, p. 10; February 7, 1919, p. 83.

36. *ÖW*, November 22, 1918, pp. 737–38; January 3, 1919, pp. 7–8.

37. *ÖW*, December 6, 1918, pp. 779–80.

38. *ÖW*, December 13, 1918, p. 800.

39. *ÖW*, January 24, 1919, p. 56.

40. See, for example, *ÖW*, October 18, 1918, pp. 659–60; November 8, 1918, pp. 705, 706–707; November 22, 1918, pp. 737–38; December 6, 1918, pp. 779–80; December 13, 1918, p. 800.

41. See, for example, *ÖW*, October 25, 1918, pp. 675–76; December 6, 1918, pp. 779–80.

42. *ÖW,* December 27, 1918, pp. 821–22. These views reiterate and accentuate the attitude toward Jewish identity articulated by Vienna's famous nineteenth-century rabbis. See Marsha L. Rozenblit, "Jewish Identity and the Modern Rabbi: The Cases of Isak Noa Mannheimer, Adolf Jellinek, and Moritz Güdemann in Nineteenth-Century Vienna," *LBIYB* 35 (1990): 103–31.

43. *ÖW,* December 27, 1918, pp. 823–24.

44. *ÖW,* January 24, 1919, pp. 55–56.

45. *Monatsschrift der Oesterreichisch-Israelitischen Union* 31, nos. 2–4 (February–April 1919): 1–5, esp. 4.

46. S. Krauss, "Die Krise der Wiener Judenschaft," *Zweimonats-Bericht für die Mitglieder der österr. israel. Humanitätsvereine "Bnai Brith"* 22, no. 1 (1919): 2–17, esp. 11–12.

47. On Bloch, see Josef S. Bloch, *My Reminiscences* (Vienna, 1923); idem, *Der nationale Zwist und die Juden in Oesterreich* (Vienna, 1886); Rozenblit, *Jews of Vienna, 1867–1914,* pp. 155–56, 181–84; and Wistrich, *Jews of Vienna,* pp. 270–309.

48. *ÖW,* June 27, 1919, pp. 390–92.

49. *Jüdische Korrespondenz,* October 22, 1918, pp. 2–3; November 1, 1918, p. 1; December 5, 1918, p. 1; January 2, 1919, p. 3.

50. See, for example, *Jüdische Korrespondenz,* April 13, 1918, pp. 1–3; May 16, 1918, pp. 3–4; December 5, 1918, p. 1; *ÖW,* December 20, 1918, pp. 814–15.

51. *Jüdische Korrespondenz,* January 2, 1919, p. 3; *JZ,* January 3, 1919, p. 6; *ÖW,* December 27, 1918, p. 824.

52. *ÖW,* January 17, 1919, pp. 34–36. See also the regular "Frauenrecht und Frauenarbeit" page that she edited for the Zionist daily *WMZ* in 1919, for example, February 2, 1919, p. 7.

53. Lachs, *Warum schaust du zurück,* p. 117. Lachs's father, Benno Schiffmann, was a Zionist.

54. On German Jews, see Eva Reichmann, "Der Bewusstseinswandel der deutschen Juden," in *Deutsches Judentum in Krieg und Revolution, 1916–1923,* ed. Mosse, pp. 511–612. See also Avraham Barkai's essay (chapter 5) in this volume.

55. Freidenreich, *Jewish Politics,* pp. 180–203. Freidenreich herself uses the term "problematic" as a label for Jewish status (p. 187). For Jews in Austria after 1934, see Sylvia Maderegger, *Die Juden im österreichischen Ständestaat, 1934–38* (Vienna, 1973).

56. Freidenreich, *Jewish Politics,* pp. 36, 72, and passim.

57. Ezra Mendelsohn, *The Jews of East Central Europe between the World Wars* (Bloomington, 1983).

58. Marion Kaplan, *The Making of the Jewish Middle Class: Women, Family, and Identity in Imperial Germany* (New York, 1991), pp. 83–84, has cogently argued that the Jewish family served the important function of protecting Jews from the ordeal of antisemitism, and of course also of fostering Jewish identity, in late nineteenth-century Germany.

59. *ÖW,* January 17, 1919, pp. 34–36.

60. J. Nina Lieberman, "Lost and Found: A Life," unpublished memoir, ALBI-NY, esp. pp. 22–36 (quotation on p. 36). On the intensity of antisemitism in Salzburg, see Marko M. Feingold, ed., *Ein ewiges Dennoch: 125 Jahre Juden in Salzburg* (Vienna, 1993).

61. Lieberman, "Lost and Found," pp. 74–75 (quotation on p. 75).

62. Otto Friedman, "Lebenserinnerungen," unpublished memoir, ALBI-NY, p. 8. Friedman's memoir also appears in Feingold, *Ein ewiges Dennoch,* pp. 466–84.

63. *Hella*, transcribed, taped reminiscence, privately printed by her children, Nelly Urbach and Willy Mautner, Washington, D.C., 1996, pp. 58–78 (quotation on p. 78). For other positive descriptions of family life in this period, see the unpublished memoirs at the LBI, especially Vinca Safar, "Aus meinem Leben," pp. 76–102; Otto F. Ehrentheil, "Part of the Honors"; Eric Fischer, "Memoirs and Reminiscences"; Egon Basch, "Wirken und Wandern: Lebenserinnerungen," pp. 35–81; Olly Schwarz, "Lebens-Erinnerungen," pp. 27–47.

64. See, for example, Margarete Klein, "Briefe aus Israel an meine Verwandten in Oesterreich," p. 11; Paul Steiner, "Autobiography" (in German), pp. 21–22, 30, 41–47; Ulrich Furst, "Windows to My Youth"; Eric Fischer, "Memoirs and Reminiscences," Section VII, unpublished memoirs, ALBI-NY. See also George Clare, *Last Waltz in Vienna: The Rise and Destruction of a Family, 1842–1942* (New York, 1982).

65. Meir Neeman, "Autobiography," unpublished memoir, ALBI-NY, pp. 1–19.

66. Freda Ulman Teitelbaum, *Vienna Revisited* (Santa Barbara, 1995), pp. 59, 63. She describes the period between 1924 and 1938 on pp. 52–56, 61–95, 100–104.

67. Segal, "You Shall Never Forget," pp. 30–32. See also Toni Stolper, "Recorded Memories," taped and transcribed by her grandson, Alister Campbell, 1982, unpublished memoir, ALBI-NY.

68. Esti D. Freud, "Vignettes of My Life," unpublished memoir, ALBI-NY, pp. 29–53.

69. Teitelbaum, *Vienna Revisited*, p. 103. See also pp. 47 and 114–51.

9

Gender, Identity, & Community

Jewish University Women in Germany and Austria

HARRIET PASS FREIDENREICH

Jewish women who attended universities in Germany and Austria in the early twentieth century demonstrated many different, intertwined identities during their lifetimes: as middle-class girls and women; as students, intellectuals, and professionals; as daughters and, in most cases, wives and mothers; as Germans or Austrians; and as Jews. Although their early education and socialization were the same as those of other Central European Jewish women, and although they exhibited a similar range of Jewish identification, their education and subsequent careers often intensified an existing sense of alienation from the Jewish community. This essay will examine the religious and ethnic attitudes and behavior of these women and will explore how they manifested both their Jewishness and their Germanness; in doing so, it will define the various factors that shaped the Jewish identities of Central European university women.

After German and Austrian universities opened their doors to women around the turn of the century, young Jewish women entered these institutions in disproportionately large numbers.[1] At the University of Vienna, on the eve of World War I, 304 Jews represented 43 percent of all women students and accounted for 59 percent of the students in the faculty of medicine and 37 percent in the faculty of philosophy. Although the percentage of Jewish women students in the Austrian capital declined to roughly 20 percent by 1933/34, their absolute numbers continued to increase. In 1934, 539 Jewish women were enrolled at the University of Vienna—261 in medicine, 222 in philosophy, and 56 in law.[2] At Prussian universities before World

War I, 189 Jewish women made up 11 percent of the total female student population, including 28 percent of the women in medicine; by 1931/32, 1,321 Jewish women constituted 7 percent of all women students in Germany.[3] Although many more Jewish men than women received a higher education, the proportion of Jewish women among female students remained roughly twice as high as the proportion of Jewish men among male students.[4]

Central European Jewish university women constituted an elite group of highly educated individuals who did not conform to many of the established norms for middle-class Jewish women. Both as Jews and as women, they often differed in their attitudes and behavior from their mothers and their less-educated sisters, as well as from the female Jewish population at large. Over the course of the twentieth century, however, higher education has become increasingly common among Jewish women everywhere. It is important to investigate Jewish identification among the pioneering generations of university women in order to understand the dissonance that still resonates when Jewish women with advanced secular degrees but minimal Jewish knowledge try to relate to their Jewishness and to the broader Jewish community. The women under discussion may be considered examples of the "New Woman," but the "New Jewish Woman" had not yet emerged.

The research findings presented in this essay form part of a larger, on-going project, a collective biography of Central European Jewish university women in the early twentieth century. The analysis is based on information gleaned primarily from published and unpublished memoirs, biographies, and biographical dictionaries, as well as from questionnaires and interviews. It focuses on a study population of 448 Jewish women who attended universities in Central Europe before the Nazi era. These women can be divided by age into two groups of roughly equal size: the older generation, or those born before the turn of the century, who began their university studies before the end of World War I; and the younger cohort, born between 1900 and 1916, who received their higher education during the interwar years. Sixty-two percent of these women were born in Germany, 32 percent in Austria-Hungary; the remaining 6 percent were from Russia or some other part of Europe.

Delimiting the identity of modern Jewish women is by no means an easy task. Generalizing about 448 women, many of whom were truly exceptional individuals, is a daunting challenge for any researcher. The characteristics that all these women had in common are Jewish descent (i.e., two parents who were born Jews); a middle-class, often upper middle-class, socioeconomic background; and a strong desire to attain personal self-fulfillment, if not economic independence, through higher education. The first generation of university women had to overcome many personal and educational obstacles before they gained access to universities. The older women in my study population generally tended to come from wealthier and more highly acculturated families than did members of the younger cohort. They were more likely to have been baptized or to have formally opted out of the Jewish community, but they were less likely to have been married. During the interwar years, once university education for women had become more widespread and socially acceptable, young women from somewhat more traditional and less affluent families began to attend universities in larger numbers. As a result of the inflationary spiral of the 1920s and the depression of the 1930s, many of these younger women lived at home and had to work at part-time jobs in order to afford their university studies. Although members of the younger group were also highly acculturated members of German or Austrian society, they were more likely to remain, at least nominally, within the framework of the *Gemeinde,* the official Jewish community.

For the most part, however, Jewish university women did not strongly identify with the organized Jewish community or its institutions before the Nazi era. Their Jewishness was often revealed in their early family life and friendships but much less frequently reflected in supplementary education, synagogue attendance, or organizational affiliation. As students and as adults, they drifted even further from a specifically Jewish lifestyle, and they did not usually join Jewish groups or women's associations. Their Jewish identity was primarily personal and private rather than public or communal in expression.

Marion Kaplan, in her excellent book *The Making of the Jewish Middle Class,* as well as in many articles,[5] has portrayed German Jewish women in the late nineteenth and early twentieth centuries as the embodiment of the "cult of domesticity"; they were middle-class wives and mothers and guardians of the Jewish home. Young women were expected to remain in their parental household until marriage, to find an appropriate mate by their mid-twenties, and then to stay at home raising children. Women who attended the university, however, were "New Women" who chose a different path. Not content with standard girls' "finishing school" training, which had provided their mothers with a good foundation in German *Bildung* (culture and refinement)—with an emphasis on literature, art, and music—they sought personal self-fulfillment in a university education that might lead to professional careers in previously all-male fields such as medicine, law, or higher education. As one woman phrased it, "I wanted to become a person *[ein Mensch]*, and not just a middle-class school girl."[6]

These young women sought greater personal freedom than was the norm for middle-class girls of their day. As teenagers, they were by and large reluctant debutantes and not primarily interested in getting married. While attending university, they often left home for several semesters, if not longer, and they learned to live independently of their families. They considered chaperones, arranged marriages, and dowries old-fashioned; instead, they developed friendships and relationships with men of their own choosing. Although, for the most part, their partners and, later, the spouses of those who married, tended to be Jews of a similar age, background, and education, 27 percent of the women in my study population remained single. Among those that eventually married, many did so relatively late in life and 40 percent had no children.

Jewish university women thus tried to avoid following in their mothers' footsteps; they did not want to give up their career aspirations in order to become full-time homemakers in accordance with the German and Jewish middle-class ideal for women. For the most part, these women evinced little interest in cooking, handicrafts, household management, or volunteer social work. For those who pursued professional careers, whether or not they ever married, their private life, and hence their Jewish life, differed from that of less-educated Jewish women. These women had sought the same secular education and often the same professions as Jewish men; their personal role models were likely to have been fathers, uncles, or brothers, not mothers, aunts, or sisters. As Jewish women with a man's education, they found themselves in limbo. They no longer felt comfortable within the confines of the gynocentric, traditional Jewish home but could not find a place within the larger androcentric Jewish community. As Jews, they sought in most cases to replicate neither the domestic Judaism of women nor the more public Judaism of men.

Among the women of Jewish origin who attended universities in Central Europe before the Nazi era, a broad spectrum of Jewish identity is evident. Interestingly enough, my study population does not reveal consistent or significant differences in types of Jewish identification according to country of birth, whether that be Germany, Austria-Hungary, or Russia. To be sure, there are some regional disparities within both Germany and Austria; women who grew up in Galicia or in Orthodox communities in Karlsruhe or Frankfurt am Main tended to have stronger, more positive Jewish identities than those raised in more highly assimilated communities such as Vienna or Berlin; but no hard and fast rule applies and exceptions abound.

Although the range of identity of Jewish university women forms a continuum, for convenience, I will define three general categories: the "Former Jews," who officially left the Jewish community; the "Just Jews," who remained nominally affiliated as Jews throughout their lives; and the "Jewish Jews," who actively affirmed their Jewishness in their public as well as private behavior.[7] Brief sketches of three women, Käte Frankenthal, Rose-Marie Papanek-Akselrad, and Rahel Goitein Straus, serve to illustrate these categories, although no one individual can be seen as "typical."

Käte Frankenthal regarded herself as a Jew by descent but not by religion or by nationality. In her memoirs, *Der dreifache Fluch* [The threefold curse], which were written in the United States in 1939, she identified the three curses that worked against her in Nazi Germany: she was a Jewish woman, she was an intellectual, and she was a socialist. Frankenthal was born in 1889 into an affluent German-Jewish family; her father was a successful merchant and her mother a devoted housewife. Although she remained deeply attached to her parents, she rejected their middle-class Jewish lifestyle and values. Whereas her father was president of the Jewish community of Kiel, religion lacked importance in her life, and she found associating with other Jews too limiting. She decided at an early age not to marry, dismissing the possibility of intermarriage but claiming to have no love for Jewish men and to be "turned off by anything Jewish in appearance or manner."[8] Rejecting the idea that Jews should have a monopoly on her interest, she formally left the Gemeinde and declared herself konfessionslos in 1923, after both her parents had died. Frankenthal was a Jew merely by fate; she was a medical doctor and socialist politician by choice.[9]

Frankenthal, who acknowledged her Jewish descent yet abandoned the Jewish community, represents the category of Former Jews; Rose-Marie Papanek-Akselrad exemplifies the much larger group that I have labeled Just Jewish. Her memoirs, like Frankenthal's, were written shortly after her emigration to the United States in 1938, and they begin as follows:

I am an Austrian. I was born and raised in Vienna and the families of both my parents resided in Austria for centuries; all of their traditions and memories were tied to this homeland. I am also a Jew, but what that was and what it meant I knew very little about in my childhood and youth. One belonged to the Jewish religious community because one's fathers and grandfathers were Jews, but otherwise one lived exactly as the other Austrian citizens who were Catholic or Protestant.[10]

Papanek-Axelrad thus presents herself as an Austrian by nationality and as a Jew by religion, although she implies that Judaism was not her own personal religion but that of her male forebears.

Papanek-Axelrad's Jewish identity was shaped largely by negative factors, such as social segregation and antisemitism, rather than by Jewish observance at home or religious education at school. Born in 1904 to Jewish parents who had migrated to Vienna from Bohemia and Moravia, she was raised in a highly acculturated family; many of her relatives had been baptized. As a student at the Hochschule für Bodenkultur, a hotbed of German nationalism in the 1920s, Papanek witnessed frequent outbreaks of violence against male Jewish students, many of whom were Zionists; but as a woman whom fellow students apparently viewed as "un-Jewish" in both appearance and behavior, she rejected Jewish nationalism and claimed not to have personally experienced overt discrimination. She seems to have associated primarily with other Jews, but her marriage in a synagogue ceremony on the eve of her departure from Vienna is the only contact with the Gemeinde that she mentions in her unpublished autobiography.[11] Papanek-Axelrad considers being Austrian by citizenship and residency more important to her personally than being nominally Jewish by religion; yet she does not attempt to leave the Jewish community. She accepts her Jewishness as an immutable fact of life, which ultimately compels her to leave her beloved homeland.

By comparison, Rahel Goitein remained a very strongly committed Jewish Jew all her life. Born in 1880 in Karlsruhe, she was among the first woman medical doctors trained in Germany. The daughter of a modern Orthodox rabbi, she had been raised by her widowed mother in a strictly observant household. She received an excellent supplementary Jewish education and became an ardent Zionist while still a teenager. Since women were excluded from male student fraternities at the University of Heidelberg, Goitein helped organize a women's student society there. When this group, like the German fraternities, expelled Jews and foreigners from membership, she formed a separate alumnae association that would accept Jews.[12]

Rahel Goitein Straus's Jewish identity had been firmly established before she entered the university and did not change radically over the years. While practicing medicine in Munich after her marriage, she maintained a kosher household, raised five children, and frequently entertained guests and visiting Jewish dignitaries in her home. Among her many activities, she established several women's Zionist groups and became involved in various feminist organizations, serving as national vice-president of the Jüdischer Frauenbund.

Whereas her lawyer husband led a private minyan (prayer group) in their summer home and served as vice-president in charge of welfare within the Munich Gemeinde, Straus limited her activities largely to the women's sphere; her widowed mother remained her role model throughout her life.[13] As a career woman and an active feminist who also assumed the traditional roles of Jewish wife, mother, and volunteer in nearly every respect, Rahel Straus is more an exception than the rule among university women.

About 10 to 15 percent of my study population can be categorized, along with Rahel Goitein Straus, as Jewish Jews on the basis of their personal religious observance, involvement in Jewish organizations, commitment to Jewish nationalism, or efforts to acquire and spread more advanced Jewish knowledge. Between 15 and 20 percent can be classified as Former Jews; like Frankenthal, they were Jews by birth with two Jewish parents, but they were among those highly assimilated Central European Jews whose identification with the Jewish community as adults was minimal or nonexistent. At least two-thirds of the university women in this study, however, belonged to the third category; like Papanek-Akselrad, they were Just Jews who acknowledged their Jewishness and remained within the Gemeinde but did not consider being Jewish a particularly important aspect of their everyday lives before the 1930s, when it became the decisive factor in their existence. Marie Jahoda, a social psychologist born in 1907 in Vienna, noted with slight exaggeration: "My Jewish identity only became a real identification for me with Hitler. Not earlier. It played hardly any role in my thinking and feeling."[14]

Jewish identity and involvement is not a static phenomenon but can change and evolve considerably over the course of a lifetime. The memoirs and other primary sources that provide the basis for this analysis can only graze the surface of what it really meant to these women to have been born Jews and of how being Jewish affected their lives and behavior. Although there are some individuals who rebelled against their upbringing and went from being Jewish Jews to Former Jews or vice versa, for the majority of Jewish university women in my study population, the most important influence in shaping their Jewish identity was probably their family background. Nevertheless, even within a single family, a wide range of personal identification could emerge. For example, of the three daughters of the Zaloscer family, born in Bosnia to Galician Jewish parents but educated in Vienna, the oldest, Hilde Zaloscer (b. 1903), an art historian and self-declared Zionist, later became a nominal Muslim in Egypt; her sister, Erna Zaloscer Sailer (b. 1908), who trained as a lawyer and, many years later, served as the Austrian ambassador to India, was a Social Democrat who converted to Catholicism and married a non-Jew; the youngest sister, Ruth Zaloscer Gutman (b. 1911), who was also a socialist but associated primarily with Jews, trained as a medical doctor, married another Jewish doctor, and, after surviving the Holocaust, eventually emigrated to Palestine.[15] If one highly acculturated Jewish family can produce an Austrian Catholic socialist, an Egyptian Muslim Zionist agnostic, and a leftist Israeli Jew, generalizations about family influences on the development of personal identity become somewhat risky!

By and large, Jewish university women, like German and Austrian Jews in general, defined being Jewish in terms of religion rather than in terms of ethnicity or nationality; yet they did not adhere to traditional Jewish beliefs or religious practices. The middle-class households in which Jewish university women were raised reflected the range of observance among Central European Jews as a whole, although Orthodox Jews were somewhat underrepresented and the more highly assimilated overrepresented, especially among the older generation. Many Just Jews, as well as most Former Jews, came from homes in which Christmas was more likely to have been observed than either Passover or the High Holidays. Descriptions of Christmas trees, gift exchanges, and family celebrations are by no means unusual in these women's memoirs.[16] By contrast, the more Jewish Jews toward the other end of the identity spectrum grew up in many cases in more traditional homes in which kosher dietary laws were more likely to be followed and Sabbath and Jewish holidays observed with festive meals.[17] Many Just Jews, however, associated Sabbath and holiday observances with their grandparents rather than their parents. As Marie Jahoda recalled:

> Neither of my parents were religious. Both grandparents were very interested in Judaism religiously and culturally. . . . And through the contact of my parents with their parents there developed a respect for Judaism without this influencing (our) daily life in any way. . . . We preferred to go to our grandparents for the major Jewish festivals. The Jewish tradition was a family tradition—but not something alive for us.[18]

The Jewish education these women received did not, by and large, exceed that of their mothers. Although the daughters, unlike their mothers, passed the *Abitur* or *Matura* (matriculation examinations), attended the university, completed certification programs and, in a majority of cases, earned doctorates, their formal Jewish education remained rudimentary. Some Former Jews received virtually no

Jewish education whatsoever and were barely aware that their families were Jewish; even if they were not baptized, they might well have
enrolled in Lutheran religious education classes.[19] Lise Meitner, a
nuclear physicist who was born in Vienna in 1878 and not baptized
until the age of thirty, received no formal Jewish education as a child.
She once commented: "I feel like an imposter when American Jews
praise me especially because I am of Jewish descent. I am not Jewish
by belief, know nothing of the history of Judaism, and do not feel
closer to Jews than to other people."[20]

Most Just Jews attended Jewish religious education classes throughout elementary and secondary school but frequently disliked them
and resented being segregated from their classmates.[21] Dodo Liebman,
who was born in Berlin in 1906, provides a fairly typical description of
compulsory Jewish education in her unpublished memoirs:

> Of course, we had religious instruction at school. We had Jewish religious
> instruction while the others had Christian religious instruction. In my
> school almost half the girls were Jewish, so we parted into two roughly
> equal groups for religious instruction. . . . The religious instruction was
> not very inspiring and I just took it as another lesson, and one for which
> we did not have to do much work. At home we did not get any religious
> instruction. . . . In spite of this we were brought up very much with the
> knowledge of being Jewish and that we were, so to speak, set aside
> socially.[22]

Mandatory religious education in public and private schools generally
provided little more than a smattering of Hebrew language instruction, Bible stories, and some Jewish history. It reinforced the notion of
Jewish separateness, but only occasionally did it leave a positive
imprint on a young girl's Jewish identity.

A fairly small group of Jewish university women attended Jewish
elementary or secondary schools, such as the Philanthropin or the
Samson Raphael Hirsch Realschule in Frankfurt. Orthodox families,
however, generally discouraged their daughters from pursuing higher
education unless they tended toward Modern Orthodoxy, as in the
case of Rahel Goitein's family and several other members of the
Karlsruhe *Austrittsgemeinde* (separatist Orthodox community).[23] Jewish Jews sometimes received supplementary Jewish education from
tutors, as well as from local rabbis and cantors, and they tended to be
more enthusiastic than Just Jews about acquiring Jewish knowledge.[24] One questionnaire respondent, who was born in Augsburg
in 1906 and later became a teacher in Palestine/Israel, reported the
following:

All Jewish holidays were celebrated in our home. On Saturday we went to school, but after school there was a special youth service for us (which we did not like). . . . During my thirteen school years we had two weekly lessons of religion, first by the local cantor and later by our rabbi. We were taught Bible stories and to read and understand the main prayers in Hebrew. We even had to write an essay on the prophets in our written Matric[ulation exam].

When she went to university, this woman chose to study in Berlin, as well as Munich, "because there was the possibility of studying Judaism, which interested me."[25] Some Jewish Jews opted to continue their Jewish education while at the university or beyond, occasionally attending lectures by Hermann Cohen, participating in Franz Rosenzweig's Lehrhaus, or writing their doctoral dissertations on Jewish topics. With notable exceptions, however, university women tended to be excluded from higher Jewish education[26] and did not play a very active role in what Michael Brenner refers to as the "renaissance of Jewish culture" in Weimar Germany.[27]

Most university women had little personal involvement with synagogues or communally sponsored Jewish activities, whether as children or as adults. Former Jews and many Just Jews rarely, if ever, mention in their memoirs attending synagogue while they were growing up; instead, several recall going to church with their Catholic governesses.[28] Some were attracted to Christianity as young girls and became jealous of their Christian friends.[29] While some university women had already been baptized as children, others opted for Christianity as adults, whether for marriage, career, or other personal reasons. Several women, including Edith Stein, the philosopher who became a Catholic nun, and Alice Salomon, the social work pioneer and feminist who converted to Protestantism during World War I, chose Christianity out of sincere religious conviction.[30] Other university women rejected religion altogether, often as teenagers; many, especially among the younger cohort, became secular humanists and turned to socialism or communism as an alternative to Judaism.[31]

The grandparents and parents of Just Jews might go to synagogue occasionally, especially for the High Holidays, but the daughters were not likely to attend regularly, especially after they left home. Ruth Feitelberg Hope, an economist born in Berlin in 1905, recalled in her unpublished memoir:

> I was raised in the Jewish faith. Neither of my parents were orthodox, but this positive attitude towards Judaism, combined with a certain tribal nostalgia, made them observe the high and sometimes the minor holidays. I do not remember that either of them went to the synagogue except on

Rosh Hashanah and Yom Kippur. The holidays were an occasion of the highest order. My father stayed home from the office, I stayed home from school. New or best clothes were donned, my father put on his silk top hat and took his prayer shawl along. Most of the service was performed in Hebrew but a few prayers and the sermon were rendered in German. . . . My parents never observed the fasting that is prescribed for Yom Kippur, while I fasted religiously during my teens, when I had a religious streak. The festive dinners, prompted by the holidays, including the Passover meals, were always taken at my grandmother's house. Somehow, any observance of the Jewish holidays has disappeared from my life. . . . I never missed them for religious reasons. They are a family and childhood memory of things past rather than a religious conviction for me.[32]

Some university women expressed negative attitudes about synagogue attendance and felt alienated because they lacked knowledge of Hebrew and because women were excluded from participation. Charlotte Wolff, who was born in West Prussia in 1897, described her impressions as follows:

We kept the big Jewish festivals of Rosch-a-Shona [sic] and Yom Kippur. Visits to the Synagogue were compulsory on those days. Both the atmosphere and the happenings in the Synagogue almost suffocated me. The religious service was held on the ground floor, which was reserved for males. Women did not participate in it, and had to sit in a gallery above. . . . The women, second-class citizens of God, chatted about children, house and clothes, and paraded their fineries to one another. They didn't understand Hebrew anyway; nor did most of the men I believe, apart from the Rabbi and Cantor. I accepted neither the discrimination between the sexes nor the hollow holiness of the religious service. After my . . . experience at sixteen, I refused visits to the Synagogue.[33]

Some Jewish Jews from traditional homes attended synagogue weekly during their childhood, but very few continued to do so as they grew older. For some young women, at least, synagogue attendance was more of a social occasion than a religious experience. In their memoirs, Orthodox women seem to mention socializing with young men in the synagogue courtyard more frequently than praying in the sanctuary.[34] In only rare cases, such as the Silving memoir, are prayer and God mentioned at all.[35] Very few women refer to synagogue confirmation ceremonies in their memoirs or questionnaires; later in life they were likely to get married in a synagogue, but even that fact is noted only rarely.

German and Jewish youth movements, like synagogues, tended to be predominantly male bastions, although several developed separate offshoots for girls. My research findings indicate that young girls planning to study at a university, especially those born in the nineteenth century, rarely belonged to youth groups or girls' clubs. The few who joined the Wandervogel found themselves rejected because of antisemitism. By contrast, those who affiliated with the co-educational socialist youth movement generally retained a Social Democratic or Communist affiliation while at the university. Although membership in socialist groups was certainly more common than participation in Jewish youth movements, for the most part, future university women tended to be loners and not joiners.

Among the younger generation, those born after 1900, several became active in the Zionist Blau-Weiss and Hashomer Hatzair or in the Liberal youth movement, Kameraden. Such groups provided co-ed social outlets as well as sports, hiking, and nature lore, along with informal Jewish education; and they often had a very strong impact on the lives and group identity of their members, sometimes transforming them into ardent Zionists against their parents' wishes.[36] Trude Weiss-Rosmarin, a Jewish educator and journalist born in Frankfurt am Main in 1908, recounts the following: "Blau-Weiss filled all my waking hours—school and home were necessary evils—Blau-Weiss was meaning and purpose."[37] These young girls belonged to a Jewish community of youth, but they were very much the exceptions, rather than the general rule among prospective Jewish university women.

As university students, Jewish women continued their pattern of individualism by rarely joining either women's student organizations or Jewish student groups. Male Jewish students organized the Kartell-Convent and Zionist Kartell Jüdischer Verbindungen in order to overcome the social ostracism and rampant antisemitism within German and Austrian student fraternities; but Jewish women students remained excluded from membership in these male fraternities, as well as from most women's student societies, which tended to be Christian and denominational. Despite their disproportionately large representation at many German and Austrian universities, Jewish women students were reluctant to establish their own organizations. My research has uncovered only cursory references to an Orthodox women's student group called Beruria[38] and a short-lived Jewish Women's Student Association at the University of Berlin immediately after World War I. According to its statutes, the primary goal of the latter organization was "to unite those Jewish women students who consciously feel themselves to be Jews and want to work together for the development of a living Judaism"; despite the very sizable number of Jewish women studying in Berlin, however, this association attracted only a few dozen members and lasted only four years.[39]

Insofar as Jewish women manifested overt signs of Jewishness while at the university, they generally did so individually rather than collectively. Religious observance of any kind was uncommon among Jewish university students; however, several women with Orthodox backgrounds, including Rahel Goitein, Selma Lewin (later Wehl) and Henda Silberpfennig (later known as Helen Silving-Rhu), made special arrangements to observe kashrut while living away from home. Henda Silberpfenning walked to her classes at the University of Vienna and refused to carry an umbrella on the Sabbath. Selma Lewin transferred universities several times in order to be able to complete her medical school requirements without taking examinations on Saturday.[40] Although, with some effort, one could maintain a private Jewish lifestyle while at university, very few women students were inclined to do so.

Antisemitism was rampant at German and Austrian universities, especially during the interwar years, and as a result, higher education did not generally serve to instill or reinforce a positive sense of Jewish identity. While at the university, female Jewish students usually did not encounter the same types of physical violence and verbal slurs that their male counterparts often experienced, especially in Vienna.[41] Like Rose-Marie Papanek-Akselrad, nearly all the women in my study population, except for some foreign-born students,[42] claim not to have personally experienced antisemitism during their student years prior to the 1930s; nonetheless, the academic climate was certainly not conducive to public expressions of Jewishness. After receiving their degrees, university women were apt to meet up with more overt antisemitism, as well as misogyny, in the form of job discrimination, especially when seeking internships, teaching jobs, and research positions.

Both German and Austrian universities were notorious for their reluctance to hire and promote unbaptized Jews and women. Therefore, with rare exceptions, only women who were Former Jews could even aspire to academic careers. The very select group of women of Jewish descent who managed to become untenured faculty at German or Austrian universities was made up overwhelmingly of baptized or unaffiliated Jews.[43] Even baptized Jews, including the philosopher Edith Stein and the Etruscan expert Eva Fiesel, had considerable difficulty attaining university positions. Jewish Jews, such as the historian Selma Stern-Täubler, failed to obtain academic appointments; other highly qualified Jewish women did not even consider applying for academic jobs.[44] Being Jewish was clearly a disadvantage for those women who wished to remain in a university setting.

Some individuals who nevertheless chose to affirm their Jewish identity became active in Zionist student groups, although they encountered difficulties, as women, in joining previously all-male societies, especially before World War I. It was Zionism, rather than Judaism, that attracted several highly assimilated Former Jews, such as Rudolfine Walltuch (later Menzel) and Emilie Melchior (later Braun), back to the Jewish fold.[45] For many Jewish Jews, including some from Orthodox backgrounds, identifying themselves as Jews by nationality and involving themselves in Zionist activities provided a vehicle for a more positive and modern identification as Jews. One woman with a doctorate in history, born in Frankfurt in 1900, wrote in a letter to me: "Why did I become a Zionist, although I was raised in the [S. R.] Hirsch [Orthodox] community? This was not a common event in those days, but it was not unusual either. Those were the happy and hopeful days after World War I and being Jewish was a matter of pride and joy."[46] Yet only about 10 percent of university women in my study population identified themselves as Zionists or Jewish nationalists.

Central European Jewish university women usually considered themselves to be Germans by language and culture. For most of these women, the attachment to German culture was so strong that becoming a Jewish nationalist was almost inconceivable.[47] As Erna Aronsohn Proskauer, a lawyer who was born in Bromberg, Posen, in 1903, expressed it, "We were so German, that the idea never came to us even in a dream to leave Germany." Her father was an anti-Zionist who found the idea of a Jewish state absurd; although she herself later emigrated to Palestine, Erna Aronsohn was completely uninterested in the question of Palestine and there were no Zionists within her circle of friends.[48] This situation was by no means unusual among Just Jews or even among Jewish Jews; Cora Berliner, an economist and organizer of Jewish girls' clubs, and Margarete Berent, a lawyer and active member of the Jüdischer Frauenbund, for example, remained committed Jewish Liberals and non-Zionists.[49]

Rose-Marie Papanek-Akselrad's self-identification as an Austrian mirrors a statement by Beate Berwin that she was "imbued with German culture to such a degree that there was no question about [her] being and feeling German." Like Papanek-Axelrad, Berwin, who was born in Silesia in 1885, claimed to "look like a German girl," but she encountered antisemitism firsthand. After receiving her doctorate in philosophy from Heidelberg University, she became a disciple of Hermann Cohen, who taught her to "understand her own origin" and provided her with a role model for being "an ardent German patriot though being a faithful Jew."[50]

Although some Jewish university women recalled patriotic feelings toward Germany or Austria during World War I, most lacked a strong sense of German or Austrian national identity. During the interwar years, when German nationalism became increasingly identified with its right-wing, *völkisch* and Nazi elements, educated Jewish women, who were predominantly liberals or leftists, or else apolitical, tended to distance themselves from ardent expressions of nationalism. After the advent of Nazi rule, however, some of these women articulated an urgent need to be accepted as Germans or Austrians and to disassociate themselves from the Jewish community and other Jews. This phenomenon is particularly conspicuous among some of the submissions for the essay competition "My Life in Germany Before and After 1933"—sponsored by Harvard University on the eve of the war—including the memoirs of Käte Frankenthal, Rose-Marie Papanek-Akselrad, Beate Berwin, and especially Paula Tobias.

Tobias, born in Hamburg in 1886, was a rural physician who was religiously unaffiliated but whose son was baptized a Lutheran. In 1933, she responded at length to an accusation in the *Deutsches Ärzteblatt* that physicians were knowingly denying their Jewish origins. She wrote:

> That I am 'non-Aryan' and a physician I admit in advance. That I am German, I can prove as true. . . . Our tragedy does not lie in self-deception as you imply. A life like ours with all its results and achievements is not built upon self-deception. That we with all our powers were never anything other than German, and then to be ejected from the midst of our own *Volk* and made without honor, that is our tragedy. . . .

In closing, she reiterated her loyalty to Germany and her love and devotion to all things German.[51] Tobias's highly patriotic assertions, which could only have been made before the Holocaust, are somewhat of an anomaly for Central European Jewish university women, most of whose memoirs were written after World War II and hence were influenced by personal or family experiences of the Shoah.

Some Former Jews, like Tobias, might only reluctantly acknowledge that they were "non-Aryans," while Jewish Jews, like Rahel Goitein Straus, openly manifested pride in their Jewishness; but many Just Jews, like Papanek-Akselrad, can be classified as *Trotzjüdinnen*. They were Jews despite a lack of strong personal commitment to either Judaism or Jewish nationalism; for them, being a Jew who belonged to the Gemeinde was merely a fact of life rather than a source of either shame or joy. Formal affiliation with a local Jewish community was not a very meaningful measure of identification for most Jewish university women, since the decision whether or not to remain within the Gemeinde and pay one's annual religious tax generally rested with a male head of household, either a father or, later, in many cases a husband. Memoirs indicate that the decision not to desert the Jewish community for opportunistic reasons in difficult times was often made not by these women themselves but by their fathers. As Beate Berwin recalled, "My father [a small-town judge in Silesia] would not hear of a change of his religion though he was quite liberal and did not cling to the dogma of his forefathers. When any of his superiors proposed to him to become converted in order to be promoted immediately after, he always rejected it saying that one must not change one's creed like a dress. I remember this phrase well."[52] For most university women, being Jewish was simply what one was, not what one did; one's sense of a collective Jewish identity was personal and not public.

In general, women were excluded from Gemeinde leadership. In nearly all Central European communities, women who were not tax-paying heads of households could not vote in communal elections, and women were not eligible to hold elected communal offices. Instead, German and Austrian Jewish women became involved in Jewish public life primarily through their volunteer efforts on behalf of Jewish women's organizations such as the Jüdischer Frauenbund and B'nai B'rith Women or various charities and social welfare agencies. Although there are notable exceptions, including Rahel Goitein Straus, Margarete Berent, and Cora Berliner, most university women tended to shun volunteer women's groups and did not become actively involved within the Jewish community or its institutions before the Nazi era.

Despite a lack of formal affiliation with Jewish groups, the friendships and social circles of most of the women in my study population tended to be made up largely of other Jews, not necessarily by conscious choice or preference. In their childhood and youth, Jewish university women sometimes had close friendships with both Jews and non-Jews, but as they grew older, they often found themselves gravitating toward other Jews. Girls began to experience the social barriers between Jews and non-Jews at a fairly young age. Several women, including Käte Frankenthal, comment in their memoirs that they were not welcome in the homes of their non-Jewish school friends and, by the age of thirteen, no longer received birthday invitations from certain classmates.[53]

The antisemitism experienced by young Jewish women was, for the most part, social in nature. While at the university and thereafter, many avoided unpleasant encounters by socializing mainly with other Jews, both men and women. Jewish Jews and Just Jews were more conscious than Former Jews of belonging to a community of fate and, as a result, they were more likely to associate with, and eventually marry, other Jews. Less than 10 percent of the unbaptized women in my study population who married intermarried. In their professional careers, as well as in their personal lives, they generally found themselves in predominantly Jewish circles.

Former Jews tended to associate primarily with, and to marry, non-Jews or other Former Jews. Although the marriage selection pool for Former Jews would appear to be much wider than for those women who remained Jewish, a disproportionately large number of the Former Jews within my study population (37 percent of Former Jews as compared to 27 percent of Just Jews and 13 percent of Jewish Jews) never married. Those socialist and communist activists who, like Käte Frankenthal, formally left the Jewish community, as well as the majority of left-wing sympathizers who remained nominally affiliated, generally belonged to circles of middle-class, left-wing intellectuals, nearly all of whom were Jews or Former Jews. With some notable exceptions, they too were likely eventually to marry other Jews or Former Jews, if they married at all.[54] Although Jewish university women often distanced themselves from Judaism and the organized Jewish community, except for those who were formally baptized, most remained Jews by association.

If, when, and whom a woman married often greatly influenced a university woman's Jewish involvement, as well as her level of Jewish practice. Women who dropped out of the university to get married or who married soon after receiving a doctorate and who did not pursue a career were somewhat more likely to conform to Marion Kaplan's prescribed norms for middle-class Jewish women by maintaining some Jewish observances in their homes and joining volunteer Jewish women's organizations. Their lifestyle more closely resembled that of their mothers and less-educated sisters than did that of Jewish university women who never married, married later in life, or had no children. Single women had a particularly difficult time finding a niche for themselves in Jewish terms, although some found employment within the communal educational and social welfare network and several became active in the Jüdischer Frauenbund.

After 1933, some Just Jewish university women rediscovered their Jewishness and turned to the Jewish community from which they had become estranged. Having lost their jobs as teachers, social workers, and administrators, they increasingly looked to Jewish schools and institutions for employment. Several established new schools for Jewish children, while others temporarily assumed leadership roles in organizing emigration and looking after the needs of those who remained. For the first time, in many cases, they were using their professional skills specifically to help other Jews.

For the most part, however, Jewish university women were marginal members of the organized Jewish community and remained on its periphery throughout their lives in Germany or Austria. This was true not only because many of them came from highly assimilated backgrounds but because they often did not assume the traditional roles of middle-class Jewish women. Highly educated women who remained single, who married late, and who had no children, or who combined both family and career, did not easily fit within the established Jewish communal and organizational framework. If they had not already distanced themselves from the Gemeinde and its institutions in their youth, many became increasingly alienated as adults.

Both as Jews and as women, Central European Jewish university women never found a Jewish community with which they could strongly identify.[55] Even the Jewish Jews among them did not fit into the Jewish mainstream very comfortably; but few of them attempted to reform the Gemeinde or the position of women within it. As educated career women, whether married or not, they generally did not feel part of the established Jewish community, which expected women to adhere to their traditional roles as wives, mothers, and volunteers.

The women in my study population tended to be exceptional individuals and loners who rarely joined either women's or Jewish organizations. For most of them, their Jewishness was a private matter, and before 1933 at least, they only occasionally articulated or manifested it publicly. Nevertheless, even if they were no longer involved in traditional Jewish family life or official Jewish communities, since most Jewish university women associated primarily with other Jews of similar background and education, they continued to belong, de facto, to informal communities of Jews. Jewish university women in Germany and Austria were thus "New Women" who, for the most part, identified as Jews in their personal lives but did not carve out a significant role for themselves within the organized Jewish community. Nevertheless, they can be seen as the vanguard of the highly educated "New Jewish Woman" of the late twentieth century.

Notes

1. Swiss universities began to accept women as matriculated students in the 1860s, but the Jewish women who attended came mainly from Russia and only a few hailed from Germany or Austria-Hungary. The University of Vienna admitted women in 1897; the universities in Baden started to accept women in 1900 and in Prussia in 1908.

2. Waltraud Heindl and Marina Tichy, eds., *"Durch Erkenntnis zu Freiheit und Glück . . ." Frauen an der Universität Wien ab 1897* (Vienna, 1990), pp. 139–49.

3. Claudia Huerkamp, "Frauen, Universitäten und Bildungsbürgertum: Zur Lage studierender Frauen 1900–1930," in *Bürgerliche Berufe: Zur Sozialgeschichte der freien und akademischen Berufe im internationalen Vergleich,* ed. Hannes Siegrist (Göttingen, 1988), pp. 208–10; Claudia Huerkamp, "Jüdische Akademikerinnen in Deutschland, 1900–1938," *Geschichte und Gesellschaft* 19 (1993): 311–31; *Deutsche Hochschulstatistik* (1932).

4. Ibid. See also Konrad H. Jarausch, *Students, Society and Politics in Imperial Germany: The Rise of Academic Illiberalism* (Princeton, 1982), pp. 96–97; Gary B. Cohen, "Die Studenten der Wiener Universität von 1860 bis 1900," in *Wegenetz europäischen Geistes II: Universitäten und Studenten,* ed. Richard Georg Plaschka and Karlheinz Mack (Vienna, 1987), pp. 296–97; Peter Pulzer, *The Rise of Political Anti-Semitism in Germany and Austria* (New York, 1964), pp. 12–13.

5. Marion A. Kaplan, *The Making of the Jewish Middle Class: Women, Family, and Identity in Imperial Germany* (New York, 1991); idem, "For Love or Money: The Marriage Strategies of Jewish Women in Imperial Germany," *LBIYB* 28 (1983): 263–300; idem, "Priestess and Hausfrau: Women and Tradition in the German-Jewish Family," in *The Jewish Family: Myths and Reality,* ed. Steven M. Cohen and Paula E. Hyman (New York, 1986), pp. 62–81; idem, "Tradition and Transition – The Acculturation, Assimilation and Integration of Jews in Imperial Germany: A Gender Analysis," *LBIYB* 27 (1982).

6. Rudolfine Menzel, "My Life in Germany Before and After January 30, 1933," Houghton Library, Harvard University, bMS Ger91, #155, p. 21.

7. For a more detailed discussion of these categories, see Harriet Pass Freidenreich, "Jewish Identity and the 'New Woman': Central European Jewish University Women in the Early Twentieth Century," in *Gender and Judaism,* ed. T. M. Rudavsky (New York, 1995), pp. 113–22.

8. Frankenthal's sexual orientation is not entirely clear in her memoir. She drank and smoked cigars, wore her hair short, and sometimes dressed in men's clothing. She seems to have preferred the company of men to that of women. The editors of her published memoirs do not indicate that she was a lesbian. However, only a handful of the unmarried women in my study population identified themselves, or were identified by others, as lesbians. The most explicitly identified Jewish lesbian university woman was Charlotte Wolff. See Charlotte Wolff, *Hindsight* (London, 1980).

9. Käte Frankenthal, *Der dreifache Fluch: Jüdin, Intellektuelle, Sozialistin* (Frankfurt am Main, 1981).

10. Rose-Marie Papanek-Akselrad, "My Life in Germany," Houghton Library, Harvard University, bMS Ger91, #175, p. 1.

11. Ibid.

12. Rahel Straus, *Wir lebten in Deutschland: Erinnerungen einer deutschen Jüdin 1880–1933* (Stuttgart, 1961).

13. Ibid.

14. Marie Jahoda, "Es war nicht umsonst," in *Die andere Erinnerung*, ed. Hajo Funke (Frankfurt am Main, 1990), p. 338.

15. Hilde Zaloscer, *Eine Heimkehr gibt es nicht* (Vienna, 1988); interviews with Hilde Zaloscer, Vienna, July 1992, and with Ruth Gutman, Philadelphia, August 1992. Cf. Edith Stein, *Life in a Jewish Family, 1891–1916: Collected Works of Edith Stein, Sister Teresa Benedicta of the Cross, Discalced Carmelite*, ed. L. Gelber and Romaeus Leuven, vol. 1 (Washington, D.C., 1986); Susanne M. Batzdorff, "Reflections in a Rearview Mirror" (unpublished memoir, Santa Rosa, Ca., 1984); Ruth Pincus-Wieruszowski, "Erinnerungen an Alfred Wierusowski," Leo Baeck Institute (LBI), New York, Memoir Collection, ME-270.

16. Marie Munk, "Reminiscences/Memoirs" (1961), LBI, Memoir Collection, ME-332, vol. 2, p. 4; Margarete Susman, *Ich habe viele Leben gelebt: Erinnerungen* (Stuttgart, 1964), p. 17; Margarete Sallis-Freudenthal, *Ich habe mein Land gefunden* (Frankfurt am Main, 1977); Alice Salomon, "Character Is Destiny," LBI, Memoir Collection, AR-3875; Käthe Leichter, "Lebenserinnerungen" in *Käthe Leichter: Leben und Werk*, ed. Herbert Steiner (Vienna, 1973), p. 303; Wolff, *Hindsight*, p. 11; Hilde Spiel, *Die hellen und die finsteren Zeiten: Erinnerungen 1911–1946* (Munich, 1989); Stephanie Braun Orfali, *Jewish Girl in the Weimar Republic* (Berkeley, 1987).

17. Straus, *Wir lebten in Deutschland*; Yaakov Wehl and Hadassah Wehl, *House Calls to Eternity: The Story of Dr. Selma Wehl* (Brooklyn, 1987); Lotte Popper, "My Life in Germany," Houghton Library, Harvard University, bMS Ger91, #179; Julie Braun-Vogelstein, *Was niemals stirbt: Gestalten und Erinnerungen* (Stuttgart, 1966); Wolff, *Hindsight*, p. 21.

18. Jahoda, "Es war nicht umsonst," pp. 336–37. Cf. Ruth Feitelberg Hope, "The Story of My Family, LBI, Memoir Collection, ME-770; Ingrid Warburg Spinelli, *Die Dringlichkeit des Mitleids und die Einsamkeit, nein zu sagen: Lebenserinnerungen* (Hamburg, 1990); Sallis-Freudenthal, *Ich habe mein Land gefunden.*

19. Charlotte Kerner, *Lise, Atomphysiker: Die Lebensgeschichte der Lise Meitner* (Weinheim, 1986); Elise Richter, "Summe des Lebens. Lebensfreuden Lebensleid" (1940), Landes- und Stadtsarchiv, Vienna, Manuscript Collection, Papers of Elise und Helene Richter, MA9, 336/47, III, 37/3, Box 3; Hilda Weiss, "My Life in Germany," Houghton Library, Harvard University, bMS Ger 91, #240; Sallis-Freudenthal, *Ich habe mein Land gefunden.*

20. Ruth Lewin Sime, *Lise Meitner: A Life in Physics* (Berkeley, 1996), pp. 315–16.

21. Nellie Friedrichs, *Erinnerungen aus meinem Leben in Braunschweig* (Braunschweig, 1983); Orfali, *Jewish Girl in the Weimar Republic;* Wolff, *Hindsight;* Spinelli, *Die Dringliche des Mitleids;* questionnaires.

22. Dodo Liebman, "We Kept Our Heads: Personal Memories of Being Jewish in Nazi Germany and Making a New Home in England" (1976), LBI, Memoir Collection, ME-394, p. 4.

23. Mordechai Breuer, *Modernity within Tradition: A Social History of Orthodoxy in Imperial Germany* (New York, 1992), p. 280.

24. Straus, *Wir lebten in Deutschland;* Helen Silving (Henda Silberpfennig), *Helen Silving Memoirs;* Judith S. Kestenberg, "Kindheit und Wissenschaft: Eine biographische Skizze," in *Psychoanalyse in Selbstdarstellungen*, ed. Ludger M. Hermanns (Tübingen, 1992).

25. Questionnaire and letter from Elisheva Stern (née Elisabeth Dann), Israel, June 1992.

26. Interestingly enough, Regina Jonas, the only woman to receive any form of rabbinical ordination in Germany, did not attend a university but received her entire training at the Hochschule für die Wissenschaft des Judentums. See Katharina von Kellenbach, "'God Does Not Oppress Any Human Being': The Life and Thought of Rabbi Regina Jonas," *LBIYB* 29 (1994): 213–26.

27. Michael Brenner, *The Renaissance of Jewish Culture in Weimar Germany* (New Haven, 1996), pp. 86, 110–11. Exceptions to this general rule include Selma Stern-Täubler, Hannah Arendt, Bertha Badt-Strauss, Paula Weiner-Odenheimer, Eva Reichmann, and Rahel Wischnitzer, all of whom published works on Jewish topics while in Germany. One might also mention Trude Weiss-Rosmarin, Nehama Leibowitz, and Lea Goldberg, who emigrated soon after receiving their doctorates.

28. Marie Langer, *Von Wien bis Managua: Wege einer Psychoanalytikerin* (Frankfurt am Main, 1986); Edith Weisskopf-Joelson, *Father, Have I Kept My Promise?* (West Lafayette, 1988); Helene Deutsch, *Confrontations with Myself: An Epilogue* (New York, 1973); Stella Klein-Löw, *Erinnerungen: Erlebtes und Gedachtes* (Vienna, 1980).

29. Lotte H. Eisner, *Ich hatte einst ein schönes Vaterland: Memoiren* (Heidelberg, 1984); Wolff, *Hindsight*.

30. Stein, *Life in a Jewish Family;* Salomon, "Character Is Destiny," pp. 120–24.

31. Steiner, *Käte Leichter;* Klein-Löw, *Erinnerungen;* Toni Sender, *The Autobiography of a German Rebel* (New York, 1939); Recha Rothschild, "Memoirs of Recha Rothschild (1880–1964)," LBI, Memoir Collection, ME-243.

32. Ruth Feitelberg Hope, "The Story of My Family," LBI, Memoir Collection, ME-770, pp. 86–87; cf. Susi Lewinsky, "Memoires" (unpublished memoir, courtesy of Andreas Lixl-Purcell, with permission of author).

33. Wolff, *Hindsight*, pp. 46–47.

34. Monika Richarz, ed., *Jewish Life in Germany: Memoirs from Three Centuries,* trans. Stella P. Rosenfeld and Sidney Rosenfeld (Bloomington, 1991), pp. 266–67. To the extent that these women prayed on a regular basis, it is likely that they did so in the privacy of their home rather than in the synagogue.

35. One of the few exceptions is Henda Silberpfennig. See Helen Silving, *Helen Silving Memoirs* (New York, 1988).

36. Menzel, "My Life in Germany"; Orfali, *Jewish Girl in Weimar Germany.*

37. Trude Weiss-Rosmarin, "Frankfurt am Main," *Jewish Spectator* (Fall 1976): 3–6 (as quoted in Barbara Straus Reed, "Trude Weiss-Rosmarin: Rebel with a Cause," paper presented to the Annual National Meeting of the Association for Education in Journalism, Boston, 1991).

38. Breuer, *Modernity within Tradition,* p. 379.

39. "Jüdischer Studentinnenverein an der Universität Berlin 1916/20," Humboldt University Archives, Rektorat/Senat No. 845.

40. Straus, *Wir lebten in Deutschland;* Wehl, *House Calls to Eternity;* Silving, *Helen Silving Memoirs.*

41. Benno Varon, *Professions of a Lucky Jew* (New York, 1992); Edmund Schechter, *Viennese Vignettes: Personal Recollections* (New York, 1983); Papanek-Akselrad, "My Life in Germany"; questionnaires and interviews.

42. One foreign student who encountered virulent antisemitism while studying in Germany in the 1920s was Hungarian-born Margaret Mahler. See Margaret Mahler, *The Memoirs of Margaret S. Mahler,* ed. Paul E. Stepansky (New York, 1988), pp. 27–39.

43. Among the prominent Former Jewish women who achieved "Habilitation"

were Elise Richter in Romance philology and Charlotte Bühler in psychology at the University of Vienna; and Lise Meitner in physics, Charlotte Leubuscher in sociology, Hedwig Hintze in history, and Lydia Rabinowitsch-Kempner in bacteriology at the University of Berlin. The exceptions, women who obtained academic appointments while remaining Jews, included Emmy Noether in mathematics at Göttingen; Hilde Geiringer in mathematics at Berlin; and Selma Meyer in pediatric medicine at Düsseldorf. See Elisabeth Boedeker and Maria Meyer-Plath, *50 Jahre Habilitation von Frauen in Deutschland* (Göttingen, 1974); Doris Ingrisch, *"Alles war das Institut!"* (Vienna, 1992).

44. Hiltrud Häntzschel, "Der Exodus von Wissenschaftlerinnen: Jüdische Studentinnen an der Münchner Universität und was aus ihnen wurde," *Exil: Forschung, Erkenntnisse, Ergebnisse* 2 (1992): 43–51.

45. Menzel, "My Life in Germany"; Emily Melchior Braun, Memoir (Israel, 1986), LBI, Memoir Collection, ME-231.

46. Letter from Rosy B. Bodenheimer, Baltimore, Maryland, May 28, 1992.

47. Wolff, *Hindsight.* Helene Deutsch, a psychoanalyst from Galicia, was an ardent Polish nationalist rather than a German nationalist. See Deutsch, *Confrontations with Myself.*

48. Erna Proskauer, *Wege und Umwege: Erinnerungen einer Rechtsanwältin,* ed. Sabine Berghahn and Christl Wickert (Berlin, 1989), p. 17.

49. Esriel Hildesheimer, "Cora Berliner: Ihr Leben und Wirken," *BLBI* 67 (1984): 41–70; Cora Berliner Papers, LBI, Memoir Collection AR-1578; Margarete Berent Papers, LBI, Memoir Collection AR-2861/2862.

50. Beate Clara Berwin (pseud. Elisabeth Moore), "My Own Development," Houghton Library, Harvard University, bMS Ger91, #26, pp. 4–5.

51. Paula Tobias, "My Life in Germany," Houghton Library, Harvard University, bMS Ger91, #235, pp. 12–14.

52. Berwin, "My Own Development," p. 1. Cf. Inka Bertz, "Helene Nathan: Eine Grossstadtbücherei und ihre Bibliothekarin," in *Leidenschaft und Bildung,* ed. Helga Lüdke (Berlin, 1992), p. 174.

53. Frankenthal, *Der dreifache Fluch;* Munk, "Reminiscences"; Emmy Klieneberger-Nobel, *Pionierleistungen für die Medizinische Mikrobiologie: Lebenserinnerungen* (Stuttgart, 1977).

54. Steiner, *Käthe Leichter;* Jahoda, "Es war nicht umsonst"; Langer, *Von Wien bis Managua.*

55. Helga Embacher, "Aussenseiterinnen: bürgerlich, jüdisch, intellektuell–links," *L'Homme. Zeitschrift für Feministische Geschichtswissenschaft* 2, no. 2 (1991): 57–76.

10

The Crisis of the Jewish Family in Weimar Germany

Social Conditions and Cultural Representations

SHARON GILLERMAN

For some, family cohesion is the basis of all state
and national welfare; for others, the family is an
outdated institution whose functions are better
fulfilled by other means. The first group
believes the family unit still exists and is
valued by the masses; the other is of
the opinion that family life has ceased
to exist altogether. Between the extremes
is the idea that affirms the family as a value
and source of individual and national
well-being but recognizes that it is
endangered by modern life.

—*Alice Salomon*[1]

In the aftermath of World War I, most social critics and reformers
agreed that the family was in the throes of an unprecedented crisis.
The terrible war casualties, along with a plummeting national birthrate, raised concerns that the German nation would never regain its
former strength. Beyond its reduced reproductive capacity, the family
was also believed to be in a state of moral decay. According to the
writer Jakob Wassermann, a seemingly indiscriminate discarding of
accepted social norms, coupled with a growing sense of individual

autonomy, particularly in the cities, had "made middle-class marriage appear more than ever a questionable institution."[2]

Given this atmosphere, it may seem surprising that the family was also enlisted as an emblem of national unity. Although the image of the model family, as depicted by public figures and medical and social work professionals, bore the distinct imprint of middle-class society, it served to offer an ideology of integration to the nation as a whole. This idealized family, drawn from a pastiche of backward-looking fantasies of preindustrial life and nineteenth-century formulations of bourgeois family life, existed well above the fray of day-to-day politics. In its capacity as the basic constituent of the nation, each family was an equal member of the national organism and every citizen a co-equal contributor to its strength. Conversely, as the moral and physical "sickness" of the family spread to *Volk* and economy, the existence of the state was believed to be in danger. "When the family is in need," read the entry in a respected encyclopedia of politics and government, "nation and Fatherland are too."[3]

Analysis of the discussion of family decline within the Jewish community during this period raises an important methodological question, one that underlies the study of modern Jews as a whole. Is it possible for historians to isolate the "Jewish" aspects of any given social practice, attitude, or even set of social conditions from their "general" or non-Jewish origins when our historical subjects are part of, indeed a product of, that general culture? Historians of German Jewry face a fundamental paradox in pursuing such questions. On the one hand, German Jews were the paradigmatic moderns. Historians therefore take it as given that there were competing claims for their loyalties and that religion and ethnicity were but two among many influences shaping an individual's identity. On the other hand, given an a priori interest in the Jews, our questions generally seek to isolate distinct aspects of the Jewish experience. We tend to dwell upon subjects such as antisemitism and Jewish communal life that primarily, if not exclusively, affected the Jews. While recognizing that Jewishness forms only one part of the modern Jewish individual, is it possible to focus on specifically Jewish aspects of experience without yielding a distorted historical picture? In other words, can we disentangle things German and Jewish without compromising the real complexity of our subjects?

This essay will focus on how both German and specifically Jewish concerns about family decline in Weimar Germany coalesced during this period of political and social transition. Based on the writings of a variety of social work professionals, lay leaders, rabbis, and feminists, I will look first at the broad features of the crisis as they were understood by both Jewish and non-Jewish Germans. I will then turn to an examination of some of the specific cultural meanings that the family had for Jews. By looking at social realities alongside their cultural constructions, I hope to highlight the apparent disjunction between the self-perception of a prominent sector of the Jewish community and the situation affecting them and their co-religionists. The interrelated set of social and economic circumstances that made up what Weimar contemporaries labeled "the crisis of the family" was not based on conditions unique to the Jewish community, although there were aspects specific to it that I will touch on here. Yet, while there was little that was exclusively Jewish about the family problems addressed by these leaders in their discussions, the problems endured by Jewish families were felt to affect German Jews in a unique way. The cultural significance ascribed to the Jewish family, its historical role for Jews, and its presumed uniqueness point to the existence of a set of beliefs about the Jewish family that served to accentuate the uniqueness of the Jews as a group. I will suggest that an ideology of Jewish uniqueness grew in significance precisely at a time when the fear of losing group distinctiveness was greatest. The more acute the sense of social change, and the more the social realities of Jewish families appeared to approximate those of non-Jews, the greater the significance of the family—as social institution and cultural con-struct—in forming and re-forming a Jewish self-consciousness al-ready noted as being constantly in flux.

The focus on family decline during periods of social transition is certainly not unique to Weimar Germany. Society's attention seems to return to the theme of "family in crisis" at significant social junctures, when certain elements of society are reeling from the impact of social change. The theme of the "family in crisis" accompanied the social revolutions of the late 1960s, and we saw it surface again in the early 1990s. Among Jews, the assumption of the social characteristics of the majority culture on the one hand, and the assertion of the unique importance of the family on the other, have been discernible in the stance of the communal leadership of American Jews who, as a highly acculturated minority group, have faced a similar set of social dynam-ics to those confronting German Jews.

Because of this, one important aspect of the Jewish crisis of the family, which went beyond the actual social distress undergone by Jewish families during the economic crises of the 1920s, was the strong desire of Jewish leaders to preserve a degree of Jewish group distinctiveness in the face of ongoing German-Jewish integration. In addition to its universally important symbolic function as an object of nostalgic longing, the family represented for Jews one of the final markers of Jewish difference within the larger society, one of the last remaining areas of Jewish group distinctiveness. For Jews who had relinquished attachment to Judaism as a religious system, the family had become a proud standard-bearer for Jewish ethnic values. In an age of nationalism, it was becoming something of a homeland for the modern Jew.

The Weimar Crisis of the Family

The idea that the modern nuclear family *(Kleinfamilie)* was facing dissolution did not originate with the Weimar Republic. During the latter part of the nineteenth century, the family had become a symbol of the social upheavals accompanying the transformation to urban industrial society. As the focal point of middle-class reform programs, the living conditions and moral qualities of working-class families in particular became a central concern for Germans witnessing the troubling impact of rapid social change. The bourgeois women's movement, for example, enthusiastically promoted the idea of "social motherhood." By encouraging women to apply their "natural" mothering skills to a broader group of recipients outside the home, the women's movement sought to bring about reconciliation and social healing among working-class youth and their families.[4] Likewise, the emerging science of eugenics aspired to control and manage female reproduction for the sake of improving existing "social material," with a significant part of its socially restorative prescriptions directed toward the biological improvement of the middle-class family. Finally, the growth of professional social work as a service-oriented, scientifically based program defined a whole new set of social problems and risks that designated the family, sexuality, and the body as sites for social work intervention. All these movements and programs arose in response to a broader perception of social disorder, generally referred to, in the mid- to late nineteenth-century, as the *soziale Frage.*

The impact of World War I, together with the military defeat and revolution that followed, served to transform the notion of the family in crisis into a major social and political issue. On the home front, family life had been disrupted by the prolonged absence of the father and older brothers, and often by the chronic worry or illness of the mother. The domestic toll exacted by the war was also exceedingly costly: there were as many civilians as soldiers among the victims.[5]

The social effects of the war on families were accompanied by physical deprivations. Children were underweight by as much as 8 to 12 percent, and their average height declined by 3 to 4 percent.[6] The perception of crisis was most evident in the idea that the bonds that held families together were breaking apart. Perhaps more than anything else, the debate over the crisis of the family conveyed a profound sense of rupture from past forms of community and social relationships. The idea of "the loosening of familial bonds" was invoked almost formulaically by those commenting on the current state of the German family. While the unraveling of family relationships was universally acknowledged to be at least partly the result of the extreme economic conditions of the Weimar period, relationships among family members and between the generations were increasingly analyzed with the help of contemporary psychological concepts.

To many Weimar observers, one of the most readily apparent manifestations of the family's declining cohesion and authority was the rising trend of youthful rebelliousness known as the *Verwilderung der Jugend* (youth going wild). World War I had brought about what Viennese psychoanalyst Paul Federn called a *vaterlose Gesellschaft* (fatherless society).[7] The prolonged absence of husbands during the war placed a double burden on both German and German-Jewish women, many of whom were forced to seek temporary employment outside the home. Images of masses of male teenagers taking possession of the streets haunted public consciousness, and in this context, the political mobilization of young people during the revolutionary period only reinforced public sentiment that the country's youth represented a threat to public safety. There was, in fact, a measure of accuracy in the perception of a disproportionately large population of youth: the plummeting national birthrate during the war skewed the population structure to the extent that ten-to-fifteen-year-olds outnumbered two-year-olds by as much as a ten to one margin.[8] Moreover, the war had produced a population of upwards of two million war orphans that demanded massive state support.[9]

The illness or death of one parent—often coupled with the unemployment of the other—appears to have been the single most important factor threatening the stability of family life. This set of circumstances led to a notable rise in male and female juvenile delinquency during and immediately after the war. By the early 1930s, for example, over 60 percent of the national *Fürsorgeerziehung* population— teenagers deemed "endangered youth" by the courts and undergoing correctional education—came from families affected by divorce, separation, or the death of at least one parent.[10] An examination of the case files of the Deutsch-Israelitische Gemeindebund's two correctional homes for wayward Jewish youth yielded similar findings.[11] The circumstances of Jewish families in trouble appear to have mirrored the situation in Germany as a whole.

The testimony of parents themselves confirms the statistical evidence and gives a picture of the often interrelated set of problems facing families in the postwar period. In a letter seeking the admission of her son to the Jewish correctional home at Repzin, the widowed Frau S. of Leipzig wrote on January 4, 1922:

> My husband died in 1918 when my boy was twelve years old. He was just at that age where he was most susceptible to all the positive and negative influences around him. At that crucial time, he had to do without the guidance and education of his father. I myself am so busy with the household responsibilities attendant to caring for my large family that the boy is almost always left to his own devices. I do not know his friends nor can I control what he does when he's out with them. From the tales he has told, I had to realize that he had been lying to me. . . . I don't have to tell you how boys at this age waste heaps of money on smoking, drinking, cafes, and even worse—you know this all too well being in Berlin.[12]

Though delinquency was the most frequently noted by-product of single-parent families, it was not the only one. Plain old generational conflict was evidently readily exacerbated by the absence of the father's "strong guiding presence." The young Herbert K., for example, exhibited political attitudes and behaviors that were suspicious enough to alarm his uncle, who wrote the following letter. In the absence of the boy's father, Adolf B. of Loslau took it upon himself to address the director of Repzin on June 3, 1920:

> I turn to you today for a very big favor. It concerns my nephew, Herbert K., the son of Emanuel K., with whom you have become quite familiar. I would like to bring him to Repzin. . . . The youth is healthy and strong but suffers from fixed Zionist ideas, as the application of my sister-in-law indicates. These ideas have already led him down the wrong path. He has not been able to keep any apprentice position he has held, and he wants only to be a farmer so he can go to Palestine. My family doctor recommended a reeducation institution in which he would have to do physical work and be educated on the basis of strict order and discipline. This is a task that my sister-in-law is too weak to accomplish.[13]

While the father's absence was believed to be a prime cause of juvenile delinquency and even political radicalization among youth, the dual images of the *Doppelverdienerinnen* (double earners) and the

New Woman evoked anxiety and resentment about the loss of what were called "traditional" gender roles, that is, the middle-class model of the sexual division of labor. Jewish women were sometimes sharply castigated by men such as Felix Theilhaber for pursuing the false idol of career and for having become alienated from their calling as housewife and mother.[14] Feminists and others who worked closely with women and their families, however, emphasized instead the economic situation that forced more women to seek employment outside the home.[15] Dr. Hanauer, a professor of Social Medicine at Frankfurt University and organizer of the Frankfurt Ehebahnung-stelle (marriage preparation bureau), noted, for example, that many middle-class Jewish women were deprived of the parental financial support needed to launch a marriage. Moreover, given the sometimes skyrocketing unemployment rates among men, married women could no longer feel secure in anchoring their economic existence in mar-riage. Like many feminists, Dr. Berg-Platau countered that married women worked outside the home in order to support their children, not because they were lusting after the achievements of men.[16]

Even with both parents at home, family relations in the postwar period were said to suffer from a widening generation gap.[17] Dr. Arthur Czellitzer, a Berlin ophthalmologist and founder of the Berlin-based Gesellschaft für jüdische Familienforschung, frequently decried the *Kluft der Generationen*, or generation gap, that he thought was becoming typical of families throughout Germany. The chief cause of the generation gap, in his opinion, was rapid and unceasing migration to the cities, since it reduced cross-generational contacts by separating children from their grandparents and other extended family mem-bers. And because Jews experienced a proportionately higher degree of geographic and class mobility, Czellitzer concluded that Jewish children and parents, more than others in Germany, ceased to share common life experiences and attitudes.

Czellitzer's was a commonly held view. The Berlin pediatrician and social hygienist Heinrich Stahl concurred with him and advised Jewish parents to be responsive to the new demands posed by their adolescent children. By the 1920s, prescriptive literature in Jewish papers reflected a new readiness to grant adolescents the indepen-dence they demanded.[18] "Youth today," wrote Stahl, "force their parents to understand them. If they don't, they risk becoming alien-ated from their children."[19] Jewish women's papers exhorted mothers to cultivate close friendships with their children as a way of bridging the differences of life experience.[20]

By the 1920s, then, the emotional and psychological aspects of family relations had become the frequent subject of lively debate. It was within the general framework of discussion about child-rearing that antisemitism was understood to be a serious problem facing Jewish families and their children.[21] Parents and psychologists worried that Jewish young people suffered from a type of double alienation. On the one hand, some young Jews, like their non-Jewish counterparts, were swept up by the cult of youth, spurned the isolation of their middle-class family lives, and repudiated the compromises made by their parents; on the other hand, they faced a social environment that was becoming increasingly inhospitable to them. The question of how to handle children's encounters with antisemitism in the school was often raised in the Jewish press, particularly in advice columns.[22] Jewish psychologists explained the predicament of the Jewish child as one in which sustained social pressure led to a permanent "inferiority complex," which, in keeping with the spirit of the times, was believed to be both organically and sociologically determined.[23] Studies of the "Jewish psyche" explored the relationship between milieu and inherited characteristics that contributed to the increasing alienation experienced by Jewish children in Germany. According to the renowned psychologist Dr. Erich Stern, "the Jewish child is more agitated, troubled, more sensitive and thin-skinned, because he is permanently on the defensive, owing to the perpetual tensions existing within him. He has the sensitivity and nervousness of one who is threatened."[24]

The sense of family crisis was widely understood to entail the breakdown of traditional family relationships. But the sense of crisis also surrounded the physical existence of the family. Propelled by wartime population losses, medical doctors and population experts hastened to blame women for the changing patterns in family formation that had begun in the late nineteenth century and continued unabated into the twentieth.[25] Where family planning in the general population had been confined to a small, well-educated sector in the nineteenth century, it was increasingly practiced by the working classes and petite bourgeoisie from the beginning of the twentieth century.[26] The *Zweikindersystem* (two-child family) was becoming the rule during the Weimar Republic, and predictions abounded that the three-person household would soon become the new middle-class norm. During periods of peak unemployment, abortion rates rose noticeably, so that in 1931 alone it was estimated that one million abortions had taken place.[27]

Among the Jewish population, a sharp drop in the birthrate was noted to have begun in the 1870s. Without exception, Jewish and non-Jewish physicians agreed that the decline in the Jewish birthrate preceded and then surpassed the declining birthrates of other Germans. While they cited varying sets of numbers, the pattern they described was decisive: the Jewish birthrate had begun to tumble at least a generation before those of Protestants and Catholics.[28] By some time in the 1920s—assessments varied—the Jewish population was said to have ceased producing enough children to maintain the population size, much less provide for growth through natural increase. In Berlin, the situation was reputed to be even more dismal. The Jewish birthrate hovered around 9.4 per 1000; 17 births per 1000 was the rate believed necessary in order to maintain replacement levels of the population. Without the Jewish population's fertile eastern sector, Theilhaber figured the birthrate might have been as low as 5 to 6 percent.

Explanations for the decline in births among Jews and non-Jews were quite similar—it was due to fewer and later marriages. It had been asserted since the middle of the nineteenth century that Jews had developed a growing distaste for marriage, entering marriage less frequently than members of other confessions. Theilhaber, for example, claimed that the "scourge of marriagelessness" afflicted 25 percent of adult, marriage-age Jews. He maintained that, owing to Jews' lower infant mortality rate, Jewish marriage rates remained some 20 to 50 percent below the German national average, even though their rate had been 10 to 20 percent higher than that of other Germans before the turn of the century.[29] Even more than the declining number of marriages, however, Jewish social critics during the Weimar era cited late marriage as the most significant reason for the diminishing numbers of Jewish offspring. Because fewer fertile years remained within which couples could produce "child-rich" families, late marriages were generally held responsible for declining infant "yields." Prior to the turn of the century, social scientists had already noted a more advanced age of marriage among German Jews, but the postwar postponement of marriage was now reportedly accelerating. By the end of the 1920s, Theilhaber was convinced, on the basis of the Jewish population survey conducted by the Preussischer Landesverband jüdischer Gemeinden, that women were hastening to join men in deferring marriage.[30] "Half of all Jewesses marry only after their twenty-seventh year," he proclaimed grimly. "Fifty percent of female Jews, therefore, have been excluded from motherhood during the first decade of their child-bearing years. Only in the second half of their fertile years do these women succeed in contracting marriages."[31]

Beyond decreasing the period of marital fertility, late marriage was thought to further exacerbate the decline in births by encouraging increased sexual activity outside marriage. Prolonging the period of being single at a time when standards governing sexual behavior were being relaxed appeared to be at the root of a rising incidence of sexually transmitted diseases.[32] The contraction of sexual diseases, in turn, was considered to be a significant contributing factor to reduced fertility since venereal diseases frequently left their victims sterile. According to the sexologists Hirsch and Nürnberg, one-half to two-thirds of all undesired infertility in Germany was due to the ravaging effects of sexually transmitted disease among both men and women. The Jewish physician Berg-Platau concluded that the "role of syphilis in causing the birth decline and the degenerative phenomena among Jews is not to be underestimated, since, thanks to their particularly high rate of late marriage, Jews are contracting sexual diseases more frequently."[33] Focusing more on the changing sexual patterns of women—since expectations of celibacy for men had long since been abandoned—Theilhaber reported "recent studies implicating the unmarried Jewess in the acquisition of sexual diseases."[34]

More than providing a strict measure of fertility, however, birthrates reflected larger changes occurring within the population as a whole. Such factors as discrepancies in the balance between the sexes, which inevitably increased after a war, the age structure of the population, emigration patterns, and the number of marriages contracted all affected the overall birthrate. For the Jewish community, outmarriage and withdrawal from the community were the unique factors contributing to the shrinking population size and thus to the apparent decline in fertility. Doctors reporting Jewish birth statistics, for example, included only the offspring of "pure Jewish marriages"— marriages contracted between two Jews. Given the high communal attrition rate anticipated from the children of mixed marriage, these physicians did not consider the offspring of such unions to qualify, at least for statistical purposes, as Jewish births.

The final assault on the health and reproductivity of the Jewish family came in the form of intermarriage. Mixed marriage, opined Ernst Kahn, "devours that remnant left after [the depletion effected by] birth control of the essence *[Substanz]* of Jewry, in particular, German Jews."[35] Like late marriage, intermarriage was also viewed as a social force sapping collective Jewish vitality. The unborn and those born without affiliation to Jewish institutional life were reckoned as total losses for the community. The findings derived from the 1905 Prussian census—that only 22 percent of the children of intermarriage were raised as Jews—were repeated in study after study to prove the utter lack of utility of mixed marriages for the Jewish community.[36]

Given the exclusion of children of mixed marriage from Jewish birth statistics, we might expect the objection to intermarriage to have been based on qualitative considerations, that is, on the fact that children were not being raised as Jews. Interestingly enough, however, interconfessional marriages were also looked upon with disapproval as being largely infertile. "They are almost all childless," noted one observer, "and thus signify no gain for Jewry, even when the women [Catholic converts to Judaism] . . . adhere zealously to their new religion."[37] While at the moral level, intermarriage was viewed as the final act of betrayal toward the community, at the biological level, mixed marriage was also deemed catastrophic for the physical continuity of Judaism because of the paucity of children produced. Kahn alleged that there were 1.5 children for every Jewish marriage in Prussia, while the issue of mixed marriages did not exceed 0.5 per marriage.[38]

In sum, the Weimar Republic represented a transitional era in defining ideas about relationships among family members, the sexual division of labor, relationships between the sexes, and the separation of sex and reproduction. Inaugurated in the presence of acute political upheaval and a sense of social collapse, the Republic was distinguished by both radical social experimentation and a desire to retreat into an idyllic past. In the face of military defeat and economic collapse, members of the older generation sensed that the old structures of authority had disintegrated and that "traditional" values were no longer honored and protected. At the same time, the younger generation was exhibiting a sharpened sense of generational consciousness and changing sexual attitudes and behaviors; more women were leaving the confines of the home to seek outside employment. All of these circumstances converged with the general sense of social malaise after World War I. Jewish and non-Jewish observers, noting the impermanence of the times, reckoned they were living through a period of great transition.[39] "Not only have we experienced a vast political revolution and are still reeling from its impact," noted Wassermann, "but we have passed through an intellectual one of similar dimensions and importance. The main result is that the old ties have disappeared, and new ones have not yet been discovered to take their place."[40]

Toward an Ideology of the Jewish Family

We have seen how the Jewish understanding of the crisis of the family had its immediate origins in the social and economic changes taking place in postwar Germany but long-term roots in the twin processes of urbanization and industrialization. It should now be evident that the Jewish crisis of the family was more than merely an internal Jewish issue that had to do only with intermarriage and assimilation. Nor were the categories used by Jews to describe and analyze the crisis of the family merely "adapted" by German Jews from their non-Jewish surroundings.

Yet discussions about the Jewish family among social critics also had a particularist character to them. While representations of the Jewish family reflected the shared categories of analysis and middle-class values of Jewish and non-Jewish Germans, they invariably stressed the Jews' anomalous history and the uniqueness of the Jewish family. An analysis of the specifically Jewish aspect of the "crisis of the family" suggests that it was more than merely a Jewish gloss on the general debate. Rather, claims of Jewish uniqueness had become a veritable article of faith amongst modern Jews attempting to reconcile Jewish particularity and universality. This central impulse underlay the Jews' redefinition of their collective existence since Emancipation.[41]

This impulse, which will be reconstructed only in its outlines, was one that transformed the traditional theological idea of Israel's cho-senness into modern secular terms. Amos Funkenstein has shown how, until the nineteenth century, these concepts were viewed by Jews as completely opposing categories. Historically, Jewish existence was considered to be unique precisely because it was not normal. As an aberration from history, the stubborn persistence of the Jews was deemed exceptional, even miraculous. The notion of Israel's chosen-ness was thus closely tied in with its anomalous historical existence.[42]

With Emancipation, Funkenstein demonstrates, western Jews be-gan to recast uniqueness and normality as potentially complementary categories. Seen in this light, the programs of the Jewish Enlighten-ment, Wissenschaft des Judentums, and Zionism all aspired to trans-form the uniqueness and eternity of Israel into secular concepts. In all of these culturally creative enterprises, Judaism's uniqueness was understood to reside in its universality.[43] Perhaps the best known example of this is the nineteenth-century Jewish historian Heinrich Graetz's interpretation of Jewish history as the embodiment of the idea of pure monotheism. Israel's distinctive tradition was thus recon-ceived as a highly refined filter for the values of Western culture.

Representations of the Jewish family during the Weimar Republic continued to reflect the ongoing effort of German Jews to reconcile the competing claims of uniqueness and normality. The Jewish family was seen as unique because of its anomalous history, but it was also set apart from the German family by the sum total of "universal" values that the Jewish family was believed to embody. The "universal" values ascribed to the Jewish family were, not surprisingly, decidedly time-bound. At the outset of the nineteenth century, for example, the unique qualities of the Jewish family had once served as proof that Jews possessed the civic virtues necessary for becoming full subjects of the state. Jewish publicists had argued that the Jewish family embodied stability, thrift, industriousness, and moral conservatism.[44] Now, a full century later, the terms of the debate, as well as the actual socioeconomic and political position of German Jews, had shifted markedly. An analysis of this discussion in the 1920s thus reflects some of the period's Jewish and non-Jewish social concerns, among them, the emphasis on individual health for the collective, the creation of ethnic identities in an age of nationalism, and the quality of emotional relationships within the family.

Although the desire for family was considered to be biologically rooted, the Jewish family was generally spoken about more in relation to the laws of history than of nature.[45] In contrast to Catholics and Protestants, who portrayed the family as a "natural" social unit and an *organische Gemeinschaft* (organic community),[46] Jewish commentators writing for a Jewish public generally portrayed the family as a social form that evolved out of their unique history. As the direct descendant of the biblical family, the modern Jewish family was called upon to showcase Jewish authenticity and antiquity both to Jews and to Gentiles. The attempts of Weimar Jewish commentators to take refuge and find contemporary meaning in history suggests that, for the most part, the categories with which they were conceptualizing their past were consistent with their history-centered tradition. Even Arthur Czellitzer, himself an enthusiastic champion of eugenics, drew a picture of the Jewish family that stressed historical development, not racial-biological explanations. It would appear that the views of this cadre of leaders had not been usurped by the racial-biological mindset that took possession of many Catholics and Protestants during this period.[47]

Discussions of the Jewish family typically adhered to a narrative style designed to establish the ancient lineage and genealogy of the modern Jewish family. In these accounts, the family was assigned a sustaining power comparable only to that of strict religious adherence in the past. In a cultural-historical sketch of the Jewish family, Hilde Ottenheimer described the family and community as the two centers and complementary spheres of Jewish life.[48] During medieval times, Jewish life was organized entirely around the two pillars of family and community.[49] "The religion encompassed both centers; both [family and community] breathed the same spirit, and they were bound into a single unit by it."[50] Jewish social commentators during the 1920s frequently pointed to the late Middle Ages and the ghetto period as eras of exemplary Jewish family life, as a time when the family-community relationship had reached its zenith.[51] Looking to history to anchor contemporary Jewish existence in a meaningful past, these accounts were manifestly ahistorical: the image of the family was that of an institution that had remained essentially unchanged from antiquity through the dawn of modernity. Jewish families of various periods and climes appeared to be united more by the precepts of Torah than distinguished by cultural, geographic, or temporal differences.[52]

A significant component of the uniqueness narrative addressed the social and cultural functions of the Jewish family. German-Jewish commentators portrayed the family as having played an unparalleled role in the history and culture of the Jewish people. According to Arthur Czellitzer, the non-Jew was able to draw life-sustaining strength from the nurturing soil of his homeland; his nation's survival was secured through a migratory influx from the countryside, which delivered "fresh blood into the veins of every people, fructifying and maintaining its culture."[53] The Jews, on the other hand, had lost possession of their land and lacked a comparable source of sustenance. Since there was no land to nurture Jewish creativity and repro-ductivity, the secret of Jewish survival would have to be found elsewhere. By the twentieth century, the answer to the age-old conundrum of Jewish survival was no longer divine intervention, as had been suggested by religious commentators from earlier periods.[54] No, the key to Jewish survival was now seen to reside in the Jew's family; indeed, the family had become the homeland of the modern Jew.[55] Having supplanted attachment to the Holy Land and faith in divine providence, the Jewish family was understood, in the eyes of Czellitzer, as

> the native soil that nurtured the ability to weather the fury of persecution, to brave the daily battles throughout the ages. Today, for this people without its own land or language, at least for many who are alienated from ritual and dogma, it is the only support that connects them to their roots and to Judaism.[56]

One further role of the Jewish family in the construction of an evolving modern Jewish identity was in warding off the attacks of antisemites. Paula Hyman has shown that supporters of the Jews in early debates on Jewish emancipation pointed to the Jewish family as a sign of Jewish moral fitness.[57] Similarly, Ismar Schorsch has demonstrated that the virtues of the Jewish family were enlisted by Jews in the defense of Judaism in the nineteenth century.[58] Even well into the twentieth century, the reputed strength and stability of the Jewish family served to answer antisemitic charges of Jewish moral and physical degeneracy. In an article on the necessity of health care for Jewish children, the Berlin physician Fritz von Gutfeld states what had by then become a very popular sentiment:

> Our Jewish family life is something very special; this is well known and recognized by all non-Jews. Even the worst Jew-hater, who would otherwise have absolutely nothing good to say about the Jews, and who would deny the great contributions made by many Jews in all areas of life, even he would say: one thing you have to give the Jews—their family life is exemplary, something we non-Jews can look to as a model. If we want to know what the chief foundation of our Jewish family life is, it is this: children's reverence for their parents and parents' love for each other and for the children.[59]

It is particularly instructive to note the specific qualities ascribed to the Jewish family that were held up as a positive model for the Gentiles. For von Gutfeld as for many other Jewish commentators, Jewish uniqueness was seen to reside in the special relationship between Jewish parents and their children. The definition of what constituted healthy family relations preoccupied social reformers, psychologists, and educators, who took particular interest in parent-child relationships in the "century of the child."[60] In her case histories of German family life, for example, Alice Salomon voiced current pedagogic thinking when she criticized the authoritarian parenting practices of working-class families.[61] By the close of the Weimar Republic, the idea of love in place of authority, self-education instead of education, and encouraging the development of the child's creative capacity had all been embraced as cardinal principles for healthy child-rearing.[62]

In light of these general concerns, it is interesting to see how Jews claimed these emotional qualities as their historical inheritance. A rabbi writing for the female readership of Die jüdische Frau claimed that Jews were keenly interested in current pedagogic thinking because "our children and their education are particularly close to our hearts. God, in his Holy Scripture, has specifically enjoined us in this holy task."[63] Likewise, Ottenheimer insisted that the intense love felt by Jewish parents for their children was, if not a Jewish invention, then at least a distinctively Jewish trait traceable to antiquity:

The education of children is a parental affair, not a public matter as it is with the Greek polis. The love of a father and mother for their children was something so primordially Jewish, that it would later appear in the mouths of the biblical prophets as a metaphor for God's love of Israel and Judah.[64]

Not all Jews viewed these unique emotional characteristics favorably, however. The socialist feminist Henriette Fürth characterized Jewish parents as beset by "enormous fearfulness and an almost pathological, exaggerated feeling of responsibility toward the children."[65] Even more emphatically, a teenage girl writing in the short-lived journal *Jerubaal* faulted Jewish parents for being overly narcissistic. Jewish children yearned for the simplicity and *Gemütlichkeit* (congenial togetherness) of Aryan families, she wrote, because Jewish children are nothing but the objects of their parents' vain desires:

> One characteristic of the Jewish civilized family is that it is always dull. It lacks the congenial togetherness of the Aryan. . . . There are Jewish children who yearn deeply for Aryan family life, for the calm simplicity and also for a certain sentimentality. Because their environment is dull, [the parents] concern themselves with the children much too much. At least, this is frequently the case with mothers. [This environment] makes the children so unchildlike that they are continually drawn into adult life. Jewish mothers are very vain about their children. The child is reared to be intelligent, talented, and always immaculately groomed. Under the constant observation of adults, the child always feels compelled to excel and be more intelligent than other children in order to satisfy the vain expectations of his parents. Everything is forgiven the child, even every impudence, so long as he can charm the grown-ups. But the inner child is left without support, and as a result, he withdraws into himself. What lends the picture of Aryan children such innocence and calm simplicity, the childlike intimacy with nature (at least in the summer months), the boundless play and camaraderie, is for the most part denied Jewish children. They are nothing but the objects of their parents' vanity, upon which the parents indulge their narcissism and carry out their predetermined pedagogic goals.[66]

A further trait attributed to the modern Jewish family was its apparent concern with health. As an issue of general social concern in Germany since the late eighteenth century, health was, from the beginning of this period, closely associated with bourgeois culture and its values. Good health implied discipline, success, good morals, and social integration. While the value of "good health" was hardly a new idea, the notion that health was subject to human control was popularized during the last two decades of the nineteenth century.[67]

In a social and political context that equated national strength and health, these socially active Jews transformed the idea of Jews' "traditional" investment in their children into the practical issue of maintaining good health. Given its importance for national regeneration, promoting an active Jewish investment in health also served an apologetic function. One observer noted, for example:

> The Jewish child should grow up with a healthy body so that the Jewish religion's high regard for caring for children as a holy task will be made evident through him. [Healthy Jewish bodies] will also let future generations know that, in a period of difficult economic depression, we found the means and time to care for our offspring.[68]

In a similar vein, Paula Ollendorf, chairwoman of the Jüdischer Frauenbund, called on rabbis to sermonize about why it was "un-Jewish" for parents to neglect the health care of their children.[69]

At the peak of German and German Jewish preoccupation with the family, a new Jewish organization was founded in Berlin to celebrate the Jewish family in all its uniqueness. In 1924, Dr. Arthur Czellitzer established the Gesellschaft für jüdische Familienforschung to serve as a central bureau for Jewish family historical research.[70] As part of an interest in genealogy that had gained popularity in Germany around the turn of the century, Czellitzer's society was responding to the apparently weakened condition of Jewish family life. In the year of its founding, the society claimed five hundred individual members and thirty corporate ones.[71] Its journal published records of genealogical interest alongside articles on genetic research and eugenics, and the society also convened well-attended evening lectures where members exchanged ideas on related themes.

Czellitzer's idea in founding the Gesellschaft für jüdische Familienforschung was to offer Jews a way to retrieve aspects of their vanishing past. Demographic mobility had put greater distance between children and their grandparents, while urban life and the decadent culture of the metropolis (Grossstadtkultur) had diminished the quality of cross-generational ties. Jewish children had thus lost their best opportunity for gaining a positive picture of Jewish history. In addition to these considerations, Jewish families faced the added problem of conversion and attrition through baptism or religious indifference which, Czellitzer maintained, widened the cultural divide between modern Jews and their ancestors.[72] Czellitzer felt that he would only realize his goal when the Jewish family was restored to its former place of glory, when Jews again felt themselves to be part of the unbroken chain of Jewish tradition:

All of our actions and strivings will only be successful if they manage to lead German Jews back to the once self-evident highly esteemed family and all the ethical and moral values which flow from it. This is the path I have taken in founding the Gesellschaft für Familienforschung. He who lovingly deals with the history of his ancestors and is aware of the inner connection of his own feelings and thoughts toward them, will himself feel the desire to have offspring. He will want to affix a new link to the chain, since he himself, temporarily at least, forms the final link! To place the Jewish family back in the center of the Jewish worldview—and to ease the future forming of families through measures of economic support—this synthesis is our slogan and our future![73]

Other contemporaries of Czellitzer, Hilde Ottenheimer, for ex- ample, recognized the cultural function of the Jewish family for her own generation. Ottenheimer saw how Jews' identification with the historical Jewish family offered them a way to affirm their ties with a unique history. On the subject of the family as an anchor for a modern Jewish self-consciousness, Ottenheimer concluded:

While the life force of the family was extinguished—announced, as it were, as an obituary—people from all quarters recalled its worth. The corpus of Jewish scholarship praised its meaning for the continuity of Judaism, they extolled it as the keystone of the entire moral world order. The competing factions of Orthodoxy and Liberalism joined together in their admiration of the family. . . . Jewish literature is particularly partial to portraying the family, family life, family connections, and family separation in a romantic, sentimental spirit. Finally, the family has also become an object of research; there are family chronicles, family histories, and family trees now being made that trace the fate of individual families through history. All in all: the proud belief in progress at the beginning of the nineteenth century gave way, at the end of this period, to a historical, backward-looking conscious- ness, which reinstated the self-conscious Jewish individual back in the chain of generations.[74]

Conclusion

The interest expressed by Jewish social commentators and reform- ers in resituating the Jewish family "in the center of the Jewish worldview" reflected one route by which some Weimar Jews tried to hold onto a distant past. They sought to find new relevance in the idea of the family at a time when the national identity of non-Jewish Germans was being anchored in another remote past. At the same time, the content of what was put forward as a unique Jewish possession included nothing that would conflict with mainstream middle-class German values. In fact, quite the opposite was true. The Jewish family was unique in the eyes of many Jews for the way it was supposed to embody the most current, in some cases the most progressive, values of the specifically liberal, middle-class milieu in which most German Jews lived.

While the family problems observed in the Jewish community were similar in nature to those affecting non-Jewish Germans, the group of Jewish leaders studied here often perceived the problems and their impact to be singularly Jewish in nature. To a significant degree, of course, this reflected the existence of a distinctive Jewish occupational distribution—the middle-classes and the elderly were hit particularly hard by the economic crises of the Republic. But at another level, the preoccupation with questions of family decline grew out of the perception that Weimar Jews faced problems that had once been the sole province of the Gentiles. Simply put, the Jews were becoming like the "goyim," and this was so precisely because Jews had succeeded to the extent that they had. Thus, the symbolic significance of the crisis revolved around the question of nothing less than the continued survival of the Jews as a group.

The attempts of social reformers to retrieve elements of a vanishing past reflected an awareness of the growing distance between modern Jews and their historic forebears. The efforts of Jewish contemporaries to rekindle memories of a noble past were thoroughly in keeping with, and indeed nurtured by, the broader feeling that modernization had stripped ordinary individuals of the deep and meaningful bonds of community. Yet, at the same time, the intensification of antisemitism in social and economic life reinforced Jewish outsider status. The potent combination of these two forces led some Jews to look for a way back to their "authentic" selves. In this context, the family took on the nature of a refuge, representing, as the title of the popular book put it, "a haven in a heartless world."[75]

The ideology of the Jewish family reinforces the observation that the immersion of Jews in majority culture did not inevitably lead to complete disappearance within the larger society.[76] The integration of ideas, habits, and beliefs from the surrounding society served not only to integrate but also to differentiate. While the ideology of the Jewish family arose out of the German ideology, Jewish leaders also enlisted the family to serve as a force to unite an otherwise diverse group of Jews. The presence of inclusionary as well as exclusionary forces in Weimar culture—and the separatist trends that it spawned—confirms the notion put forth by Shulamit Volkov that in some aspects of their communal lives, German Jews—even before Weimar—had begun a process of "dissimilation," reversing the effects of assimilation.[77] That Jews used the very tools and ideas that gave them entrée into European society to continue to strengthen the distinctive aspects of their community and culture is testimony to the dynamic modern impulse to invent new forms of ethnicity and identity.

Notes

1. Alice Salomon and Marie Baum, *Das Familienleben in der Gegenwart. 182 Monographien,* vol. 1, *Bestand und Erschütterung der Familie in der Gegenwart* (Berlin, 1930), p. 9.

2. Jakob Wassermann, "Bourgeois Marriage," in *The Book of Marriage. A New Interpretation by Twenty-Four Leaders of Contemporary Thought,* ed. Hermann Keyserling, trans. W. H. Hilton-Brown (New York, 1926), p. 203.

3. Hermann Sachen, ed., *Staatslexikon der Görresgesellschaft,* 5th ed., *s.v.* "Familienfürsorge" by M. Helm (Freiburg im Breisgau, 1931).

4. On social motherhood, see Christoph Sachsse, *Mütterlichkeit als Beruf. Sozialarbeit, Sozialreform und Frauenbewegung 1871–1929* (Frankfurt am Main, 1986); Susanne Zeller, *Volksmütter mit staatlicher Anerkennung: Frauen im Wohlfahrtswesen der zwanziger Jahren* (Düsseldorf, 1987); Dietlinde Peters, *Mütterlichkeit im Kaiserreich. Die bürgerliche Frauenbewegung und der soziale Beruf der Frau* (Bielefeld, 1984) (Wissenschaftliche Reihe); Susanna Dammer, *Mütterlichkeit und Frauenpflicht; Versuchung der Vergesellschaftung 'weiblicher Fähigkeiten' durch eine Dienstverpflichtung* (Weinheim, 1988).

5. Robert Weldon Whalen, *Bitter Wounds. German Victims of the Great War, 1914–1918* (Ithaca, 1984), p. 69.

6. Whalen, *Bitter Wounds,* p. 78.

7. Reinhard Sieder, *Sozialgeschichte der Familie* (Frankfurt am Main, 1987), p. 213. See also Karin Hausen, "Mothers, Sons and the Sale of Symbols and Goods: The 'German Mother's Day' 1923–1933," in *Interest and Emotion: Essays on the Study of Family and Kinship,* ed. Hans Medick and David Sabean (Cambridge, 1984), p. 402. Hausen cites Paul Federn, *Zur Psychologie der Revolution. Die vaterlose Gesellschaft* (1919). His thesis was that the paternal state, having failed to protect the "motherland," left the sons with an irreparable sense of insecurity and a feeling of disappointment with the fathers.

8. Richard Bessel, *Germany after the First World War* (New York, 1993), p. 209.

9. Jewish communities in Germany and Austria had the added obligation of caring for orphans created by the pogroms that spread across Eastern Europe during and immediately after the war. On the pogroms, see William O. McCagg, Jr., *A History of Habsburg Jews, 1670–1918* (Bloomington, 1989), p. 203; Ezra Mendelsohn, *The Jews of East Central Europe between the World Wars* (Bloomington, 1983), pp. 40–41.

10. Carola Kuhlmann, *Erbkrank oder Erziehbar? Jugendhilfe als Vorsorge und Aussonderung in der Fürsorgeerziehung in Westfalen von 1933–1945* (Weinheim, 1989), p. 88.

11. This is based on my examination of one hundred case files from Bundesarchiv Potsdam, 75C Ge1: Akten betreffend Fürsorgeerziehung. See also the essay by Claudia Prestel (chapter 11) in this volume.

12. Bundesarchiv Potsdam, 75C Ge1 DIGB 769.

13. Bundesarchiv Potsdam, 75C Ge1 Akten betreffend FE.

14. Zentralwohlfahrtsstelle der deutschen Juden, *Jüdische Bevölkerungspolitik. Bericht über die Tagung des Bevölkerungspolitischen Ausschusses des Preussischen Landesverbandes jüdischer Gemeinden vom 24. Februar 1929*, ed. Felix Theilhaber, Schriften der Zwst/Nr.II (Berlin, 1929), p. 9.

15. While the increase in the number of women in the workforce, particularly married women, is undisputed, assessments of its significance differ. Renate Bridenthal and Claudia Koonz argue, for example, that while female employment rose from 36 to 38 percent by the end of the Republic, a comparable increase took place within the male working population as well. Nevertheless, the impression that women were entering the workforce in greater numbers, particularly for conservative members of the middle class, reinforced the notion that women were choosing work over family and abandoning home for career. See Renate Bridenthal and Claudia Koonz, "Beyond Kinder, Küche, Kirche: Weimar Women in Politics and Work," in *When Biology Became Destiny: Women in Weimar and Nazi Germany*, ed. Renate Bridenthal, Atina Grossmann, and Marion Kaplan (New York, 1984), pp. 44–45.

16. Berg-Platau, in *Jüdische Bevölkerungspolitik*, ed. Theilhaber, p. 26.

17. For a contemporary account of the problem, see Günther Krolzig, *Der Jugendliche in der Grosstadtfamilie. Auf Grund von Niederschriften Berliner Berufsschüler und -schülerinnen*, vol. 4, *Forschung über Bestand und Erschütterung der Familie in der Gegenwart* (Berlin, 1930). See also Renate Bridenthal, "Something Old, Something New: Between the Two World Wars," in *Becoming Visible. Women in European History*, ed. Renate Bridenthal, Claudia Koonz, and Susan Stuard, 2nd ed. (Boston, 1987), p. 490.

18. Anna Beatte Nadel, "Neue Lebensformen der Frau," *Die jüdische Frau* 1 (June 1925): 1–2.

19. Heinrich Stahl, in *Jüdische Bevölkerungspolitik*, ed. Theilhaber, p. 45.

20. See, for example, Nadel, "Neue Lebensformen," pp. 1–2; idem, "Alltag und Alltägliches," *Die jüdische Frau* 1 (October 22, 1925): 8; J.R., "Die Stunde der Entscheidung," *Die jüdische Frau* 1 (August 7, 1925): 10. *Die jüdische Frau* was a short-lived liberal women's biweekly founded by Regina Isaacsohn and Anna Beate Nadel; it ran from 1925 to 1927.

21. See Hugo Rosenthal, "Zur Psychologie jüdischer Frauen und Mädchen II," *Blätter des jüdischen Frauenbundes* 8 (July 1932): 5–7.

22. See, for example, the regular exchange among women writing in the public discussion forum of *Die jüdische Frau*. Among the many articles appearing in the Jewish press on the subject, see Michael Müller-Claudius, "Das jüdische Kind in der Schule," *Der Morgen* 3, no. 1 (April 1927). For a discussion of Jewish responses to antisemitism in public schools during Weimar, see the first chapter in Yfaat Weiss, *Schicksalsgemeinschaft im Wandel: Jüdische Erziehung im nationalsozialistischen Deutschland 1933–1938* (Hamburg, 1991).

23. See Erich Stern, "Zur Psychologie des jüdischen Kindes," *Der Morgen* 3 (February 1928): 555–74; idem, "Über die Bedeutung religiöser Formen für die Erziehung," *Der Morgen* 4 (December 1928): 433–44; Rosenthal, "Zur Psychologie jüdischer Frauen und Mädchen," pp. 5–7. N. M. Feldmann's book *The Jewish Child, Its History, Folklore, Biology and Sociology* (London, 1917) was reviewed by Siegfried Bernfeld in *Der Jude* 4 (1919–1920): 95–96.

24. Stern, "Zur Psychologie des jüdischen Kindes," p. 570.

25. For a full discussion of the decline in the Jewish birthrate, see Sharon Gillerman, "Between Public and Private: Family, Community and Jewish Identity in Weimar Berlin," Ph.D. diss., University of California, Los Angeles, 1996, chapter 2. See also Claudia Prestel, "Mediniyut demografiah b'hevrah ha-yehudit: bitui le'zehut yehudit?" in *Yehudei Weimar: Hevrah be-mashber ha-moderni'ut, 1918–1933* [The Jews of Weimar: A society in the crisis of modernity], ed. Oded Heilbronner (Jerusalem, 1994), pp. 214–62.

26. Ute Frevert, *Frauen-Geschichte. Zwischen bürgerlicher Verbesserung und neuer Weiblichkeit* (Frankfurt am Main, 1986), pp. 181–82. According to Frevert, women relied predominantly on douches and coitus interruptus. Condoms and pessaries were either inaccessible or too expensive to be used by women of the working class.

27. Ibid. On the campaign to decriminalize abortion during the Weimar Republic, see Atina Grossmann, "Abortion and Economic Crisis: The 1931 Campaign against Paragraph 218," in *When Biology Became Destiny,* ed. Bridenthal, Grossmann, and Kaplan, pp. 66–86; and Karen Hagemann, *Eine Frauensache. Alltagsleben und Geburtenpolitik 1919–1932. Eine Dokumentation* (Pfaffenweiler, 1991).

28. The Jewish birthrate in Prussia had dropped from 31.7 per 1000 births in 1876–1880 to 10.8 per 1000 births in 1928. By comparison, the overall German birthrate had dropped from 40 per 1000 to 18.6 per 1000 during the same period.

29. Felix Theilhaber, *Der Untergang der deutschen Juden. Eine volkswirtschaftliche Studie,* 2nd ed. (Berlin, 1921), p. 82.

30. The survey was conducted between 1928 and 1929 by the Population Policy Committee of the Preussischer Landesverband jüdischer Gemeinden. See Theilhaber, in *Jüdische Bevölkerungspolitik,* pp. 72–85.

31. Ibid., p. 77.

32. No definitive proof exists concerning the reported increase of venereal disease. Richard Bessel suggests that the picture of a postwar upsurge in VD may have been overdrawn. Contrary to widespread belief at the time, Bessel reports that the proportion of soldiers with VD was no greater during the war than it had been before. See Bessel, *Germany after the First World War,* pp. 233–39.

33. Cited in Berg-Platau, in *Jüdische Bevölkerungspolitik,* ed. Theilhaber, p. 23.

34. Theilhaber, in *Jüdische Bevölkerungspolitik,* p. 10.

35. Ernst Kahn, *Der internationale Geburtenstreik. Umfang, Ursachen, Wirkungen, Gegenmassnahmen?* (Frankfurt am Main, 1930), p. 37.

36. See, for example, Gustav Löffler, *Wie fördern wir den religiösen Sinn der jüdischen Jugend? Mischehe, sexualethische Forderungen, Frühehe und soziale Umschichtung der jüdischen Jugend Deutschlands* (Berlin, 1919), p. 17. (The pamphlet was published by the Verband der jüdischen Jugendvereine).

37. Eugen Wolbe, *Selbstmord oder neues Leben? Ein Wort zur Bevölkerungspolitik der deutschen Juden* (Oranienburg, 1918), p. 17. The author was referring to one hundred annual conversions by lower-class Catholic women to Judaism, "out of love for their Jewish suitors."

38. Kahn, *Der internationale Geburtenstreik,* p. 38. His figures were for the year 1927.

39. Anonymous, *Jüdisches Addressbuch für Gross Berlin* (1929–1930), p. 388.

40. Wassermann, "Bourgeois Marriage," p. 203.

41. My thoughts on this subject have been shaped by my talks with the late Amos Funkenstein, and I am grateful that he discussed this material in detail with me. On the secularization of the uniqueness myth in Zionist thought, see Amos

Funkenstein, "Zionism, Science, and History," in idem, *Perceptions of Jewish History* (Berkeley, 1993), pp. 338–50.

42. Ibid., pp. 344–46.

43. Ibid., p. 345.

44. Paula Hyman, "The Modern Jewish Family: Image and Reality," in *The Jewish Family. Metaphor and Memory*, ed. David Kraemer (New York, 1989), pp. 170–80.

45. Anonymous, "Ausstellung 'Die Frau,'" *Blätter des jüdischen Frauenbundes* 9 (March 1933): 5.

46. See, for example, Hermann Muckermann and Friedrich Zahn, "Wie die Familie—so das Volk. Die kinderreiche Familie im Lichte der Eugenik" (Munich, 1927), pp. 26–35.

47. On the ascendancy of biological thinking among German Protestant women in the early twentieth century, see Doris Kaufmann, *Frauen zwischen Aufbruch und Reaktion. Protestantische Frauenbewegung in der ersten Hälfte des 20. Jahrhunderts* (Munich, 1988).

48. Hilde Ottenheimer, "Die jüdische Familie. Eine kulturgeschichtliche Skizze," *Blätter des jüdischen Frauenbundes* 14 (September 1938): 3.

49. Ibid.

50. Ibid.

51. Bertha Pappenheim, "Weh dem dessen Gewissen schläft," draft of an article for *Allgemeine Zeitung des Judentums* (December 12, 1916), Bundesarchiv Potsdam, 75C Ge1 903/ZWST.

52. See, for example, Dr. rer. pol. Gerhard Schmidt, "Die Umwelt der jüdischen Familie," *Jüdische Familienforschung* 2 (March 1926): 124–25.

53. ALBI-NY, Arthur Czellitzer Collection, founding statement of Gesellschaft für jüdische Familienforschung, p. 2.

54. Funkenstein cites the Maharal's resolution on this question. For the Maharal, nature dictated that the character and uniqueness of a people were shaped by its land; if a people were to be cut off from its land, its only fate would be extinction. The Jews, however, were never governed by the laws of nature, since they were subject to direct divine guidance. See Funkenstein, "Zionism, Science, and History," p. 344.

55. See also the fairy tale by M. Frank on a similar theme, "Der Liebe Heimat," in *Die jüdische Frau* 2 (June 1926): 5.

56. Czellitzer, "Gesellschaft für jüdische Familienforschung," p. 2.

57. Paula Hyman and Steven Cohen, eds., *The Jewish Family: Myths and Realities* (New York, 1986), pp. 3–4.

58. Ismar Schorsch, "Art as Social History: Oppenheim and the German Jewish Vision of Emancipation," in *Moritz Oppenheim: The First Jewish Painter* (Jerusalem, 1983), pp. 413–39. See also Richard Cohen, "Nostalgia and 'Return to the Ghetto': A Cultural Phenomenon in Western and Central Europe," in *Assimilation and Community. The Jews in Nineteenth-Century Europe*, ed. Jonathan Frankel and Steven J. Zipperstein (New York, 1992), pp. 135–38.

59. Dr. med. Fritz von Gutfeld, "Ärtzliche Beobachtungssprechstunden für Jugendliche," *Gemeindeblatt der jüdischen Gemeinde zu Berlin* 16 (September 1, 1926): 189–90.

60. The title of the book by Ellen Key, *The Century of the Child* (New York, 1909).

61. Salomon and Baum, *Das Familienleben*, p. 72 and passim.

62. See, for example, Margarete Kamensky, "Die Neue Erziehung," *Die jüdische Frau* 1 (July 1925): 6.

63. Rabbiner Dr. Strassburger, "Erziehung," *Die jüdische Frau* 2 (October 1926): 1.

64. Ottenheimer, "Die jüdische Familie," p. 3.

65. Henriette Fürth, "Der Geburtenrückgang bei den Juden," *Blätter des jüdischen Frauenbundes* 6 (April 1930): 3.

66. Anonymous, "Wie ist unser Verhältnis zu unseren Eltern jetzt tatsächlich? Diskussionsbemerkungen eines Mädchens in dem Sprechsaal des jüdischen Mittelschülerbundes in Wien," *Jerubaal. Eine Zeitschrift der jüdischen Jugend* 1 (1918–1919): 413.

67. See Ute Frevert, "The Civilizing Tendency of Hygiene. Working-Class Women under Medical Control in Imperial Germany," in *German Women in the Nineteenth Century,* ed. John C. Fout (New York, 1984), pp. 322–23.

68. Anonymous, *Jüdisches Addressbuch zu Berlin* (Berlin, 1931), p. 52.

69. Paula Ollendorff, in *Jüdische Bevölkerungspolitik,* ed. Theilhaber, p. 33.

70. Czellitzer, "Gesellschaft für jüdische Familienforschung," p. 1.

71. Ibid., p. 3.

72. Ibid., p. 2.

73. Czellitzer, *Jüdische Bevölkerungspolitik,* ed. Theilhaber, pp. 42–43.

74. Ottenheimer, "Die jüdische Familie," p. 3.

75. Christopher Lasch, *Haven in a Heartless World* (New York, 1978).

76. Michael Graetz demonstrates this in *Ha-Periferyah hayeta la-merkaz: perakim be-toldot Yahadut Tsarefat ba-me'ah ha-19: mi-San-Simon li-yesod 'kol Yisrael haverim'* (Jerusalem, 1982).

77. Shulamit Volkov, "The Dynamics of Dissimilation: *Ostjuden* and German Jews," in *The Jewish Response to German Culture: From the Enlightenment to the Second World War,* ed. Jehuda Reinharz and Walter Schatzberg (Hanover, 1985), pp. 195–211.

11

"Youth in Need"

Correctional Education and Family Breakdown in German Jewish Families

CLAUDIA PRESTEL

In German Jewish society of the nineteenth century, though problems of family life such as single motherhood, neglect of children, and intergenerational conflict were not unknown, institutionalization was not an option: Jewish society dealt with the problem of illegitimacy and wayward children by financially supporting the mothers or by placing children with foster families. Adolescents were given training in crafts and trades, and emigration to America was encouraged by the community.[1]

As of the turn of the century, however, a growing number of Jewish children were forced by state intervention into reform schools; according to the Prussian law of July 2, 1900, these schools had to be separated along religious lines.[2] Implementation of this change fell upon the central Jewish organization, the Deutsch-Israelitische Gemeindebund (DIGB), which established Jewish reform schools for boys in Repzin (1901) and for girls in Köpenick (1902).

Faced with the problems in Jewish family life, the spokesmen of the DIGB blamed modernity and argued that Jewish society had to bear both the positive and the negative consequences of emancipation. One of the negatives was juvenile delinquency.[3] But there was no willingness to confront such issues as violence in the family and great reluctance to explore other possible explanations for juvenile dysfunction.

In this essay I will concentrate on two areas: first, the background and origin of male inmates in Repzin (I will deal with the experience of wayward girls in a subsequent study), and second, the changes in correctional education in the late 1920s.

The first half of the twentieth century witnessed the development of new theories in social work, education, and psychology; and the conditions in reform schools led to considerable public discussion. In 1929 Peter Martin Lampel published his *Jungen in Not. Berichte von Fürsorgezöglingen*,[4] a collection of reports by inmates of reform schools that shocked the public and especially circles engaged in education and social work.[5] Furthermore, revolts in reform schools *(Fürsorgeer-ziehungsanstalten)* in the late 1920s and the subsequent court cases—which revealed disturbing conditions of brutality and ill-treatment by teachers, guards and educators[6]—caused a public uproar and forced the authorities to rethink their measures and alter fundamentally the upbringing of institutionalized children. A change in the legal system—the *Reichsjugendwohlfahrtsgesetz* from 1922 declared the education of every German child and the prevention of waywardness to be the responsibility of the state—made possible the realization of new ideas.

The Beginnings of the Jewish Reform School in Repzin

On May 1, 1901, the Israelitische Fürsorge-Erziehungs-Anstalt of the DIGB–Berlin was opened in Repzin, a small village in Pomerania, five hours by train from Berlin. According to law, all male children above the age of six who were placed in correctional education by the state had to be accepted. Furthermore, parents or even third parties could send children or adolescents to Repzin.[7] As I will show, some Jewish parents willingly institutionalized their children, a clear indication that they did not accept their responsibilities and delegated the task of upbringing to outsiders. At first there was a shortage of places, but from 1912 onward, sixty children and young adults could be accommodated at any given time. This proved adequate to meet the demand.

The reform school was run from 1903 until 1929, the year it was moved to Wolzig, by A. Baronowitz—a teacher by profession and former director of the Jewish orphanage in Pankow—and his wife. His personality and ideas of education were the decisive influence on the institution, but his wife also played a major role. Although she remains largely invisible in the sources, there are some indications of her importance in administration and the running of the household. She was expected to influence the education of the inmates through her gender-specific characteristics of kindness and gentleness.[8] The role model presented to the young adults was thus that of the

bourgeois family with its strictly gendered role distribution and patri-
archal family structure.

Apart from the director and his wife, the staff included a teacher
and several craftsmen. The craftmen's task was twofold: to provide the
inmates with vocational training, and to support the director and
teacher in reeducating the boys and adolescents. One of the major
problems was that the craftsmen were anything but trained educators.
A further complication arose from the role and composition of the
"educational committee" of the DIGB, which supervised the reform
school. Apart from a few teachers and rabbis, the majority of members
were businesspeople who had not been trained to understand the
problems of children from dysfunctional families. Thus, very often
unsuitable people decided the fate of the inmates.[9]

The Ideal of Jewish Family Life in Question: The Origins of Wayward Boys in Repzin and Wolzig

The origins of the children who at one point in their lives ended up
in reform school can be placed in two categories: children from
families that were seemingly intact, and children from homes that
recognizably did not conform to the ideal. The latter category included
children who were born out of wedlock and children whose parents
had, for various reasons, come into conflict with the law or had
neglected and abused the children. In these cases, the reasons for
Verwahrlosung (waywardness) were clear, and sympathy for the children's fate was shown—but only if they responded to the educational
efforts of the reform school. There was, however, no tolerance for the
antisocial behavior of children who came from "normal" families.[10]
These young adults suffered condemnation, and the bourgeois family
model remained unquestioned. Their rebellion was not seen as a sign
of family dysfunctionality, manifested in rigid upbringing and strict
role divisions. The motto seems to have been: "When in doubt: blame
the child."

In order to reconstruct the social environment of the inmates, we
cannot rely on the adolescents themselves because they left very few
letters or diaries; when they did, they made no reference to their
childhood. There are, however, letters from parents and reports by the
director. Some of the more important letters are those between Hans
Gross and his mother, which allow a detailed analysis of Hans Gross's
upbringing and family background.

Hans Gross was born in 1916. When his mother requested correctional education in July 1932, his father was no longer alive. The reasons for Hans Gross's admission to Wolzig can be considered stereotypical: he did not receive a sufficient education at home, he never tried to get a job, he was often absent from home, and he associated with bad company and engaged in shoplifting. Official documents do not relate his behavior to his upbringing. An analysis of his mother's letters, however, reveals the boy's problematic and dysfunctional childhood. Of particular note in the following passage is the mother's total ignorance of her son's needs. The many orthographical and syntactical mistakes, as well as the poor German, indicate that not all Jews in Germany were *gebildet* (well educated):

> My dear Hans! Why are you always so bad to me. Do you have so little common sense and don't know that today I am very poor. I hardly have to eat—not even money for a cup of coffee. Why don't you want to believe me. . . . Be reasonable and understand that I don't have the money to come to you. . . . Believe me I am longing to see you & cry every day that I cannot come to you. . . . But you have to get vacation for the Jewish holidays and I will absolutely make it possible that I speak with the director personally. [There follows a promise to come as soon as she has the money.] But if you respect your mother so that you always have to threten me then I have to be ashamed to have a son like you. You should be pleased that your mother has what to eat & and not talk badly about her all the time. I don't know what you want from me . . . So be reasonable & prey every day that your mother is alive. Because when I am no longer Alive you will be lost forever. Behave well & learn so that you can support your dear mother later a little. I am very poor & I feal very weak. But I do not want to complain & satisfied that I have my food. [The mother announces that she will try to come the following Sunday.] But if I should come don't be unreasonable & don't scold me again like you have done already in the past. I believe that you are now reasonable. So don't be sad & be happy I am always thinking about you my beloved child. You know that I only love you & that will do everything when I will only be capable then everything will be good for you again. Be content that you are among Jews and not among kristian antisemites as you were. I am very happy that you are in Wolzig again. . . . Be greated and kissed for today a thousand times from your deeply loving mother who thinks only about you.[11]

In this letter, which amounts to emotional blackmail, the gender-specific upbringing of the ethnic context becomes apparent. Which role was the sixteen-year-old Hans supposed to play? After the death of his father, a change in role distribution took place: the mother expected her only son to assume some of the roles of the husband in providing emotional and financial support. The purpose of professional training and education was not to enable Hans to step up the social ladder and break out of the vicious circle of poverty and control but to make life easier for his mother.

This was too much for a boy in puberty. In reaction to the mother's threat to his masculinity, he began to search for other company. In childhood he did not learn how to form constructive relationships since his upbringing consisted of ineffective threats, half-hearted warnings, suffocating considerateness, and instructions about the choice of friends, including injunctions against mixing with non-Jews. Tearfully the mother demanded respect, but without treating her son with respect and dignity. In this family, the mother could offer neither help nor guidance to the young man, and it is hardly surprising that he ended up in reform school. After he was institutionalized, the mother's lack of support became evident. In this emotionally disturbed family, the son's disappointment could be expressed only through aggression and destructive behavior. The reform school could not offer him what he desperately needed: love and understanding from his mother, nor did correctional education offer him other people he could relate to. Education in Wolzig had little impact on his behavior. He demonstrated "bad behavior, boastful manners and a negative and inconsistent attitude," and in the end he escaped from the institution.

Whereas the case of Hans Gross provides us with an important insight into family structure, the following cases demonstrate family breakdown without providing much information about upbringing. However, they all have one thing in common: the families wanted to send away a child and thus admitted their failure.

In 1924, Max Chaimoff from Breslau described his brother's deviant behavior: "My brother, 16 years old, is degenerate and ill-mannered. . . . He attended secondary school but made scarcely any progress. . . . He cannot stay at home since he is ruining the health of my parents in an irresponsible manner. They are over 60 years old and through his foolish pranks he only causes inconvenience to parents and siblings."[12]

Psychologists have argued that extreme views regarding religion can also lead to dysfunctionality in the family since following rules takes precedence over the relationship between the various family members.[13] It is therefore not surprising that some children from Orthodox backgrounds were to be found in reform schools. A certain J. von Gelder, Jr., from Hamburg, for example, wanted to send his nineteen-year-old son to Repzin since "in his business transactions, my son has not fulfilled the expectations to which I hold him, as he comes from a good and orderly home."[14] In the end, the father decided against Repzin because, in his eyes, the institution was not sufficiently Orthodox; the fate of the young man remains unknown. In another case, Mendel Broch removed his son from Wolzig because he feared it would have a bad influence on his Orthodox upbringing.[15] In both cases, there was a refusal to contemplate any deviation from strict adherence to Orthodoxy.

Autobiographies shed further light on the strict upbringing in Orthodox families. Rahel Straus describes how the children suffered from such rigid principles.[16] The Straus family belonged to the Neo-Orthodox in Karlsruhe, and it was expected that the children would follow in their father's footsteps. Samuel Straus had even informed his eldest son, Elias, at his mother's grave about his priorities: "I would rather see my children lying down below, next to their mother, than see them become impious."[17] This had a devastating impact: Elias Straus never visited his hometown again and felt constantly guilty.[18] The youngest son, Gabor, who was only five years old when his mother died, suffered from severe emotional distress when trying to follow his father's strict orthodoxy and in his early twenties killed himself.[19] He apparently saw no other solution when he realized that his father's way was not his way.

Problems also arose from adolescent rebellion against the bourgeois values of the parents and German *Bildung* or education, manifested in prestigious and demanding educational institutions. One sixteen-year-old, the son of a wholesaler and a student at an *Ober-Realschule* (science-oriented secondary school), embezzled money and was sent by his father to Repzin. The life of another youth, Rudolf Seelig, was characterized by social decline. He had been a secondary-school student, became an apprentice, carried out dishonest acts, ran away from home, and tried to commit suicide.[20]

Even Zionist sentiments were considered grounds for institutionalization. In 1920 a woman from Breslau wrote that her son had read many books about Zionist ideas and as a result had gone astray. The mother requested that he be admitted to Repzin because she feared his influence on his younger siblings. Even though he had a clear idea about his future—he wanted to learn farming in order to emigrate to Eretz Israel—he was not allowed to pursue his ideals. What is interesting in this context is not only the mother's behavior but the reaction of the board of trustees. They did not rebuke the mother but fully supported her, even though the son's wish to become a farmer was regarded by the leaders of German Jewry as a most desirable goal. The case shows the parents could exercise unlimited power over their children, a power that was sanctioned by society. In this case, however, when the mother asked for state intervention, the board of

trustees recommended that the mother demand correctional education not on grounds of her son's Zionist ideas but because he had run
away from home in order to go to Palestine. At the same time, the
board suggested an alternative: sending him to a Jewish *Siedlungs-
genossenschaft* (settlement co-operative).[21] In the end, mother and state
based their decision on financial considerations and sent him to
Repzin. The fate of the boy could be described as "Al parashat der-
akhim"—at the parting of the ways—between reform school and a
farm in Eretz Israel.

How a child's interests became of secondary concern is also illustrated in the following case. When Fredi Treuherz's mother remarried,
the boy's stepfather threatened to leave his wife if the young man was
not removed from their home. The boy's father, who wanted custody
of his son, had married a Christian woman and both the mother and
the maternal grandfather opposed the father's request, despite the
mother's position. It is interesting that official Jewish organizations
agreed to institutionalize the child in order to avoid his being brought
up by a Christian stepmother; the child's wishes were not taken into
consideration.

With regard to the social class of these young people, it is important
to note that the boys and young men in these particular cases came
from respected bourgeois families. This was also true of those who
went to the reform school when it moved to Wolzig. Fritz Hirsch, one
of the educators, remembers that the majority of boys belonged to the
middle class and had received proper schooling.[22] He regarded this as
an advantage, because he hoped for easier access to the adolescents.
To some extent, he linked schooling with correctional education and
assumed that the problems of middle-class children could be solved
more easily than those of children who were less educated. German
respect for *Bildung* is apparent here. But class background is important for the construction of a theory of family breakdown, which
must accommodate its incidence among those in the middle class, not
merely outsiders in Jewish society.

In the cases described above, the family did not fulfill its function;
nevertheless it showed some interest in the child. There were, however, also cases of total neglect. Werner Katz was an illegitimate child
born in 1904; he had no contact with his mother. He was brought up
in a Jewish orphanage and lost several apprenticeships because of
fraud and lies. He lived with a guardian whom he did not obey, and he
was often absent from home. In keeping with predominant German
family values, the guardian requested that Werner be placed in a strict
institution.[23]

What did the family members hope for after they admitted that their methods of upbringing had failed? Their request for a strict education was a call for help; however, these families did not realize that strict upbringing at home could in itself cause rebellion and deviant behavior. In such cases, even stricter institutional upbringing could reinforce the problems instead of solving them. If, not surprisingly, the parents lacked this insight, it would have been the task of those responsible for education and social work in Jewish circles to draw attention to this fact. However, they failed equally until fundamental changes took place in correctional education in the late 1920s.

The previous examples relate to children who were institutionalized. While the primary sources are not rich, there are nevertheless many examples of dysfunctionality that were not regarded as anything out of the ordinary and did not lead to institutionalization.

Klara Caro was born in 1886 and wrote her autobiography in a nursing home as occupational therapy in 1979; she recalls a "rather bleak childhood," which was characterized by "overage parents, my mother totally non-understanding[;] we lived in limited circumstances." She regarded her upbringing as "completely false" partly because she was spoiled as the so-called "latecomer."[24] Bruno Stern recalls that being beaten was regarded as normal;[25] and in his autobiography, Theodor Lessing describes his hatred of his parents.[26]

What we would today regard as child abuse was seen as nothing unusual in certain circles. This becomes apparent from the correspondence between one educated and financially well-off woman—who held a doctorate in chemistry—and her mother. In her letters she discusses toilet training her baby when he was just a few months old, and she mentions severely beating him and tying him to the bed at the age of three when he refused to go to sleep.[27]

An extreme case is evident in the family of Charlotte Salomon,[28] which had a history of suicide. The fact that Charlotte's grandmother committed suicide in 1940 seems understandable under the circumstances in Nazi-occupied Europe. But the steps to end their lives taken by her great-grandmother, her aunt, her grandmother's sister, and her own mother can only be interpreted as a sign of extreme dysfunctionality. It was not a gender-related disposition. Charlotte's great-uncle had drowned himself at the age of twenty-eight after his mother forced him to marry for money and the marriage turned out to be very unhappy. The death of the son had a devastating impact on his mother, who as a result tried repeatedly to escape the care of two nurses in order to take her life. She finally succeeded after eight years. The pattern of suicide extended also to some who married into the family.[29]

Through painting Charlotte tried to come to terms with loneliness,

sadness, and feelings of guilt[30] following her mother's suicide when
she was still a young child. Her mother's suicide is understood clearly
as a reaction to her strict upbringing, and Charlotte's stepmother
explicitly blamed the grandmother for her children's death. "Grandmother had stifled every natural impulse in her children by bringing
them up to be stiff and formal, . . . had imposed the example of her
own perfection on them in such a way that, in the certainty of their
own imperfection and, on the other hand, impelled by strong natural
instincts, they found themselves in such violent inner conflicts that
their only escape was through death."[31]

Further examples of dysfunctional families could be given but for
lack of space. What is the relevance of the few cases discussed here? It
is clear that we can never come to a representative view—expressed in
numbers and percentages—if only because of the lack of sources. But
such evidence as we have strongly indicates that family breakdown,
dysfunctional families, and unhappy childhoods were not unusual in
Jewish society, although it is possible that there was less breakdown in
Jewish families than in those that were non-Jewish. Jewish children
were significantly underrepresented in correctional education. In
1930, for example, the Jews made up 1.1 percent of the population in
Germany but only 0.4 percent of children in reform schools.[32] Several
factors must be considered in any attempt to explain this. One of these
is certainly class. In non-Jewish society the children of the lower class
ended up more frequently in reform schools than children of middle-
class parents. Since Jews in Germany were more strongly represented
amongst the middle class, this might explain the relatively low number of children in correctional education. This evidence may tell us
more about the attitude of the state toward the institutionalization of
children—that is, a greater willingness to target the working class for
reform—than the actual incidence of dysfunctionality in families.

From Authoritarian One-Man Rule to Self-determination: Changes in Correctional Education

While changes in the education system were widely discussed in
the Jewish and non-Jewish public during the Weimar period, life in
Repzin remained for the most part unchanged. In 1923 the director
still declared that the educational principles of the institution were
Strenge, Arbeit und *Belehrung* (rigor, work, and instruction).[33] This
stance contradicts the theory that Jews were at the forefront of social

reform. When it came to correctional education that was definitely not the case.

The necessary changes were undertaken only after the youth office ordered the closure of Repzin because it did not meet the pedagogical standards of the time and the buildings were dilapidated and unsanitary.[34] The twenty-year-old Robert Kummer, for example, had spent two years in Repzin and not learned a profession. He felt betrayed because the institution had not trained him to make a living after his release.[35] This changed in November 1929 when the director, who had absolute rule in the institution, was replaced by a man who espoused progressive educational views. A pediatrician by profession, Hans Lubinski had the necessary qualifications to carry out Wilker's educational principle of *Hinführen zur Freiheit durch Freiheit* (leading to freedom through freedom).[36] The inmates in Repzin had high expectations from the new system, as can be seen in the "Lied der Aktivisten" [Song of the activists].

> Wir kamen von Repzin her . . .
> Da gab's nur Kommandieren, ein Glück, wir sind da raus.
> Hier schaffen wir uns Neuland–
> hier muss es anders sein. . . .[37]

> [We came from Repzin . . .
> There were only orders, thank God we are out of there.
> Here we create New Land–
> here things have to be different. . . .]

The hopes of the young men were not unreasonable. In contrast to the previous system, education was now based on self-rule, as it is in modern non-Jewish reform schools. At least this was the theory, although in reality the director quickly learned that the transition from the authoritarian rule of his predecessor to progressive principles was not an easy one. The new principles demanded much from both inmates and educators, and it took some time for the system to work. Hans Lubinski later admitted frankly that in the beginning he was too optimistic, and after two months he gave up the idea of total self-administration. He realized there was a need for gradual adaptation since otherwise the adolescents and young men would feel overburdened by the new responsibilities and duties.[38] After some adjustment, the system worked adequately; by 1931 it was reported that decisionmaking included allocation of work and even details of the menu.[39]

A first effort to let the inmates decide on punishment was made under the old system in 1919 but was abandoned at their request; they had greater confidence in the director than in their peers.[40] Furthermore, their decisions on punishment seemed too severe to Baronowitz. It comes as no surprise that adolescents who knew only a violent language from early childhood regarded beating, for example, as appropriate punishment for stealing.[41] This was interpreted by Baronowitz as a sign of incapacity and irresponsibility, and he used it to discredit the new ideas of self-rule as inappropriate for Repzin.

In Wolzig change was initiated by the director. He was far more successful than his predecessor because he had greater understanding of the psychological difficulties of young men from dysfunctional homes. Unfortunately we know very little about the director's and the other educators' methods regarding the reeducation of youth used to violence from an early age. Lubinski, unlike Baronowitz, had neither the time nor the need to pour out his heart to his superiors. However, some major changes can be determined.

The ages of the inmates changed: rather than accepting children from the age of six to twenty-one, Wolzig now accepted only youths from fourteen to twenty; and in the 1920s, the average age was eighteen. This might have been far more challenging since the behavior pattern of older boys is far more difficult to change, a fact that greatly concerned Lubinski.[42] Unlike Repzin, however, there were more educators for this difficult task. In Repzin there was only one teacher and between one and three guards, and they had not received any special training that would have qualified them to supervise and educate children and adolescents with severe emotional problems.[43] In Wolzig, eleven educators took care of the sixty-eight inmates. Furthermore, most of them had been trained,[44] and the two functions of guard and craftsman were separated.

Wolzig educators were ardent supporters of the youth movement, which made it easier to reach an understanding with the young men who, like non-Jewish reform school inmates, were highly politicized and had their own ideas about the structure of society and the place of the youth in changing it. The youth movement played an important role in supporting the education efforts at Wolzig for another reason: the apprentices in Wolzig had built a youth hostel nearby, and direct contact existed between the inmates and members of youth groups who stayed there. A group of *Chaluzim* (pioneers), for example, brought about fundamental change since their example taught the inmates *Gemeinschaftsgeist* (community spirit), and they became more prepared to take responsibility for the well-being of the group.[45]

Unlike Repzin, the young men in Wolzig were not cut off but had contact with the outside world. And part of the reeducation process was to establish a healthy, nonsexual relationship based on equality and freedom between the sexes. The achievement of this goal was hindered by gender segregation in the reform schools, and some reformers demanded the introduction of co-education.[46]

Lubinski acknowledged the disadvantages of gender-segregated education and sought a solution. The contact with mixed groups from the youth hostel provided one means of breaking down gender barriers and also exposed the inmates to the ideological issues facing their peers in the general community. The inmates in Wolzig could confront these ideas since freedom of speech, thought, and expression was not limited. In contrast to the bourgeois world, socialism had not only become acceptable, but socialist ideas were shared by some of the educators. The changes in correctional education must also be seen in the context of the growing influence of Zionism: in Wolzig it was possible to learn Hebrew, take courses in Jewish history, and discuss questions of Jewish existence and identity, as well as issues concerning Eretz Israel.[47]

Wolzig was not surrounded by fences and the young men could, theoretically, leave at any time. So that the young men could get used to life outside the institution, they were allowed to go out on some weekends and every second Sunday were allowed to remain out until eleven o'clock at night—after they had learned the rules of this less oppressive system. The fact that very few attempts to escape took place—in contrast to Repzin—must be interpreted as a sign that the new system was far more appropriate for the needs of the young men.

Other changes reflected respect for individual privacy, such as freedom of correspondence. Furthermore there was no ban on smoking, which was of importance to the inmates since it meant that their desire to be part of the adult male world was taken seriously.

With regard to outward appearances, the changes were obvious: Wolzig was a modern institution with central heating and electrical cooling. It was the largest and most modern building in the neighborhood and filled the non-Jewish rural population with envy. Whereas occupational training for the inmates at Repzin was completely unsatisfactory,[48] in Wolzig it was provided, albeit in professions that were regarded as appropriate for this particular group of Jewish youth and that were in accordance with the aspirations of the German Jewish leadership in a period of restructuring. In occupations such as carpentry, tailoring, shoemaking, farming, and gardening it had become increasingly difficult to make a living in a time of rising antisemitism and economic crisis;[49] for most, such vocational training proved to be useful only in the context of emigration, especially to Palestine. Since the success of reformatory education depended upon the availability of work, occupational choice was of vital importance. The economic climate of the late 1920s and early 1930s, however, made it increasingly difficult to make a decision that would ensure employment. Language has always been indicative of attitudes and values. The change in the institution's name from Fürsorgeerziehungsanstalt into Jüdisches Jugend- und Lehrheim was therefore more than merely cosmetic: it reflected altered principles of education. Furthermore, Wolzig, unlike Repzin, was not situated in a "godforsaken region near the North Pole," as one of the early teachers had described it,[50] but sixty kilometers from Berlin in a village of one thousand inhabitants. The fact that it was close to the cultural and political center of Weimar Germany was important and facilitated education geared to both nature and culture. In the beautiful summers of the village, the young adolescents could swim—occasionally naked[51]—and they could go ice-skating in winter. In the institution's sailboat, the older inmates could go sailing without supervision. Every Wednesday evening a film was shown,[52] and once a month the inmates participated in cultural events in Berlin, which provided them not only with freedom but the opportunity to take part in the excitement of city life. Wolzig also had a radio and a record player. The inmates were thus aware of the political and cultural world outside the institution and could spend their leisure time in more interesting ways.

Monthly hiking tours in the Märkische Heide as well as two- to three-week trips once a year fostered a positive relationship between an educator and his group:

> If we did not find a youth hostel, we slept in a barn, sometimes under the cover of trees in the forest. This form of gathering, which had been unfamiliar to the boys, turned into an experience for everyone. Thus a comradely relationship developed between the educator and the boys, and not even the most difficult boy was willing to remove himself from it.[53]

Even allowing for some degree of overstatement, this was a fundamental change from the old system where educators had created distance between themselves and the inmates. The dedication of the educators, however, had its price, for they had hardly any privacy; they were with their groups from six o'clock in the morning until bedtime. Fritz Hirsch remembers that it was "often nerve-racking for the educator. . . . Not only did he need a good physical constitution but also a proper degree of idealism and empathetic ability in order to do justice to the problems of each boy."[54]

Changes in the principles of education were also reflected in the work ethos that fostered the inmates' sense of self-worth and enabled them to enjoy the fruits of their labor. They received weekly pocket money geared to their productivity and a productivity bonus;[55] with this money they could buy goods manufactured in Wolzig, including shoes and clothes. Unfortunately we don't know whether the products satisfied the taste of the individual, but any clothes were welcome, and fashion was unlikely to have been a major issue. During the last years of the Repzin home, very little winter clothing was available and spending time outdoors was more or less impossible.[56]

Hygiene—the famous German *Sauberkeit*—was central to the German education system and played a vital role in the reform schools. However, while it was in little evidence beyond rhetoric in Repzin (inmates had to live without hot water for almost a year since there was no money to fix the water heater), in Wolzig each of the four groups into which the inmates were divided—at the most twenty adolescents—had showers and two baths.

Whereas in Repzin the only place for an inmate to be alone might be the toilet—and even there the time was limited in order to prevent masturbation—in Wolzig the need for privacy was respected and each group had four individual rooms and two communal bedrooms (each one for seven to eight boys).[57]

Fostering Jewish identity played a role in both institutions. But while it was a formal Jewish education in Repzin—based on religious instruction alone—Wolzig offered secular Jewish culture as well. As mentioned above, Hebrew was offered, and the burning question of a Jewish future in Germany or Eretz Israel was discussed. Zionism, Socialism, and other progressive movements had become a realistic alternative for the *Fürsorgezöglinge*. Furthermore the institution endorsed religious freedom, although this was limited by the requirement that every inmate participate in the prayers in the synagogue on Shabbat and strictly uphold the holidays.

Masturbation and homosexual activities were a cause of major concern in both Jewish and non-Jewish bourgeois society and were severely punished in the reform schools. While masturbation and homosexuality were contrary to Jewish law, Baronowitz based his views on prevailing the scientific opinion that masturbation caused severe health problems such as softening of the brain, myelomalacia, nervous debility, and greensickness, and was expected to lead inevitably to sterility and the inability to lead a healthy sex life. Homosexuality was simply stigmatized as a perversion that had to be exorcized through severe beating. In the 1920s, however, this theory was challenged by physicians, sex reformers, educators, and progressive

214

forces in Weimar Germany.[58] Unfortunately there is no evidence how the problem was treated in Wolzig, but it is reasonable to assume that the changes in general values were also reflected in sex education. We know that masturbation was no longer punished by beating since the use of force had been totally forbidden under the new educational philosophy. The educators might have advised the youth not to masturbate in order to encourage them to learn self-control,[59] but the rigid controls that were common in Repzin[60] were out of the question. Homosexuality[61] was no longer taboo but was regarded more or less as a disease requiring treatment.[62]

In Repzin, humiliation, physical violence, forced hair cuts for attempts to escape,[63] beatings not only for masturbation and *sexuelle Schweinereien* (that is, engaging in some sort of homosexual activities), but also for an endless list of infractions (not eating enough or pilfering food, not paying attention in class, impudence) were part of the "daily life" of inmates. One could argue that these educational methods were nothing unusual, that the director did not know any better, and that he was convinced he did the best he could for the inmates in order to turn them into respectable citizens. But this argument must be dismissed for several reasons. First, even contemporaries spoke of abuse and ill-treatment in some cases (without, however, interfering in favor of the children);[64] and second, extensive research undertaken in education and psychology since the turn of the century had discredited such practices. The 1920s, in particular, saw the publication of books and articles—above all the work of Alfred Adler[65]—that dealt with the devastating impact of corporal punishment on physiological and psychological well-being.[66] Journals such as the *Zeitschrift für Kinderforschung* and the *Zeitschrift für Pädagogik, Pathologie und Therapie* had declared since the end of the nineteenth century that beating intensified the tendency to violence and that brutal behavior had its origins in early childhood ill-treatment.[67] Furthermore, it was believed that a causal link had been established between beating and a heightening of the sex drive, which led to activities such as masturbation.[68] Since masturbation had to be prevented by any means, an end to corporal punishment was the logical consequence. While the readership of these journals was limited to specialists, personal memoirs such as those of August Forel had the potential to reach a wider audience. In his *Erinnerungen eines Waisenknaben*, published in 1910, Forel described the feelings aroused by brutal punishment, clearly depicting its impact on the individual.[69]

None of the above-mentioned brutal methods of education survived the reform of the late 1920s. An inmate's body was no longer an object on which the director and other educators could take out their frustrations and aggressions.[70]

How did Wolzig fit into the general picture of *Fürsorgeerziehung* in Weimar Germany? According to Fritz Hirsch, a non-Jewish educator and athletics instructor who worked in Wolzig from June 1930 (and who was accorded the title of a "Righteous among the Gentiles" in recognition of his behavior and attitude), Erziehungsheim Wolzig was one of the few progressive institutions in Germany.[71]

Little is known of the fate of young men after they left Wolzig. They were required to leave the institution at the latest at the age of twenty-one. Those engaged in social work and education argued that while educational efforts normally ended at this point, further assistance was required. The transition from the restrictive but protected environment of the reform school was not an easy one for a twenty-one-year-old confronted with the difficulties and challenges of a society in crisis. While the old system had included no program that supported integration and a smooth transition, a Jüdisches Jugendwohnheim was established in Berlin in April 1931 under the new regime. This institution was supposed to assist young men in finding employment and to provide them with an opportunity for creative and socially acceptable leisure-time activities. The social worker Friedel Joseph recalls that the young men went to the theater, to concerts, and to sports events, and that they even attended evening classes.[72]

Can the new principles of correctional education that were applied in Wolzig be called a success? The new system was only in operation for four years, between November 1929 and June 1933 (when the Nazi state closed down the institution and incarcerated educators and inmates in prison and concentration camps).[73] Some indication of success during this brief period lies in the fact that there were few attempts to escape. There is also evidence that some inmates who had previously been in various non-Jewish institutions preferred Wolzig.[74] However, as the case of Hans Gross demonstrates, his stay at Wolzig was to no avail. His behavior remained unchanged, and society continued to regard him as an outcast. Complete success would not have been a realistic expectation, but a certain degree of success might be measurable by a young man's integration into society. The difficulty in making this assessment is that hardly any evidence is available on the young men's experience after they left the institution; and in any case integration was especially difficult in the circumstances of the early 1930s.

There is no doubt, however, that new educational principles based on freedom and respect, which supplanted oppression, beatings, and other repressive measures designed to break the inmates' spirit, opened up new and more promising alternatives. Furthermore, Lubinski and the other educators at the institution were familiar with Adler's *Individualpsychologie* and had realized the folly of concentration on symptoms if underlying causes were ignored.[75]

Why did these revolutionary changes take place relatively late in comparison with the non-Jewish world? It is important to realize that progressive reforms in correctional education in Germany began shortly before the end of World War I, although at first they failed. Karl Wilker was forced to leave Lindenhof after almost four years in October 1920 because the other educators, as well as the city council, were not yet ready for far-reaching changes.[76] When the leaders of German Jewry reformed the system, it was a reform from above and in accordance with the general climate. In the case of Jewish correctional education, it is also important to note that reform had become a matter of honor, especially after 1925 when Repzin was labeled a disgrace to German Jewry.[77] Finally, the relationship between the director and the board of trustees of the reform institution changed fundamentally, since organizations apart from the DIGB had gained influence on the board.[78] While Baronowitz was treated as an employee, Lubinski was part of the leadership and played a role in the development of the theory and practice of social work. He thus had the authority to implement his progressive ideas in the institution.

I do not wish to idealize the changes in correctional education; the limited nature of the reforms must be recognized. One severe shortcoming was most certainly the lack of therapy in the institutions. Progressive forces had demanded the cooperation of psychologists and had pointed out the importance of psychology or psychoanalysis for the success of correctional education since it could help eliminate the underlying reasons for waywardness, not merely its symptoms.[79] In reality, however, hardly any steps were undertaken. Two reasons can be identified—one financial, one ideological. First, individual therapy for every inmate would have been too expensive; and second, the contrasts between various psychoanalytical and psychological schools made it increasingly difficult to sort out which one was the "right" one.[80] Nevertheless, Lubinski recognized the importance of these developments and hoped to make more use of the insights of modern psychology in the future.[81] As the sources show, he was familiar with Adler's ideas of individual psychology and utilized them in his work with the young men.[82]

The importance of population policy, which was becoming a factor in the public debate in the late 1920s,[83] played a significant role in restructuring correctional education. This might be the reason why the development in Jewish society diverged from that of the mainstream. As a result of the economic crisis of the late 1920s, as well as the widespread popularity of eugenic and racial thought, correctional education had become a bone of contention between the various ideological camps in Germany. More and more the conviction gained ground that deviancy was determined by genetics, not the environment. Those individuals who did not respond to correctional education were categorized as *unerziehbar* (uneducable). Government funding for institutions was cut in the late 1920s, partly as a response to the economic crisis but also as a consequence of the influence of deterministic racial ideas.

Although Jewish society shared many of the tenets of the dominant racial ideas, it did not embrace this deterministic approach to social problems. At least in its rhetoric, Jewish society espoused the need to transform every single Jew into a useful Jewish citizen instead of giving up on undesirable individuals. German Jewry was convinced of its important contribution to the Jewish and non-Jewish world, and thus its efforts to save every single German Jewish human being became an expression of Jewish identity and ethnicity. Yet at the same time this was only a beginning; and even its most progressive manifestation, the reform school in Wolzig, could not free itself totally from lapsing into a language that stigmatized the inmates. Hans Gross, for example, was described as showing "bad . . . boastful, erratic, and defiant behavior." Even more revealing of the conflict in which progressive educators found themselves is Lubinski's decision not to admit the most difficult adolescents.[84] Thus, similar to the non-Jewish correctional education system, the success rate was achieved by exclusion of the most problematic youth—those who needed help the most.

It should also be noted that gender played a role since reform efforts did not include wayward girls. Wolzig was an institution for male inmates, and even though changes were undertaken in the reform school for girls, they were not as extensive as those made on behalf of the male adolescents. One could argue that there was less need for reform because fewer girls were identified as requiring institutionalization[85] and because of the existence of Isenburg, Bertha Pappenheim's institution for female outsiders and deviants.[86] From 1931, Isenburg became the institution where young Jewish girls requiring correctional education were sent.[87] But it might also be correct to assume that the reeducation of girls and young women was simply not regarded as of major importance.

Conclusion

The 1920s was a period of transition for correctional education. Lubinski argued that Wolzig would continue to develop and be more successful as it incorporated the insights of modern psychology into its methods and if it received increasing support from a Jewish community in sympathy with its objectives.[88] Clearly, a process of major change in the reformatory system was under way, and Jewish society was again at the forefront of social work, including correctional education. This process came to an abrupt halt with the Nazi closure of the Jewish reform institution in 1933.

Notes

1. See Claudia Prestel, "Zwischen Tradition und Moderne. Die Armenpolitik der Gemeinde zu Fürth (1826–1870)," *Tel Aviver Jahrbuch für Deutsche Geschichte* (1991): 135–62; idem, "Jüdische Unterschichten im Zeitalter der Emanzipation dargestellt anhand der Gemeinde Fürth 1826–1870," *Aschkenas* 1 (1991): 95–134.

2. *Mitteilungen des DIGB* 54 (1900): 17.

3. *Mitteilungen des DIGB* 56 (1901): 34.

4. Peter Martin Lampel, ed., *Jungen in Not. Berichte von Fürsorgezöglingen* (Berlin, 1929).

5. In the same year, Lampel's *Revolte im Erziehungsheim* was performed in theaters and stimulated public debate.

6. See, for example, Curt Bondy, *Scheuen. Pädagogische und psychologische Betrachtungen zum Lüneburger Fürsorgeerziehungs-Prozess* (Berlin, 1931).

7. *Mitteilungen des DIGB* 56 (1901): 30, 42, 46; ibid., 71 (1908): 21; ibid., 80 (1912): 33.

8. Bundesarchiv Koblenz (hereafter BAK), former Zentralarchiv Potsdam, 75 C Ge 1 DIGB 817.

9. *Mitteilungen des DIGB* 71 (1908): 19; ibid., 56 (1901): 30; BAK, 75 C Ge 1 DIGB 794.

10. See, for example, a letter written by the Orthodox rabbi of the Adass Isroel in Königsberg about the parents of a boy frequently found on the streets: "But the parents are not capable of enforcing a strict upbringing upon the boy, despite their best intentions and faultless life conduct" (BAK, 75 C Ge 1 DIGB 769).

11. Brandenburgisches Landesarchiv (hereafter BLA), Pr. Br. Rep. 2 A Reg. Potsdam I Pol 1915.

12. BAK, 75 C Ge 1 DIGB 769.

13. Robin Norwood, *Wenn Frauen zu sehr lieben. Die heimliche Sucht gebraucht zu werden* (Hamburg, 1986), p. 33; see also David Mark Mantell, *Familie und Aggression. Zur Einübung von Gewalt und Gewaltlosigkeit* (Frankfurt am Main,

1978); Alfred Adler, *Das Leben gestalten. Vom Umgang mit Sorgenkindern* (originally published in 1930 in New York under the title *The Pattern of Life*) (Frankfurt am Main, 1981); Otto Rühle, *Zur Psychologie des proletarischen Kindes*, ed. Lutz von Werder and Reinhart Wolff (Frankfurt am Main, 1975).

14. BAK, 75 C Ge 1 DIGB 769.
15. BAK, 75 C Ge 1 DIGB 837.
16. Rahel Straus, *Wir lebten in Deutschland. Erinnerungen einer deutschen Jüdin 1880–1933* (Stuttgart, 1961), p. 115.
17. Ibid., p. 106.
18. Ibid., p. 105.
19. Ibid., p. 199.
20. BAK, 75 C Ge 1 DIGB 789.
21. BAK, 75 C Ge 1 DIGB 768.
22. Joseph Walk, "Das Ende des jüdischen Jugend- und Lehrheims Wolzig (1933)," *BLBI* 66 (1983): 5.
23. BAK, 75 C Ge 1 DIGB 768.
24. ALBI-NY, AR-Z. 983 Caro, Klara 4808.
25. "Pranks were punished with a good spanking" (Bruno Stern, *Meine Jugenderinnerungen an eine Württembergische Kleinstadt und ihre jüdische Gemeinde* [Stuttgart, 1968], p. 60).
26. Theodor Lessing, *Einmal und nie wieder* (Prague, 1935).
27. Central Archives for the History of the Jewish People, Jerusalem, P 154.
28. Charlotte Salomon was born in 1917 and killed in Auschwitz in 1943.
29. Charlotte's grandmother's brother-in-law, for example, committed suicide as well. Charlotte Salomon, *Charlotte: Life or Theater? An Autobiographical Play*, with an introduction by Judith Herzberg; trans. Leila Vennewitz (New York, 1981), pp. vii, 707; Charlotte Salomon, *Charlotte. A Diary in Pictures* (New York, 1963).
30. Charlotte interprets her mother's suicide as a reaction to her own naughtiness and her father's unavailability: "No, she could never be happy with that husband and with that child. . . . For even when quite small she was very cheeky, often annoying her mother. (. . .) And I will be Professor. Don't disturb, please don't disturb me. And I will be Professor." Salomon, *Life or Theater*, pp. 132, 134, 136.
31. Ibid., p. 94.
32. *Jüdische Wohlfahrtspflege und Sozialpolitik* 1, NF (1930): 198. In 1928, of the 97,571 children in correctional education, 300 were Jewish. However not all of the 300 were in Jewish institutions. In 1929, only 123 were in Jewish institutions and a year later only 98. See ibid., 3, NF (1932): 145.
33. BAK, 75 C Ge 1 DIGB 769.
34. From the beginning, the building was in an unsatisfactory and primitive condition; it was described by Heinemann Stern as "an old building, full of mice and rats and nine kilometers away from the next city where there was a physician, a pharmacy, and deliverymen"; see Heinemann Stern, *Warum hassen sie uns eigentlich? Jüdisches Leben zwischen den Kriegen. Erinnerungen*, ed. with commentary by Hans Ch. Meyer (Düsseldorf, 1970), p. 70.
35. BAK, 75 C Ge 1 DIGB 747.
36. Hannah Karminski, Paula Kronheimer, and Georg Lubinski, "Zur Reform der jüdischen Fürsorgeerziehung für Schulentlassene in Heimen," *Zeitschrift für jüdische Wohlfahrtspflege* 1 (1929): 139. Lubinski's principles were in accordance with progressive ideas at the time when he argued that in order to change the

attitude of a young human being, he has to be placed in a community that understands him. One can have the trust of a young person only if he feels that he is an equal part in the community. He not only has to trust the educator but also his comrades. BAK, 75 C Ge 1 DIGB 747.

37. BLA, Pr. Br. Rep. 2 A Reg. Potsdam I Pol 1915.

38. *Jüdische Wohlfahrtspflege und Sozialpolitik* 1, NF, no. 9–10 (September–October 1930): 357–58.

39. *Israelitisches Gemeindeblatt Mannheim*, no. 2, February 16, 1931, p. 8.

40. BAK, 75 C Ge 1 DIGB 748.

41. It seems hypocritical when Baronowitz argues that the punishment seemed too severe since that is what the young men had learned in the institution. BAK, 75 C Ge 1 DIGB 799.

42. *Jüdische Wohlfahrtspflege und Sozialpolitik* 1, NF, no. 9–10 (September–October 1930): 357.

43. The guards themselves were often alcoholics, and many were involved in fights or with girls; many committed embezzlement, and antisemitic talk was common. Since the guards were mostly non-Jews, it was difficult for Baronowitz, according to the board of trustees, "to educate in a Jewish sense." However, it was not a question of origins alone, since the Jewish gardener also beat the children, did not meet the institution's demands, and was not able "to adapt to the spirit of the institution." BAK, 75 C Ge 1 DIGB 525.

44. Some had graduated in the theory and methodology of education as well as in psychology, and some had experience in social work. The majority of the educators were *staatlich geprüfte Wohlfahrtspfleger* (state-certified social workers). BAK, 75 C Ge 1 DIGB 840, 756.

45. *Jüdische Wohlfahrtspflege und Sozialpolitik* 1, NF, no. 9–10 (September–October 1930): 358.

46. Paula Kronheimer, "Erneuerungsbestrebungen und Möglichkeiten im jüdischen Heimwesen," *Mitteilungen des Reichsausschusses der jüdischen Jugendverbände* 2, no. 1, special issue, *Soziale Woche in Seesen*, March 1929, p. 13.

47. *Jüdische Wohlfahrtspflege und Sozialpolitik* 1, NF, no. 9–10 (September–October 1930): 360.

48. BAK, 75 C Ge 1 DIGB 774.

49. An article in 1931 mentioned the difficulties the young men experienced when seeking work. See *Breslauer jüdisches Gemeindeblatt*, no. 10, October 1931, pp. 136–38.

50. Heinemann Stern was one of the first teachers in Repzin. He was employed from 1903 to 1906, and he compared his trip there with a trip to the North Pole. See Stern, *Warum hassen sie uns eigentlich?* p. 69.

51. BLA, Pr. Br. Rep. 2 A Reg. Potsdam I Pol 1915.

52. BAK, 75 C Ge 1 DIGB 838.

53. Walk, "Das Ende," p. 7.

54. Ibid.

55. Their income could be as much as seven reichsmarks per week. Thirty percent was received at the end of the week, 20 percent was placed in a communal fund, and 50 percent was banked on their behalf. *Breslauer jüdisches Gemeindeblatt*, no. 10, Oktober 1931, pp. 136–38.

56. BAK, 75 C Ge 1 DIGB 757.

57. Walk, "Das Ende," p. 5.

58. See, for example, Magnus Hirschfeld and Ewald Bohm, *Sexualerziehung. Der Weg durch Natürlichkeit zur neuen Moral* (Berlin, 1930), pp. 154, 155–57; Wilhelm

Stekel argued that masturbation was an expression of health, intelligence, and talent. Wilhelm Stekel, *Onanie und Homosexualität*, 2nd ed. (Berlin, 1921), p. 14. Werner Villinger warned that psychoneurotic disorders were the consequence of suppressing masturbation. Werner Villinger, "Über Onanie im Kindesalter," *Zeitschrift für Kinderforschung* 31 (1926): 111–34.

59. Georg Löwenstein, for example, argued that masturbation weakens willpower and advised the young workers not to engage in it. Georg Löwenstein, *Arbeiterjugend und sexuelle Frage* (Munich, 1930), p. 22.

60. In the late 1920s, Baronowitz still suggested that a night guard be employed to prevent the inmates from masturbating and from mutual sexual activities. BAK, 75 C Ge 1 DIGB 748.

61. It is doubtful whether it is appropriate to talk of "real" homosexuality and not "forced" homosexuality. Oswald Schwarz described this phenomenon as "Entwicklungshomosexualität," which was not to be understood as an expression of homosexuality. Oswald Schwarz, *Sexualität und Persönlichkeit* (Vienna, 1934), p. 54. Since no other sources of emotion and sexuality were available, the most feminine boys served as substitutes for girls and women and were often subjected to abuse and rape. Peter Martin Lampel, ed., *Jungen in Not. Berichte von Fürsorgezöglingen* (Berlin, 1929).

62. *Zeitschrift für jüdische Wohlfahrtspflege* 1 (1929): 140.

63. In May 1926, Baronowitz reported that one of the inmates had tried to run away. When he objected to the usual punishment of having his hair cut, he was slapped in the face. BAK, 75 C Ge 1 DIGB 799.

64. Even Baronowitz, who often beat the children, realized that the teacher was too brutal and called on the board of trustees to interfere. The teacher was rebuked but continued his beatings and received tenure a few years later. BAK, 75 C Ge 1 DIGB 822, 805.

65. See, for example, Alfred Adler, *Schwer erziehbare Kinder* (Dresden, 1927).

66. See, for example, Hans Zulliger, *Psychoanalytische Erfahrungen aus der Volksschulpraxis* (Bern, 1921), p. 3; Otto Rühle, *Das verwahrloste Kind* (Dresden, 1926); Ruth Künkel, *Das sexuell frühreife Kind* (Dresden, 1926); Ada Beil, *Das trotzige Kind* (Dresden, 1926).

67. *Zeitschrift für Kinderforschung* 19 (1914): 87, 89; ibid., 14 (1909): 25–29; ibid., 9 (1904): 157–60; *Die Kinderfehler. Zeitschrift für Pädagogik, Pathologie und Therapie* (1896): 169, 173.

68. *Zeitschrift für Kinderforschung* 9 (1904): 157–60.

69. August Forel, *Erinnerungen eines Waisenknaben. Von ihm selbst erzählt* (Munich, 1910); see also *Ich suche meine Mutter. Die Jugendgeschichte eines Findelkindes.* Retold by Max Winter (Munich, 1910); Wolf Ritter, *Der Drahtzaun. Aufzeichnungen des Fürsorgezöglings Günther Rodegast* (Hamburg, 1926), in which he describes the stupidity, nastiness, and bigotry of the teachers and educators.

70. Even the board of trustees realized that there was a connection between one of the teacher's frustrations and his beating of children; however, no steps were taken to restrain him. BAK, 75 C Ge 1 DIGB 822.

71. Walk, "Das Ende," p. 5.

72. ALBI-NY, AR-C.1913 Friedel Joseph 4982; Paul & Friedel Joseph, "Das jüdische Jugendwohnheim in Berlin," *Jüdische Wohlfahrtspflege und Sozialpolitik* 4 (April 1932): 118–21.

73. The staff of the institution was sent to prison and relased after a short time, but the inmates were kept for five months in Oranienburg. After their release they were brought to the Jewish hospital in Berlin to recover from their

experiences in the concentration camp. Some returned to their parents, a few subsequently emigrated to Palestine. Walk, "Das Ende," pp. 12, 17, 18.

74. Hans Blumenthal, who had contrived to escape from various non-Jewish institutions, found Wolzig to his liking. BLA, Pr. Br. Rep. 2 A Reg. Potsdam I Pol 1915.

75. *Mitteilungen des Reichsausschusses der jüdischen Jugendverbände* 2, no. 1, special issue, *Soziale Woche in Seesen* (March 1929): 11.

76. Karl Wilker had become director in 1917 of the Fürsorgeerziehungsanstalt für schulentlassene männliche Zöglinge der Stadt Berlin in Berlin-Lichtenberg; it was later known as Lindenhof. Karl Wilker, *Der Lindenhof. Werden und Wollen*, 2nd ed. (Kettwig an der Ruhr, 1924).

77. BAK, 75 C Ge 1 DIGB 525.

78. After April 1930, the Jewish community of Berlin took over responsibility for Wolzig from the DIGB. *Breslauer jüdisches Gemeindeblatt*, no. 10, October 1931, pp. 136–37.

79. See, for example, August Aichhorn, *Verwahrloste Jugend. Die Psychoanalyse in der Fürsorgeerziehung* (Leipzig, 1925).

80. See, for example, *Das Problem der Schwererziehbaren in der Fürsorgeerziehung. Referate des AFET* (Berlin, 1931), p. 13.

81. BLA, Rep. 2 A I Pol 1914.

82. Hans Lubinski, "Zwei Jahre Erziehungsarbeit in Wolzig," *Jüdische Wohlfahrts- pflege und Sozialpolitik* 4 (April 1932): 114–15.

83. Claudia Prestel, "Population Policy in Jewish Society: An Expression of Jewish Identity?" in *Yehudei Weimar: Hevra be-mashber ha-moderni'ut, 1918–1933* [The Jews of Weimar: A society in the crisis of modernity], ed. Oded Heilbronner (Jerusalem, 1994), pp. 214–62 (in Hebrew) (German version, "Bevölkerungs- politik in der jüdischen Gesellschaft in der Weimarer Republik–Ausdruck jüdi- scher Identität?" *Zeitschrift für Geschichtswissenschaft* 41 [1993]: 685–715).

84. BAK, 75 C Ge 1 DIGB 747.

85. According to official statistics, boys made up two thirds of the inmates. Ernst Siefert, *Psychiatrische Untersuchungen über Fürsorgezöglinge* (Halle, 1912), p. 140. In the Jewish institutions, they represented nearly 75 percent. Wolzig and Repzin usually had between fifty and sixty inmates, while there were about twenty girls in Köpenick. *Jüdische Wohlfahrtspflege und Sozialpolitik* 1, NF (1930): 482.

86. Marion A. Kaplan, *Die jüdische Frauenbewegung in Deutschland* (Hamburg, 1981); Claudia Prestel, "Uneheliche Kinder und ledige Mütter in der jüdischen Gemeinschaft im 20. Jahrhundert: Eingliederung oder Ausschluss? – Ein Beitrag zur deutsch-jüdischen Frauengeschichte," *L'Homme. Zeitschrift für Feministische Geschichtswissenschaft* 2, no. 5 (1994): 81–101.

87. *Jüdische Wohlfahrtspflege und Sozialpolitik* 4 (April 1932): 121.

88. BLA, Rep. 2 A I Pol. 1914.

12

Decline & Survival of Rural Jewish Communities

STEVEN M. LOWENSTEIN

In the Black Forest of southwest Germany, three towns symbolize the fate of small-town Jewry in the Weimar Republic. Less than five kilometers east of the small town of Horb (population in 1933: 2,806) lay the village of Nordstetten, whose greatest claim to fame was that it was the hometown of Berthold Auerbach (1812–1882), the Jewish author of the widely popular *Black Forest Village Tales*. Auerbach's popularization and sentimentalizing of German village life in literature did not seem to persuade his Jewish former neighbors of the glories of rural life, since they moved out of the village in droves. Nordstetten's Jewish community went into rapid decline. In 1867, 201 of the village's 900 inhabitants were Jews; by 1900 this number had fallen to 65, and in 1925 only 11 were left. An hour's walk from Horb in the opposite direction lay the village of Rexingen, about the same size as Nordstetten and equally overwhelmingly Catholic. But in Rexingen the Jews did not move out. The number of Jews, which hovered around 350 in the late nineteenth century, remained at 307 in 1925, making it one of the largest village Jewish communities in Germany. It was unique among all German Jewish communities in forming the core of an emigrant group that founded an agricultural settlement in Palestine at Shavei Zion between Haifa and Naharia. The third community, Horb, the site of the railroad station that served all three towns, was somewhat larger than the other two and was the local commercial center. The first Jews came to Horb in the 1870s, presumably from the nearby villages; the community grew to over one hundred members by the twentieth century, then declined slightly during the Weimar period.

Small-town Jewry in the Weimar Republic generally fell into one of the categories symbolized by the three towns. Most of the hundreds of Jewish communities in villages of one thousand or fewer inhabitants followed the pattern of Nordstetten and shrank drastically, in some cases losing their viability as communities. (The size of a viable Jewish community in German villages was quite small by the standards of today's America. One hundred Jewish inhabitants was generally considered a thriving community, and even communities as small as thirty or forty individuals were usually considered viable.) No more than a few dozen village communities retained much of their Jewish population and remained lively centers of Jewish life the way Rexingen did. The Jews of rural cities of two thousand to ten thousand inhabitants had a different history. In the early stages of Jewish migration out of the villages, many villagers moved to the nearest regional town, swelling the local Jewish population.[1] But for many Jews, the small towns were mere way stations, which they left within a generation to move to large cities such as Berlin, Frankfurt am Main, or Stuttgart.[2] Some small cities shared the intensely traditional atmosphere of village Jewish communities, but many experienced it only in muted form.

In 1925 about one in every six German Jews lived in a town of ten thousand or fewer inhabitants. They were the remnant of what had once been the vast majority of German Jewry. Small-town Jewry was very much reduced in influence by the loss of the provinces of Alsace and Posen in the aftermath of World War I—two provinces that had large non-urban Jewish populations. In the Germany of 1910, 31.8 percent of the Jewish population lived in towns of twenty thousand or fewer inhabitants, but if one omits the areas which Germany lost in the war, the percentage for 1910 was only 26.9 percent.[3] Those who remained in the small towns generally came from families which had lived in the town for several generations and were buried in the local Jewish cemetery. Few new families and almost no East European immigrants settled in the small towns after the mid–nineteenth century. Usually in small villages most men were born in the town, often living in the ancestral family house, but many of their wives were born elsewhere. (Sometimes, although less commonly, the reverse was true). In small cities, many Jewish inhabitants were born in other towns and villages of the region. The communities had their inherited traditions symbolized by synagogue, Jewish teacher, cemetery and local customs. They were far less affected by the twin trends of assimilation and modernist culture than their co-religionists in the large cities. In communities which retained a viable size, most Jews retained a clear sense of identity as members of a Jewish community, alongside their equally strong sense of belonging as German citizens and part of the village community.

There are important regional differences in the nature of small-town Jewry in Germany. The settlement pattern of Posen, and West

Prussia, most of which was returned to Poland after 1918, was similar to the shtetls of Eastern Europe. In 1816 the vast majority of Prussian Jewish communities with more than 500 members were in those provinces and a number of towns had a Jewish majority. In the early nineteenth century, several Posen province shtetlekh rivaled Berlin in Jewish population. Many of these Jewish communities survived with reduced Jewish populations into the early twentieth century but virtually all disappeared when the areas came under Polish administration.[4] In most of the rest of northern Germany, as well as neighboring areas in Holland, there were quite a few substantial Jewish communities in towns of two thousand to ten thousand but relatively few in villages of under two thousand.[5] The unique cultural pattern of Jewish village life which will be described below was present in much clearer form in the South German states of Bavaria (including Palatinate), Hesse, Baden and Württemberg and the southern Rhineland districts of Trier and Koblenz than in the north. Beyond the borders of Weimar Germany it was also to be found in Alsace and Lorraine. (See table 12.1.)

Even within the core area of Jewish village life in South Germany there were noticeable regional differences in degree of Orthodoxy or intensity of antisemitism. Although, overall, Jewish life in villages and small towns preserved more of the traditional rhythm and practices of Jewish life than urban communities, the assumption that they were all deeply Orthodox has been shown to be much exaggerated. A folk variety of Orthodoxy with strict observance of the Sabbath, kashruth, and even of the agriculture *halakhot*, as well as use of the ritual bath by married women was widespread in certain regions such as Lower Franconia in Bavaria and the northern part of Hesse. On the other hand, Jacob Borut has shown that most small-town Jews in the Rheinland, Westphalia, and the Palatinate observed mainly the High Holidays and rites of passage but were extremely lax about Sabbath observance and abandoned the use of the ritual bath.[6] With regard to the degree of good or bad feelings between Jews and Gentiles, there were again important differences. Besides areas of strong traditional antisemitism, for instance in northern Hesse, there was a general tendency for relations in the Weimar Republic to be somewhat better in Catholic than in Protestant areas. This pattern was the rule in the years 1928–1933, when the NSDAP usually gained a much larger percentage of the rural vote in Protestant than in Catholic areas; but it is not necessarily true earlier.[7] It would also seem that towns that experienced a rapid decline in Jewish population between 1880 and 1925 were the site of stronger antisemitism than villages where the Jewish population remained fairly stable. Here it is not clear which

Table 12.1. Number of Communities with over Fifty
Jewish Inhabitants in 1911 (by Town Size)

	General Population of Town		
	over 10,000	2,000–10,000	below 2,000
North Germany within the borders of the Weimar Republic			
East Prussia	10	26	5
Brandenburg	18	25	0
Pomerania	12	27	0
Silesia	38	30	0
Prussian Saxony	19	2	0
Schleswig-Holstein	5	2	0
Hanover	19	22	9
Westphalia	30	33	13
Northern Rhineland (Düsseldorf, Cologne, Aachen districts)	37	29	10
Saxony (Kingdom)	7	0	0
Mecklenburg (Schwerin and Strelitz)	5	1	0
Oldenburg (north German part)	1	2	0
Smaller principalities	20	13	6
Total	221	212	34
South Germany within the borders of the Weimar Republic			
Upper and Lower Bavaria	4	0	0
Upper Palatinate (Bavaria)	3	2	1
Rhine Palatinate (Bavaria)	9	16	20
Franconia (Bavaria)	11	35	74
Bavarian Swabia	2	5	5

| | General Population of Town | | |
	over 10,000	2,000–10,000	below 2,000
Baden	13	35	36
Württemberg	9	10	18
Hohenzollern	0	1	1
Hesse (Grand Duchy)	7	55	60
Hesse-Nassau (Prussia)	13	45	73
Birkenfeld (Oldenburg)	0	2	3
Southern Rhineland (Koblenz and Trier districts)	8	28	32
Total	80	264	323

Beyond the borders of
Weimar Germany

	over 10,000	2,000–10,000	below 2,000
Posen	9	61	18
West Prussia	13	53	2
Alsace-Lorraine	13	51	80
Total	35	165	100

is the cause and which the effect. Were Jews more likely to move out of towns where the atmosphere was more hostile, or did the rapid outmigration of Jews make the Christian population more uneasy about the Jews in their midst?[8]

Despite the important differences from place to place, there were many traits shared by small-town Jewry in general. One is struck at how many times the same motifs are repeated again and again in local histories.[9] The role of Jews in many rural German communities is extremely well documented. Town and regional archives preserve tax records and other material on economic relations. Real estate records show where Jews lived in the villages. Local newspapers and school teachers' reports add much additional detail. Many memoirs of former

Jewish village residents have been preserved, and many of them have been published. A number of local histories and regional studies have made ample and sophisticated use of this documentation. In addition, they have engaged in in-depth interviews and fieldwork among local inhabitants and their former Jewish neighbors. All of this enables us to discuss aspects of daily life and intergroup relations not often available to historians.[10]

One of the most basic characteristics of the position of Jews in small towns was the lack of anonymity. Everyone knew who was a Jew and who a Christian. The boundaries between the two groups were clearly drawn, and although Jews and Christians often interacted in a friendly and neighborly manner, there was never any doubt about who belonged where. Relationships between Jews and non-Jews, whether friendly or unfriendly, were highly personalized. Everyone knew everyone by name and often had strong opinions about individual members of the village community. Identity problems were not significant in village Jewry and intermarriage and conversion were extremely rare.[11]

Intergroup relations on the village level simultaneously showed remarkable integration and remarkable separateness. In most villages, both Jews and Christians shared a respect for traditional religious forms. They attended their own religious services regularly, observed religious holidays at home and at the house of worship, and respected religious leaders.[12] This entailed a certain level of respect for the religious conventions of the other group. It is likely that the influence of the piety of the Christian population was a factor that motivated the Jews to keep up at least the public observance of Jewish rites.[13] There are numerous descriptions of rural Jews decorating their homes for Christian festivals, especially for the Corpus Christi procession,[14] and of Christians knowing not to do business with Jews on their holidays. Sometimes rural Jews, otherwise quite pious in their Jewishness, even participated in the prayers of their Christian schoolmates in the local one-room schoolhouse.[15] When a villager died, all neighbors and friends followed the funeral procession regardless of their religion, a practice that the Nazis had difficulty eradicating.[16] For Passover, Jews brought their neighbors matzohs as a gift in exchange for which they often received colored Easter eggs.[17] Christians in *Judendörfer* (Jewish villages) knew about and showed curiosity about such public displays of Jewishness as the outdoor *sukka*, the masquerades on Purim, and the wearing of white shrouds on the High Holidays.[18] In some villages, Christians continued to bake the Jewish Sabbath bread *(berches)* even after World War II when their Jewish communities had been wiped out.[19] In many rural areas Jewish men who had no time to say their morning prayers upon rising early for business trips recited them and put on tefillin in railroad waiting rooms and even village inns.[20] It was characteristic of much village Jewish religion that it was practiced unselfconsciously in the public eye.

Jews in most towns with Jewish communities were active in local political and organizational life during the Weimar Republic. Beginning around the 1880s and continuing until 1933, it was a common practice in most villages with viable Jewish communities to have one or more Jewish members on the town council. The first Jewish councilman in Schenklengsfeld was chosen in 1898 at the same time as three-class suffrage (based on wealth) was introduced. This suffrage gave the Jews a majority on the council despite the fact that they were a minority of the population. In Gailingen a Jew served as mayor from 1870 to 1884, something that Jews generally avoided even in towns where Jews had a majority on the town council. Jewish public influence was less significant in the Weimar Republic than before, both because of the declining Jewish population and the abolition of the class-based curiae that had given Jewish voters disproportionate leverage. Still, Jewish council members continued to be active in communal affairs, often helping to introduce such innovations as railroad stations, electricity, and running water.[21] In organizational life, most village histories speak about Jews as active (sometimes founding) members of volunteer fire departments, veterans associations, singing societies, the Red Cross chapter, sports clubs, and even (quite frequently) the marksmanship association *(Schützenverein)*.[22] Also quite frequently described is the presence of at least some Jewish men among those regularly meeting for a drink at village taverns and playing cards there.[23] At village dances at the turn of the century, it was common for Jews and Christians to dance together, but this became less common in the Weimar period.[24]

In Weimar times, Jews interacted with Christians as neighbors, fellow citizens, buyers and sellers, employers and employees. Among the Christians most integrated into Jewish life were domestic servants who knew Jewish customs intimately and often retained close personal ties to their employers even after leaving their service. Maids and former maids in Jewish homes were overrepresented among those who helped their Jewish fellow villagers during the Nazi persecution.[25]

But often the very relationships that brought Jews and Gentiles into close proximity and even intimacy demonstrated the barriers that existed to integration and were the cause of deep misunderstanding and distrust. This was most obvious in the economic sphere. Jews played an important role in the economy of the rural regions in which they lived. In the 1920s, the chief occupations of rural Jews were cattle dealing (often the most common Jewish occupation), shop keeping (especially dry goods and groceries), and dealing in grain, agriculture machinery, etc.[26] In some fields such as the cattle trade, Jews had a virtual monopoly. In almost every Jewish village the contrast between a Christian population concentrated in small-scale farming and a Jewish population concentrated in trade was clear and sharp. (This is not to say that Jews did not also engage in some farming. However, Jewish landholdings were generally small and were mainly used as a supplement to other main economic activities such as cattle trading; Jews usually had hired hands to do much of the agricultural work.)

The average taxable wealth of Jews far exceeded that of their Gentile peasant neighbors. Frequently a Jew was the richest inhabitant of the town. Nevertheless, there was generally a considerable gap between the small number of wealthy Jews in small towns and the more modest majority. Such a gap between a small number of wealthy Jews and the majority of the Jewish community, many of whom were middle class but some of whom were poor, is evident in most villages for which we have information. In Gaukönigshofen in 1933, for instance, the Jewish community consisted of an upper class of fifteen members, a middle class of twenty, and a lower class of seventeen members.[27] The greater prosperity of the Jewish population and the clear wealth of a small number of the village Jews became much less common during the hard times of the Weimar Republic. In Gailingen, for instance, the Jewish share of town taxes fell to 27.5 percent in 1924 from 44 percent in 1918. In Gaukönigshofen, the major Jewish farm machinery business went bankrupt in 1930, and many small Jewish businesses had trouble paying their taxes in the 1920s and had to ask for tax relief.[28] Similar cases of Jews unable to pay their taxes in the 1920s and the Depression are found in Niederwerrn.[29] Relative Jewish wealth may also have been exaggerated by tax records, since Jews owned only a small proportion of the farmland in the villages. In Gailingen in 1918, for example, Jews paid 83 percent of the taxes on capital but owned only 30 percent of the real estate. This figure includes the value of Jewish homes, which was often higher than that of Christian-owned houses. In Gaukönigshofen, the total amount of farmland owned by all Jews combined was only about fifty acres, while eighteen houses were owned by Jews.[30]

The non-Jewish residents needed their Jewish neighbors when they wished to buy or sell cattle, get their grain to market, or buy machinery, seeds, or fertilizer. Often they needed the credit offered by Jewish businessmen, and some Christian residents found employment as servants, cattle drivers, field hands or commercial assistants of Jews. In Michelbach an der Lücke, which had 130 Jewish inhabitants in 1890, twenty-six Christians were full-time employees of Jews, and thirty more were part-time workers or day laborers for Jews. In Gaukönigshofen, the Jewish-owned farm machinery company employed eighty persons in 1919 (but only forty-six in 1927).[31] Although this Jewish economic activity was often vital for the town, many Christians resented the fact that they were economically dependent on the Jewish minority. Many villagers considered the trade of the Jews to be parasitical, not real work like the physical labor of peasants and craftsmen. Such practices as advertising and holding sales, engaged in by village Jewish businesses but not by their Christian competitors, were looked upon by many as unethical.[32]

The lifestyle of the village Jews was often noticeably different from that of non-Jews, a fact that could lead to tension. The Jews are frequently described as more urban, middle class, and modern in their way of life than their neighbors. The Jewish Sabbath, with consumption of sumptuous meals that included much meat, elegant city-style clothing, and promenades around or outside of town, exhibited a type of luxurious living rare among peasants even on Sunday. Jews often had more modern furniture (such as sofas, china closets, etc.), owned pianos and other musical instruments, and showed more interest in reading and high culture than their neighbors. In the Weimar Republic it became usual for the children of village Jews to go on for secondary education, still a rarity among non-Jews. Those who did not go on to high school usually went to other towns or cities for training in commercial skills or other trades. Fewer and fewer young Jews remained in the small towns.[33]

On the local level Jews are frequently described as cultural pioneers. Often they were the first to have telephones, a radio, or an automobile, or to wear makeup. In Horb in 1900 there were thirty telephones, twenty-four of them belonging to Jews.[34] Jews traveled more and often had a broader view of the world than their neighbors. In Gaukönigshofen, wealthy Jews went on vacations at spas, something unheard of in the Christian population. Towns with substantial Jewish populations often seemed to have a more urban appearance than others, with large Jewish homes built in urban style and more fashionable dress than elsewhere. Some such Judendörfer were nicknamed Little Paris or Little Stuttgart, a fact that was not always to the liking of the non-Jewish population.[35]

The differences between Jews and Christians were often also noticeable in politics. Unlike the Christian villagers who generally voted for peasant parties or the Catholic Center, their Jewish neighbors tended to support first the liberal German Democratic Party (DDP) and later the Social Democrats (SPD). The contrast between the liberal Jewish voters and the conservative peasants sometimes led to tension, even occasionally to the creation of separate "Jewish" and "Christian" party lists. Despite the relative prosperity of village Jews, they sometimes found political allies among the village poor or rural working class but rarely among the landowning farmers. In the later years of the Weimar Republic (and in some places much earlier), this traditional political dichotomy was much exacerbated by the growth of a local Nazi party constituency.[36]

On the social plane, there were barriers as well as cooperation. Although some Jews did spend some spare time in the village tavern, they often stood out by the fact that they drank little and played cards with each other or with members of the village elite. Jews engaged in small talk with fellow villagers, traded favors with their neighbors, and belonged to some village organizations; but they rarely exchanged social visits with non-Jews. In traditional Jewish communities, religious practice, especially the observance of kashruth and the Sabbath, made socializing with non-Jews in the home more difficult. The rhythm of the life of the Jews was different from that of Christians. Jewish men were often away during the week on business and returned home only for the Sabbath. They rose early but sometimes had time to sit in taverns and cafes in the afternoons when farmers were still working in the fields. Jewish women ran their household and sometimes a shop but unlike Christian women rarely worked in the fields. Labsch-Benz's study of Nonnenweier, Baden, provides us with the following outline of the contrasting picture that Christians in Nonnenweier had of Jews and Christians:

Jews	Christians
always traveling	stationary
intellectually superior	intellectually inferior
physically weak	physically strong
lazy	hard-working

Among the signs of "Jewish laziness" she mentions are the reports of Christian residents that the Jews let others plant their fields, came back home in the early afternoon when their work was done, sat in the tavern after work, and went for walks in the village on the Sabbath.[37]

The difference in religious practices and beliefs, sometimes exacerbated by the way the local pastor taught the stories of the New Testament, also constituted a strong barrier. Although Christians knew about some of the more public Jewish practices such as the sukka, Sabbath rest, or not eating certain foods, there were many aspects of Jewish practice that were unknown to them. Often peasant informants describing Jewish practices mixed up the various holidays, misinterpreted the meaning of Jewish ritual, or believed in secret and sinister Jewish rites. Included among these were widespread beliefs that Jews strangle dying co-religionists to put them out of their misery and sporadic charges of ritual murder. Jews often knew more about the practices of the Christian majority, but they too often felt uneasy about Christian beliefs and about Christian imagery.[38]

The social distance between Jews and non-Jews increased in the younger generation, which grew up during and after World War I. Younger village Jews were less likely than their parents to participate in village social life at dances, the tavern, or local celebrations. They were much more likely to pursue advanced education than either their parents or their non-Jewish contemporaries. Often they are described as having sophisticated friends from the big cities who visited them and whom they visited. Some peasants complained that young Jews thought they were better than everyone else and looked down on their neighbors. (There are similar descriptions of the attitudes of Jewish women.)[39]

A change that may have pushed in the opposite direction—toward greater Jewish integration—was the demise of the Jewish elementary school. In the nineteenth century, many rural and small-town communities had their own separate, state-subsidized one-room Jewish school. The number of such schools decreased tremendously in the first decade of the twentieth century, and by the 1920s most rural Jewish children attended the same elementary school as their Christian neighbors—often a school with markedly Christian denominational features.[40]

Changes in the rural Jewish ethos also became more and more noticeable in the twentieth century. Rural Jewish families began limiting the size of their families long before their Christian neighbors. By the Weimar Republic families with one or two children had become the norm. Some couples had no children. According to the Jewish sociologist Felix Theilhaber, the rural Jewish family decreased in average size from 3 to 1.9 children in the period between 1891 and 1912. Rural Jews had thus begun to duplicate the pattern of low fertility that had earlier become the rule for Jews in the cities.[41]

The picture given by much of the descriptive literature on village life in the Weimar Republic is of an aging and demographically troubled population. In general it was the young who were most likely to leave the villages for the big cities, leaving behind a population more and more aged. There was considerable variation from village to village, however, and not all Jewish villages shared the unfavorable demographic profile. Some villages had a larger percentage of young people than Jewish populations in Germany as a whole, but most did not. In any case German Jews everywhere were a more aged population than non-Jewish Germans.[42]

Because it was difficult to find Jewish marriage partners in the small village communities, a difficulty that became greater as communities declined in size, Jews searched for spouses over an ever greater distance. They were much more likely than their non-Jewish neighbors to marry someone from out of town. In most places the majority of brides were not born locally. Although impressionistic descriptions speak of many Jews remaining unmarried in the villages, this is not generally confirmed by analysis of lists of Jewish inhabitants.[43] On the other hand, there is considerable evidence to back up the impression that village Jews were marrying cousins and other close relatives in increasingly large numbers.[44]

A final characteristic noticeable in the Weimar period was a decline in piety. This decline varied greatly in degree from area to area. In some villages and small towns, even in the relatively traditional areas of South Germany, ever-increasing numbers of the young spent the Sabbath traveling by car out of town, secretly (or sometimes openly) ate non-kosher food away from home, and in some cases (almost always males) found themselves Christian lovers. In other towns, the violation of traditional mores were less extreme, but even in strongly traditional villages (for instance Geroda, Unterfranken) practices such as shaving with a razor, skipping weekday services, and ignoring minor fasts became widespread.[45]

The decay of traditional life was more evident in towns with sharply decreased Jewish populations than in those where the Jewish population was more stable. Towns such as Gailingen, Ichenhausen, Rhina, and Rexingen still had hundreds of Jewish inhabitants in the 1920s. Although the number of such large communities in small towns was much less than it had been a century or even two decades earlier, a considerable percentage of the surviving rural Jewish population still lived in them.[46] Many of the memoirs and descriptions of rural Jewish life from the Weimar period come from these larger more viable communities.[47] This may be one of the reasons why our picture of small-town Jewish life is one of vibrant tradition, a picture less accurate for the smaller communities.

In larger rural Jewish communities there was generally a well-developed network of Jewish organizations—not only the traditional burial society or charity groups found elsewhere, but also Jewish sports clubs, youth groups, veterans associations, and Centralverein chapters. Many such communities still had Jewish taverns or cafes. In Gailingen (with 375 Jews in a population of 1500) the celebration of Purim rivaled the Christian carnival, with public masquerades, balls, even floats and a Jewish jesters' society (Narrenverein Fidelius). The 1920s Purim celebrations in Gailingen were modern enough to include chorus lines with high-kicking male and female dancers.[48] Sometimes these large communities served as meeting places for smaller communities in the region or even for conventions of national Jewish youth organizations. In such towns where it was easier for Jews to socialize with other Jews, the degree of social interaction with Gentiles was probably smaller than elsewhere. Although the Jews in these surviving large communities were a well-known factor in the life of the town, they were also more isolated than elsewhere. This isolation may have led to increased hostility toward Jews in some places, but this is not necessarily the case. In Rexingen, for instance, where the Jews are described as a socially isolated group, the Nazi vote was extremely small before 1933, and relations remained relatively good even in the first years of Nazi rule.[49] In Gailingen, there were some local residents whose anti-Jewish feelings made them early adherents of the Nazis. On the other hand, there were also non-Jews who joined their Jewish neighbors in breaking up or preventing Nazi meetings.[50] In other towns, some of them still with substantial Jewish populations, there was a considerable tradition of dislike of Jews and an early rise in support for the Nazis.[51] Whether the local atmosphere was relatively favorable to the Jews or strongly antisemitic in the Weimar Republic, the village Jews were among the first to suffer physical attacks and economic boycott when the Nazis came to power. Their numbers dropped rapidly under Nazi rule, although in many towns a community hung on till it was too late to emigrate. From 1940 to 1943, the last remnants of village and small-town Jewry were deported to their deaths.

The Jews of rural and small-town Germany represent a cultural phenomenon quite different from small-town life either further east or further west. Unlike the more or less isolated small-town communities of many Western countries, they remained centers of tradition rather than outposts with little Jewish life.[52] Unlike the small communities of Eastern Europe, they demonstrated a kind of integration into the social life of their Christian neighbors unknown in the shtetlekh and villages of Poland and Russia. What makes them unique is their combination of strong integration and strong separateness, often in an unstable equilibrium but sometimes with seemingly little sense of contradiction.

In the Weimar Republic, small-town Jewry was in its next to final stage. In terms of numbers, it had only a small fraction of the weight within German Jewry that it had in the early nineteenth century. Most communities were severely shrunken in size and had to give up some of their institutions for lack of funds. Yet, in the dozens of towns and especially the villages where viable Jewish communities survived in the Weimar Republic, the traditions of rural German Jewry lived on, although in modernized form. Much of the picture we have of German Jewry overall—its cultural contributions, identity problems, far-reaching assimilation—was not true of rural Jewry. In numerous, mainly South German small towns, there remained groups of Jews who were both a part of the overall village community and apart from it, both clearly Jewish and deeply German.[53] They were sophisticated compared to many of their peasant neighbors. but they remained far more traditional and far less complex than their coreligionists in the big cities. Although no longer typical of German Jewry, they remained one of the many-sided elements that made up the Jewish community of Germany.

Notes

1. Although Nordstetten and Rexingen are examples that show there was no absolute and necessary correlation between the town's overall size and the tendency of Jews to move out, there was a general statistical tendency for such a pattern to hold. See the following chart for an example of the pattern in the Bavarian district of Unterfranken:

Overall size	1816	1925	1925 (as a percentage of 1816)
Under 500	1,827	476	26.1
500–999	5,518	1,896	34.4
1,000–1,499	2,466	824	33.4
1,500–1,999	383	438	114.4
2,000–9,999	1,384	2,197	158.7
Over 10,000	310	3,739	1,206.1

(Drawn from database analysis of figures for individual communities given in *Pinkas Hakehillot, Germania, Bavaria* [Jerusalem, 1973], pp. 379–580.)

Figures for 1816 show large Jewish communities in towns of varying size with little correlation. By 1925, even in relatively rural South Germany, there was a close correlation between the size of the Jewish community and the size of the town. Very few large communities remained in towns of fewer than one thousand inhabitants.

2. In Horb, for instance, the first Jewish inhabitant, Hugo Frank, arrived from Nordstetten in 1874. He became prosperous in the town and moved to Stuttgart in 1899. (See the memoirs of his son, Fritz Frank, in *Jüdisches Leben in Deutschland. Selbstzeugnisse zur Sozialgeschichte im Kaiserreich*, ed. Monika Richarz [Stuttgart, 1979], pp. 169–80.)

3. Usiel O. Schmelz, "Die demographische Entwicklung der Juden in Deutschland von der Mitte des 19. Jahrhunderts bis 1933," *Zeitschrift für Bevölkerungswissenschaft* 8, no. 1 (1992): 40, table 3.

4. Bruno Blau, "Die Entwicklung der jüdischen Bevölkerung in Deutschland von 1800 bis 1945" (manuscript, Leo Baeck Institute, New York), pp. 33–34. In 1817, Berlin had 3,699 Jews (1.9 percent of the total population of the city). In the province of Posen, the largest communities in 1817 were Posen, 4,025 Jews (17.7 percent); Lissa, 3,644 Jews (46.0 percent); Kempen, 2,406 Jews (52.4 percent); Inowraclaw, 1,784 Jews (46.9 percent); Krotoschin, 1,586 Jews (33.9 percent); and Grätz, 1,455 Jews (48.8 percent). Posen was the only one of these towns with a total population of over ten thousand. In 1905, by contrast, the Jewish populations of the same towns were Berlin, 98,393 (4.2 percent); Posen, 5,761 (4.2 percent); Lissa, 995 (6.2 percent); Kempen, 804 (13.7 percent); Inowraclaw, 1,050 (4.3 percent); Krotoschin, 525 (4.1 percent); and Grätz, 240 (4.4 percent). Only Kempen and Grätz still had fewer than ten thousand inhabitants.

5. See, for example, *Pinkas Hakehillot. Holland* (Jerusalem, 1983), based on the figures from the 1941 census.

6. Jacob Borut, "Hayei hadat bekerev yehudei hakefarim vehaayarot bema-arava shel Germania bitekufat Weimar" [Religious life among the Jews of villages and small towns in western Germany in the Weimar Period], in *Yehudei Weimar: Hevra be-mashber ha-moderni'ut, 1918–1933* [The Jews of Weimar: A society in the crisis of modernity], ed. Oded Heilbronner (Jerusalem, 1994), pp. 90–107. For a map showing the approximate division between Orthodox and Liberal Judaism in Germany, especially in the countryside, see the chapter on religion in *Integration in Dispute, 1871–1918*, vol. 3 of *German-Jewish History in Modern Times*, ed. Michael A. Meyer (New York, 1998). Clearly Orthodox areas are found in northern Bavaria, northern Hesse, northern Baden, and northern Württemberg, as well as in East Frisia; leading non-Orthodox areas included almost all areas that were later in communist East Germany, Westphalia, most of the Rhineland and the Palatinate, and much of Lower Silesia and Pomerania.

An explanation of the reasons for the regional differences between more Orthodox and more "Liberal" rural Jewry is quite complex. Some of the factors that seem to correlate with greater Orthodoxy, but with many exceptions, are a high percentage of Catholics in the population, relative economic backwardness, high rates of churchgoing among the Christian population, and a relatively low percentage of urbanization in the district.

7. James F. Harris, *The People Speak! Anti-Semitism and Emancipation in Nineteenth-Century Bavaria* (Ann Arbor, 1993), esp. chapter 5, documents much greater opposition to Jewish emancipation in Catholic areas than in Protestant ones. In the Kulturkampf of the 1870s, anti-Jewish feeling among Catholics was also quite high.

Statistical analysis of decline in rural Jewish populations seems to indicate that it was somewhat more rapid in Protestant than in Catholic areas, but this may be due to other factors, such as the relative degree of economic development or the relative size of Protestant and Catholic villages.

8. Utz Jeggle, *Judendörfer in Württemberg* (Tübingen, 1969), pp. 300–301.

9. But perhaps some of this is the result of the fact that the more serious local histories are influenced by reading the same books (especially Jeggle's work; see previous note).

10. The number of local histories of Jewish communities in rural Germany is very large. Many of these works are fairly rudimentary, but quite a few make extensive use of archival materials or professionally conducted interviews and are methodologically sophisticated. Among the sources used in this essay are the following superb studies: Jeggle, *Judendörfer,* and Elfie Labsch-Benz, *Die jüdische Gemeinde Nonnenweier. Jüdisches Leben und Brauchtum in einer badischen Landgemeinde zu Beginn des 20. Jahrhunderts* (Freiburg, 1981), sociological-anthropological studies on a regional and local basis, respectively. I have also drawn on Thomas Michel, *Die Juden in Gaukönigshofen/Unterfranken (1550–1942). Beiträge zur Wirtschafts-und Sozialgeschichte,* vol. 36 (Wiesbaden, 1988); Regina Schmid, *Verlorene Heimat. Gailingen – ein Dorf und seine jüdische Gemeinde in der Weimarer Zeit,* Schriftenreihe des Arbeitskreises für Regionalgeschichte Konstanz, no. 7 (Konstanz, 1988); and *Geschichte der jüdischen Gemeinde Schenklengsfeld* (Schenklengsfeld, 1988), which are particularly rich in statistical and archival data.

11. *Geschichte der jüdischen Gemeinde Schenklengsfeld,* p. 131; Jeggle, *Judendörfer,* pp. 279–81; Frances Henry, *Victims and Neighbors: A Small Town in Nazi Germany Remembered* (South Hadley, 1984), pp. 20–21, 62–65, 110; Labsch-Benz, *Jüdische Gemeinde Nonnenweier,* pp. 60, 101–102. In towns where the Jewish community had shrunk to a tiny size, intermarriage was somewhat more common (Jeggle, *Judendörfer,* p. 268).

12. Michel, *Die Juden in Gaukönigshofen,* p. 412.

13. Borut, "Hayei hadat," pp. 105–106. The influence of the Christian example was most noticeable in attendance at worship services and rite-of-passage ceremonies, where it even induced rural Jews in non-Orthodox areas to keep up the basics so as not to appear irreligious in the eyes of their Christian neighbors. More distinctively Jewish practices such as the sukka, kashruth, and others were less likely to be influenced by the Christian example.

14. Jeggle, *Judendörfer,* p. 271; Borut, "Hayei hadat," p. 106; Schmid, *Verlorene Heimat,* pp. 116–17, 208 note 155. An example of Christian participation in Jewish affairs was the attendance by Christians at the inauguration of Rabbi Bohrer of Gailingen in 1927 (Schmid, *Verlorene Heimat,* p. 114).

15. Michel, *Die Juden in Gaukönigshofen,* pp. 317, 458–59, 577–78; Hermann Fechenbach, *Die letzten Mergentheimer Juden und die Geschichte der Familien Fechenbach* (Stuttgart, 1972), pp. 59, 63–64.

16. Jeggle, *Judendörfer,* pp. 243–44, 283–86; Schmid, *Verlorene Heimat,* p. 114; Michel, *Die Juden in Gaukönigshofen,* pp. 382, 652; Labsch-Benz, *Jüdische Gemeinde Nonnenweier,* pp. 112–13.

17. Jeggle, *Judendörfer,* pp. 260–61; Michel, *Die Juden in Gaukönigshofen,* pp. 382, 414–15; Fechenbach, *Die letzten Mergentheimer Juden,* p. 106; Labsch-Benz, *Jüdische Gemeinde Nonnenweier,* pp. 46, 110; Hugo Mandelbaum, *Jewish Life in the Village Communities of Southern Germany* (New York, 1985), p. 77.

18. Jeggle, *Judendörfer,* pp. 263–64, 266; Schmid, *Verlorene Heimat,* p. 123; Michel, *Die Juden in Gaukönigshofen,* pp. 381–82.

19. Jeggle, *Judendörfer,* p. 223.

20. *Geschichte der jüdischen Gemeinde Schenklengsfeld,* pp. 144, 165–66; Mandel-baum, *Jewish Life,* p. 46.

21. Jeggle, *Judendörfer,* pp. 255–56; *Geschichte der jüdischen Gemeinde Schenk-lengsfeld,* pp. 125–26; Schmid, *Verlorene Heimat,* pp. 108, 124, 133–34; Michel, *Die Juden in Gaukönigshofen,* pp. 399–405; Mandelbaum, *Jewish Life,* p. 30; Henry, *Victims and Neighbors,* p. 157; Karl-Heinz Grossmann, *Die Niederwerrner Juden 1871–1945* (Würzburg, 1990), pp. 46, 107–108.

22. Jeggle, *Judendörfer,* pp. 247–50, 253–54; *Geschichte der jüdischen Gemeinde Schenklengsfeld,* pp. 87, 131; Schmid, *Verlorene Heimat,* p. 116; Michel, *Die Juden in Gaukönigshofen,* pp. 318–22, 406–11; Grossmann, *Die Niederwerrner Juden,* pp. 47, 86–90. Among the organizations mentioned in these local histories are the veteran's society (Kriegerverein, four different towns), volunteer fire depart-ment (two, but in one town it is explicitly stated that Jews did not participate), sports and gymnastics association (four), choral society, bicycle riding association (2), horsemanship society (Reitverein), marksmanship association (Schützenver-ein), garden society (Obst-und Gartenbauverein), and St. Joseph kindergarten society. In Niederwerrn, thirteen of the twenty-three women in the Red Cross were Jewish.

23. Jeggle, *Judendörfer,* pp. 240–41; Michel, *Die Juden in Gaukönigshofen,* pp. 416–17; Schmid, *Verlorene Heimat,* p. 114; Labsch-Benz, *Jüdische Gemeinde Non-nenweier,* pp. 74–75; Werner J. Cahnman, "Village and Small-Town Jews in Germany—A Typological Study," *LBIYB* 19 (1974): 124.

24. Jeggle, *Judendörfer,* pp. 278–79.

25. Ibid., pp. 224–25; Grossmann, *Die Niederwerrner Juden,* pp. 135–37.

26. Jeggle, *Judendörfer,* pp. 229–35; *Geschichte der jüdischen Gemeinde Schenk-lengsfeld,* pp. 89–90; Michel, *Die Juden in Gaukönigshofen,* pp. 341–71; Grossmann, *Die Niederwerrner Juden,* pp. 67–73; Labsch-Benz, *Jüdische Gemeinde Nonnenweier,* pp. 53–55. In Schenklengsfeld in 1931, for instance, fifteen of thirty-five em-ployed Jews were cattle dealers (sometimes also engaging in horse trading) and another nine sold dry goods *(Manufakturwaren).* In Ermershausen, in the Unter-franken district of Bavaria in 1935, nine of sixteen Jews with a listed occupation were cattle dealers.

27. See Jeggle, *Judendörfer,* pp. 188–89; Jews in Buttenhausen made up 22 percent of the population in 1925 and paid 62.6 percent of the taxes. See *Geschichte der jüdischen Gemeinde Schenklengsfeld,* p. 83; in 1880–1881, Jews made up 13.4 percent of the population and paid 34 percent of the assessment tax *(Klassensteuer).* See also Schmid, *Verlorene Heimat,* p. 99; in 1918, Jews made up 28 percent of the population of Gailingen and paid 44 percent of all taxes (53 percent of assessment taxes).

In Gaukönigshofen in 1898, eleven Jewish taxpayers had an average of 6.5 tax votes as against 3.3 for the Christian taxpayers. The wealthiest two Jews had seventeen and twenty-three votes, respectively, while the wealthiest Christian had only ten votes. There were five Jewish taxpayers with five or six votes and four with only one to three (Michel, *Die Juden in Gaukönigshofen,* pp. 268, 371–72).

In Schenklengsfeld in 1904, the highest-paying Jewish taxpayer paid 360 marks, two paid 105, and three paid 42 to 45 marks. These wealthy taxpayers were only six of the forty-two Jewish taxpayers in town. Of the rest, three were too poor to pay any taxes, five paid less than six marks, and twenty-seven paid between 12 and 30 marks. The three richest Jews paid almost half of all taxes paid by Jews *(Geschichte der jüdischen Gemeinde Schenklengsfeld,* pp. 83–84).

28. Michel, *Die Juden in Gaukönigshofen,* pp. 359–71; Schmid, *Verlorene Heimat,* p. 104–106.

29. Grossmann, *Die Niederwerrner Juden*, p. 93.

30. Schmid, *Verlorene Heimat*, pp. 99–100; Michel, *Die Juden in Gaukönigshofen*, p. 562–63. On Jewish landowning and farming, see also Cahnman, "Village and Small-Town Jews," p. 112; Labsch-Benz, *Jüdische Gemeinde Nonnenweier*, p. 53–54; and Mandelbaum, *Jewish Life*, pp. 58, 60.

31. Jeggle, *Judendörfer*, pp. 229–31; Michel, *Die Juden in Gaukönigshofen*, pp. 350, 357.

32. Jeggle, *Judendörfer*, pp. 160–62, 234–35. In the 1860s, the first advertisements in the *Horber Chronik* were placed by Jewish businesses. See also Michel, *Die Juden in Gaukönigshofen*, pp. 329–31.

33. Jeggle, *Judendörfer*, pp. 167–68, 220–23, 226, 276–77; Michel, *Die Juden in Gaukönigshofen*, pp. 420–24, 641.

34. Jeggle, *Judendörfer*, pp. 223–24, 226–27; Schmid, *Verlorene Heimat*, pp. 108–10; Labsch-Benz, *Jüdische Gemeinde Nonnenweier*, p. 55.

35. Schmid, *Verlorene Heimat*, pp. 106, 108, 123; Jeggle, *Judendörfer*, p. 223; Michel, *Die Juden in Gaukönigshofen*, pp. 327–28, 421–23; Labsch-Benz, *Jüdische Gemeinde Nonnenweier*, pp. 54–55.

36. Schmid, *Verlorene Heimat*, pp. 135–95; Michel, *Die Juden in Gaukönigshofen*, pp. 403–405.

37. Jeggle, *Judendörfer*, pp. 240–43; Michel, *Die Juden in Gaukönigshofen*, pp. 323–24, 416–17; Fechenbach, *Die letzten Mergentheimer Juden*, pp. 63–64; Labsch-Benz, *Jüdische Gemeinde Nonnenweier*, pp. 67–68.

38. This was the case, for instance, in Gaukönigshofen, where Jews complained about the Christian imagery used in the World War I memorial. Christians resented the Jewish objections, and there was considerable unpleasantness between the two groups as a result.

Another example of the way religion could be a dividing line was the fact that certain objects of Jewish ritual, especially the sukka, could be the target of vandalism or minor violence (stone throwing, etc.). See Jeggle, *Judendörfer*, pp. 264–65.

39. Ibid., pp. 246, 286–89; Michel, *Die Juden in Gaukönigshofen*, pp. 405–406, 417–19. In Gaukönigshofen between 1919 and 1933, there were nine Jewish children of the age to attend fourth to seventh grade. Seven of these attended schools that led to secondary education rather than the village school.

40. The number of Jewish elementary schools in Prussia fell from 241 in 1901 to 96 in 1926. In Bavaria the number went from 124 in 1871 to 78 in 1901 and 20 in 1925. In Niederwerrn, the Jewish school closed in 1921, while in Schenklengsfeld it was abolished only in 1933. See Mordechai Breuer, *Jüdische Orthodoxie im Deutschen Reich 1871–1918. Sozialgeschichte einer religiösen Minderheit* (Frankfurt am Main, 1986), p. 94; *Pinkas Hakehillot, Germania, Bavaria*, p. 12; *Geschichte der jüdischen Gemeinde Schenklengsfeld*, p. 111; Grossmann, *Die Niederwerrner Juden*, p. 65.

41. Michel, *Die Juden in Gaukönigshofen*, pp. 340, 340–41 note 8. See Grossmann, *Die Niederwerrner Juden*, p. 190; in Niederwerrn, 110 Jewish children were born between 1876 and 1900 but only nine between 1900 and 1918. In Gaukönigshofen, only two of eleven families in the Weimar period had more than two children (three and five, respectively), while five children was the rule among Christians.

42. In the towns and years for which we have data, there was considerable variety in age distribution. Between the three small-town communities of Schenklengsfeld (1933), Ermershausen (1935), and Mergentheim (1933–1942), the percentage under age twenty varied widely, from 16 to 30 percent, the latter

figure indicating a much younger population than the overall Jewish population in Germany. The percentage over sixty varied from 11 to 20 percent. Certain towns seem to have had much older populations. In the town of Laupheim, Württemberg, with a Jewish population of 231 in 1933, only 18 percent were under twenty years of age and 50 percent were fifty or older. In nearby Buchau, forty-five of 165 Jews (27 percent) were over sixty, and eighty-nine (54 percent) were over fifty, while only twenty-one (13 percent) were under the age of twenty (*Pinkas Hakehillot, Baden Württemberg*, pp. 57, 103).

43. One case that does seem to confirm the impression is that of Buchau, Württemberg. Of eighty-nine Jews over the age of fifty in 1933, thirty were married, twenty-five were widowed, and thirty-four were single (*Pinkas Hakehillot, Baden Württemberg*, p. 57).

44. In Hohenzollern, there was an 11 percent rate of marriage to relatives (5 percent to first cousins) among Jewish couples who died before 1922; of those still alive in 1922, the rate had increased to 22 percent (16 percent to first cousins). These rates were several times as high as the rates for Christian marriages. See Wilhelm Reutlinger, "Über die Häufigkeit der Verwandtenehen bei Juden in Hohenzollern und über Untersuchungen bei Deszendenten aus jüdischen Verwandtenehen," *Archiv für Rassen- und Gesellschaftsbiologie* 14 (1922): 301–303, quoted by Marion Kaplan *The Making of the Jewish Middle Class: Women, Family, and Identity in Imperial Germany* (New York, 1991), p. 273 note 206. See also Cahnman, "Village and Small-Town Jews," pp. 122–23, for an impressionistic discussion of the same phenomenon.

45. Jeggle, *Judendörfer*, p. 287; Michel, *Die Juden in Gaukönigshofen*, pp. 389–91; Schmid, *Verlorene Heimat*, pp. 41–42; Mandelbaum, *Jewish Life*, p. 41; Cahnman, "Village and Small-Town Jews," p. 119. In Gailingen, besides declining observance, there are also contrary forces. Rabbi Bohrer, for instance, attempted to make adherence to tradition stricter than before.

46. In Lower Franconia in 1925, of the villages that had Jewish communities, only twenty-six of ninety-five villages of fewer than two thousand inhabitants (27 percent) had fifty or more Jewish inhabitants; but 2,051 of the 3,634 Jews living in towns of under two thousand (56 percent) lived in these larger communities.

The following fifty-three towns with fewer than ten thousand inhabitants in southern Germany had at least 125 Jewish residents in 1925 [* = general population under four thousand; number of Jews in parentheses]:

Hesse: Bad Nauheim (290), Alzey (237), Alsfeld (216), Dieburg (175), Gross Gerau (161), *Büdingen (148), Seligenstadt (146 in 1933), *Gedern (146), Lauterbach (139)

Hesse-Nassau: *Schlüchtern (308), *Rhina (228), Gelnhausen (215), *Kirchhain (189), Langenselbold (186), *Guxhagen (159), *Burghaun (152), Bad Wildungen (152), *Schenklengsfeld (149), Bergen (148), *Borken (145), *Rotenburg a.d. Fulda (143), *Gross-Krotzenburg (137), Bebra (136), Witzenhausen (134), Treysa (130)

Bavaria: Bad Kissingen (504), *Ichenhausen (356), Nördlingen (233), Gunzenhausen (219), *Thüngen (180), *Markt Breit (164), *Bad Neustadt a.d. Saale (162), *Fischach (153), *Mellrichstadt (151), *Brückenau (128)

Baden: *Gailingen (375), Emmendingen (364), *Breisach (287), *Königsbach (162), Mosbach (159), Bretten (155), *Kippenheim (153), *Schmieheim (134), *Eichstetten (129)

Württemberg: *Rexingen (307), Laupheim (225), *Haigerloch (213), Bad

Mergentheim (213), *Buchau (202), Crailsheim (196), Öhringen (159), *Oberdorf (137), *Buttenhausen (133)

The number of large Jewish communities in small towns was much smaller in 1925 than earlier. Compared to eighty Bavarian towns with over 125 Jews but fewer than ten thousand inhabitants in 1816, there were only sixty-two in 1867, thirty in 1900, and ten in 1925.

47. One noticeable exception is Geroda, the town in which Hugo Mandelbaum lived (see note 17 above). Geroda's Jewish population in 1925 was only forty-nine, yet, according to Mandelbaum, it had a lively Jewish community.

48. Schmid, *Verlorene Heimat*, pp. 57–66, 117. In Gailingen, there were separate Jewish and Christian choral societies and theater groups (ibid., pp. 64–65).

49. Jeggle, *Judendörfer*, pp. 296–300, gives statistics on the Nazi vote in various villages of the district of Horb. The Nazi vote in July 1932 was highest in the Protestant village of Hochdorf (65.4 percent) and lowest in the Catholic village of Grünmettstetten (2.8 percent). The Nazi vote in towns with Jewish populations varied greatly. In Nordstetten, 30.3 percent voted for the NSDAP as against only 5.6 percent in Baisingen and 4.9 percent in Rexingen. Interestingly, Baisingen and Rexingen were the only villages in the district that still had substantial Jewish populations in 1933.

50. Schmid, *Verlorene Heimat*, pp. 160–90. The Nazis did better in national elections in Gailingen than they did in local elections. In town council elections in 1930 and 1931, they won from 11 to 13 percent of the vote. In the Reichstag election of July 1932, they received 21 percent of the vote, and in March 1933, 34.1 percent. Since about one-third of Gailingen's voters were Jews, this means that about one-half of the Christians voted for the NSDAP in 1933.

51. *Geschichte der jüdischen Gemeinde Schenklengsfeld*, pp. 130–31, 203; Labsch-Benz, *Jüdische Gemeinde Nonnenweier*, pp. 26–27, 77–80. The Schenklengsfeld party organization *(Ortsgruppe)* was founded as early as 1925, the first in the county. Three years earlier, the extreme rightist organization Bund Oberland had thirty members in the village.

52. There are undoubtedly parallels with small-town Jewish life in the West (in the United States, England, and France outside Alsace-Lorraine) and in some of the patterns described in this essay, especially in the areas of economic life and intergroup relations. The main difference is that village communities in Germany were frequently several hundred years old and had the weight of generations of local tradition behind them, unlike small-town communities further west. Small-town Jews were an important source of Jewish traditionalism in Germany as a whole. This was a role that in the West was played more by the urban metropolises than by the small town communities.

53. Although most of the examples given in this essay have concentrated on the Jewishness of the rural Jews, much of what we have discussed also indicates their deep sense of Germanness. First was their sense of rootedness on the local scene, expressed both in their pride in their generations of residence in the same place and on their almost total lack of interest in Zionism. Second was the considerable degree to which, despite the limitations, they socialized with their non-Jewish neighbors. In addition, one can cite their locally tinged German speech (although it may sometimes have been tinged with some Jewish peculiarities), and their participation in local political and organizational life.

CONTRIBUTORS

Avraham Barkai is a member of Kibbutz Lahavat Habashan and serves on the executive board of the Leo Baeck Institute in Jerusalem. His publications have traced the social and economic history of German Jewry throughout the nineteenth and twentieth centuries. His most recent publications in English include *From Boycott to Annihilation: The Economic Struggle of German Jews, 1933–1943* (1989) and "Renewal and Destruction, 1918–1945," in *German Jewish History in Modern Times* 4 (1998).

Jacob Borut is a research fellow at Yad Vashem, Jerusalem. He edited *Pinkas Kehillot Germaniyah*, vols. 5 and 6, and has published numerous articles on the history of German Jewry during the Second Empire and Weimar Republic. He is the author of a forthcoming book on the social, economic, and political history of German Jewry at the fin de siècle.

Michael Brenner is Professor of Jewish History and Culture at the University of Munich. He is the author of *The Renaissance of Jewish Culture in Weimar Germany* (1996) and *After the Holocaust: Rebuilding Jewish Lives in Postwar Germany* (1997). He is the assistant editor and co-author of the four-volume *German Jewish History in Modern Times* (1996–1998).

David Ellenson is I.H. and Anna Grancell Professor of Jewish Religious Thought at Hebrew Union College–Jewish Institute of Religion, Los Angeles. He is the author of several books, including *Rabbi Esriel Hildesheimer and the Creation of a Modern Jewish Orthodoxy* (1990). He is co-author of the forthcoming volume *"For the Sake of Heaven": Conversion, Law, and Politics in Modern Jewish Orthodoxy*.

Harriet Pass Freidenreich is Professor of History at Temple University in Philadelphia. She is the author of *The Jews of Yugoslavia: A Quest for Community* (1979) and *Jewish Politics in Vienna, 1918–1938* (1991) and of various articles on Balkan and Central European Jewry. She is presently writing a book on Jewish university women in Central Europe in the early twentieth century.

Sharon Gillerman is Assistant Professor of Near Eastern and Judaic Studies at Brandeis University. Her doctoral dissertation, which is under revision for publication, is entitled "Between Public and Private: Family, Community, and Identity in Weimar Berlin."

Jack Jacobs is Associate Professor of Government at John Jay College of the City University of New York. His publications include *On Socialists and "the Jewish Question" after Marx* (1992) and numerous articles on the relationship between Jews, leftist politics, and labor movements.

Steven M. Lowenstein is the Isadore Levine Professor of Jewish History at the University of Judaism in Los Angeles. He is the author of *Frankfurt on the Hudson: The German Jewish Community of Washington Heights, 1933–1983* (1989); *The Mechanics of Change: Essays in German Jewish Social History* (1992); and *The Berlin Jewish Community: Enlightenment, Family, and Crisis, 1770–1830* (1994).

Michael A. Meyer is Adolph S. Ochs Professor of Jewish History at Hebrew University College–Jewish Institute of Religion in Cincinnati. His books include *Response to Modernity: A History of the Reform Movement in Judaism* (1988) and *Jewish Identity in the Modern World* (1990). He is the editor of the four-volume *German Jewish History in Modern Times* (1996–1998).

Derek J. Penslar holds the Zacks Chair in Jewish History at the University of Toronto. He is the author of *Zionism and Technocracy: The Engineering of Jewish Settlement in Palestine, 1870–1918* (1991) and is completing a book titled *Shylock's Children: The Jews, Economics, and Ethnic Identity in Modern Europe.*

Claudia Prestel is Senior Lecturer in Jewish History at Monash University. She is the author of *Jüdisches Schul- und Erziehungswesen in Bayern 1804–1933* (1989) and of numerous articles on modern Jewish social history and women's history.

Marsha L. Rozenblit is Associate Professor of History at the University of Maryland, College Park. A specialist in the social history of the Jews in Austria-Hungary, she is the author of *The Jews of Vienna, 1867–1914: Assimilation and Identity* (1983). She is currently completing a book on the impact of World War I on the Jews of Austria-Hungary.

Shulamit Volkov is Professor of Modern History and Director of the Graduate School of History at Tel Aviv University. Her publications include *The Rise of Popular Antimodernism in Germany* (1978), *Jüdisches Leben und Antisemitismus im 19. und 20. Jahrhundert* (1990), and *Die Juden in Deutschland, 1780–1918* (1994).

INDEX

acculturation, x, 94, 156, 178
Adler, Alfred, 214, 216
Anschluss, 128, 135, 145, 147–48
antinomianism, 40, 51
antisemitism, xi, 8, 9, 11–12, 71, 211; anti-Zionism and, 86; in Austria, 9, 124, 134, 135, 136, 137–38, 145–49, 159; crisis of family and, 183; dashed hopes for assimilation, 79; in education, 67, 159, 165, 166; in German youth movements, 57, 59, 165; impact on Jewish women and girls, 169–70, 196n22; in Imperial Germany, 75; Jewish family as refuge from, 189–90, 194; Jewish schools and, 99, 111n24; in rural Germany, 225, 227, 235; struggle against, 75–76, 143, 144; in Weimar Republic, ix, 74; Zionism and, 82–85. *See also* nationalism; Zionism
anti-Zionism, 16, 86, 167; Bundism and, 116, 118, 122; of Centralverein, 70, 78–79, 80, 84–85. *See also* Zionism
artists/artisans, 97–98, 102–104, 156
assimilation, xi, xii, xiii, 94, 157, 171, 187; in Austria, 140–43; Austro-German rejection of, 135; crisis of family and, 178–79; culture and the arts, 102–104; degree of in various countries, 146; "dissimilation" and, 195; education and, 96, 98–99; individual character of, 4–13, 160, 161; in rural Germany, 224, 236; sports associations, 68; Zionist rejection of, 80, 93, 97
athletic societies. *See* sports associations
Auerbach, Berthold, 9, 223
Austria, Republic of, ix, xiii, 5; Bundism in, 115–33; Jewish ethnic identity in, 134–53; subcultures in, 94. *See also* Austro-Hungarian Empire; Vienna
Austrittsgemeinden, 37, 44, 162
Austrittsgesetz. See Law of Secession (1876)
Austro-Hungarian Empire, 116, 120, 121, 136–37, 155, 157; collapse of, 134–35, 141, 145. *See also* Austria, Republic of; Vienna

Baeck, Rabbi Leo, 19–20, 32n35, 35n66, 42, 70, 83, 85
Balfour Declaration (1917), 79, 82
Bar Kochba (sports association), 68, 100, 104
Bar Kochba (student society), 57
Baronowitz, A., 201, 210, 213, 221n64

Bauer, Otto, 118, 128
Bauman, Zygmunt, 5, 6, 9
Berger, Peter, 36–37
Berlin, xii, 9, 87, 157, 224, 225; concentration of Jews in, x, 74; elections in, 74–75, 81–82, 86, 96; Jewish women university students in, 165; in nineteenth century, 15–16; synagogues in, 8, 15, 16, 23, 26–27, 30; youth rebellion in, 181. *See also* Germany; Prussia; Weimar Republic
Berwin, Beate, 167, 168, 169
birthrates, decline of, 183–85, 197n25, 197n28, 233, 240n41
Blau-Weiss (youth movement), 59, 61, 62, 63, 165
Blind, Yitzhok, 127–28
Blumenfeld, Kurt, 76, 79, 85, 109n4
B'nai B'rith, 98, 143, 144, 169
Borut, Jacob, xiii, 225
bourgeois society: assimilation and, 9, 11, 12, 94, 95; concern with health, 191–92; cultural activities and, 102, 105; family model of, 202
Braun, Siegfried, 92, 93
Brenner, Michael, xii, 99, 163
Breuer, Isaac, 44, 61–62
Breuer, Mordechai, 39, 42
Breuer, Solomon, 45, 46
Brodnitz, Friedrich, 70, 81–82, 85
Buber, Martin, xi, 18–19, 20, 21, 24, 34n59, 57; influence on youth, 57, 60–61, 63, 66
Bukharin, Nikolai, 117
Bukovina, 118, 120, 136, 137
Bundism, xiii, 115–33. *See also* communism; socialism

cabarets, 103, 107
Catholicism, 22, 97, 108, 158, 161, 163; antisemitism and, 225, 227, 237n7; birthrate, 184; conversion to Judaism, 186, 197n37; *Kulturkampf* and, 11, 237n7; in rural Germany, 223, 237n6, 237–38n7; view of family, 188; workers' organizations and, 102, 107. *See also* Christianity; Protestantism
Centralverein (CV), xiii, 10, 69–70; history of, 88–89n6; ideological divisions within, 74–91; in rural areas, 235; subcultures and, 93, 94, 95; Zionism in, 86
Central Zionist Archives (Jerusalem), 111n28

Christians/Christianity: churches, x, 9, 22; Jewish conversion to, 163; in rural Germany, 227, 228–34, 235, 237n6, 238n 13; schools, 96, 162; women in, 21, 33n 35. *See also* Catholicism; Protestantism
Christian Social Party (Austria), 120, 124, 146
Cohen, Hermann, 26, 39, 163, 167
communism/communists: in Austria, 121, 122, 127; in Germany, 31n5, 56, 93, 97, 102, 107, 163, 165, 170; in Hungary, 121, 126; in Russia, 127; Third International, 123
community: decline of, xiv, 36, 51; in Jewish tradition, 49, 52; renewed sense of, xii, 12, 71; synagogue design and, 23; varieties of, ix–x; volkish ideology and, 87. See also *Gemeinschaft*
Conservative Judaism, x, 55n43
conversion, 9, 228
correctional education. *See* reform schools
Czechoslovakia, 139, 147
Czellitzer, Arthur, 182, 188, 189, 192, 193

delinquency. *See* youth rebellion
Deutsch-Israelitische Gemeindebund (DIGB), 181, 200, 202, 216
Deutschtum (Germanness), 76, 96, 140–43, 242n53
Diaspora, 64, 65, 100
discrimination, 8, 9, 76, 95
Dohm, Christian Wilhelm von, 6

economic crisis: antisemitism and, 134; breakdown of family relations and, 180, 182; correctional education and, 211, 217; effect on university women, 156; Jewish community affected by, xi, 5, 12, 194, 211; unemployment and, 121, 182
education: of children, 190; correction of troubled youth, 200–222; decline of Jewish schools, 96, 98–99, 111n24, 233, 240n40; for Jewish adults, 104–105, 113n62; Jewish university women, 154–75; in rural Germany, 231, 233; Schulen der jüdischen Jugend, 64–68
Einheitsgemeinden, xii, 38, 41, 44, 46, 49–50, 53
Einstein, Albert, ix, 16
emancipation, 5–6, 8–9, 74, 103, 136, 187
Eretz Israel, 205–206, 211, 213. *See also* Israel, state of; Palestine
Esra (youth organization), 59
eugenics, 188, 192, 217

Falkenberg, Hermann, 25, 28, 30, 35n63
families, 146–49, 152n58, 153n63; correc-

tional education for troubled youth, 200–222; crisis of, 176–99; Jewish identity and, 160–61
fathers, absence of, 179, 180, 181, 195n7
feminism/feminists, 159–60, 177, 182, 191
Ferdinand Lassalle club, 118, 119, 122, 125
film, 104, 107, 132n55
Frankenthal, Käte, 158, 160, 168, 169, 170, 172n8
Freidenreich, Harriet, xiii, 115, 126, 146
French Revolution, 5
Friedländer, Josua Falk, 25, 27
Fuchs, Eugen, 76, 78–79, 84
Funkenstein, Amos, 187, 197–98n41, 198n 54

Galicia (East European region): antisemitism in, 137, 138; in Austro-Hungarian Empire, 136; Jewish migration to Austria from, 120, 132n58, 137, 157; Jewish socialists in, 118, 119, 122, 125, 127. *See also* Poland
Gay, Peter, ix, 56, 63
Geiger, Abraham, 25–26, 34n60
Gemeinde (Jewish community), ix–x, 2; *Gemeinschaft* within, 25–30; position of women in, 156, 158–60, 168, 169, 171; religious ferment in, 15–18, 19
Gemeinschaft, ix–xi, 18–24, 36, 51, 70; art and literature, 105; within *Gemeinde*, 25–30; masculinity and, 62–63; notion of organic community, 188; youth movements and, 60, 62, 64. *See also* community
Gemeinschaft und Gesellschaft (Tönnies), x
generational conflict, 181, 182, 186, 200
Gentiles. *See* Christians/Christianity
George, Stefan, 62, 63
German language, 21, 26, 27, 28, 34n59; Austrian Jews and, 135, 137, 140, 142; synagogue services in, 164
Germany: crisis of family in, 178, 179–80, 182, 183–84, 187, 194; impact of World War I, 176–77, 186; Imperial, x, 11, 75; Jewish disillusion in, 1–14; Jewish university women in, 155, 157; Nazi, 30, 145, 158, 215; subcultures in, 94, 100, 102; tolerance for minorities, 97; volkish ideology in, 57, 58, 60; youth movements in, 56–73, 106. *See also* Berlin; Prussia; Weimar Republic
Gerson, Hermann, 60–61, 64
Gesangvereine (singing societies), 102–103, 107
Gesellschaft für Familienforschung, 182, 192, 193
Gesellschaft, x, xi, 18, 36, 51

Gross, Hans, 202–204
Grossmann, Henryk, 119, 130n14
Grünewald, Rabbi Max, 66–67
Gutman, Feliks, 119, 129–30n14

Habsburg monarchy. *See* Austro-Hungarian
    Empire
Haggadah, 28, 34n57
Halakah, 40, 50
Hamburg Temple, 21, 23
Hasidic Tales (Buber), 63
Hasidism, 60, 65, 120
Haskalah (Jewish Enlightenment), 94, 103,
    187
Hebrew language, 29, 57, 61, 65, 106, 162,
    163; synagogue services in, 17, 26,
    27, 28, 34n59, 164; taught in reform
    schools, 211, 213; theater in, 103
Heimat (fatherland), 142–43
Heine, Heinrich, 9
Herzl, Theodor, 55n46, 65, 143
High Holy Days, 16, 27, 32n29, 33n49, 161,
    163, 229
hiking, as group activity, 58, 62, 66, 212
Hirsch, Rabbi Samson Raphael, xii, 37, 38,
    44, 58
Hitler, Adolf, 2, 3, 23, 160
Holländer, Ludwig, 77–78, 84
Holocaust, ix, 147, 161, 168
homosexuality, 172n8, 213–14, 221n61
Hungary, 121, 126, 136

I and Thou (Buber), 19
identity, 10, 11, 70, 96, 160; Jews in Ger-
    man Austria, 134–53; in rural areas,
    228, 236
Imperial Germany, x, xvn3, 75
individualism, 19, 20, 60
integration. *See* assimilation
intermarriage, 9, 20, 158, 187; children of,
    185–86, 206; incidence of, 16, 170; rab-
    bis and, 31n6; in rural Germany, 228,
    238n11
Israel, state of, 1, 63, 161, 162. *See also* Eretz
    Israel; Palestine
Israel (faith community), 28, 43, 46, 47, 48,
    187, 191
Italiener, Rabbi Bruno, 23–24

Jewish Agency, 70–71, 82, 83, 85
Jewish National Councils, 139, 140
"Jewish Question," 74
Jewish Social Democratic Party of Galicia
    (ZPSD), 118–19, 121, 122, 131n27
Jewish Women's Student Association, 165
Jews: Austrian patriotism of, 137, 150n9;
    Bundist movement and, 115–33; com-

munity organizations, xiv, 4, 6, 10, 64,
    92–93, 94, 235; cultural achievements
    of, 8; ethnic identity in Austrian Repub-
    lic, 134–53; ethnic *versus* religious com-
    munity, x; family life, xiii–xiv, 7, 9, 19,
    146–49, 152n58, 153n63, 176–99, 200;
    German patriotism of, 71, 76, 78–79,
    84, 85, 96–97, 167–68; in high culture
    and the arts, 102–104; impact of Hitler's
    rise to power, 1–3, 12; as individuals
    versus as a group, 4–13, 46–47; Jewish
    establishment, 69–71; position in soci-
    ety, xi, 8, 15; religious life of, 15–35;
    rural communities, 223–42; as a tribe
    (Stamm), 78; uniqueness and universal-
    ity of, 187–88, 197–98n41, 198n54; in
    United States, x, 8, 29, 55n43, 149, 158,
    178; as veterans of Austrian military,
    120; as veterans of German military,
    xi, 8, 69, 86, 101, 107, 229; youth in
    Weimar Germany, 56–73. *See also* Juda-
    ism; *Ostjuden*
Jogiches, Leo, 124
Judaism, x, 9, 12, 28, 40–41, 52, 144, 147;
    confessionalism and, 7, 44, 52; educa-
    tional institutes and, 104; gender and,
    157; historical meaning of family, 187–
    89; ideal of Jewish unity and, 77; Jewish
    education and, 161–62; as opposed to
    "Jewishness," 70; relinquished attach-
    ment to, 22, 141, 160, 170, 179; return
    to, 56; synthesis of *Deutschtum* and *Juden-
    tum*, 74–91, 96–97, 105, 167, 194; in
    university life, 166; youth movements
    and, 60, 61, 64. *See also* Jews
Jude, Der (journal), xi, 21, 57–58
Judentum. See Judaism
Jüdische Liberale Jugend (JLJ), 59–60, 65
Jüdische-Liberale Zeitung (newspaper), 84–
    85, 86, 87, 101
Jüdischer Frauenbund, 99, 159, 167, 169,
    170, 192
Jüdische Volkspartei (JVP), 23, 75, 85, 99,
    106
Jung Jüdischer Wanderbund (youth move-
    ment), 59

Kadimah (youth organization), 65
Kafka, Franz, 57
Kaiserreich. *See* Imperial Germany
Kameraden (youth organization), 59, 60,
    61, 63, 80, 165
Kaplan, Marion, 156, 170
kehillah (congregation), 29, 37
Keren Hayesod, 82, 85
kibbutzim, 59
Klal Yisrael, 43–44, 47

Köpenich (reform school), 200, 222n85
Kulturkampf, 11, 14n15, 237n7
Kultusgemeinde, 115, 128, 133n67

Landauer, Gustav, 18
Landjuden (rural Jews), 62
Lassalle club. *See* Ferdinand Lassalle club
Law of Secession (1876), 37, 43, 45, 55n28
leaders, youth admiration of, 58, 60–61
Lebensfragn (journal), 116–17, 129n5
Lehrhaus (House of Study), 65, 67, 104, 113n64, 163
Liberal Judaism, x, xii–xiii, 16–18, 20, 23, 24, 25, 28, 83; anti-Zionism and, 84–87; in Austria, 138, 141–45; education and, 67; opposition to Jewish schools, 99; relations with Orthodoxy, 39–41, 45–51, 193; in rural Germany, 237n6; social work and, 35n63; sports clubs and, 69; youth movements and, 59–60, 64, 66, 165; Zionism and, 55n46, 98, 102, 104–105, 108–109, 110n19, 113n68. *See also* Judaism; Orthodox Judaism; Reform Judaism
"Liberal Synagogue of the North" (Berlin), 27–30
Liebknecht, Karl, 124
Löwenfeld, Raphael, 75–76
Lubinski, Hans, 209, 210, 216
Luxemburg, Rosa, 124

Maccabi (sports association), 100, 107
Making of the Jewish Middle Class, The (Kaplan), 156
marriage, 182, 184, 234, 241n44
Marxism, 116
masculinity, 62–63
mass society, 19–20
masturbation, 213–14, 221nn58–60
Mecklenburg, Georg, 80, 83
Medem, Vladimir, 116, 117, 129n5
Mendelssohn, Moses, 6, 7, 34n60
Middle Ages, 36, 49, 77, 188–89
middle class, xi, 1, 4, 7, 27, 30; Jewish university women, 154, 155, 156–57, 161, 170; marriage and family, 177, 182, 183, 194; party affiliation of, 85; in rural Germany, 230, 231; youth rebellion and, 56, 64, 206, 208
Misrachi Youth, 59
Mittelstand. *See* middle class
modernism/modernization, 194, 224
Modernity and Ambivalence (Bauman), 5
Morgen, Der (journal), 24, 78
Moscow, archives in, 86, 89n6
Moses, Siegfried, 85, 87

music, 102–103, 156, 231

nationalism, 14n15, 109n6, 179; in Austria, 150n7; in Austro-Hungarian Empire, 136–39; ethnic identity and, 188; following Napoleonic wars, 9; German, x, 3, 59, 64, 85, 145–46, 159, 175n47; Judaism and, xi, 78; Polish, 175n47. *See also* Jews, Austrian *and* German patriotism of; Nazism; volkish ideology; Zionism
National Socialism. *See* Nazism
nature, romantic love of, 59, 62
Naumann, Max, 83, 86, 87
Nazism, 12, 24, 64, 86, 111n24, 156, 158, 169, 215; in Austria, 147–14; Centralverein and, 89n6; degree of support in rural Germany, 225, 227, 228, 229, 232, 235, 242nn49–50; German nationalism and, 168; Jews driven out of German cultural life, 102; return of Jewish ghetto and, 30, 109; rise of, 74, 145; workers' participation in, 107; Zionism compared to, 85. *See also* antisemitism; nationalism; volkish ideology
New Synagogue (Berlin), 15, 16, 23, 27
"New Woman," 155, 156, 171, 172n7, 181–82
Nobel, Rabbi Nehemiah Anton, xii, 37, 38–44, 59, 61

Orthodox Judaism, x, 16–17, 25, 97; in Austria, 145; education and, 68, 98; relations with Liberal Judaism, xii, 36–55; in rural Germany, 225, 237n6; women and, 157, 162, 164; youth movements and, 58, 59, 61, 66; youth rebellion and, 204–205, 218n10. *See also* Judaism; Liberal Judaism; Reform Judaism
Österreichische Wochenschrift (newspaper), 138, 139, 142, 144
Ostjuden (East European Jews), 62, 75, 79, 120; Austro-German Jewish rejection of, 144; Bundism and, 119, 121–22; in culture and the arts, 103, 104; Jewish schools and, 98; organizations of, 97, 109; in Vienna, 126, 130n23, 132n55, 132n58; voting rights of, 83; World War I and, 137; Zionism and, 105–106, 108. *See also* Jews
Ottenheimer, Hilde, 188, 190, 193

Palestine, 70, 80, 86, 140, 167; agricultural settlements in, 223; British mandate over, 79, 82; emigration to, 4, 59, 64, 149, 161, 181, 205–206, 212; women's

organizations and, 100. *See also* Eretz
Israel; Israel, state of
Papanek-Akselrad, Rose-Marie, 158–59,
160, 166, 167, 168
"passing," 7, 8, 9
Passover, 28, 161, 164, 228
Poalei-Zion party, 118, 126, 130–31n27
Poland: Bundism in, 116, 125, 127, 129n2,
133n65; formerly German territory of,
225; Jewish cultural integration in, 146,
235. *See also* Galicia
Polish Workers Council, 124–25
politics, 8, 12, 19, 232
private sphere, 37, 52, 146
professional associations, 95, 97
Protestantism, 11, 22, 35n63, 40, 158, 162,
198n47; antisemitism and, 225, 227;
birthrate, 184; Jewish conversion to,
163, 168; in rural Germany, 237–38n7;
view of family, 188. *See also* Catholicism;
Christianity
Prussia, 5, 6, 11, 37, 97, 154–55, 185–86,
224–25. *See also* Germany
psychoanalysis/psychoanalysts, 180, 216
public sphere, 37, 52, 146
Purim, 31n7, 229, 235

rabbis, xii, 7, 27, 32–33, 90n33; crisis of
family and, 177, 202; intermarriage and,
31n6; Jewish youth movements and,
66; positions on Zionism, 83–84, 137;
Richtlinien and, 39, 41–42; view of Jewish identity, 137, 152n42; women in
rabbinical ordination, 21, 33n35, 174n
26
Rathenau, Walther, ix, 9, 14n13
Reform Judaism, x, 8, 21, 29, 39, 45, 50–51.
See also Judaism; Liberal Judaism; Orthodox Judaism
reform schools, 200–222
Reichsvertretung der deutschen Juden, xiv,
82, 86, 87
religion: confessionalism and, 7; consigned
to private sphere, x, 37, 49, 51–52; *Gemeinschaft* and, 18–19; indifference to,
16, 77–78, 83, 158, 163, 192; Jewish
identity and, 143–45, 161, 177; morality and, 40; renewal of, xii; in rural
Germany, 225, 227, 228–34, 238n13,
240n38; social work and, 35n63. *See also*
Christianity; Judaism; synagogues
Religionsvolk, Jews as, 143
Repzin (reform school), 181, 200, 204–206,
208–10, 210, 213, 216
Richtlinien, Die, 39–41
romanticism, 58, 59, 60

Rosenmann, Lippe, 122, 126, 127
Rosenzweig, Franz, 26, 34n60, 57, 65, 113n
64, 163
Russia, 3, 155, 157; Bundism in, 116, 125,
126, 132n58; separatism of Jewish life
in, 235; war with Austria, 137

Schicksalsgemeinschaft (community of fate),
x, 38, 71, 78, 81, 145
Scholem, Gerhard, 57–58, 62–63
Schreiber, Heinrich, 139, 142
Schulen der jüdischen Jugend, 64–68
Schwarze Fähnlein, Das (youth organization), 61, 86
Second Temple, 49
secularism/secularization, 16, 116, 163, 187
Segal, Erna, 139, 148
Seligmann, Rabbi Caesar, 83–84
separatism, 37, 38, 43, 45–46, 50–51, 52,
162, 194
Shavei Zion (settlement in Palestine), 223
Social Democratic Party: Austrian, 118, 120,
122, 123–24, 127, 139; German, 11,
14n15, 93, 96, 124, 165, 232; Russian,
117
socialism, x, xii, 56, 65, 158, 163, 170; in
Austria, 115, 121, 124–25, 128; *Gemeinschaft* and, 18; influence on correctional
education, 211, 213; Polish, 124; ruptures within, 93; as subculture, 106–
107, 113n75; youth movements and,
59, 165. *See also* Bundism; communism
sociology, x, 36–37, 65, 233
Sorkin, David, 94–95
soviets (workers' councils), 121, 122
Spartacist uprising, 124
"spiritual ghetto," 92, 93, 109
sports associations, 68–69, 94, 95, 100–101,
109, 229, 239n22
Stahl, Heinrich, 87, 182
Stammesgemeinschaft (community of descent), x, 78, 81, 144
Stamm (tribe), 137, 144
Stein, Edith, 163, 166
Stern, Heinrich, 20, 35n66
Straus, Rahel Goitein, 158, 159–60, 166,
168
Stricker, Robert, 140, 151n29
student organizations, 57, 61–62, 94, 98,
99, 159
subcultures, 93–95, 129
Switzerland, 116, 172n1
synagogues, xi, 15–35, 31n4, 102, 156, 163

Talmud, 61, 89n7
Talmudists, 38, 39

taxes, x, 18, 27, 31n5, 50; in archival records, 228; education and, 68; Jewish share of, 230, 239n27; as male responsibility, 169
Teilkultur (partial culture), 95–96, 99, 100, 106, 108
theater, 102, 103, 104, 125
Theilhaber, Felix, 182, 184, 233
"three-day-a-year Jews," 17, 26
Tietz, Ludwig, 70, 81–82, 85, 86
tolerance, 134–35, 147
Tönnies, Ferdinand, x, 18, 36
Torah, 24, 46
trade unions, 97, 125
Trennungsorthodoxie, 37–38, 44, 45, 47–48, 49
Trotsky, Leon, 117
Trotzjüdinnen (casual Jews), 168–69

United States, x, 8, 29, 55n43, 149, 158, 178
Unna, Rabbi Isak, xii, 37, 38, 44–51
urbanization, xiv, 36, 62, 67, 179, 187, 237n6

Varnhagen, Rahel, 9, 13n8
Veker, Der (Bundist journal), 122, 123–24
Verband National-deutscher Juden, 4, 83
Vereine (associations), 5, 8, 108
Vereinigung für das liberale Judentum (VLJ), 83–86, 103–104
veterans' associations, 229, 239n22
Vienna, x, 9, 45, 134, 137, 157, 158; Bundism in, 115–33; concentration of Jews in, 119–20; revolution in, 125–26, 128. *See also* Austria, Republic of; Austro-Hungarian Empire
volkish ideology, 57, 58, 60, 99–100, 105, 168; in Austria, 137, 141, 143; as "community of blood," 86–87; concept of *Stamm* (tribe), 78; in First Austrian Republic, 135. *See also* nationalism; Nazism; Zionism
Volksgemeinde, 105, 113n68
Volksgemeinschaft, x, 145

Walk, Joseph, 61, 68
Wandervogel, 58, 59, 60, 165
Warschauer, Rabbi Malwin, 30–31n3, 32n35
Wassermann, Jakob, 176, 186
Weimar Republic, 9, 11, 12–13, 74; correctional education for youth, 200–222; crisis of Jewish family in, 176–99; Jewish community organizations in, 97; Jewish religious life in, 16–30; Jewish youth in, 56–73; Orthodox Judaism in,

36–55; rural Jewish communities in, 223–42; socialism in, 106–107; Zionist subculture in, 92–114. *See also* Berlin; Germany; Prussia
welfare organizations, 95, 104, 106
Weltsch, Robert, 71, 74, 150n18, 151n26
Wolzig (reform school), 201, 203, 205, 206, 210–15, 217–18
women: associations of, 99–100; changing gender roles and, 35n64, 181–84; employment outside the home, 180, 186, 196n15; in German and Austrian universities, xiii, 154–75; reform school girls, 200, 217, 222n85; in rural Germany, 232, 233; "social motherhood" movement, 179, 195n4; synagogue attendance, 16, 21, 26, 32n25, 32–33n35, 156, 164, 174n34; youth movements and, 63; Zionism and, 147
working class: family life, 190; family planning and, 183, 197n26; organizations of, 11; revolution and, 121, 123, 124; rural, 232; socialist subculture and, 106–107, 113n75; youth rebellion and, 208
World War I, ix, 59, 67, 142, 147, 165; Bundists and, 116, 119, 122; as "catastrophe," xi; changes in Centralverein and, 69; collapse of Austro-Hungarian Empire, 134, 137–38; commemoration of in Germany, 240n38; correctional education during, 216; crisis of family and, 176, 179–80, 185, 186; German subcultures and, 93; growing antisemitism preceding, 57; impact of on Jews, 150n12; loss of German territory following, 224–25; revolutions following, 126; sociology and, x; Zionism and, 97
World War II, 168, 229
World Zionist Organization (WZO), 150n18, 151n26
Woyda, Bruno, 84, 86–87

yiddishkeit, 81
Yiddish language: Bundism/socialism and, 119, 126, 132n55; theater in, 57, 104, 106, 125
Yom Kippur, 28, 164
youth movements, xii–xiii, 56–73, 80, 86, 94, 97; girls in, 164–65; subcultures and, 99, 100
youth rebellion, 180–83, 200–201, 218–22; changes in correctional education, 208–17; Jewish reform schools, 201–202; origins of, 202–208

Zeirei Misrachi (youth movement), 59, 103

Zionism, x, xiii, 2–3, 10, 12, 16, 20, 23, 187; antisemitism and, 83; in Austria, 122, 138–41, 145, 159; Centralverein and, 75–76, 78–80; culture and the arts, 103–104; idea of Jews as nation, 137, 138–43; influence on correctional education, 211, 213; Judaism and, 42, 55n46; rural Jews and, 242n53; sports associations and, 69, 95, 100–101, 104, 107, 110n16; student organizations and, 167; subculture in Weimar Republic, 92–114; women's organizations and, 99–100; youth movements and, 57–62, 64–65, 67–68, 70–71, 107; youth rebellion and, 181, 205–206. *See also* antisemitism; anti-Zionism; nationalism; volkish ideology

Zionistische Vereinigung für Deutschland (ZVfD), 75, 78–79, 80, 85, 87

Zweig, Stefan, 28, 66